The Short Oxford History of Germany

Weimar Germany

The Short Oxford History of Germany

Weimar Germany

Edited by Anthony McElligott

OXFORD
UNIVERSITY PRESS

This book has been printed digitally and produced in a standard specification in order to ensure its continuing availability

OXFORD
UNIVERSITY PRESS

Great Clarendon Street, Oxford OX2 6DP

Oxford University Press is a department of the University of Oxford.
It furthers the University's objective of excellence in research, scholarship,
and education by publishing worldwide in

Oxford New York

Auckland   Cape Town Dar es Salaam   Hong Kong   Karachi
Kuala Lumpur Madrid Melbourne Mexico City   Nairobi
New Delhi Shanghai Taipei Toronto
With offices in
Argentina Austria Brazil Chile Czech Republic France Greece
Guatemala Hungary Italy Japan South Korea Poland Portugal
Singapore Switzerland Thailand Turkey Ukraine Vietnam

Oxford is a registered trade mark of Oxford University Press
in the UK and in certain other countries

Published in the United States
by Oxford University Press Inc., New York

ISBN 978-0-19-928006-3

The Short Oxford History of Germany

The *Short Oxford History of Germany* series provides a concise, readable, and authoritative point of entry for the history of Germany, from the dawn of the nineteenth century to the present day. The series is divided into five volumes, each one dealing with a distinct phase in the country's history. The first two volumes take the reader from the dying days of the Holy Roman Empire, through unification under Prussian leadership in 1871, to the collapse of the Wilhelmine Reich at the end of the First World War. The subsequent three volumes then focus on the Weimar period from 1919 to 1933; the calamitous years of the Third Reich and the Second World War; and Germany since 1945, first as two separate states on the front line of the Cold War and later as a reunified country at the heart of Europe.

NOW AVAILABLE:

Germany, 1800–1870

Imperial Germany, 1871–1918

Weimar Germany, 1919–1933

Nazi Germany, 1933–1945

Contents

    Karl Christian Führer

       The public promotion of art and culture   261
       Art as leisure   269
       Arts and the public   276

    Further Reading   282
    Chancellors of the Weimar Republic, 1919–1933   299
    Chronology   300
    Map   307
    Index   309

Glossary of terms
and abbreviations

Arbeiterwohlfahrt	Workers' Welfare
Ausnahmestaat	the 'extra-legal' or 'exceptional' state
BdF	Bund deutscher Frauenvereine (League of German Women's Associations)
Belagerungszustand	state of siege
Bund für Mutterschutz	League for the Protection of Mothers
Burgfrieden	social peace
BVP	Bavarian People's Party
CIAM	Congrès Internationaux d'Architecture Moderne
CV	Central-Verein deutscher Staatsbürger jüdischen Glaubens (Central Association of German Citizens of the Jewish Faith)
DDP	German Democratic Party
Deutscher Werkbund	German Work Federation
DNVP	German National People's Party
DST	Deutsche Städtetag (German Congress of Cities)
DVP	German People's Party
GDP	gross domestic product
Gleichschaltung	administrative synchronization
Heimat	localism or locality
IFFF	Internationale Frauenbund für Frieden und Freiheit (Women's International League for Peace and Freedom)

JFB	Jüdischer Frauenbund (League of Jewish Women)
JVP	Jewish People's Party
Kleinkinderfürsorge	early childhood welfare/infant welfare
Kleinrentner	pensioners
KPD	Kommunistische Partei Deutschlands (German Communist Party)
Kriegsbeschädigtenfürsorge	war-damaged welfare
Kriegswohlfahrtspflege	wartime welfare
Kulturnation	nation defined by culture
Länder	regional (federal) states
NDP	national domestic product
Neue Sachlichkeit	New Objectivity
NSDAP	Nationalsozialistische Deutsche Arbeiter Partei (National Socialist German Workers' Party)
Ostjuden	Eastern European Jews
Reichsexekution	suspension by the Reich of a federal state
Reichsrat	Reich Council of Ministers
Reichsreform	constitutional reform
Reichsstädtebund	association of small towns
Reichsstädteordnung	national municipal charter
Reichswehr	German army after 1918
RFB	Rotfrontkämpferband (Red Front Fighters' League)
Sonderweg	special path (denoting German peculiarity)
soziale Fürsorge	social relief
Sozialrentner	pensioners of the social insurance system
Spartacists	left-wing precursor to the KPD

SPD	Socialistische Partei Deutschlands (German Social Democratic Party)
Staatsstreich	*coup d'état*
Stahlhelm	Steel Helmets (right-wing veterans' association)
Truppenamt	successor to the General Staff from 1918
Ufa	Universum Film Aktiengesellschaft (Universal Film Company)
USPD	Unabhangige Sozialistische Partei Deutschlands (Independent Socialists)
Vereinigung	Zionist Organization
Vernunftrepublikaner	pragmatic republicans
völkisch	folkish (with racial connotations)
Volksgemeinschaft	people's community
Volkskrieg	people's war
Volksstaat	citizen state
Wehrhaftmachung	getting fit to fight
Weltanschauung	ideology
Weltpolitik	world politics
Wohlfahrtspflege	social welfare
Zentrum	Catholic Centre Party

List of contributors

JOHN BINGHAM is Assistant Professor of History at Dalhousie University, Toronto. He has published articles on urban cultures and political relations between the local and central state. He is the author of the recently published *Weimar Cities: The Metropolis between Isolation and Assimilation in Modern Germany, 1919–1936*; and is working on a long-term research project: *Crime under a Criminal Régime: The German Underworld in Nazi Berlin, 1933–1945*.

KATHLEEN CANNING is Arthur F. Thurnau Professor in History at the University of Michigan, Ann Arbor. She is the author of several acclaimed works on the Weimar Republic and on gender history, including *Gender History in Practice: Historical Perspectives on Bodies, Class, and Citizenship* (Ithaca, NY, 2006); *Gender, Citizenships and Subjectivities*, co-edited with Sonya O. Rose (London, 2002); she won the Central European Book Prize for 1996/7 for her monograph *Languages of Labor and Gender: Female Factory Work in Germany, 1850–1914* (Ithaca, NY, 1996). Her current research includes citizenship and gender in the Weimar Republic, European histories of the body, political violence in the aftermath of war, and the politics of social reform and social hygiene in the nineteenth and twentieth centuries. She is now writing a book entitled *Embodied Citizenships: Gender and the Crisis of the Nation in Germany, 1916–1930* and is editing together with Kerstin Barndt and Kristin McGuire *Weimar Publics, Weimar Subjects: Rethinking the Political Culture of Germany in the 1920s* (forthcoming 2009). She is the former North American co-editor of *Gender & History* and is currently on the editorial boards of the *American Historical Review* and *Central European History*.

WOLFGANG ELZ is Senior Lecturer of History, Johannes Gutenberg-Universität, Mainz, where he teaches modern European history. He is an internationally recognized authority on the foreign policy of Germany during the nineteenth and twentieth centuries. His main publications are *Die europäischen Großmächte und der kretische Aufstand 1866–1867* (= Quellen und Studien zur Geschichte des östlichen Europa 28, Stuttgart, 1988); editor with Winfried Baumgart and Werner Zürrer, *Preußische Akten zur Geschichte des Krimkriegs*, ii: *9. August 1854 bis 15. April 1856* (Munich, 1990); editor, *Weimarer Republik, Nationalsozialismus, Zweiter Weltkrieg (1919–1945)*, Part 2: *Persönliche Quellen* (= Quellenkunde zur deutschen Geschichte der Neuzeit von 1500 bis zur Gegenwart, ed. Winfried Baumgart, vol. 6, Darmstadt, 2003); editor, *Quellen zur Außenpolitik der Weimarer Republik 1918–1933* (= Ausgewählte Quellen zur deutschen Geschichte der Neuzeit. Freiherr-vom-Stein-Gedächtnisausgabe, vol. 32, Darmstadt, 2007).

KARL CHRISTIAN FÜHRER is Adjunct Professor of History, University of Hamburg, and Associate Senior Fellow, Institute for the Study of National Socialism and Contemporary History, Hamburg. He was formerly editor of *Archiv für Sozialgeschichte*, and has held a number of posts in German universities. He has written extensively on the social, economic, and cultural history of the Weimar Republic and Germany in the early twentieth century. Among his many publications are three important essays on media and culture: 'A medium of modernity? broadcasting in Weimar Germany, 1923–1932', *Journal of Modern History*, 69 (1997) and 'German cultural life and the crisis of national identity during the Depression, 1929–1933', *German Studies Review*, 24 (2001); 'Öffentlichkeit—Medien—Geschichte: Konzepte der modernen Öffentlichkeit und Zugänge zu ihrer Erforschung' (with Knut Hickethier and Axel Schildt), *Archiv für Sozialgeschichte*, 41 (2001); and the following monographs: *Wirtschaftsgeschichte des Rundfunks in der Weimarer Republik* (Potsdam, 1997); *Mieter, Hausbesitzer, Staat und Wohnungsmarkt: Wohnungsmangel und Wohnungszwangswirtschaft in Deutschland 1914–1960* (Stuttgart, 1995); *Arbeitslosigkeit und die Entstehung der Arbeitslosenversicherung in Deutschland: 1902–1927* (Berlin, 1990).

YOUNG-SUN HONG is Associate Professor of History, SUNY, where she teaches German and European history. She has written a number of important essays on welfarism and modernity, including the path-breaking 'The contradictions of modernization in the German welfare state: gender and the politics of welfare reform in First World War Germany', *Social History*, 17 (1992); her book *Welfare, Modernity, and the Weimar State, 1919–1933* (Princeton,

1998) is the seminal study of welfare under the republic. She is currently completing a study of poor relief and welfare in Germany from the Enlightenment to the First World War with a focus on social discipline and state formation, and is planning a future project that will investigate social hygiene, gender, and modernist aesthetics in twentieth-century urban planning and architecture. Her other interests include state theory and the public sphere, the culture of capitalism in post-war Europe, and history and memory.

HAROLD JAMES is Professor of History, Princeton University. He was previously a Fellow of Peterhouse, Cambridge, for eight years until 1986. An internationally acclaimed scholar of Germany, he is the author of a study of the inter-war depression in Germany, *The German Slump* (Oxford, 1986); an analysis of the changing character of national identity in Germany, *A Germany Identity 1770–1990* (London, 1989); and *A History of International Monetary Cooperation since 1945* (Oxford, 1996). His most recent work is *The End of Globalization: Lessons from the Great Depression* (Cambridge, Mass., 2001). He was also co-author of a history of the commercial bank Deutsche Bank (*Deutsche Bank*, 1995), also published in German by C. H. Beck, Munich, and which won the Financial Times Global Business Book Award in 1996. He recently published *The Deutsche Bank and the Nazi Economic War against the Jews* (Cambridge, 2001). He is a member of the Independent Commission of Experts investigating the political and economic links of Switzerland with Nazi Germany and of commissions to examine the roles of Deutsche Bank and Dresdner Bank, and is Chairman of the Editorial Board of *World Politics*.

ANTHONY D. KAUDERS is Lecturer in European History at the University of Keele. He has research interests in twentieth-century Germany, modern Jewish history, German-Jewish history, anti-Semitism, and the history of psychoanalysis. He is the author of many important essays on Jewish history, Weimar, and twentieth-century Germany. Among his publications are three monographs: *German Politics and the Jews: Düsseldorf and Nuremberg 1910–1933* (Oxford, 1996); *Democratization and the Jews: Munich 1945–1965* (Lincoln, Nebr., 2004); *Unmögliche Heimat: Eine deutsch-jüdische Geschichte der Bundesrepublik* (Munich, 2007). He has edited *Jüdische Geschichte lesen: Texte der jüdischen Geschichtsschreibung im 19. und 20. Jahrhundert* (together with M. Brenner, N. Roemer, and G. Reuveni) (Munich, 2003); *Jüdische Geschichte: Alte Heraus-forderungen, neue Ansätze* (together with E. Bar-Chen) (Munich, 2003).

ANTHONY MCELLIGOTT is Professor of History, University of Limerick, where he is also Director of the Centre for Historical Research. A founding member of the Hamburg History Workshop, among his publications are: *Contested City: Municipal Politics and the Rise of Nazism in Altona, 1917–1937* (Ann Arbor, 1998); *The German Urban Experience, 1900–1945: Modernity and Crisis* (London, 2001). He has edited with Tim Kirk *Opposing Fascism: Community, Authority and Resistance in Europe* (Cambridge, 1999) and the festschrift *'Working Towards the Führer': Essays in Honour of Sir Ian Kershaw* (Manchester, 2003); with Jordan Goodman and Lara Marks, *Useful Bodies: Humans in the Service of Medical Science in the Twentieth Century* (Baltimore, 2003). He is an editor of *Cultural and Social History: The Journal of the Social History Society*. He is currently finishing a book on authority under the Weimar Republic and a study of murder in Munich in the 1930s.

WILLIAM MULLIGAN is Lecturer in History, University College Dublin. He won the T. Desmond Williams Prize, University College Dublin (1997), and held the Robert Gardiner Scholarship, University of Cambridge (1997–2000). He has published a number of important articles on the army and the Weimar Republic, including 'Civil–military relations in the early Weimar Republic', *Historical Journal*, 'Restoring trust in the *Reichswehr*: the case of the *Vertrauensleute*', *War & Society*, and 'The Reichswehr, the Republic and the primacy of foreign policy, 1918–1923' in a recent special issue of *German History* devoted to the primacy of foreign policy which he edited together with Brendan Simms. His monograph *The Creation of the Modern German Army: General Walter Reinhardt and the Weimar Republic* was published by Berghahn in 2006.

ADELHEID VON SALDERN is Professor Emeritus in history at the University of Hanover. She is one of Germany's most distinguished social and cultural historians, being a founder member of the German Social History Workshop and a member of several international editorial boards and funding committees.

She has been a Visiting Scholar at Johns Hopkins University, Baltimore, the University of Chicago, and the Center for European Studies, Harvard University. She has published extensively over the past three decades on the history of the Weimar Republic and the Third Reich, most notably: *Häuserleben: Zur Geschichte städtischen Arbeiterwohnens vom Kaiserreich bis heute* (Bonn, 1995; 2nd edn. 1997); *Bauen und Wohnen in Niedersachsen während der fünfziger Jahre* (Hanover, 1999); she edited with Ulfert Herlyn and Wulf Tessin *Neubausiedlungen der 20er und 60er Jahre: Ein historisch-soziologischer Vergleich* (Frankfurt am Main, 1987); *Amerikanisierung: Traum und Alptraum im Deutschland des 20. Jahrhunderts* (Stuttgart, 1996) with Alf Lüdtke and Inge Marßolek; and with Inge Marßolek *Radiozeiten: Herrschaft, Alltag Gesellschaft* (Potsdam, 1999); a collection of her most important writings was published in English as *The Challenge of Modernity: German Social and Cultural Studies, 1890–1960* (Ann Arbor, 2002).

Introduction

Anthony McElligott

It is a wonder that the Weimar Republic, besieged from the outset
by hostile forces, should have lasted for as long as it did: fourteen
years. The early years were turbulent: revolution threatened from
the left; attempted *coups d'état* were staged from the right; political
assassination claimed the lives of many democrats, notably ministers Matthias Erzberger and Walther Rathenau, and the leaders
of the left-wing Spartacists, Karl Liebknecht and Rosa Luxemburg;
monetary instability ruined the lives of millions; in the later years
of the republic, from 1930, economic depression tore deep into the
social and political fabric and propelled the republic towards its
end. Even the so-called years of relative stability, between 1924 and
1929, were not without their difficulties: many investors and small
savers were left feeling cheated by the revaluation of the currency
that followed stabilization in 1924; tensions arose between the
judiciary and parliament over the proposed expropriation of the
princes in 1925; nationalists revolted against Locarno in the same
year; morality groups raged over alleged indecency on the stages of
Berlin's theatres; the Ruhr lockout in 1928, when employers took a
combative stance vis-à-vis iron and steel workers, finally killed off
the industrial accommodation symbolized by the Stinnes-Legien
agreement of 1918; in the north German countryside unrest was
brewing among peasant farmers who in 1929 besieged and bombed
tax offices; the introduction of the Young Plan provided grist to
the mill of nationalists; Chancellor Brüning's policies deepened the
economic depression, alienating and radicalizing the population,
finally pushing 37 per cent of the electorate towards Hitler in
July 1932. By the end of that summer Weimar Germany appeared

I am grateful to Liz Harvey for her helpful comments.

critically weakened and its democratic institutions immobilized. Lacking in authority and with its dwindling supporters unable to withstand the forces attacking it, the republic had little chance for survival.

And yet only a few years before, the republic had been stabilized and Germans had much to look forward to. A progressive constitution was in place; by 1926 Germany was reintegrated into the international community as a result of a successful conciliatory foreign policy, as Wolfgang Elz shows in his chapter to this volume; political differences were channelled through parliament, which, as seen in the contribution by the present author, functioned reasonably well; economic disputes were resolved via arbitration boards. Participation in elections remained high throughout the life of the republic, frequently over 60 per cent and rising to over 80 per cent respectively at communal, regional, and Reich elections. Similarly, workplace elections showed a strong participation; while membership of unions and white-collar associations was high, around seven and a half million in 1929, or roughly a fifth of the working population. Industrial unrest had waned considerably by the second half of the 1920s, with about a third of the working population covered by collective wage agreements. Another indicator of 'stake holding' could be found in the republic's vibrant associational life, providing a dense network of social, cultural, and educational activity with a strong emphasis upon local identity and traditions, especially in the provinces where the traditional idea of *Heimat* (locality) did not necessarily conflict with republican identity, as Celia Applegate found in her study of the Pfalz region.[1] The German people positively participated in the republic and to a lesser or greater degree, and in spite of its inherent contradictions, reaped the benefits of the welfare state, as we can read in the contributions to this volume by Adelheid von Saldern and Young-Sun Hong.[2]

Praise for the republic and its achievements was not confined solely to the self-congratulatory speeches and publications of 1929 that celebrated ten years of republican democracy. The very dry two-volume *Handbuch des Deutschen Staatsrechts* ('Manual of German Constitutional Law', 1931/2) pointed to the great strides made by Germany as a republic since 1919. Foreign observers commented favourably on the republic's social infrastructure, and notably its

housing programme, while visitors such as the young Stephen
Spender and Christopher Isherwood found the cultural atmosphere of the metropolises—described by John Bingham as 'urban
republics'—positively liberating, as too did the diplomat Harold
Nicolson. To be sure, 'Weimar culture' was famously restricted
to Berlin and a few other cities, such as Hamburg, and hardly
impinged upon the provinces, as Karl Christian Führer argues
at the end of this volume. Nevertheless, Weimar's cities came to
epitomize the republic—and its ambiguities, as too did Germany's
newly emancipated female population and its most important
minority, the Jews, as Kathleen Canning and Anthony Kauders
argue below. But among European societies in the post-war years,
Weimar Germany was an advanced polity with social and racial
integration.

But it had its critics, especially on the right, ranging from obvious candidates such as Oswald Spengler (whose *Decline of the West*,
originally published in 1918, referred to the alleged degeneracy of
Wilhelmine society!) to the constitutional theorist Carl Schmitt.
Critics could also be found on the left. Traditional elites viewed
the republic with scepticism, if not downright hostility, but were
nonetheless prepared to try and shape it, at least temporarily, as
William Mulligan shows. In the same year that Friedrich Stampfer
edited the anniversary volume *Zehn Jahre Republik* ('Ten Years
Republic'), Kurt Tucholsky published *Deutschland Deutschland
über alles* ('Germany, Germany above all else'), a damning indictment of Weimar governments' failure fully to deliver reforms leading to material improvement and social justice for all; this was an
indictment graphically echoed in the 1932 film *Kuhle Wampe oder
wem gehört die Welt?* ('Kuhle Wampe or who owns the world?'), a
collaboration between the director Slatan Dudow and playwright
Bertolt Brecht, when the depression was at its height. Meanwhile
the left-wing weekly journal *Die Weltbühne* ('The World Stage'),
with which Tucholsky was intimately associated, kept up a steady
stream of criticism.[3] But left-wing criticism was confined to a
loud but marginalized and ideologically desiccated Communist
movement. Towards the end of the 1920s, there was little in the
republic's origins, its recent past, and nothing in its present to
indicate the shape of things to come. To be sure, there were problems that remained unresolved during the good years, not least

the triple burden of social welfare, taxation, and reparations, as
Harold James argues; but paradoxically it was not strictly speaking
these burdens that brought Hitler to power. The conclusion that
James leaves us with is that had not the depression lifted when
it did (it had reached its nadir in the summer of 1932), Hitler's
cabinet would not have lasted and Weimar Germany's place in
history would have looked rather different.

The 'doomed' republic

Until recently, the idea of a 'doomed republic' grafted onto an
innately conservative social body that eventually rejected it was the
meta-narrative of Weimar Germany, in spite of its achievements. It
was already a theme among conservatives before the Third Reich,
when, for instance, in 1928, August Winnig, the former Social
Democrat *Oberpräsident* (provincial governor) of East Prussia (the
province described at the time by the *Herald* journalist Morgan
Philips Price as the 'Vendée of Weimar reaction'), gave a bleak
account of the republic's chances for survival.[4] In this reading, the
republic was hastily improvised with little substance of thought or
planning, without spiritual compass; a mere provisional construct.
The idea that the political arrangement that emerged from the
chaos of defeat in 1918 was merely a temporary fix was aired at
the time by *The Times*, and was held by some of the key players,
not least Paul von Hindenburg, and shared even by those national
liberals who had come to terms with the republic out of pragmatic
considerations rather than any deeply felt sentiment, the so-called
Vernunftrepublikaner. The historian Friedrich Meinecke, in his
classic study *The German Catastrophe*, written in the mid-1930s
but published a decade later, described the Weimar Republic
as an 'emergency construction' (*Notbau*).[5] This suggestion of a
makeshift polity lodged between two authoritarian regimes gained
widespread currency after 1945, finding its typical expression in a
collection of essays published in the early 1960s by the German
historian Theodor Eschenburg who, like his contemporary Golo
Mann, had come of age under the republic.[6]

Outside Germany there was a victors' history to explain the path to war in 1939. British and American historians applied their own standards of measurement to the republic. The former pointed the finger of blame at Weimar's proportional representation under the Constitution: this is what let the Nazis in the door in the first place, and as such was seen as a key flaw. The latter applied in abundance a sometimes crude political science and social psychology to tell us that the German people were not ready for democracy; in both approaches, Prussian militarism with all its atavistic connotations was to blame. It is of no surprise, therefore, that historians tend to view the republic and its actors through a dim lens. One of the leading German historians of the period, Hans Mommsen, pointed out some years ago that this negative discourse, originally stemming from the camp of the republic's detractors, has cast a 'long shadow' over historical discussions and, indeed, continues into the present day. Even the immensely gifted and critical historian the late Detlev J. K. Peukert, whose synthesis, published originally in 1987 and translated into English four years later as *The Weimar Republic: The Crisis of Classical Modernity*, offered a fresh approach to its history, in the end could not escape the prevailing paradigm of a republic thwarted at every turn by structural flaws, immaturity, and enemies. As recently as 2001 the German cultural historian Wolfgang Schivelbusch in a study of the impact of lost wars on civil societies alluded to the republic's 'culture of defeat', while Paul Nolte referred to Weimar's 'insecurity' and 'disorder' as the republic's defining features, thus echoing Peukert's diagnosis a decade earlier.[7]

The idea of a doomed republic is difficult to shake off, even among a new generation of younger scholars.[8] There is hardly a title without some reference to the impending disaster awaiting the republic and which places the republican experience firmly in the antechamber of the Third Reich. This approach to the republic continues to permeate secondary school curricula and still invades university lecture halls. And yet the picture is problematic, not least for the obvious reason that as historians we are trained not to read history backwards and yet we seem prepared to lapse when it comes to the Weimar Republic. For what these histories have in common is that they look back from the vantage point of '1933'. But to approach the history of Weimar Germany from this perspective in order to ask: 'How was Hitler possible?' and: 'Was the Nazi "seizure of power" avoidable?' skews our historical vision, as the German historian Eberhard Kolb has noted, and it militates against a nuanced understanding of the complex interplay of forces that shaped and reshaped the republic from its beginning. The fact is, in 1918 the republic's future was open and its history yet to be determined; Hitler was neither its predestined nor its obvious conclusion.[9] Weimar's history, therefore, should not be told through this lens alone.[10]

Weimar and the limits of 'crisis years of classical modernity'

If, as I suggest above, Detlev Peukert could not ultimately escape the 'doomed republic' paradigm, he nonetheless challenged historians to rethink the Weimar Republic by casting his approach to it in a different chronological and conceptual mould than had been the case up to that point. For Peukert, following on from David Blackbourn and Geoff Eley's attack against the *Sonderweg* (literally, special path) thesis that postulated a German singularity to explain the phenomenon of Hitler,[11] there was little to differentiate German development since the mid-nineteenth century from that of much of West and Central Europe. Indeed, when set against the wider European landscape, there was little that was 'special' or different about Germany's development in the nineteenth century. Landed elites exerted influence and power over the polity almost everywhere in Europe; newer social forces thrown up by industrial and financial capitalism were emergent in many European societies; the character of state institutions comprised a mixture of both reaction and reform; every European society nurtured a mythologized romanticism rooted in nationalist soil. The crucial 'peculiarity'—if that is the right term to use—was that modernization in late nineteenth- and early twentieth-century Germany was more attenuated than elsewhere.

Drawing heavily from the writings of the German philosopher Jürgen Habermas, Peukert reframed the republic within the idea of a 'crisis of classical modernity' in which European society in the three decades from the turn of the century faced a series of ruptures brought about by the wrenching changes associated with economic, social, and cultural modernization.[12] In the vanguard of European modernity and its contradictions, Germany experienced these transformations more acutely than elsewhere because here the transformations were more jagged and widespread. By demythologizing German history and casting it in an alternative and broader context, Peukert sought to release Weimar from the determinist shadow of the Third Reich. His approach restored contingency to the republic; but he was nonetheless still left with the vexed question, given that most of the industrial world was struck by similar multiple crises around 1930, why Germany's path led to the catastrophe of Hitler. Nevertheless, Peukert's approach opened new doors for the study of Germany in the first half of the twentieth century.

Peukert's approach in *Crisis of Classical Modernity*, with its greater emphasis on the social, culture, and the 'everyday', reflected the shift that had been taking place among historians in Germany since the 1970s, and was path-breaking. Peukert's book was to have an enormous impact on scholarship in the following two decades, and arguably established itself as one of the paradigms for studying Weimar. This influence notwithstanding, Weimar as a 'crisis' of 'classical modernity' is now in need of some elaboration, as contributors to a recent symposium at the Humboldt University in Berlin argued.[13] Recent research has begun to extend the paradigm to considerations of both the periodization and nature of modernity. Social and cultural historians of the *experience* of Germany's modernization (the latter is here defined as a conscious project of change, while the former is understood as modernity) have gone back to the works of Georg Simmel (1903), Siegfried Kracauer (1927), and Ernst Bloch (1935), to name just three of its most important critics, to gain a better understanding of what was taking place in Germany at this time. These authors, in different ways, had sought to delve below the surface of modernity in an attempt to capture the sensory and 'inner' experiences of change. Building on their approach, increasingly social historians are adopting a more elastic periodization that now extends into the 1950s and beyond. There is an increasing acceptance that there was not a single path to modernity; nor indeed was modernity itself one dimensional but polyvalent, as Peukert argued, and as is emphasized in this volume by Hong and von Saldern. On closer examination Weimar's 'crisis' need not be interpreted as a 'crisis of modernity' *per se*, but instead as one where there was an ongoing tension between these different paths to modernization. For this reason, we prefer to talk of 'ambiguities' rather than 'crisis' of modernity. What is meant by this should become clearer as we develop our arguments below.

Weimar and the ambiguities of 'classical modernity'

As suggested in the foregoing, the question of the Weimar experience as 'modernity in crisis' is problematic, for it posits the notion that there was only one type of modernity (a liberal parliamentary model), and so ignores the potential for other meanings or types of modernity, and not least those of a more authoritarian or reactionary nature as described some years ago by Jeffrey Herf.[14] The ambiguities of 'classical modernity' can be traced in most of the contributions to the present volume. For instance in his discussion of Weimar's political culture, Anthony McElligott focuses on the competing visions for political order that accompanied the republic from its beginnings. Here important ideas regarding the nature and role of political leadership were crucial: whether that leadership should reside in a single person, or a small executive, or be collectively shared, as implied by parliamentary democracy. In 1918/19 contingency shaped the contours of Weimar Germany's political order and favoured the latter; ten years on a different set of contingencies demanded a different model of governance.

McElligott emphasizes the importance of perception in dictating action. The type of republic that emerged in the winter of 1918/19 was very much the product of a perception of catastrophe in which crisis management demanded a political pragmatism that allowed hostile forces to unite in an uneasy alliance to save the Reich. Germany had lost the war; its sovereignty was vulnerable and its borders under challenge; quite apart from the tumult on the streets, it faced the threat of fragmentation as secessionist voices grew louder—particularly in Bavaria; its economy was severely strained by the cost of war and demobilization. Against this background, the new political leaders of Germany and the old elites acted to stabilize the country as quickly as possible and in the process adopted an authoritarian politics: parliamentary sovereignty was accorded second place to executive power, enhanced by special laws and later Article 48. While it is unlikely that the pre-republican elites lost much sleep over this question, the new parliamentary elites displayed a more complex, indeed, ambiguous, attitude to the question of government, as their discussions over the constitution and extraordinary powers reveal. The Weimar Constitution was not only a compromise between particular sectional interests, not least that of women, as Kathleen Canning points out, but also between philosophical ideas as to the visible form of the state. The inherent tensions in the ideas and practices of politics and the most appropriate form of leadership in any given circumstance remained not far below the surface, and in more than one way defined the republic. In the end, Weimar's political institutions were contested sites for power between those who favoured a citizen state (*Volksstaat*) and those who favoured an executive state. Thus the ambiguities of Weimar's political culture lay in the fact that, at the surface level, it was a constitutionally determined parliamentary democracy, but below the surface inclined towards authoritarianism. Thus democracy and authoritarianism were minted from the same coinage of modernity.

The post-1918 state *per se* was not in contention with the old elites. As we can see in Wolfgang Elz's chapter, senior civil servants, the bastion of Wilhelmine *Weltpolitik* (world politics), after the humiliation of Versailles were nonetheless pragmatic enough to go with the grain under the republic as long as it served the interests of the 'eternal' Reich (Mulligan). These hitherto autonomous policy makers and advisers had to attune themselves equally to the international sphere in which they traditionally operated and to the domestic pressures arising from Germany's democratization. No longer the arcane and autonomous sphere it had appeared to be under the empire, Weimar foreign policy had to take into account domestic political factors in its formulation and practice.

It is clear now that foreign policy, and especially that associated with Gustav Stresemann, was framed by public perceptions of Germany's international role after the First World War, as it was by the signing of the Versailles Treaty that set the boundaries of the republic's foreign policy and by international considerations during the 1920s. Elz's nuanced picture of public pressures on and responses to foreign policy under the republic shows how the early policy confusion gave way to a more expansive, considered, and for the most part forgiving approach that was by and large accepted by the public. Stresemann's policy of 'quiet revisionism' was partly dictated by the emasculation of the military under the terms of the Treaty. This changed after Stresemann's death in 1929 when internal and external conditions were no longer conducive to international conciliation or restraint, and nationalist voices grew more strident, not least within military circles. Calls for the revision of the Treaty were as much part of political rhetoric as real: by the beginning of the 1930s many of the indignities (though by no means all) had in fact been removed. While foreign policy under the republic was determined to a large degree by the contingencies arising from the Versailles Treaty, there were larger issues at stake that transcended the post-war arrangements, not least the faltering steps towards some sort of idea of European unity, at least as a market area, suggesting tantalizing continuities with later developments.[15] The aim of Stresemann's policy of conciliation was to restore Germany as an international power, but through peaceful means and within a European context. What emerges, however, is the highly ambivalent nature of foreign policy thinking, both before, during, and after Stresemann. When reconsidered from the angle of either Peukert's 'crisis years of classical modernity' or simply modernity's ambiguities, Weimar's foreign policy throws up completely different questions from those constrained by the straitjacket of 1919.

In a similar vein, William Mulligan shows how the military, another prime example of Weimar's 'reactionary modernists' (Herf), believed that while the Reich was 'eternal' its political form need not be. Leading officers, such as Generals Reinhardt and Groener, did not reject the republic out of hand but tolerated it as long as it facilitated military aims. They were pragmatists who had an interest in the stability of the republic in order to pursue their goal of restoring post-Versailles Germany to its former status as a Great Power. What is clear from reading Mulligan's account is that the attitude of officers towards the republic is more complex than normally assumed. Mulligan shows how the 'primacy of foreign policy' underwrote military calculations in the 1920s. But military thinkers were not in total agreement on the means to achieving a restoration of power status. There were differing visions on how this should be achieved, and these are the focus of Mulligan's discussion.

Army leaders were united in their concern on the need for a national regeneration (here also reminiscent of post-1806 Prussia), but differed on how best to achieve this. If Reinhardt, Seeckt, and Groener were pragmatists who worked with the grain of Weimar politics, then Blomberg, Stülpnagel, and Schleicher inclined more towards a radical utopian vision that envisaged the thorough reordering of civil society into a militarized national community (here there are links to the Ludendorff–Hindenburg Programme of 1916 and to Germany after 1938) and a dynamic rearmament programme, both of which ran counter to domestic imperatives and Stresemann's policy of quiet revisionism, examined in Elz's chapter. All of these officers were prepared to cooperate at various stages with the Weimar state, which they saw as the servant of the military, not vice versa. By the early 1930s, it had become clear to the army leadership that the republic was making little progress on military aims, leading it to jettison the parliamentary system in favour of dictatorship. The Nazi Party, with its mass support and overtly nationalistic, militaristic aims, appeared to represent a domestic political precondition to the pursuit of international power politics. Blomberg and others thought they saw a community of aims between the *Reichswehr* and the Nazi movement and for this reason supported Hitler in 1933. However, this community of aims proved to be a mirage ending in a loss of control over questions of national security to Hitler by 1938. Mulligan argues in his chapter that this well-documented shift had already begun under the Weimar Republic with the formulation of increasingly radical solutions to the inter-war military crisis that eventually paved the way for the developments of the later 1930s that were to refashion German society as a military national community.

The military national community of Ludendorff–Hindenburg had failed in 1918. Weimar Germany was a civil national community in which the people—in theory at least—were sovereign. This raised the question of their suitability as determiners of the new republican polity. The military technocrats discussed by Mulligan had their counterparts in Weimar's social workers (among others, including architects) who, as 'technicians of social modernity', were entrusted with the task of carrying out the national project of civic rehabilitation. Different, and yet similar, therefore, were the visions of shaping 'the people' into a national community after 1918. Social and welfare agencies believed they faced a society in which the majority had been stymied by rapid industrialization and squalid living conditions in overcrowded towns and cities, exacerbated by wartime privations; the 'people' were weakened biologically and spiritually, having lost their moral compass as the collapse of the 'home front' purported to show. The end of the old order promised a new beginning; an opportunity to refashion the nation according to principles of modern science, enabled by technology and modernized technocratic organization.[16] After 1918, social policy became 'constitutionalized' (Peukert), turning the physical and inner worlds of the working class into the prerogative of the state to shape and regulate.

As Young-Sun Hong argues in her chapter, the relationship between citizenship and social welfare in the republic was defined in important ways by the dialectic of emancipation and social discipline, the two contradictory elements of the ambiguities of the modern liberal state. On the one hand, the Weimar Constitution postulated a close relationship between citizenship and social welfare, and the republic witnessed the proliferation of rights-based discourses of social welfare among ordinary Germans. On the other hand, social welfare services became increasingly indispensable for inculcating civic values into those actual and potential recipients of social services. Through its practices underpinned by rationality and rationalization, welfare imposed normative models upon individuals (and society). Jürgen Habermas has referred to this process as a form of 'inner colonization' of the individual's private sphere by the state in its attempt to shape society more broadly.[17] Welfare became a general term designating not simply the various forms of assistance to the poor, but all forms of interventions directed towards the production and reproduction of the normal subject. Building on the work of Peukert, Hong examines this contradictory and often contested nature of the Weimar social welfare system, in particular the infant, youth, and maternal welfare programmes, which formed the backbone of the system and which had their origins in war welfare. Hong's examination of the vision and experience of citizenship and modernity in the conflict-ridden process of making the Weimar welfare system reveals that concepts such as 'social disciplining' (Foucault) are ambiguous and problematic in the Weimar case, where many of the initiatives were welcomed by ordinary citizens, who also however resented their emasculation at the hands of state policy. She notes the latent proclivities of welfare to recategorize people into those for whom welfare can work and those deemed beyond redemption. Hong nevertheless warns against making too trite a connection to the racial policies of the Third Reich. There was, in the end, a distinction between Weimar's welfare modernity, which was largely predicated upon 'nurture', and that of the Third Reich, with its emphasis upon 'purifying' and which ultimately proved eliminationist in both intention and practice.[18]

Although a number of European countries in the post-war period embarked upon social programmes, Weimar Germany stood in the vanguard of this social modernization. The welfare programmes discussed by Young-Sun Hong focused on the body; but to be successful, the built environment also had to undergo reform. At a fringe meeting of municipal representatives at the Social Democratic Party Congress in 1920, Paul Hirsch, who briefly became Prussia's first prime minister and himself was an expert on municipal affairs, told his colleagues, 'good apartments, cheap apartments, plenty of apartments, produce a good social life, a good family life, and this creates stability which makes the workers industrious and honourable'. As Adelheid von Saldern notes, new directions in mass housing go to the heart of the social-political visions under the Weimar Republic as to how the future was to be shaped. The republic went on to build around 2 million, largely subsidized, housing units before the economic depression ended construction. The housing estates built by Ernst May in Frankfurt, Martin Wagner and Bruno Taut in Berlin, and the ideas of Walter Gropius, who founded the Bauhaus in Weimar in 1919, and its subsequent directors, Hannes Meyer and Mies van der Rohe, just to name the better-known socially engaged architects and city planners associated with the collectively termed movement of New Construction (*Neues Bauen*), became the visible hallmark of the Weimar state. Indeed, even though the avant-garde estates of *Neues Bauen* constituted barely 5 per cent of construction under the republic, they nonetheless cast in stone the ethos of reform and they exposed in heightened form the ambiguities of modernity.

These new estates were designed according to Fordist principles of rationalization and normative principles of behaviour. Residents, and, in particular, housewives, were to act functionally in their apartments and so be able to manage with a minimum of living space (determined by cost of land). The resulting ethos of 'new living' implied social disciplining with a strong emphasis placed on order and cleanliness, so-called *Wohnhygiene*, according to strict rules with regard to communal life and to the contents and internal arrangements of the apartments themselves. But the flip side to social disciplining was emancipation of the individual—and in this case, women. The rationalized organization of life in the new home was intended both to elevate housework as a social function and to create free time in which women would educate themselves, as befitted them as newly enfranchised citizens of the republic state. As Kathleen Canning also notes, here the ambiguous nature of Weimar's modernity, with its contradictory claims upon women, could be found. Central to the project of reconstructing Germany was the search for an organic totality (*Ganzheit*) of the national body, as historians from Peter Gay to Paul Nolte have noted.[19] But the project of reconstructing Germany via its new housing policy was hampered by a number of economic, social, political, and cultural crises that beset the republic after 1930. Von Saldern concludes that the social and political divisions of the imperial period which were seen as the root of the divided nation were not overcome, but given an even greater spatial configuration. Moreover, the new housing itself became both an ideological and physical site of political conflict, like much else under the republic, as competing visions clashed. In much the same way as Hong and other contributors to this volume, von Saldern emphasizes the ambiguity inherent in Weimar modernity. Like Hong, she posits a link between the polyvalent nature of Weimar social and physical hygiene and the radical racial version incorporated into the Third Reich, while at the same time being cautious not to overstate the continuity between the two versions of modernity.

The mobilization of the home population for the war effort brought women and state into direct contact, radically transforming the relationship in the process as the war progressed. With their menfolk mobilized, women's expectations and perceptions of themselves were greatly altered both as a result of their contributions to the war effort and also as a result of their own privations and sacrifice as wives and mothers. Kathleen Canning argues that although one should be careful not to overstate the emancipatory effect of the war on women, the experience nonetheless created a heightened consciousness of women as actors; this paved the way for citizenship in the 1920s. The war thus set the parameters for gender relations under the republic. Death in the trenches created a female 'surplus' in the population that was only overcome in 1928; the horrific maiming and trauma of war destabilized traditional masculinity; political empowerment was matched by sexual empowerment and a confidence as producers and consumers. Younger women especially were not about to retreat to the now-idealized conventions of home and hearth of pre-war Germany. In short women—and especially young, single women—became visible emblems of Weimar modernity that led to anxiety (in some quarters) that the nation was being feminized. In a discourse that paralleled fears about Jews as the 'other' (see the discussion below), the visibility of Weimar's 'new women' came to represent a disordering moment in national life. Carl Gustav Jung spoke for many, notably conservatives, when he declared that women's emancipation endangered not only the institution of marriage but also the whole spiritual balance between the masculine and feminine principle. Canning makes the point that much of the (misogynistic) negativity surrounding women was stimulated by a public image that emphasized the new woman as 'glamorous', a frivolous consumer, capricious, ungovernable, and childlike (an image that was reinforced by depictions of the 'new woman' in the popular media, and especially cinema). Canning shows that visibility was also due to the enlargement of the public sphere after 1918, generated in part by female activism and growing numbers of economically active women. For instance, women's organizations expanded after 1918, large sectors of the economy, notably assembly-line light manufacturing and services, became 'feminized', and trade union growth owed much to female membership; meanwhile the half-million or so war widows became a powerful lobby (and formed a sizeable portion of the welfare recipients discussed by Hong); welfare and family became national imperatives; and campaigns for control over reproductive rights, especially in the depression years, thrust women and women's issues to the forefront of Weimar politics. While this enlarged sphere recorded women as citizens, at the same time it exposes how they (and especially their bodies) were also sites of intervention, as the social state sought to literally rehabilitate the national body via those of women. Attitudes towards women's position after 1918, like that of the republic and the general reception of modernity, were filled with ambiguity, as contemporary surveys, such as that conducted by Erich Fromm in 1929, showed.[20] Conflicts over gender roles were apparently resolved by the Nazi takeover and a resurgence of conservative models of womanhood—though it quickly became clear that National Socialism's policies on women and the family owed little to traditional conservatism and far more to the twin goals of racial hygiene and the mobilization of human resources for war.

The precise relationship between the ambiguities of modernity and the crisis of the republic needs to be examined carefully. Wolfgang Elz's chapter throws into stark relief the limitations of 'modernity in crisis' as a hermeneutic model for studying foreign policy under the republic. Karl Christian Führer in this volume also challenges the conventional picture of Weimar's 'cultural modernity'. Führer argues that the traditional notion of Germany as a *Kulturnation* (a nation defined by culture) rather than as a society steeped in 'Americanization' took on greater meaning for Germany's educated classes during the Weimar period. In the wake of defeat, German culture not only became a last resort of national pride, it became also a means of moral rehabilitation and spiritual regeneration that stood at the heart of Weimar cultural policy and which was now the responsibility of state and municipal administrations that had taken over, for the most part, theatres, museums, and similar cultural institutions. Historians have mostly posited a 'hothouse' idea to Weimar culture. But, as Führer argues, this is based on a selective post-1945 memory of 'Weimar culture' that has skewed our understanding of the historical reality.[21] In much the same way that *Neues Bauen* only ever constituted a small part of housing construction, as Adelheid von Saldern points out in her chapter, so too 'Weimar culture' as expressed through the generation of avant-garde artists (some of who were also linked to the Bauhaus), or the sumptuous revues of Berlin's West End and Mitte districts, or risqué cabarets, or the luxury consumption of the major department stores, or above all by the cinema and such iconic films as Robert Wiene's *Das Cabinet des Dr. Caligari* (1919/20), or F. W. Murnau's *Nosferatu* (1921), or Fritz Lang's *Metropolis* (1927), or Josef Sternberg's *The Blue Angel* (1931), only ever constituted a small part of Weimar's cultural modernity. Not the heady atmosphere of Berlin, Führer argues, but the mundane province, not 'high life' but the 'lowbrow' of prosaic forms of both traditional and 'light' entertainment with their inclination towards nostalgia, characterized Weimar's cultural landscape. This is not to say that 'culture' under the republic was not a site of discord. Since the inflation, 'culture', like welfare, had largely become the prerogative of the local state; it cost money—and this was usually supplied grudgingly by the local taxpayer. And there was discord too as competing understandings of 'German culture' jostled with one another and conflicted with the 'international style' favoured by modernist architecture; the idea of Weimar as a 'crisis of culture' (*Kulturkrise*) exemplified by the modernist aesthetic was mounted by nationalists as a surrogate field of battle with the republic that undermined its cultural stability, eventually allowing for the Nazi purge of 'degenerate art' in the 1930s. In some ways the conclusion reached by Führer also resonates with the experience of Jews, as Anthony Kauders's examination of Weimar's Jews, their communal relations, diverse cultures and outlooks, and political behaviour, shows.

Between 1918 and 1933 Jews comprised barely 1 per cent of the population of Germany, and yet their impact has been important for obvious and not so obvious reasons. Given the smallness of numbers, Kauders asks, 'why study Jews?' The answer, as he goes on to argue, is because they perhaps more than any other group epitomized the very contradictions of Weimar modernity. Their cosmopolitanism shared certain similarities with Weimar's internationalism and its attempts to reconstitute itself as a nation after defeat; Jewish identity in the 1920s was buffeted between cultural globalization and social separation, but at the same time it was intimately bound together with Weimar liberalism, to which its affiliation was stable. As Kauders shows, Weimar's Jews were not a homogeneous group: they organized in religious and sometimes linguistic communities, participated in political organizations, and were identified by social standing (sometimes all these elements came together in a spatial context as in the lower-class district of 'Scheunenviertel' near Alexanderplatz in Berlin or in the area between Dammtor and Grindelberg in Hamburg). The hybrid identity that could result from this (German, Pole, Russian, secular Jew, *fromme Jude* (pious Jew), Zionist, nationalist, conservative, liberal, middle class, working class, and so forth) could be found in other groups, for instance the much larger religious community of Catholics. But in the case of Weimar Jews it seemed to single them out. If Weimar modernity was characterized by fluidity and tempo, Jews, as *the* paradigm of multiple identities, non-fixity, and mobility in its social, cultural, and geographical senses, embodied the transgressive: and as such were disordering and disorderly in an age that sought fixity. Indeed, the sociologist Zygmunt Bauman refers to the modern period as the 'age of gardening', when design and cultivation predominated as societal paradigms of orderly modernization (this is a metaphor that is also entirely appropriate to Weimar's social welfare policy).[22] The very fact of their cultural and social and political propinquity to Weimar modernity and to the republican polity made Jews all the more 'dangerous' in a society lacking confidence in itself. Indeed, the attitude towards Jews among Gentiles in Weimar Germany was marked by an ambiguity that turned increasingly hostile—paralleling that towards the republic itself. Because of their apparently amorphous identity, Jews were cast as the disorderly 'other' and after 1933 became destined for 'weeding out' (Bauman) in order to create space for and to nurture a racially homogenized Germany.

Tensions within the republic were not only of a political, class, cultural, or racialized nature; they also ran along a centre–periphery faultline. To be exact, there were tensions within the state itself, and this too was very much a product of the contradictions arising from early twentieth-century modernity.

On the one hand, Germany's strong localism embedded in its administrative and civic culture since 1808 was itself 'constitution-alized' (Article 127); on the other hand, a feature of modernization was its demand for more centralized powers, inevitably at the expense of localism. A good example here was the reform of the tax system from 1917 and culminating in the Erzberger tax reforms of 1920 that arrogated to the Reich direct taxation at the expense of the local and regional states. But the irony is that it was precisely the local and regional authorities that carried the reforms of Weimar Germany in an effort to rebuild the nation after war and defeat. Its great (and lesser) cities especially promoted the new international-style architecture alongside the old, concentrated wealth, drove consumption, fostered some of the most remarkable artistic experi-mentation of the twentieth century, and formed the laboratories of the burgeoning welfare state. Thus Weimar's cities stood in the vanguard of modernity, but also suffered from its ambiguities. For all their vibrancy and apparent power, cities occupied positions of curious political, financial, and cultural weakness in Germany after the First World War, not least because of the tax reforms referred to above. Although some Germans viewed with pride their cities' achievement and industry, others (foremost conservatives and the Nazis) hated the speed and impersonality of urban life and rejected as alien the new shapes and forms in the built environment, loathed and feared working-class politics, and looked beyond the growing social and economic centrality of the city to the central state as the proper caretaker and administrator of the German nation.

As John Bingham shows, these tensions surfaced in the cities' campaign in the late 1920s for a constitutional restructuring of the Reich to their benefit. Arguing that their vastly increased social responsibilities after the war required a comparable increase in resources, mayors demanded greater revenue, closer ties with central institutions, a vast reform to standardize the existing patchwork of legislation across regional and state governments, and a strong collective voice in the national (Reich) government. This was little short of a claim to reshape the republic's administration and constitutional structure in favour of the cities, where, after all, over a third of the population lived in 1925. But the decentralized unitary state advocated by Oskar Mulert and his colleagues in the Deutsche Städtetag (German Congress of Cities, or DST), the body that represented the cities, never materialized for a variety of reasons, not least because of the stand-off between powerful vested interests and because of the distractions facing government after 1930. Nonetheless, a *Reichsreform* (constitutional reform) creating the unitary state did eventually come about, but *after* 1933. However, the longed for equalization of local government vis-à-vis the central and regional states failed to materialize. Thus it is ironic that the demands for standardized principles of self-government and an end to the states' wilful interference in municipal affairs were realized in 1935 with the passing of a new Reich Local Government Statute (lauded at the time as a new basic constitution for the Reich) but at the cost of local autonomy. Nevertheless, as Bingham stresses, at its core Hitler's 'urban modernity', while departing in some aspects radically from that of the republic, arguably contained many of the same imperatives to modernize, and it continued to harbour many of the old tensions and ambiguities too. Thus the ambiguities of modernity did not stop at the gates of '1933' but continued well into the 1940s. Indeed, the tension between local and central states was only resolved in the post-Second World War period.

If, in the beginning, there was Versailles (Elz), then in the end, it was the economy. The enormous responsibilities of government in the modern period, especially those associated with welfare and social rehabilitation after the Great War, burdened the Weimar Republic. Other European countries also had to face the economic costs of reconstruction, but the extensive nature of the modernization programme set Weimar Germany apart and demanded that some sort of consensus based on compromise was formed. As Harold James argues in his contribution to this volume, the fate of the Weimar Republic depended upon the ability of its politicians to successfully maintain a consensus between the traditionally hostile camps of capital and labour. This required the state to play an active role in the distribution of wealth, on the one hand, protecting wage demands and standards of living through social programmes in welfare and housing, and, on the other hand, helping industrialists and business to maintain their profits. Thus the republic stood in the vanguard of what we today call corporatism or social partnership—a strategy mix of control and market (a model that was to stabilize Europe in the decades after 1945), but which failed to deliver. As James shows, this strategy worked initially in overcoming the political crisis of the early years of the republic (thus partly contributing to the inflation of that period), but increasingly the policy of consensus came under attack during the years of so-called 'relative stabilization' (1924–9), as employers and labour unions battled over the size of the wage packet against a background of low productivity and dislocated markets that limited corporate profits and investment in the late 1920s, and in turn led to sluggish growth and budget deficits. The conflicts climaxed at the height of the depression in 1932, when the twin crises in the economy and in political life intersected in cataclysmal fashion to end the parliamentary system. Thus it is to the depression years that we look to when trying to gauge Weimar's crisis of modernity, and here the intersection between economy and politics becomes critical. How far could the German economy have been cushioned by the vagaries of the international economy, of which it was an integral part, in the early 1930s? Was Chancellor Brüning's pro-cyclical (deflationary) policy the correct one to follow, or should he have embarked upon a counter-cyclical policy to reflate the economy?

The type of modern economy that was emerging in early twentieth-century Europe (and which was to last until the mid-1970s) was one which required political will in order to develop macro-economic planning and to manage consensus among the participating parties. In Germany, the experience of the First World War had pointed to the importance of economic planning, but republican administrations failed to grasp fully the meaning of its changed role (even though its attitude was different with respect to the provision and management of social policies) with regard to the latter. Moreover, by 1930 government under Brüning was becoming increasingly partisan. Within two years Germany's captains of industry and finance were actively interested in ending the 'democratic experiment', seeking instead a return to once again becoming 'masters in their own house', mirroring the aims of radical conservatives in politics and bureaucracy and in the military. By the turn of the year 1932/3 they saw in Hitler albeit a temporary stop-gap en route to restoring this twin authority and disengaging government from the economy. But their reading of events and their timing was poor. Hitler was the beneficiary of the international economic upturn, of the renegotiated terms of reparations, and was prepared to embark upon a counter-cyclical programme in June 1933 in an attempt to put the country back to work (and thus stabilize his government in the process); he also interfered in the market by imposing a policy of price and wage controls, while at the same time passing legislation in the spring of 1934 that restored authority to the employers. In other words, the unstable compromise of Weimar's mixed economy gave way to the imposed settlement of the Third Reich. That the latter version of economic modernity was also inherently destabilizing is well known and ended with a 'flight into war' in 1939.[23] But it requires us to look again at Weimar Germany in a longer and more fluid trajectory, one in which competing models of economic modernization vie with one another for hegemony and require either a more forceful government than that on offer under the republic or the free hand of the market.

Conclusion

There are two distinct histories here which nonetheless are fated to share the same space. The Weimar Republic was in one sense a political contingency, but it was also the product of secular transformations that we collectively refer to as 'modernity'. Weimar Germany as a republic was marred by crises that derived from internal conflicts as well as external pressures. It nonetheless was able to withstand these crises for as long as the forces that carried it were prepared to act together. As some of the chapters in this volume show, the ending of that consensus represented an opportunity to regain what certain elite circles thought they had lost in 1918. At the same time, Weimar incubated and promoted at astonishing speed the modernization of Germany as a social state. But the very essence of this transformation was itself contested. For some the parliamentary system in the end could not deliver—or at least, not quickly enough—the aims and aspirations of broad sections of the population; while for others it was viewed as inimical to fulfilling ideals of *Weltpolitik*. The ending of the democratic republic in 1933 did not bring to an end the project of modernity—it was not 'incomplete' (Habermas) in that sense, but, as the authors of this volume suggest, continued beyond the republic. What ended in 1933 was a particular political and social consensus for delivering modernization *per se*. As we have seen, modernity itself was highly ambiguous, poised as it was between benign and coercive reform. This contradiction ran through the life of the republic both constituting and resulting in what historians refer to as the 'crisis' of Weimar Germany in the years of classical modernity.

Notes

1. Celia Applegate, *A Nation of Provincials: The German Idea of Heimat* (Berkeley and Los Angeles, 1990), chapter 6 in particular.
2. For comprehensive accounts see Ludwig Preller, *Sozialpolitik in der Weimarer Republik* (Düsseldorf, 1978; 1st pub. 1949); Werner Abelshauser, 'Die Weimarer Republik: Ein Wohlfahrtsstaat?', in idem, *Die Weimarer Republik als Wohlfahrtsstaat: Zum Verhältnis von Wirtschafts- und Sozialpolitik in der Industriegesellschaft* (= Vierteljahrsschrift für Wirtschaftsgeschichte Beiheft 87, Stuttgart, 1987), 9–31.
3. Istvan Deak, *Weimar Germany's Left-Wing Intellectuals: Political History of the 'Weltbühne' and its Circle* (Berkeley, 1968). For both left and right, see the contributions in Anthony Phelan (ed.), *The Weimar Dilemma: Intellectuals in the Weimar Republic* (Manchester, 1985).
4. August Winnig, *Das Reich als Republik 1918–1928* (Stuttgart, 1928). For a comprehensive account of anti-republicanism in East Prussia see Andreas Kossert, *Ostpreussen Geschichte und Mythos* (Munich, 2007), 196–273, *passim*.
5. Friedrich Meinecke, *Die Deutsche Katastrophe* (Berlin, 1947), 88.
6. Theodor Eschenburg, *Die improvisierte Demokratie: Gesammelte Aufsätze zur Weimarer Republik* (Munich, 1963). Golo Mann, *Reminiscences and Reflections: Growing up in Germany* (London, 1990; orig. German 1987).
7. Wolfgang Schivelbusch, *Culture of Defeat: On National Trauma, Mourning, and Recovery* (London, 2003; orig. *Die Kultur der Niederlage*, Berlin, 2001). Paul Nolte, *Die Ordnung der deutschen Gesellschaft: Selbstentwurf und Selbstbeschreibung im 20. Jahrhundert* (Munich, 2000), 64, 72, 74. Detlev J. K. Peukert, 'The Weimar Republic:

old and new perspectives', *German History*, 6/2 (1988), 139. Hans Mommsen, 'Der lange Schatten der untergehenden Republik: Zur Kontinuität politischer Denkhaltungen von den späten Weimarer zur frühen Bonner Republik', in Karl Dietrich Bracher, Manfred Funke, and Hans-Adolf Jacobsen (eds.), *Die Weimarer Republik 1918–1933: Politik, Wirtschaft, Gesellschaft* (Düsseldorf, 1987), 552–86.

8. Two recent examples, both in German, are Andreas Wirsching, *Die Weimarer Republik: Politik und Gesellschaft* (Munich, 2000), and Ricardo Bavaj, *Von Links gegen Weimar: Linkes antiparlamentarisches Denken in der Weimarer Republik* (Bonn, 2005).

9. Friedrich Stampfer, *Der 9. November: Gedenkblätter zu seiner Wiederkehr* (Berlin, 1919), 36; Meinecke, *Katastrophe*, 95–7.

10. For the 'rise of the Nazis' during the Weimar Republic that avoids this, see Peter Fritzsche, 'The NSDAP 1919–1934: from fringe politics to seizure of power', in Jane Caplan (ed.), *Nazi Germany*, Short Oxford History of Germany (Oxford, 2008).

11. David Blackbourn and Geoff Eley, *The Peculiarities of German History: Bourgeois Society and Politics in Nineteenth-Century Germany* (Oxford, 1984).

12. Jürgen Habermas, 'Modernity: an incomplete project', *New German Critique*, 22 (Winter 1981), 3–15. William Outhwaite, 'Habermas: modernity as reflection', in Bryan Cheyette and Laura Marcus (eds.), *Modernity, Culture and 'the Jew'* (Cambridge, 1998), 157–70.

13. Now published as Moritz Föllmer and Rüdiger Graf (eds.), *Die 'Krise' der Weimarer Republik* (Frankfurt, 2005).

14. *Reactionary Modernism: Technology, Culture and Politics in Weimar and the Third Reich* (Cambridge, 1984).

15. Peter M. R. Stirk (ed.), *European Unity in Context: The Interwar Period* (London, 1989).

16. See Christoph Asendorf, *Batteries of Life: On the History of Things and their Perception in Modernity* (Berkeley and Los Angeles, 1993). Anthony McElligott, *The German Urban Experience 1900–1945: Modernity and Crisis* (London, 2001), chapters 4 and 5.

17. Jürgen Habermas, *Theorie des kommunikativen Handelns* (Frankfurt am Main, 1981), ii. 522 ff. Outhwaite, 'Habermas: Modernity as Reflection', 159.

18. See Jill Stephenson, 'Inclusion: building the national community in propaganda and practice' and Nik Wachsmann, 'The policy of exclusion: repression in the Nazi state, 1933–1939', both in Caplan (ed.), *Nazi Germany*. Michelle Mouton, *From Nurturing the Nation to Purifying the Volk: Weimar and Nazi Family Policy, 1918–1945* (Cambridge, 2007).

19. Peter Gay, *Weimar Culture: The Outsider as Insider* (New York, 1968); Nolte, *Ordnung*, 67.

20. Erich Fromm, *Arbeiter und Angestellte am Vorabend des Dritten Reiches: Eine sozialpolitische Untersuchung* (Munich 1983; 1st pub. 1929), 168, 170–1.

21. This is an argument also made recently by Paul Betts in relation to the reception of the Bauhaus after 1945; see Paul Betts, 'Die Bauhaus-Legende: Amerikanisch-Deutsches *Joint-Venture* des Kalten Krieges', in Alf Lüdtke, Inge Marßolek, and Adelheid von Saldern (eds.), *Amerikanisierung: Traum und Alptraum im Deutschland des 20. Jahrhunderts* (Stuttgart, 1996), 270–90.

22. Zygmunt Bauman, 'Allosemitism: premodern, modern, postmodern', in Cheyette and Marcus (eds.), *Modernity, Culture and 'the Jew'*, 152–3.

23. See Adam Tooze, 'The economic history of the Third Reich', in Caplan (ed.), *Nazi Germany*.

Political culture

Anthony McElligott

It is not my intention in this chapter to retread the now familiar ground of the republic's political narrative told through its various parties and organizations. Instead, I want to address its political culture (broadly defined) in terms of the tension between the concept of a state in which representative democracy had primacy, what Hugo Preuß in 1917 referred to as the *Volksstaat* (citizen state), and the argument mostly put forward by conservative intellectuals such as Carl Schmitt, for a strong state with powers concentrated in an executive body or directory, not unlike the wartime dictatorship of General Ludendorff and Field Marshal Hindenburg, but based on popular acclamation.[1] For here, in these two radically different visions, that of the *Volksstaat* and a plebiscitary state, we find the underlying faultline of the Weimar Republic. From its beginning, the ideal of the parliamentary *Volksstaat* was challenged by the contingency of political, social, and economic turmoil, against which government had to find quick and tough measures if it was to maintain the integrity and authority of the republican state. Ultimately this quest for authority flowed into an authoritarian politics that found its culmination in four important events between July 1932 and June 1933: Chancellor Franz von Papen's *Staatsstreich*—the *coup d'état*—against Prussia; the Reichstag Fire Decree at the end of February 1933, establishing legal terror; the Enabling Act of 23 March dismissing parliament; and the series of laws and decrees between March 1933 and February 1934 leading to the so-called *Gleichschaltung* (administrative synchronization) of *Land* governments, which effectively brought about the long-discussed unitary state. These measures together established the authoritarian plebiscitary state as long sought after by ultra conservatives, before being swiftly overtaken by Hitler to create the Nazi dictatorship.

The republic as contingency

That the Weimar Republic came about by default is well known. As is often the case, events on the ground combined with pressures coming from elsewhere to set the pace for change. The truculence of the Kaiser in the face of Wilson's Third Note finally forced the hand of the Majority Social Democrats to demand his abdication. But Friedrich Ebert and Philipp Scheidemann's petition to Prince Max von Baden on the 7th was also the consequence of rank and file pressure within their own party—from the party newspaper *Vorwärts* ('Forward') and in particular from the crowds on the streets. A general strike called by the Workers' and Soldiers' Council of Berlin for 9 November pushed further the floodgates, already forced open by the overturning of the Wittelsbach monarchy the previous evening when the Independent Socialist Kurt Eisner declared Bavaria a republic.[2]

To bring crowds onto the streets can have unforeseen consequences, as events in Petrograd a year earlier proved, and no doubt this accounts for Ebert's plea to the public to stay off the streets. Meanwhile rumours of an impending putsch, and reports that the Spartacist leader Karl Liebknecht was on his way to the Hohenzollern palace in central Berlin where he intended to declare a socialist state, forced Scheidemann to interrupt his lunch in the Reichstag canteen and to address the crowd gathering in front of the parliament. By all accounts, the situation in front of the Reichstag was confused when Scheidemann uttered the fateful words: 'That old and rotten thing, the monarchy, has collapsed. Long live the new! Long live the German republic!' Scheidemann may have been carried away by the moment, but he was also a shrewd politician. A bolshevik-style revolution, as advocated by the extreme left, would have invited foreign intervention or civil war. As far as the SPD leadership and its liberal allies were concerned, most political goals—if not all—had been achieved with the constitutional reforms of 28 October that asserted the authority of parliament vis-à-vis the monarchy.

The revolution produced its own institutions, the workers' and soldiers' councils based on the example of the Petrograd Soviet; however, these were ad hoc bodies and by no means coherent in terms of ideology or aims. In practice they sought to maintain order on the ground. For a while the provisional government, the Council of People's Representatives made up of six delegates, three each from the Majority Socialists and the Independent Socialists, led respectively by Ebert and Hugo Haase (who was assassinated a year later), had to coexist alongside a Council of Delegates, representing the Workers' and Soldiers' Council of Greater Berlin, with its own agenda and claim to power (indeed, the Council of Representatives was in theory subordinate to the Workers' and Soldiers' Council). Thus the councils themselves briefly became sites of a power struggle between moderates espousing a 'social republic' and radicals proclaiming a 'socialist republic',[3] in which the Majority Socialists triumphed over the Independent Socialists and other radicals. In Hamburg, for example, Walther Lamp'l, a young lawyer and a rising star within Social Democracy, quickly ousted the radical intellectual Heinrich Laufenberg, thereby steering the revolution in Germany's second city into calmer waters.[4] By the time delegates met at the General Congress of Workers' and Soldiers' Councils in mid-December, the councils no longer represented a so-called 'third way' between bourgeois parliament and soviet dictatorship. Instead, they became the channels through which Germany would pass to parliamentary democracy.[5]

Dominated by the Majority Socialists, the Congress voted overwhelmingly for elections to a National Assembly to take place at the earliest opportunity. In doing so, Congress effectively declared the revolution ended. Thus a consensus emerged that winter, ranging from the SPD leadership through to the army's quartermaster general, Wilhelm Groener (who had replaced General Ludendorff in October 1918), and Field Marshal Hindenburg, that the best way of curbing revolution was to bring forward the timetable for elections and to channel popular aspirations from the streets into parliament. For conservatives, such as Hindenburg, an SPD-led government and a democratized parliament were the price for

POLITICAL CULTURE | 29

salvaging the remains of the Reich. And judging from the results of that election in January 1919, this is what the majority of Germans wanted too. Over three-quarters of those who voted in the election on 19 January supported those parties that underwrote the republic; this was evidence of an overwhelming desire to return as quickly as possible to something resembling normalcy under a democratic parliamentary system.

The republic's first cabinet formed on 3 February was a centre-left coalition recalling the wartime inter-party Reichstag group and comprised Majority Socialists, liberals, and the Catholic Centre Party (together they had 75 per cent of the vote) led by Scheidemann. And even though the formidable electoral majority of this 'Weimar coalition' was to fade (though not disappear) at the first Reichstag election in June 1920, Germany's future nevertheless pointed towards democratic institutions. Until the onset of the depression, Weimar's democratic institutions, and above all the Reichstag, as we shall see, functioned well. Electoral participation remained high, and support for the two pillars of the so-called 'Weimar coalition' (the Centre Party and the Social Democratic Party) remained by and large firm. Even at the height of the multiple crises in 1932, roughly one-third of electors voted for parties that either explicitly or generally favoured the Constitution, and a further fifth supported parties that, while not explicitly pro-democracy, nonetheless were not openly fighting the republic. To assert that the Weimar Republic was a 'republic without republicans' is simply wrong.

The republic between *Volksstaat* and plebiscitary state

In 1919 the challenge from the streets continued unabated, and left-wing unrest, especially in Berlin, forced the National Assembly to convene in the small Thuringian town of Weimar on 6 February, where it elected Friedrich Ebert as the republic's first (provisional) president five days later. As well as pondering Germany's position vis-à-vis the victors at the looming peace talks at Versailles, the National Assembly also debated the proposals for a new constitution, to be drafted by a committee led by Hugo Preuß, a respected liberal theorist on constitutional issues and a member of Scheidemann's cabinet. Preuß, whose wartime writings had been highly critical of Germany's middle classes, faced a truculent bourgeoisie and an insurgent working class, both of which had been alienated from the state by the war and its aftermath. The six successive constitutional drafts produced by his committee mirrored this specific domestic context, and sought to work around it.[6]

The Constitution that was finally agreed by the Assembly at the end of July after three intensive debates, and which came into being on 11 August, was progressive for its time, but it also represented a compromise between the SPD and the liberal spectrum. It raised popular expectations for the 'social' republic (e.g. Arts. 17, 20–2, 109, 114–18, 123, 124, 163), while at the same time trying to accommodate the vested interests of an advanced capitalist society (e.g. Arts. 151, 153, 154, 164, 165).[7] As such, the constitution determined that the political culture of the republic would be based on class compromise, a sort of refashioned *Burgfrieden* or 'social peace' (in contrast to the failed wartime accommodation).[8] Nonetheless, most scholarly works read the Constitution from a later perspective, emphasizing the 'flaws' that are said to have brought down the republic, notably proportional representation (leading to a fragmented political landscape and parliamentary instability, which allowed Hitler a foot in the door[9]); a plebiscitary presidency (creating a dualist model of authority); Article 48, which arrogated extraordinary powers to the executive at the expense of parliament. I shall concentrate on the latter two aspects.

There were few choices of state form available to Germany in the late autumn of 1918. The attempt at constitutional monarchy, which in effect had been introduced with the reform of late October, had passed into history with the Kaiser's departure on 9 November. The Council of People's Representatives was a provisional body and never envisaged as a permanent institution of government. The idea of a small governing civilian directory, something similar to the Ludendorff–Hindenburg regime and favoured by conservatives, was considered briefly and pushed aside (although it reappeared at intermittent periods, as we shall see below). In 1919 such a directory would have run counter to the moment. There was broad agreement that the republic needed a new constitutional basis, government founded on a popular franchise, and a president as head of state.

The question in 1918 was: how to balance the powers of parliament and those of the head of state? On the one hand, Scheidemann believed that sovereignty should lie with parliament and the president should be a mere constitutional head without any real powers; Ebert, on the other hand, was keen to see a more active role for the president, and in this he reflected ideas that were current among some of the leading constitutional and political thinkers of the day.[10] Preuß's committee had to steer a course between these two visions, which essentially derived from the French and American experiences. Eventually his committee opted for a compromise between the two: a 'strong' president, but tempered by parliamentary checks. Nevertheless, in practice the president was the stronger element under the constitution.

At the time Preuß and his colleagues Max Weber, Friedrich Naumann, and Friedrich Meinecke did not see any contradiction between a strong executive and parliament: they were the two sides of the same coin.[11] The argument for this was that a strong plebiscitary president (Art. 41 I) would function as a counterweight to the 'tyranny' of a party-dominated parliament. Nonetheless, the fact that the president had a term longer than that of parliament (seven years over four years), and enjoyed a raft of sweeping powers—notably Article 25, the power to dissolve parliament and call new elections; Article 53 empowering the president to appoint and dismiss a chancellor and cabinet ministers; Article 48, enabling government by decree, and the right to remove an elected state government if the security of the Reich was endangered (the so-called *Reichsexekution*)—meant that ultimately the balance was heavily tipped in favour of the executive. Indeed, as the constitutional historian Rudolf Weber-Fas has observed, the president under the democratic republic was, technically speaking, more powerful than the Kaiser.[12]

Nonetheless, in 1919, neither a plebiscitary president nor dictatorial powers (Art. 48) elicited the misgivings that were to be aired later. Indeed, Article 48 was conceived as an instrument that would allow the president to swiftly enact laws or take special measures to safeguard the Reich in times of crisis when the machinery of the Reichstag would prove too cumbersome and slow.[13] The fact that from 1930 it turned from this to become an alternative to parliament could not have been anticipated in 1919.

Revolution and reaction

Both Scheidemann and Ebert thought of themselves first and foremost as German patriots, not as revolutionaries; for them social democracy was a bulwark against bolshevism and the forces of disorder.[14] Ebert's alleged declaration that he detested revolution like the plague was not mere rhetoric; he meant it. It was from this consideration that in the early days of December Ebert entered into secret negotiations with senior army officers in order to secure the republic against the extreme left and its attempt to initiate a 'second wave' of revolution. Whether or not the pact with the army was one with the devil, Ebert believed he had little choice.[15] In his eyes the country was teetering on anarchy, as radicals loosely gathered under the banner of the Spartacists and led by Karl Liebknecht and Rosa Luxemburg fomented insurgency. To be sure, mass protests and strikes couched in political language were almost a daily occurrence, especially among poor rural workers in the east Elbian countryside, on the shop floor in the metal factories and mines of the industrial Ruhr, and, notably, among dock workers in Hamburg, where anarcho-syndicalists and extreme left splinter groups tilled fertile ground. Indeed, until the late autumn of 1923, the republic appeared to be in a permanent state of insurrection. And even though the state was never really in danger of succumbing to this,[16] the government reintroduced the hated *Belagerungszustand*—state of siege—almost as soon as it had been abolished in November 1918; after the Constitution came into effect in August, it added Article 48 to its arsenal. But in order to impose order Weimar's government had to rely on military force.

In an ironic twist of fate, the security of the republic was handed by the army minister Gustav Noske, a Social Democrat, to the army under General Hans von Seeckt and to the so-called 'regiments of students and lieutenants', NCOs, and assorted adventurers who made up the various paramilitary formations. Between 1919 and

1923, the army declared a state of emergency in different parts of the Reich at least thirty-seven times; in 1923 it was declared throughout the Reich.[17] Under the guise of countering revolution, the army broke up strikes and dispersed demonstrators protesting over lack of food and other material shortages, in spite of the growing concern in the Reichstag over its use internally.[18] Ministers were divided on this issue as too were government advisers. On the one hand, Friedrich Freund and Hermann Pünder, respectively from the Prussian and Reich finance ministries, were convinced that Article 48 and military force were the only means to save the republic from bolshevism, whilst on the other hand, the Social Democrats Carl Severing and Arnold Brecht warned against over-exaggerating the threat and thereby drawing the army too one-sidedly into domestic politics, with the consequence that the republic would lose popular support.[19]

There was a marked contrast in the brutal way the army dealt with the left and its soft-glove approach to the right, which (as Chancellor Wirth declared after Rathenau's murder in 1922) posed the greater threat to the republic. Its inertia during the Kapp–Lüttwitz Putsch in 1920 exposed its superficial adherence to democracy and contrasted radically with its behaviour against workers in the Ruhr who had mobilized against the putsch. Its ambivalence towards republican democracy had not lessened three years later during Hitler and Ludendorff's so-called Beer Hall Putsch in Munich. A month before this the government of Saxony reported how regular army units were liaising with illegal right-wing paramilitary organizations, notably the Roßbach Free Corps, while other members of Army Group IV were attending meetings with the NSDAP.[20] In marked contrast to events in Bavaria where the army leadership under General von Lossow and the civilian administration under von Kahr's commissarial authority were themselves implicated, Thuringia's left-wing coalition government faced the threat of a *Reichsexekution* as a result of General Reinhardt's exaggerated claims of a 'red terror'. Using powers under the 'state of siege', Reinhardt carried out mass arrests of well-known activists, councillors, and politicians and dispersed striking miners. On 8 November troops occupied Weimar and stationed themselves in front of the Landtag in a blatant show of force that was replete with anti-parliamentary symbolism.[21]

Republican Germany was facing multiple crises in the autumn of 1923, and Stresemann's cabinet was barely able to meet the challenges. With de facto power entrusted to him and the army through Article 48, Seeckt briefly saw an opportunity to enact a 'silent coup' after the expected demission of Stresemann's second cabinet. His military confidant Major-General Otto Hasse was convinced that 'the cry for a strong man must come' within weeks. In this scenario, with the army behind him and with the support of Oskar Hergt and Count Kuno von Westarp from the German Nationalist People's Party (DNVP), Seeckt would step forward to lead a directory as 'military chancellor': that is, govern without parliament.[22] Even though the plan came to nought, it nevertheless illustrates not only the right's contempt for parliamentary democracy but also the allure of the 'strong leader' in times of crisis.

The reliance on Article 48 and the *Belagerungszustand* both offered a quick route to internal security and 'won' over the army to the government (or at least that is what republican politicians thought), but it was also a lazy convenience in that it allowed a challenged cabinet to assert authority without having to rely on parliament.[23] Throughout the crisis in October, Stresemann used Article 48 not only to restore political authority, but to carry out everyday business 'in the interests of the Reich'. Between mid-October and the middle of the following February, sixty-three emergency decrees were passed, none of them dealing with the political crisis, but instead with economic, financial, and labour market issues. The complaint by Hugo Preuß shortly after the reintroduction of the *Belagerungszustand* in late 1918 might equally have applied in 1923.

In the former authoritarian state the citizen had hardly a voice, in the present one he has absolutely nothing to say whatsoever. Now, more than ever before, the people in its entirety is simply an object of a government that swathes it with unfathomable pieces of advice, only that these are not based on divine right (*Gottesgnadentum*), but on a just as intangible popular right. Legal title is with the one as with the other, based on power, or more accurately, the belief in a superior force backing it. In brief, it is in essence the mirror image of the authoritarian state.[24]

And as Gustav Schmoller dryly noted in 1922, 'Even in the red republic, the people as such have never and nowhere governed.'[25]

In these early years, Weimar's new governing class opted for presidential power over parliament to avert crises that would have undermined the authority of the state. It also accepted the use of force (including the excesses of rogue *Freikorps* units and exceptional courts) to suppress political challenges (but selectively, as the inaction over the Kapp and Munich putsches shows). However, these extraordinary measures using Article 48 were deployed within the constitutional framework and were not intended to overturn it This is the paradox that Alexander Rüstow in 1929 referred to as 'dictatorship within the parameters of democracy'.[26] For Ebert and others at the time, this was not so much a paradox as a necessity to avoid what they believed would otherwise be a national catastrophe.[27] The suspension of the *Volksstaat* was precisely that: a postponement until the multiple crises confronting Germany had been overcome. But the combination of Article 48 and the *Belagerungszustand*, together with the Law for the Protection of the Republic (1922), with its wide-ranging and ill-defined enemies, in effect created a template for the 'extra-legal' state (*Ausnahmestaat*) that anticipated the Nazi exceptional state after the passing of the Emergency Decree for the Protection of the People and the State in February 1933.

The *Volksstaat*

Under Article 54 a chancellor and his ministers had to have the confidence of the Reichstag in order to govern. This clause was Preuß's attempt to subject the executive to democratic controls; but it inadvertently created a tension at the highest level in Weimar's political culture, for by passing a vote of no confidence the Reichstag could cause a government to fall. Here the tension between parliament and the executive was brought to a head. Writing in 1926, Martin Schiele (DNVP), who had been a minister in Hans Luther's first cabinet (January–October the previous year), argued that Article 54 was 'totally unacceptable' because 'As long as this situation exists, it prevents the German Reich from having strong leadership.'[28] Indeed, during the life of the republic there were over thirty such motions, but on only two occasions,

both in the years of so-called relative stability, did a cabinet fall as
the consequence of such a vote. Less often cited is the fact that over
the same period the Reichstag voted its confidence in government
twenty-four times.[29]

Nonetheless Weimar cabinets managed for the most part to work
consensually, and when they did break up it was usually because
ministers faced pressure from within their own party, forcing
them to adopt positions that they might otherwise have avoided.
Thus conflict leading to the break-up of a cabinet was often not
between ministers, but between party machines and cabinet.[30]
This is how both Stresemann's administration in October 1923
and Heinrich Müller's coalition in March 1930 came to grief.
The constitutional theorist Carl Schmitt, like many of his fellow
conservatives, saw in this the symptom of Weimar's inability to
forge national unity.[31]

To be sure, cabinets appeared to come and go with alarming
frequency—twenty times between 1919 and 1932 (half of these
between the elections of January 1919 and May 1924). But not
all contemporaries were necessarily disturbed by this. For Gustav
Schmoller such changes were par for the course in coalition politics
and more often than not ministers were forced to seek compromise;
a positive factor of German democracy.[32] And no less a figure
than the eminent legal expert Hermann Heller noted in 1931 that
Weimar's parliamentary democracy *per se* was perfectly stable;
what was destabilizing 'Above all . . . [was] the politically naive
German thinking that was enthral to any sort of mass hypnotic
or dictatorial superstitious miracle'.[33] Heller was certainly taking
a side swipe at Carl Schmitt and the increasingly loud calls for
a 'strong man'. Moreover, when viewed in a wider European
context, frequent cabinet changes were not a peculiarly German
phenomenon, as the case of France shows.

Indeed, for the most part the members of Weimar's political class
worked reasonably well together in spite of ideological differences.
This consensus was founded upon social and cultural factors,
as Thomas Megerl recently demonstrated in his important study
of the Reichstag. A cursory look at the social data of the deputies
in the Reichstag, and of the cabinet members in particular, shows
a fairly cohesive political class, similar in age, education, social

and political experience. Indeed, Gustav Schmoller noted as early as 1922:

A certain common mental-moral atmosphere permeates our ministers and deputies. This understanding is by and large possible despite the frequently large differences in [their] convictions. The common training, the common understanding for the necessities of state connects conservatives and liberals, Catholic as well as Protestant officials, National Liberals and Progressives [sic], and now also, more and more, the Social Democrats, who for 20 years have been cooperating in self-government with the representatives of bourgeois parties.[34]

Until the summer of 1932, there appeared to be almost a game of musical chairs where cabinet posts were concerned, so much so that the popular Munich caricaturist Thomas Theodor Heine was moved to comment ironically, 'The new cabinet?! Its physiognomy appears familiar to me' (while depicting a row of ministers' bottoms). The pool of ministers sharing 223 ministerial posts in the republic's nineteen cabinets, serving ten chancellors, stood at 79, of which 40.5 per cent held office just once; the same proportion held office between two and four times; importantly, 19 per cent, or nearly a fifth, held office five times or more.[35]

A good illustration of this ministerial stability can be found with the liberal deputy Otto Geßler, first appointed in late March 1920 as minister for reconstruction in Gustav Bauer's cabinet and who then remained in government as army minister until June 1928, serving thirteen different cabinets. Another example is the Centre Party politician Heinrich Brauns, who joined Konstantin Fehrenbach's cabinet in June 1920 and served under various chancellors for eight years, leaving government at the same time as Geßler. Another, and more prominent, cabinet member was, of course, Gustav Stresemann, who led two ill-starred administrations in 1923, before successfully serving as foreign minister in seven cabinets until his death in 1929. Neither Geßler nor Brauns nor Stresemann was unusual, and this should caution us against accepting too easily the idea that government under the republic was unstable simply because of cabinet changes.

Finally, continuity of chancellors and ministers meant that policy seldom changed in any fundamental way before the crisis of 1930–2. The six cabinets led by Wilhelm Marx and Hans Luther, for example, pursued an almost seamless domestic and foreign policy in the mid-years from June 1924 to June 1928. As Lindsay Rogers and his colleagues at Columbia University observed at the time, 'Cabinet changes mean a new deal of the same cards rather than a different deck.' Arguably, Weimar's parliamentary system was quite stable in spite of the superficial changes signalled by cabinet reshuffles and the odd spat in the Reichstag; even under Chancellor Brüning, whose dismissal in May 1932 spelt the 'death knell of responsible cabinet government'.[36]

Towards the plebiscitary state

As we have already noted, there were precedents for using Article 48 to govern without parliamentary approval, and not just in the crises-ridden years before 1924. During the minority cabinets of Wilhelm Marx and Hans Luther between 1926 and 1927, for example, the executive resorted to government by decree after the SPD (by this time in opposition) withdrew its 'quiet' support for the cabinet. In spite of Hindenburg's belief that the socialists were incapable of forming a stable government, they did so after the elections of May 1928, and governed under Hermann Müller at the head of a grand coalition for the next two years. But after its collapse in early 1930, and Heinrich Brüning's appointment as chancellor, the dynamics of Weimar's political culture changed drastically.

As we know, Brüning had little support for his policies in an increasingly fractious Reichstag. His situation worsened after the landslide election of September 1930 when the NSDAP increased its number of deputies from 12 to 107. After this date, he became dependent on the toleration of the SPD in order to push through his policies, and in October the following year owed his survival to their support in a motion of 'no confidence' tabled by the NSDAP.[37] Without a majority in parliament, and dependent on the SPD and assorted liberal factions, Brüning was vulnerable to the political vagaries of the Reichstag—he was in effect its prisoner. As long as parliament was sitting, his entire political and economic programme was at risk because of the Damocles sword of Article 54.

On the other hand, resorting to Article 48 to force through policies also weakened Brüning by making him dependent on the president rather than responsible to the Reichstag. Increasingly, Brüning relied on Hindenburg to support him by signing off emergency decrees.[38] There is little to suggest that Brüning was intent on destroying Weimar's parliamentary democracy, but he had taken the first step on the path towards the dissolution of the republic as a parliamentary system.[39]

In the early months of Brüning's chancellorship, few liberal commentators were overly concerned, remembering the earlier usage of Article 48 (by Ebert and Hindenburg) which had not boded ill for the republic.[40] Indeed, a number of factors spoke in favour of a presidential cabinet, not least the continuing economic crisis and a Reichstag dominated by Nazis and Communists, and worsening political conditions on the streets. In this context, Brüning, Hindenburg, and Article 48 were seen as the 'lesser evil' and for this reason tolerated.[41] Thus government by decree was based on a 'silent' consensus of the middle and the democratic left. Under Brüning's first cabinet parliamentary democracy was not so much abandoned as laid to one side, as Article 48 was invoked to overcome crisis as in 1923; its usage fell within the model analysed by Rüstow in 1929.[42] However, from October 1931, when Brüning formed his second cabinet, Weimar's wider political culture was swiftly shifting to the right, signalled by the establishment of the Harzburg Front, and a changed attitude from Hindenburg. In this climate Article 48 in Brüning's hands was no longer a safeguard of republican democracy; the Reichstag, which had been already reduced to an awkward irrelevance—up to that point it had sat forty-one times, less than half compared to the previous year, while the number of emergency decrees signed off by Hindenburg had risen from five to forty-four—was suspended until the following February. Thus by the time Brüning was dismissed from office at the end of May 1932, 'just one hundred metres from his goal' as he later claimed in his memoirs (but in reality a spent force), parliament had become a mere spectator rather than an actor; Weimar's political culture was now being shaped by a court camarilla of intriguers—not least among them General Kurt von Schleicher (described by Wilhelm Abegg, the former state secretary in the Prussian Interior Ministry, as a 'duplicitous fox' and an 'incorrigible intriguer'[43]) and the ubiquitous and Machiavellian cabinet secretary Otto Meissner—and by violent political gangs on the streets. Within the higher echelons of the ministerial bureaucracy and in industrial circles there were renewed calls for a radical reform of the republic's constitutional arrangements that would favour a more authoritarian state.

Plebiscitary dictatorship

If, as Hans Boldt has remarked, Germany under Brüning slipped into legislative dictatorship,[44] under von Papen's brief and fatal administration from 1 June to 3 December, it was consciously steered towards plebiscitary dictatorship. Appointed as Brüning's successor, von Papen was not the charming if somewhat dilettante politician that some, and not least his mentor, Schleicher, believed. The aristocratic von Papen was a shrewd, calculating, and ruthless political operator who was prepared to utilize the law in order to break with the Constitution, and who had few qualms in ditching his erstwhile 'mentor' (Schleicher) when the occasion arose.

According to the historian Friedrich Meinecke, Papen's agenda was to restore the status quo ante October 1918.[45] But this over-simplifies von Papen's aims. True, as *Paris Soir* noted on his appointment, von Papen was an out and out monarchist, but his conservatism dovetailed with more modern conceptions of the state, too. Ever since the crisis year of 1923, Papen had favoured government by a small executive body untrammelled by the machinery of parliament, and conditions in the early summer of 1932 seemed to favour this option. Germany was facing ruin and von Papen believed only exceptional powers would allow him to tackle the multiple crises facing the country. His authoritarian views chimed with many conservatives who urged the final break with democratic institutions. Addressing the influential Langnamverein, the industrialist association in the Ruhr, in the summer of 1932, the constitutional theorist Carl Schmitt also spoke of the need for 'strong government' freed from parliamentary controls.

I believe that today a legal government, if it decides to make use of all constitutional means [at its disposal], can accomplish substantial reforms and programs. A government dependent on parliament, however, has not even the possibility of accomplishing even a five year plan.[46]

Schmitt's views were by now common currency among broad circles in Germany, and ultimately pointed towards a 'plebiscitary dictatorship' based on popular acclamation.

In early October 1931, during a speech in the town of Dülmen, von Papen had called for a *rassemblement* of the right to seize the opportunity for power.[47] The problem for von Papen and his 'cabinet of barons' was that they were too far removed from the broad mass of the people needed to achieve this *fronde*; and even though it was severely hamstrung, the Reichstag was still breathing; on 12 September a resounding 90 per cent of deputies voted 'no confidence' in his regime (it was duly dissolved for a second time under von Papen and new elections set for 6 November). The only party on the right that commanded broad support was, of course, the NSDAP, but a large section of the traditional right, not least Hindenburg himself, was still sceptical about Hitler's intentions. Moreover, attempts to bring the NSDAP into government had foundered on Hitler's 'all or nothing' demands.[48]

Using Article 48 von Papen's cabinet had forced through highly unpopular policies that only exacerbated material distress and furthered political radicalization, now sweeping the country. By the summer of 1932 political violence had become an everyday occurrence, so much so that talk of 'civil war' conditions on Germany's streets and in the countryside was commonplace.[49] As in the earlier period, the spectre of Communist insurgency was used as an excuse for taking draconian measures, the most notorious of which was the illegal suspension of Prussia's caretaker administration on 20 July, after ostensibly failing to adequately deal with political violence and for alleged secret negotiations with the Communist Party.[50] This action transferred powers from Prussia to the Reich, much to the consternation of the other regional governments, not least Bavaria. Unlike the Kapp Putsch in 1920, Papen's coup against Prussia met with little resistance on the ground. The Prussian administration supported by other *Land* governments took the Reich to court—and won its case, but to little effect.[51] Von Papen's attack upon Prussia was in effect the first step towards a much-vaunted constitutional and administrative reform of the Reich, which had been under discussion for several years and which only found its completion after 1933.[52]

It was observed that von Papen's usage of Article 48 was more extensive (nearly a quarter of the 232 emergency acts passed between October 1919 and September 1932) and more draconian than the hated emergency legislation under Ludendorff and Hindenburg during the war.[53] Indeed, while many of these decrees addressed Germany's economic problems, increasingly their political purpose was unmistakable. Decree after decree gave the police and judicial authorities sweeping powers, while the army hovered in the background preparing itself for the eventuality of martial law.[54] The American political scientist Lindsay Rogers asked whether von Papen's cabinet dictatorship was going to be merely an interregnum until the crisis was over or a permanent form of government.[55] At the beginning of December, Papen was thinking the latter.

The sources show that Hindenburg became increasingly uneasy with von Papen's actions and not least with the threat of further legal action over the continuing use of Article 48. Cabinet dictatorship—even with the army in reserve—was simply not working, and brought with it a genuine fear of civil war. Von Papen's cabinet had already resigned on 17 November but continued in a caretaking function until a new cabinet could be formed. In his final cabinet meeting on 3 December von Papen expressed his satisfaction to have led an administration that had governed 'in the spirit of conservative state-leadership that spelled the end of the liberal era', and expressed his confidence that the new cabinet led by von Schleicher would continue in this vein.[56] This wish was to be disappointed. Hardly a democrat of the first degree, von Schleicher instead sought a broad consensus that steered him away from plebiscitary dictatorship and apparently towards parliamentary politics, based on a rapprochement with the trade unions, the Centre Party, and the so-called left wing of the NSDAP gathered around Gregor Strasser. In other words he appeared to be returning to a form of *Volksstaat* extremely unpalatable to some sections of the right. And this was his undoing, for it alienated him from the bedrock of Germany's elite; not even his own generals supported him. Within weeks of his appointment, he found himself politically isolated from all sides and without the support of Hindenburg. On

28 January, von Schleicher laid out the alternatives to the president: a majority cabinet under Hitler, a minority cabinet under himself, or the continuation of the presidial regime. Hindenburg did not want to continue with the latter; a minority cabinet under the isolated chancellor also did not come into consideration; that left Hitler.[57]

The turn to Hitler was the final attempt to find a consensus based on the unity of an invigorated national body. The presidential and Reichstag elections in the spring and summer had shown that Hitler was able to cut across class, gender, and generational lines; his personal vote in the second round of the presidential elections, for instance, had topped a third of the electorate; and even though his party had lost votes in November, it still garnered the greatest number of votes in the country. While it would be overstating the case to say that Hitler's appointment in January 1933 was predetermined, there was an air of inevitability that his time had come, especially among influential industrialists from the Langnamverein, including the magnate Fritz Thyssen and Paul Reusch, who, by late November 1932, universally favoured a Hitler cabinet.[58] But as Franz Bracht (a minister in both the Papen and Schleicher cabinets) noted in private correspondence,

It seems to do less with a change in favour of Hitler than with the belief that a Hitler government cannot be avoided any longer. Under these circumstances one must accelerate Hitler's entry into government, even if he does not prove himself satisfactorily, and his government, as sceptics in industrial circles assume, only lasts a few weeks.[59]

When von Papen was appointed chancellor *Paris Soir* commented that 'Germany has a feudal government today, and will have a Hitler government to-morrow . . . Soon the Hohenzollerns will be back.' While the newspaper erred on the latter point, it was prescient on the former. Papen more than any other politician worked towards Hitler's inclusion into government, and, in the final analysis, manoeuvred him into power. The gamble was that a Hitler cabinet would finally break the impasse that had developed in conservative politics, thereby facilitating the restoration of Germany's fortunes through a strengthened plebiscitary state.[60] After touch and go negotiations between 27 and 30 January, brokered by Papen, Hitler was appointed by Hindenburg to lead a government of 'national unity' and 'renewal'. This was to be the republic's twenty-first and last cabinet.

Among the items for discussion at Hitler's first cabinet meeting at 5 p.m. on 30 January was a proposal by von Papen to introduce an Enabling Act that would allow cabinet to govern without the inconvenience of the Reichstag. The following day, during the discussion of Göring's earlier proposal to dissolve the Reichstag and call new elections, von Papen went further, stating that 'it is for the best to fix now that the coming elections to the Reichstag shall be the last, and that a return to a parliamentary system is to be avoided for ever'.[61] This time von Papen got his way. The (heavily compromised) Reichstag dismissed itself on 23 March, initially for four years (to be recalled only on those occasions when Hitler needed it for acclamatory purposes). Meanwhile the idea of cabinet dictatorship was taken a step further by Hitler who, as *Führer* from 1934, came to embody the state as its plebiscitary dictator.

Notes

1. Hugo Preuß, *Staat, Recht und Freiheit aus 40 Jahren deutscher Politik und Geschichte* (Tübingen, 1926); Carl Schmitt, 'Diktator und Belagerungszustand: Eine staatsrechtliche Studie', in *Zeitschrift für die gesamte Strafrechts* (1917), 138–62.
2. Herbert Michaelis and Ernst Schraepler (eds.), *Ursachen und Folgen: Vom deutschen Zusammenbruch 1918 und 1945 bis zur staatlichen Neuordnung Deutschlands in der Gegenwart*, 26 vols. (Berlin, 1958–79, hereafter *Ursachen und Folgen* followed by volume), iii. 104–5. See the accounts in Philipp Scheidemann, *Das historische Versagen der SPD: Schriften aus dem Exil* (Lüneburg, 2002), 98; and former state secretary and chief of staff of the chancellery 1926–32 Hermann Pünder, *Der Reichspräsident in der Weimarer Republik* (Frankfurt am Main, 1961), 12, who refers to the Kaiser's (forced) abdication as 'revolution from above'.
3. Friedrich Stampfer, *Der 9. November: Gedenkblätter zu seiner Wiederkehr* (Berlin, 1919), 17 ff. *Ursachen und Folgen*, iii. 9–10, proclamation of the Berlin Arbeiter- und Soldatenrat, 10 Nov. 1918; Pünder, *Der Reichspräsident*, 13.
4. Walther Lamp'l, *Die Revolution in Groß-Hamburg* (Hamburg, 1921); Richard Comfort, *Revolutionary Hamburg: Labor Politics in the*

Early Weimar Republic (Stanford, Calif., 1966); Völker Ullrich, *Die Hamburger Arbeiterbewegung vom Vorabend des ersten Weltkrieges bis zur Revolution 1918/19*, 2 vols. (Hamburg, 1976).

5. Friedrich Meinecke, 'Die Revolution: Ursachen und Tatsachen', *Handbuch des Deutschen Staatsrechts*, 1 (1931), 115–19; *Ursachen und Folgen*, ii. 574–5 and iii. 23, 38–47; Harry Graf Kessler, *Tagebücher, 1918–1937* (Frankfurt am Main, 1961), 22. Overviews in Reinhard Rurüp, 'Problems of the German revolution 1918–19', *Journal of Contemporary History*, 3/4 (Oct. 1968), 109–35; Eckehard Jesse and Henning Köhler, 'Die deutsche Revolution 1918/19 im Wandel der historischen Forschung: Forschungsüberblick und Kritik der "herrschenden Lehre" ', in *Aus Politik und Zeitgeschichte* (1978), B45, 2–232; Ulrich Kluge, *Die deutsche Revolution 1918/19* (Frankfurt am Main, 1985).

6. Ludwig Richter, 'Reichspräsident und Ausnahmegewalt: Die Genese des Artikels 48 in den Beratungen der Weimarer Nationalversammlung', *Der Staat*, 37 (1998), 221–47.

7. Elmar M. Hucko (ed.), *The Democratic Tradition: Four German Constitutions* (Oxford, 1987), 147–90; Hans Boldt, 'Die Weimarer Verfassung', in Karl Dietrich Bracher, Manfred Funke, and Hans-Adolf Jacobsen (eds.), *Die Weimarer Republik 1918–1933: Politik, Wirtschaft, Gesellschaft* (Düsseldorf, 1987), 59.

8. Friedrich Meinecke, *Republik, Bürgertum, Jugend: Vortrag gehalten im Demokratischen Studentenbund zu Berlin am 16. Januar 1925* (Frankfurt am Main, 1925), 17; Waldemar Besson, 'Friedrich Meinecke und die Weimarer Republik', *Vierteljahrshefte für Zeitgeschichte*, 7/2 (Apr. 1959), 119.

9. In the case of proportional representation, the German historian Eberhard Jäckel believes that had there been a 5% threshold (as later in the Bonn Republic) the NSDAP (which entered the Reichstag for the first time in May 1924) would have been banished to the political wilderness after the election in May 1928 on the basis of its 2.6% share of the vote (which saw the number of deputies halved from 32 to 14). But this has little bearing on its performance from 1929 in the Prussian local elections where it made strong gains, and, particularly, in the Reichstag election in September 1930 when it took over 18.3% of the vote, spurred on by the state's looming fiscal crisis and deteriorating material conditions. The NSDAP's successes were due to a groundswell in support fanned by its extra-parliamentary activities and by the disintegration of the conservative 'middle' to provide adequate representation. There is, in fact, no causality between proportional representation and the Nazis' coming to power

in 1933. Moreover, had such a threshold operated, neither the liberal DDP in 1928, nor the right of centre DVP—Stresemann's party—in 1919, 1930, and 1932, nor the Bavarian People's Party (BVP), for all nine elections, would have entered the Reichstag. Eberhard Jäckel, *Das deutsche Jahrhundert* (Frankfurt am Main, 1999), 100.

10. Martin Needler, 'The theory of the Weimar presidency', *Review of Politics*, 21/4 (Oct. 1959), 692–8.

11. Max Weber, *Deutschlands Künftige Staatsform* (Frankfurt am Main, 1919; 1st pub. in the *Frankfurter Zeitung*, Nov. 1918); Besson, 'Meinecke', 125.

12. R. Weber-Fas, *Deutschlands Verfassung vom Wiener Kongreß bis zur Gegenwart* (Tübingen, 2001; 1st edn. 1997), 122. See also Heinrich Pohl, 'Der Reichspräsident und die Reichsregierung', *Handbuch des Deutschen Staatsrechts*, 1 (1931), 467, 482; Pünder, *Der Reichspräsident*, 15; Needler, 'Theory', 695–6.

13. Carl Schmitt, 'Die Diktator des Reichspräsidenten nach Art. 48 der Reichsverfassung', in Karl Bilfinger (ed.), *Der deutsche Föderalismus: Referate [der] Verhandlungen der Tagung der deutschen Staatsrechtslehrer zu Jena am 14. und 15. April 1924* (Jena, 1924). Pünder, *Der Reichspräsident*, 17.

14. Scheidemann, *Das historische Versagen*, 48–51, 99, 104, 110. August Winnig, 'Die Reich als Republik 1918–1928' (Stuttgart, 1928), 127; Wilhelm von Schramm, *Radikale Politik: Die Welt diesseits und jenseits des Bolschewismus* (Munich, 1932), 55; Meinecke, *Republik*, 27.

15. Scheidemann, *Das historische Versagen*, 108; Stampfer, *Der 9. November*, 25, 31. See the debate between Reinhard Rürup and Eckehard Jesse, 'Friedrich Ebert und das Problem der Handlungsspielraüme in der deutschen Revolution 1918/19', in Rudolf König, Hartmut Soell, and Hermann Weber (eds.), *Friedrich Ebert und seine Zeit: Bilanz und Perspektiven der Forschung* (Munich, 1990), 69–110.

16. Bundesarchiv Berlin-Lichterfelde (hereafter BArch), R3001/22069, Bl. 200–4, RMdI, June 1921.

17. BArch R3001/22071 Bl. 160–80, Zusammenstellung 1919–23. Ibid., R3001/6623, Bl. 325; R3001/6626 Bl. 183; R3001/6627, Bl. 35.

18. BArch R3001/6668, Bl. 114–15.

19. BArch R3001/22069, Bl 35, 99, 204–5; *Akten der Reichskanzlei Weimarer Republik:* Das Kabinett Scheidemann: 13. Februar bis 20. Juni 1919 prepared by Hagen Schulze (Boppard am Rhein, 1971), 142, 157: nn. 17, 18; Pünder, *Der Reichspräsident*, 18.

20. *Akten der Reichskanzlei Weimarer Republik. Die Kabinette Stresemann* I u. II 13. August bis 6 Oktober 1923 and 6. Oktober bis 30. November

1923 prepared by Karl Dietrich Erdmann (Boppard am Rhein, 1978), ii. 496, Doc 117, Cabinet meeting 6 Oct. 1923.

21. Ibid. 995 n. 3 (report 6 Nov. 1923).

22. Ibid., Anhang 1, 1176–203; Hasse quote is on 1184.

23. Lindsay Rogers, Freda Forester, and Sanford Schwarz, 'Aspects of German Political Institutions', Part I, *Political Science Quarterly*, 47/3 (Sept. 1932), 347, for the contrary argument.

24. Hugo Preuss, *Staat Recht und Freiheit: Aus 40 Jahren Deutscher Politik und Geschichte* (Tübingen, 1926), 365.

25. Gustav Schmoller, *Walther Rathenau und Hugo Preuss: Die Staatsmänner des neuen Deutschlands* (Munich, 1922), 28–9.

26. 'Dokumentation: Zur Frage der Staatsführung in der Weimarer Republik', *Vierteljahrshefte für Zeitgeschichte*, 7/1 (Jan. 1959), 85–111. For Pünder, *Der Reichspräsident*, this exercise of 'healthy authority' did not pose a threat to democratic authority.

27. Jesse, 'Problem', in König et al., *Friedrich Ebert und seine Zeit*, 108; Dieter Rebentisch, 'Verpaßte Chancen und verhinderte Katastrophen: Friedrich Ebert und sein Platz in der deutschen Geschichte', in König et al., *Friedrich Ebert*, 161–73.

28. Martin Schiele, 'Innere Politik', in Walther Lambach (ed.), *Politische Praxis 1926* (Hamburg, 1926), 53. Pünder, *Der Reichspräsident*, 24, speaks of proportional representation as the 'basic evil' (*Grundübel*) besetting the republic.

29. Rogers et al., 'Aspects', Part I, 344. Ernst Rudolf Huber, *Deutsche Verfassungsgeschichte seit 1789*, vi: *Die Weimarer Reichsverfassung* (Stuttgart, 1981), 875.

30. Rogers et al., 'Aspects', Part I, 349.

31. Carl Schmitt, 'Der Begriff der modernen Demokratie in seinem Verhältnis zum Staatsbegriff', *Archiv für Sozialwissenschaft und Sozialpolitik*, 51 (Tübingen, 1924), 821.

32. Schmoller, *Walther Rathenau und Hugo Preuss*, 33.

33. Hermann Heller, 'Genie und Funktionär in der Politik', in *Probleme der Demokratie = Politische Wissenschaft Schriftenreihe der Deutschen Hochschule für Politik in Berlin und des Instituts für Auswärtige Politik in Hamburg*, 10 (Berlin, 1931), 68.

34. Schmoller, *Walther Rathenau und Hugo Preuss*, 42–3; Thomas Mergel, *Parlamentarische Kultur in der Weimar Republik* (Düsseldorf, 2005), chapter 2, *passim*; Rogers et al., 'Aspects', Part I, 347; Martin Schumacher, *M.d.R.: Die Reichstagsabgeordneten der Weimarer Republik in der Zeit des Nationalsozialismus* (Düsseldorf, 1994), 'Forschungsbericht', 28; G. Best, 'Elite structure and regime (dis)continuity in

Germany 1867–1933: the case of the parliamentary leadership groups',
German History, 7 (1990).

35. Rogers et al., 'Aspects', Part I, 344–6.
36. Rogers et al., 'Aspects', Part I, 322–3, and 344 for the quote.
37. Huber, *Verfassungsgeschichte*, vii. 883; Helmut Heiber, *The Weimar Republic*, trans. W. E. Yuill (Oxford, 1993), 180; Jäckel, *Das deutsche Jahrhundert*, 101.
38. Ernst Rudolf Huber, *Dokumente zur deutschen Verfassungsgeschichte*, 3 vols. (2nd edn. Stuttgart, 1961–66), iii. 160–2, for a list of these.
39. Highly critical of Brüning, Karl Dietrich Bracher, *Die Auflösung der Weimarer Republik: Eine Studie zum Problem des Machtverfalls in der Demokratie* (Düsseldorf, 1984), 151; and in his defence: William J. Patch, *Heinrich Brüning and the Dissolution of the Weimar Republic* (Cambridge, 1998).
40. Pünder, *Der Reichspräsident*, 24.
41. Heinrich August Winkler, 'Choosing the lesser evil: the German Social Democrats and the fall of the Weimar Republic', *Journal of Contemporary History*, 25/2–3 (May–June 1990), 205–27; idem, *Weimar 1918–1933: Die Geschichte der ersten deutschen Demokratie* (Munich, 1994), 444–76.
42. For damning assessment of Brüning, see Arthur Rosenberg, *A History of the German Republic* (New York, 1965); Hans Mommsen, *Die verspielte Freiheit: Der Weg der Republik von Weimar in den Untergang 1918 bis 1933* (Berlin, 1989).
43. BArch N2001/113, Nachlaß Wilhelm Abegg, Bl. 36
44. Hans Boldt, 'Der Artikel 48 der Weimarer Verfassung: Sein historischer Hintergrund und seine politische Funktion', in Michael Stürmer (ed.), *Die Weimarer Republik: Belagerte Civitas* (Königstein, 1980), 298.
45. Meinecke, *Katastrophe*, 104 f.
46. Carl Schmitt, 'Gesunde Wirtschaft im Starken Staat', unidentified newspaper cutting (1932), BArch N2035/2 Nachlaß Bracht, Bl. 132.
47. Theodor Eschenburg, 'Franz von Papen', *Vierteljahrshefte für Zeitgeschichte*, 2/5 (1954), 161, 163. Manfred Funke, 'Republik im Untergang: Die Zerstörung des Parlamentarismus als Vorbereitung der Diktatur', in Bracher, Funke, and Jacobsen (eds.), *Die Weimarer Republik*, 512.
48. Huber, *Verfassungsgeschichte*, vii. 907, 909.
49. Dirk Blasius, *Weimars Ende: Bürgerkrieg und Politik 1930–1933* (Frankfurt am Main, 2008).
50. *Ursachen und Folgen*, viii. 557 ff. See the astute commentary in the *Cape Times*, 22 July 1932.

51. *Preußen contra Reich vor dem Staatsgerichtshof* (Berlin, 1933);
Dr Schwalb, 'Die Einwendungen gegen das Staatsgerichts-Urteil vom
25 Oktober 1932 in der Preußensache', *Die Justiz*, 8/5–6 (1933),
217–39; *Akten der Reichskanzlei Weimarer Republik*, Das Kabinett
von Papen, prepared by Karl-Heinz Minuth, ii (Boppard am Rhein,
1989), Doc. 215, 960. BArch N2001/128, Bl. 30 on secret discussions in
June/July (1932?) regarding the possible detention of von Papen and
Hitler.

52. *Akten*, Kab. v. Papen, Doc. 96, 353 (von Leyden); see the pamphlet
by Bavaria's Social Democrat prime minister Dr Heinrich Held, *Das
preußische-deutsche Problem* (Berlin, 1929).

53. Dr F. Friedensburg, 'Fünfzehn Notverordnungen in zwei Jahren', *Die
Justiz*, 8/7 (1933), 314–22; Boldt, 'Der Artikel 48', 293–4, 301; Funke,
'Republik im Untergang', 530; Heiber, *Weimar Republic*, 180, has
slightly differing figures.

54. BArch R3001/6670 (22087), Bl. 6, 79, 85; *Akten*, Kab. v. Papen,
Doc. 239b, 1037 f.n. 10; Wolfram Pyta, 'Vorbereitungen für den
militärischen Ausnahmezustand unter Papen/Schleicher', *Militär-
gechichtliche Mitteilungen*, 51 (1992), 385–428. Eberhard Kolb and
Wolfram Pyta, 'Die Staatsnotstandsplanung unter den Regierungen
Papen und Schleicher', in Heinrich August Winkler (ed.), *Hand-
lungsspielräume und Alternativen in der deutschen Staatskrise 1930–1933*
(Munich, 1992), 153–79.

55. Rogers et al., 'Aspects', Part II, 577–82.

56. *Akten*, Kab. v. Papen 2, Docs. 215 f., 240.

57. *Akten der Reichskanzlei, Weimarer Republik*, Das Kabinett von
Schleicher 3 Dezember 1932 bis 30 Januar 1933, prepared by Anton Golecki (Boppard am Rhein, 1986), LXV–LXX; Funke, 'Republik
im Untergang', 516–17.

58. *Akten*, Kab. Schleicher, Docs. 71, 77, and 79 *passim*.

59. BArch N2035/2, Nachlaß Bracht, Bl. 169.

60. BArch N2001/126, Nachlaß Abegg, Archiv-Auszug. Still useful is David
Abraham, *The Collapse of the Weimar Republic: Political Economy and
Crisis*, 2nd edn. (Princeton, 1986).

61. *Akten der Reichskanzlei Regierung Hitler 1933–1938*, vol. i, 30. Januar
bis 31 August 1933, part 1, prepared by Konrad Repgen and Hans
Günter Hockerts (Boppard am Rhein, 1983), Docs. 1 and 2, p. 6 for
the quote. Bracher, *Auflösung*, 465 ff.

Foreign policy

Wolfgang Elz

'In the beginning was the Treaty of Versailles in 1919': as a characterization of the Weimar Republic's foreign policy this statement would hit some nails on the head but it would also miss others.

The true part would be that German foreign policy between 1919 and 1933 was indeed constantly directed towards the revision of this treaty: it inflicted too deep an injury on the self-perception of the German public and politicians for even a single one of its basic clauses to be left in place.

Fundamental were naturally first and foremost the territorial secessions: the return of Alsace and those parts of Lorraine that Germany had pocketed from France in 1871 as war booty; the fifteen-year transfer of the Saar region to the League of Nations, which permitted France to exploit its coal mines; the small, largely German-speaking industrial area round Eupen and Malmédy, which after a questionable plebiscite went to Belgium; the loss of northern Schleswig to Denmark after another plebiscite; and, worst of all from the German point of view, the large-scale secessions in West Prussia and the whole of Posen (Poznań) to a re-emergent Poland, which created a sizeable German minority in the new state and together with the creation of the 'Free City of Danzig' (which lay under League protection with special rights also granted to Poland) formed the so-called 'Corridor' cutting off East Prussia from the rest of the Reich. Further consequences of the Versailles Treaty were the territorial losses in Upper Silesia, of which following a plebiscite in 1921 the League of Nations transferred a part—the economically more important part—to Poland; in the Memel (Niemen) region, which by a circuitous route came to Lithuania in 1923/4, and in the tiny Hultschiner Ländchen (Hlučínsko), which went to the Czechoslovak Republic. Other territorial stipulations included the prohibition of union with the Republic of Austria, the modest remnant of the former Habsburg empire, which at first called itself *Deutsch-Österreich* (German Austria) after what was now its majority population, and—territorially the most extensive, economically almost the least significant, having always been a financial liability—the loss of all colonies in Africa, Asia, and Oceania, which were awarded as League of Nation mandates to the victorious powers.

Sensitive too was the restriction of sovereignty resulting from the occupation of the Rhineland. This was divided into three zones from north to south; it subjected the left bank of the Rhine and three extended bridgeheads on the right bank at Cologne, Koblenz, and Mainz to the occupying forces of the victorious powers; the zones were to be evacuated, on condition of good behaviour in the future by Germany and meticulous fulfilment of the treaty, after five, ten, and fifteen years respectively. The occupation of the Rhineland had been chiefly a French concern in the negotiations: it was intended to offer a guarantee and form a glacis, and was linked to further dispositions of a military nature. The west bank of the Rhine and a strip 50 km wide to the east were to be demilitarized, so that no German soldier could be stationed there and no German fortification maintained. But that was only one of the restrictions. The army could consist of only 100,000 serving soldiers (which meant in practice that it could not train reservists), and, moreover, it could not be equipped with heavy weapons; the navy, except for some small units, was to be surrendered to the victors; Germany was forbidden to possess the new weapons of the world war—tanks, submarines, and an air force. The result was that after this treaty Germany neither would be able to launch an attack, nor defend itself against its now much stronger neighbours, France and Poland.

Especially serious too, in German eyes, was Article 231, which laid the sole blame for the war on Germany and its allies. True, this 'war guilt article' had been devised by the Allies primarily as a legal justification for demanding that Germany should pay reparations for the entire cost of the war. But in Germany it was taken above all as a moral condemnation. This new rule of international law, of determining who had caused a war and thereby justifying the payment of reparations (as against the older practice of excluding the question of causes from peace treaties and making the loser pay), arose for two main reasons. The prolonged social mobilization necessary for total war among all belligerent countries had only been possible as a result of the exceedingly massive and hitherto unknown intensity of propaganda, which presented the other side not only as the people to be defeated, but as a veritable demon. This propaganda would long continue after the war to have an influence on both sides and place almost insuperable social obstacles in the way of any rapprochement.

The demand for comprehensive German reparations can be also explained by domestic imperatives: Lloyd George fought the election campaign immediately following the end of the war with the slogan 'The Germans will pay' in order to give credibility to his promise of sweeping—and urgently needed—social measures in an England battered by crises, while in France the politicians comforted a population hard hit by four years of war on French soil with the hope that everything would be restored to its previous level by German payments. The actual total of reparations, however, was not laid down in the treaty, but only an advance payment. Establishing the exact amount was left to the victors, in whose hands it became a throttle that France above all wished to use; the French were by no means satisfied with the outcome of Versailles, but saw that their hopes of sidelining Germany in the long term and preventing a return to hostilities had not really been fulfilled. Besides reparations, other provisions, such as those on special German export duties and one-sided most-favoured-nation clauses, were an attempt to refill the empty coffers of the European victors (themselves heavily indebted to the USA) and to prevent a rapid German recovery.

But the statement with which we began this chapter is also imprecise, since it describes only half the truth, principally the way in which the peace treaty was perceived in Germany. First of all, the treaty's reception as a national humiliation may be explained by German wartime propaganda which was able to build on the widespread and deep conviction from before the war that it was the enemy who was to blame for hostilities, having 'encircled' Germany, forcing a pre-emptive strike in order to escape the annihilation threatening it sooner or later. Secondly, until shortly before the war ended propaganda had nurtured confidence in victory, especially on the political right, which branded any initiative for a compromise peace as defeatism. Lastly, as late as 3 March 1918 the Treaty of Brest-Litovsk had supposedly brought a brilliant end to the war in the east (which, incidentally, as a draconian peace that exceeded the conditions of the Versailles Treaty showed how Germany could deal with those in its power). When a mere six weeks before the armistice of 11 November 1918 the military leadership, in a sudden volte-face, admitted that victory was no longer possible, the political leadership immediately banked on Wilson's 'Fourteen Points' that seemed to promise Germany, all things considered, a 'just' peace. Thus both politicians and people later felt that they had been grossly deceived, and that the peace treaty did not accord in every aspect with these Fourteen Points.

If people in Germany had not been subject to these various self-deceptions, they could have viewed the Treaty of Versailles more soberly: to be sure some 13 per cent of German territory, including economically important regions, was lost, but the potential for being a Great Power with some 60 million inhabitants and still the strongest economy in Europe remained. This was due simply to the fact that this peace arose from a compromise between the important victors, the USA, Great Britain, and France. It was above all neighbouring France that harboured far more draconian ideas: Paris dreamt of dismantling the Reich and returning Germany to the state of affairs before 1871 or even 1866; at the very least of detaching the Rhineland, to be either annexed or turned into a buffer state that would sooner or later gravitate towards France.

In defeat those who had been responsible for the victory pro-paganda searched for domestic scapegoats and found them in the parties which since spring 1919 carried the new republic, namely the so-called 'Weimar Coalition' of Social Democrats (SPD), the left-liberal German Democratic Party (DDP), and the Catholic party, the Centre. In particular the Social Democrats were subjected to the allegation that they had 'stabbed the army in the back', which later was exposed as a myth. This accusation was made by prominent right-wingers (whose chief organization was the anti-republican German National People's Party, DNVP), and sanctified by the pronouncements of leading military men, including the last supreme commander Paul von Hindenburg. Thus responsibility for defeat lay not with the imperial army, which had remained 'undefeated in the field', but with left-wing politicians on the home front through their support of strikes and, above all, in the final days of the war, with the naval mutiny that had led directly to the fall of the monarchy. The military had planned cleverly ahead by having the armistice agreement, against all normal practice, signed on 11 November 1918 by those politicians who had come to power just two days before through the unceremonious disappearance of the imperial regime and who found themselves at Compiègne facing the commanders of the victorious armies.

Thus the horror of losing the war and the supposedly draconian peace were early on associated with the distress that very many in the middle class felt at the loss of imperial rule. The revolution of November 1918—modest as it was, at least in its effects—was linked by many liberals and above all the right with the 'shame of Versailles'. But even on the left—beyond the Social Democratic leadership—the revolution had not fulfilled every dream of greater social justice. As a consequence, from the very beginning not many people were prepared to make a success of the republic by identifying with the fresh start it offered. It was only in the few middle years of the republic that social divisions were to some extent overcome, and not by accident was a relatively realistic foreign policy possible in this period.

The Versailles Treaty

But let us return to our original point concerning the treaty. Illusions that the victorious powers were bound by Wilson's 'Fourteen Points', and obligated by the armistice, were also harboured by the representatives of those political parties that from 1917—albeit with little effect—had pursued a compromise peace. Even these moderate politicians had been infected (or feared the allegation of treason) and did not believe that they could simply accept the draft treaty handed on 7 May 1919 to the new German foreign minister Brockdorff-Rantzau, an aristocratic diplomat 'converted' from imperial service to the republic.

Even the Social Democratic chancellor of the republic, Philipp Scheidemann, allowed himself to be drawn into the rising tide of objections by stating before the National Assembly that the 'hand . . . must wither' that signed this peace. But protests led only to trivial modifications to the treaty text. When it became clear that no substantial amendments to the treaty could be attained, the entire cabinet followed the foreign minister in resigning, and a new minority government was formed without the DDP. There was a brief boom in plans for refusing to sign the treaty. But it took the declaration of the high command that, given the current power relations, any refusal to sign would be futile and might lead to an invasion by the victors, ending with Germany crushed, to bring about the bitter recognition that there was no realistic alternative. Even the last attempt to get the Allies at least not to insist on the 'points of honour' (the 'war guilt article' 231, the demand for the extradition of the numerous alleged war criminals and the ex-Kaiser, now living in Dutch exile) failed in the face of the ultimatum to sign without 'ifs' or 'buts'. The National Assembly, which had made its acceptance conditional on the deletion of these clauses, did not really consent to the signing performed under humiliating conditions on 28 June 1919 by the German minister sent to Versailles. Nonetheless, a large majority voted for a parliamentary declaration that the deputies who had supported signing the treaty had acted 'only from patriotic motives'—an expression that was swiftly forgotten, at least on the right.

The First World War with its numberless victims had a lasting traumatic effect on society in every state affected. But whereas the population in the victorious countries could at least draw some satisfaction, in Germany there was a spreading atmosphere of impotence and humiliation, which became a burden the republic could hardly bear. All in all, what was signed in Versailles was at any rate not a peace that brought peace, and probably could not be, given the totality of the war, the first of its kind in world history. Immediately after the signing and then after the ratification of the treaty on 10 January 1920, Germany sought to partially avoid fulfilment. There was resistance especially on the question of 'points of honour'. To be sure the Dutch failure to hand over Wilhelm II, who had inspired British propaganda even during the war to the cry of 'hang the Kaiser', was not really the consequence of a German initiative, but originated in The Hague. But the Reich government successfully refused to surrender 'war criminals', and the stand-off over this issue in February 1920 ended in the compromise that Germany itself would investigate and try them before the newly constituted Reich court in Leipzig—which apart from a few trials and a handful of convictions was largely a dead letter.

This early success at avoiding fulfilment may have frustrated the attempts made just after the war by the German Foreign Office and the Reich government to return to reality through a clear orientation towards the West (and in particular the USA), and replaced them with the illusory hope of quick successes in other aspects of revision. First of all there were efforts to put off the reduction in the size of the Reichswehr. This attitude on the government's part was not motivated only by foreign-policy considerations. The forced withdrawal of the remaining German troops in the Baltic after the armistice had brought into the Reich a further serious potential source of disorder at the very time when the *Freikorps*, who the government repeatedly relied upon to suppress attempted uprisings on the left, were facing disbandment. Thus the victors' ultimatum for a further reduction of the army to 200,000 men, issued in February 1920 immediately after the Treaty of Versailles had come into force, was not the least of the factors leading extreme right-wing forces around Wolfgang Kapp, the former leader of the Vaterlandspartei, and General Walther Freiherr von Lüttwitz, joined in the background by Erich Ludendorff, who by the end of the war had been the ruling spirit of the Supreme Army Command, to attempt in March 1920 a putsch against the republic.

To be sure the amateurism of the putsch—which nevertheless drove the government out of the capital to Dresden and then to Stuttgart—and the determined resistance of workers, who had swiftly responded with a general strike, put paid to it after a few days. However, when in its aftermath the trade unions' demands for a more Socialist policy turned into local uprisings in the Ruhr, and the Reich government sent in troops (and that after the Reichswehr's ambivalence during the Kapp Putsch), who temporarily crossed the demarcation line of the neutralized region, the victorious powers, in particular France, reacted mercilessly: as punishment they occupied Frankfurt and its environs, which hitherto had lain outside the zone of occupation. The Reich government was thus shown in a manner that left no room for misunderstanding that breaches of the treaty, especially of its military clauses, would not be tolerated even when the authority of Berlin was in danger; the Reichswehr was thus not allowed even to remain as an instrument for maintaining order within the Reich.

A quite different hope for revision entered several heads early on, namely that of cooperation with the other pariah of the post-war order, Soviet Russia. Thus the contacts broken off at the end of the war were slowly resumed, stopping short of full diplomatic relations. To be sure, the vague expectation that a Russian victory in the war against Poland in 1920–1 would afford the opportunity for a renewed partition proved to be illusory in the light of the Poles' unexpected success and the Treaty of Riga in 1921; but Poland, as the common enemy and a target for revision, remained the bond between Berlin and Moscow, at times fragile, and always strained by ideological differences and the activity of the Comintern in Germany. This constellation was also a counterpart to the French plan of building close ties with Poland and Czechoslovakia, in order to contain Germany within a pincer grip should the need arise. Moreover, the Reichswehr early on saw the opportunity offered by the rapprochement of avoiding the treaty limitations on armaments. Reichswehr officers could be trained in arms that Germany had been forbidden to possess. In return, the Soviet Union, as it was officially called from 1922, hoped for German help in building up the Red Army. Finally, there were also hopes within German economic circles that they could do good business by rebuilding the Russian market.

A far more pressing consideration was that of reparations. Here too German foreign policy attempted to bring about a speedy revision. But a series of conferences and decisions by the Allies or their Reparations Commission (Spa 1920, London 1921) culminated in 1921 in the final demand of 132,000,000,000 gold Marks. After Berlin refused to comply, the victors, led by France and with

English participation, by occupying Düsseldorf, Duisburg, and Ruhrort and confiscating the harbour dues raised there, again clearly demonstrated that they did not intend to allow any room for negotiation. Under consideration were not only their own debts to the USA and the immense costs of reconstruction. For the French, the reparations question served above all as a political means to exorcize the fear that their neighbour on the right of the Rhine might regain its strength—an attitude regarded with due scepticism in London, where, even during the Paris peace negotiations, there had been a disinclination to allow France to slip into the prominent role that Germany had occupied before the First World War. This scepticism peaked several times, but never led to an open breach—not least for the very reason that London harboured the false hope that in view of its own problems in the empire and the newly acquired territories in the Near and Middle East, it could maintain the status quo in Europe with as few major squabbles as possible.

The cabinet of Chancellor Joseph Wirth (1921–2) had finally to bow to pressure in the reparations question and recognized that only a 'policy of fulfilment', an attempt to meet Allied demands as far as possible, would demonstrate that they could not be fulfilled. In parallel, however, quite different initiatives were undertaken. Wirth's minister for reconstruction (and, from January 1922, foreign minister), Walther Rathenau, took soundings with his French counterpart about a scheme for payment mainly in goods and labour, in order to protect German currency. Such moves in Germany towards a readiness to cooperate foundered on the resistance of the French right and French industry, but they were also hampered by the fact that in the heated state of German public opinion, further inflamed by the extreme right, any apparent German concession passed for treason.

One factor intensifying this attitude and which drove Germany closer to the Soviets was a decision by the League of Nations affecting Germany's eastern border. Under the Treaty of Versailles, Germany was initially debarred from membership. Since the USA too, after Wilson's failed effort at getting the treaty ratified in Congress, had turned its back on Europe as regards politics, the League quickly attained the reputation of being a tool of the European victors. In March 1921, in a plebiscite in Upper Silesia, a region of mixed population, which had taken place amidst skirmishes between German and Polish irregulars, some 60 per cent voted to remain in Germany. The League now recommended to the victors in October 1921 to act on the result in such a way that the eastern, more industrialized part should go to Poland and only the larger but economically less significant remainder stay German. In Germany this reignited the charge of bad faith against the victors who dominated the League, and refuelled considerable hatred towards Poland.

Such auspices boded ill for foreign minister Walther Rathenau's plan of willing cooperation. Instead he let himself be drawn into an action that in the long term further diminished what little faith there was amongst the victors in German trustworthiness. On 16 April 1922, on the fringe of the conference in Genoa summoned on the initiative of Lloyd George and intended to advance the rebuilding of the shattered European economy by also reintegrating the Soviet Union into the market, Rathenau, behind the backs of the western delegates, struck a treaty with the Russians in the little seaside resort of Rapallo. The preliminaries had been conducted some time before, chiefly by his secretary of state at the Foreign Office, Ago von Maltzan, who favoured cooperation with Moscow against Poland. However, the actual decision to conclude the treaty was taken in haste by the German delegation, because Maltzan postulated the danger that the Soviet Union would settle with the Western Powers at Germany's expense and could then assert its hitherto dormant claims for reparations. Taken only on its content, the Treaty of Rapallo was merely one of normalization: full diplomatic relations were to be resumed; each side renounced its claims on the other—respectively reparations and compensation after Soviet confiscations—and gave assurances of good economic cooperation. The result, however, was a grave setback to German relations with the Western Powers. This was not only because they wrongly believed in the existence of a secret article on military cooperation, but also because they judged Rapallo to be an attempt at confronting the victors with a bloc. So understood, 'Rapallo' retained until after the Second World War an almost mythical significance as a byword for the threat of German–Soviet cooperation. Rathenau was not really comfortable with such an eastward-looking policy. Indeed his moderation towards the victorious powers cost him his life on 24 June at the hands of members of the 'Organisation Consul', which had been responsible for a series of assassinations, including that of Matthias Erzberger in 1921, the Centre Party politician who had signed the armistice in 1918.

No direct path leads from Rapallo to the occupation of the Ruhr in January 1923, when France, accompanied by Belgium, sent first 60,000, later 100,000, soldiers—thinly disguised as protection for a 'party of engineers'—into the Ruhr area, the industrial heart of Germany. Poincaré had once again become French prime minister at the beginning of 1922 and he still held firmly to his aim of weakening Germany. He thus exploited a slight delay in German fulfilment of delivering coal and mining timber to extract a ruling from the Reparations Commission that there had been a serious breach and thus procure himself a lawful excuse to treat the Ruhr itself as a 'productive pledge'. Thus began a sequence of developments in German foreign and domestic politics that brought the country close to collapse.

This scenario, however, was not immediately apparent. The call by the Reich and the affected *Länder* (regional states) for passive resistance to the Ruhr occupation, condemned as an illegal act of violence, and against the attempt to collect the reparations directly by exploiting the mines, was maintained by civil servants and workers over the whole area. However, the Reich government, now led by Wilhelm Cuno, refrained from denouncing the entire Treaty of Versailles as the radical right demanded. Cuno knew that this would result in the destruction of Germany just as surely as any violent resistance as demanded by the emergent *völkisch* parties. Furthermore, isolated instances of such violent resistance were mercilessly repressed by the French, who administered the area under martial law, and repeatedly led to death sentences and executions that merely increased beyond all measure German hatred towards the occupiers.

German foreign policy hopes rested on British intervention. London had firmly dissociated itself from the Franco-Belgian invasion and continued to make its disapproval clear. But Berlin's hope for stronger English pressure on France and the expectation that the initial failure of the attempted economic exploitation of the Ruhr would at least cause Paris to resume negotiations proved deceptive. Thus the *Ruhrkampf* or 'Struggle for the Ruhr' became a race against time. France erected a tariff barrier around the newly occupied area, cutting off the occupied territories from the Reich; the military administration expelled a great many civil servants with their families eastwards across the line of occupation (the number is estimated at in excess of 130,000); this made provision of the Ruhr and Rhineland from within the Reich steadily more difficult. Yet Berlin could not shrug off its duty to support the region. And this caused one problem to run out of control, though it was not new and was not actually caused by the *Ruhrkampf*: namely, inflation, as the Reichsbank completely lost control of the currency in the face of the immense costs of financing the resistance.

The Stresemann era

By August 1923 the Cuno government had to recognize that its policy of all-out non-compliance with Paris had failed. For the next few months, the chancellorship fell to Gustav Stresemann, who led a grand coalition from his own centre-right German People's Party to the SPD. Over the following years Stresemann clearly dominated, and to a large extent personified, German foreign policy until his early death in 1929. Born in 1878 into a lower-middle-class family in Berlin, Stresemann had a youthful career in trade and economic associations behind him and even before the world war represented the then still unfamiliar type of the professional politician. During the war he had been a fervent annexationist and only with difficulty got over the fall of the imperial government, the defeat, and with it the end of his dreams. But with his native pragmatism Stresemann had gradually brought himself and his party around to the republic, since he saw no realistic alternative. His political ideal was the creation of a broad 'people's community' (*Volksgemeinschaft*, a term later much misused by the Nazis), which also envisaged a stronger social integration of workers. Politically this vision demanded cooperation with the SPD and possibly also its incorporation into his government. In the following years, however, it was always a laborious task for him to create a willingness to cooperate with the SPD among the economic wing of his party, dominated as it was by Rhineland industrialists.

When Stresemann became chancellor in August 1923, it quickly became clear that his government had no other option but to call off the *Ruhrkampf*. Last desperate efforts to force Paris, either directly or indirectly from London, to negotiate the matter peacefully were unsuccessful. Poincaré insisted on total German capitulation, meaning the end of passive resistance without any promise of concessions. Faced with the hyperinflation that made financing the *Ruhrkampf* increasingly impossible, the Reich government had finally to give way and at the end of September called off the resistance.

But this produced new dangers that seemed virtually impossible to control, for the eight months of passive resistance had mobilized the population to such an extent that a return to normality was no simple matter. And at the extremes of the political spectrum there were forces ready to exploit this public mood. This was especially the case in Saxony (and neighbouring Thuringia), where the Comintern-inspired KPD (German Communist Party) had a hold on the state apparatus through its participation in government and sought to bring about a revolutionary situation. In Bavaria, politicians on the extreme right harboured vague plans for restoring the old order in the Reich, to be kick-started from Munich. Lastly, the situation in the occupied Rhineland and Ruhr was also explosive. For some weeks the abandonment of resistance left the region entirely exposed to the occupiers' whim, and given the financial straits of Berlin no further support could for the moment be expected. Hence the businessmen of the Ruhr sought direct contact with the occupiers. But they also wished to improve the competitiveness of their mines and factories by reversing some social improvements resulting from the revolution. As a result there was a ferocious struggle over the eight-hour day in the coal mines, which the working class regarded as the most important symbol of the successes of 1918.

The desperate situation in the Rhineland and Ruhr gave rise locally to very different schemes for a solution. One was for autonomy within the Reich with more intensive contacts with France, backed for instance by the lord mayor of Cologne, Konrad

Adenauer. Another scheme included the more radical plans of the separatists, who in autumn 1923—with the connivance of the French occupation regime, which had still not given up hopes of realizing the plans for the Rhineland it had drawn up in 1918–19—sought through actions at local and regional level to bring about the total separation of the Rhineland from the Reich and for some weeks took over de facto power in some districts. The resistance to these actions by the population at large—with massive support from the Reich, some of it secret—contributed to the end of the separatist rebellion along with the now quite unambiguous signal from London that Paris had gone too far.

The *Ruhrkampf* had proved a Pyrrhic victory for France, and this provided a new opportunity for German foreign policy. The franc had collapsed, and now Great Britain and above all the USA, which despite its political isolationism towards Europe had a strong economic interest in the continent, made their presence felt by denying France the means of using the reparations question as a political instrument. Washington and London compelled Paris to transfer the problem to an economic commission of experts, and in so doing made clear that they would no longer let French reparations policy torpedo their own interests in the economic recovery of Europe. Thus 1923 marked the climax of the post-war period in Europe: the last great attempt by France to bring about, unilaterally and by force, the security it believed it had not achieved in the Paris peace negotiations, and the parallel recognition in Germany that nothing was to be gained by head-on confrontation with France and no quick revision of the Versailles Treaty was thinkable.

Stresemann preferred to stake his policy on Anglo-Saxon interest in the reintegration of Germany in the world economy. This also coincided with his own idea of how his country could be a Great Power again, namely through renewed realization of its great potential in that economy. But this could be achieved only in cooperation with the other powers and in a largely peaceful Europe. This aim was, at least for the foreseeable future, to govern foreign policy. Stresemann was principally concerned with German interests, but in this approach he was no different from his French and British negotiating partners, Aristide Briand and Austen Chamberlain, who likewise put their national interests above all else. More decisive was the paradigm shift in his methods: whatever Stresemann may have dreamt of as the goal of German foreign policy (which given the contradictory evidence can probably never be established beyond all doubt), peaceful means of bringing about an economic rehabilitation of Europe were incompatible with a frontal assault on the key elements of the Treaty of Versailles. It was this principle (in which Carl Schubert, his secretary of state from 1924, concurred) that fundamentally distinguished Gustav Stresemann's foreign policy from that of his predecessors—and also, as we shall see, from that of his successors.

But much work was needed before this policy bore fruit. In the spring of 1924 the commission of experts under the American banker and later vice-president Charles Dawes presented its recommendation for a restructuring of reparations. It was initially discussed in summer by the victors at a conference in London, before—signalling a new departure in post-war policy—a German delegation was admitted for genuine negotiations and not merely to receive an ultimatum. The details of the Dawes Plan accepted at the end of the conference need only be outlined: the Allied demands for reparations were modified in such a way that safeguarding the German currency, in the interests of world economic development and thus above all of the Anglo-Saxon states, became an equally important aim; the sums to be paid each year were to begin with relatively small amounts and rise only gradually; at each stage economic experts were to examine whether Germany could afford the proposed annual payments without serious damage. Reparations were thus largely taken out of politics and subjected to economic considerations. The Dawes Plan showed quick results: investment poured into Germany from the USA, which for the time being brought relief, but at the end of the decade would prove to be an insidious danger.

However, the London Conference also revealed the dilemma that confronted Stresemann throughout the following years: in order to obtain domestic support for his foreign policy, he had to be able to point to counter-concessions from the Allies so as not to become a victim of propaganda, especially from the DNVP, alleging a sell-out of German interests. In London he achieved this with French agreement to withdraw from the Ruhr within a year. This made possible the two-thirds majority in the Reichstag for the Dawes Plan, made necessary in view of the constitutional change entailed by removing the Reichsbahn from direct Reich ownership, and which in future would guarantee reparations. In spite of the campaign against it, some DNVP deputies voted for it after coming under pressure from agrarian and industrial interest groups. Stresemann was for ever after constantly performing a high-wire act in domestic politics in order to sell each step he took in foreign policy, either with real or possible concessions by the victors, or in the expectation of 'returns', especially with regard to the occupied Rhineland. The nationalistic tone to be found in several of his speeches and writings can be simply explained by this need.

The fact is that Stresemann had recognized that only empathy with the unsatisfied French need for security and a solution to this problem could make progress possible. When in January 1925 it became known that, owing to German failure to fulfil certain disarmament terms the Allies would not, as provided in the Versailles Treaty, withdraw from the northern occupation zone in the Rhineland, at the same time as the threat was growing that Great Britain would make an anti-German treaty of guarantee with France and Belgium, he went on the diplomatic offensive. Supported by the British ambassador Lord D'Abernon, Stresemann proposed a security pact to London and Paris. At its core was to be the mutual inviolability of Germany's western border with France and Belgium as drawn up in Versailles: that is, a voluntary confirmation by Germany rather than a forced signature, and France's renunciation of any changes in its favour. The following months were marked by intensive diplomatic negotiations, in the course of which pressure was placed on Paris by London and Washington to accept the initiative.

There were two main potential stumbling blocks: France pressed for similar guarantees from Germany for its eastern border with its allies Poland and Czechoslovakia, which Stresemann rejected as totally impossible. The other Allied demand related to German entry into the League of Nations. After the prohibition at Versailles, this now passed for the precondition for reintegrating Germany in European politics and no doubt also for controlling it. Entry into the League, however, would not only stir up the hatred manifested especially on the right against this allegedly anti-German instrument of the victors, but under the League constitution Berlin would be in the unwelcome position of having to offer at least indirect assistance to any anti-Soviet policy the Western Powers might adopt, thus cutting the 'wire to the East' that had existed since Rapallo.

Both problems were eventually solved. At the Locarno conference in October 1925 the delegates initialled the 'Treaties of Locarno'. At their core was the undertaking by Germany, Belgium, and France not to change their common borders by force, which was sealed by Great Britain and Italy as guarantors of these agreements together with the permanent demilitarization of the Rhineland. The pact was completed by arbitration treaties involving France, Belgium, Germany, Poland, and Czechoslovakia. Germany's treaties with its eastern neighbours, however, did not provide for any strict obligation and were thus distinctly less binding than those with its neighbours to the west. Stresemann had thus succeeded in keeping open the question of the eastern border and its possible revision. In respect of German entry into the League, agreement was made possible by a last-minute concession from the Western Powers, who ruled out de facto any anti-Soviet obligations on Germany. Both Briand and Chamberlain went a good deal of the way towards Germany and Stresemann, since they too had an interest in resolving the security question and together recognized that only the reintegration of Germany into European politics at Locarno would make it possible.

Even so, the Locarno Treaties resulted in a ferocious political storm in Germany. At the beginning of 1925 the DNVP had for the first time accepted governmental responsibility in a centre-right coalition under the non-party chancellor Hans Luther. In the second round of the presidential elections that April, Paul von Hindenburg, the candidate above all of the DNVP, emerged as the successor to Friedrich Ebert, who had died unexpectedly at the end of February. This election was enough to show that a relative majority of the German population preferred to bask in the faded glory of past victories, and encouraged the anti-republican DNVP to hope that it could now pursue a decidedly 'national' foreign policy. It was therefore unsurprising that the coalition collapsed over the question of the treaties after the DNVP rank and file compelled its leaders to leave the cabinet, since Locarno was perceived as the 'politics of abdication'. Even Stresemann's references to revisions eventually leading to the recovery of full sovereignty in the occupied Rhineland were of little help. Nevertheless, Luther's minority cabinet could rely in its foreign policy on the opposition SPD, which, regardless of whether it was in or out of government, provided a bulwark for Stresemann's policy of compromise. As a result the Reichstag voted by a majority for the Locarno Treaties, which were finally signed in London on 1 December 1925. True, German entry into the League of Nations was delayed until September 1926, since its demand for a permanent seat on the Council was contested by other states with similar ambitions. Nonetheless, the treaties led to the reintegration of Germany and a new phase in European foreign policy, which, in the close collaboration of Stresemann, Briand, and Chamberlain at their regular meetings, strongly resembled the maintenance of peace by the nineteenth-century 'Concert of Europe'.

German–French rapprochement

The conclusion in April 1926 in Berlin of a German–Soviet friendship treaty did little to harm Stresemann's overture to the West. This agreement was intended to appease Moscow, where the new course in German foreign policy was jealously watched. Thus the Treaty of Berlin was received with comparative equanimity by London and Paris, even though it contained mutual promises of neutrality in case of war that ruled out de facto French intervention in a Soviet–Polish war.

More important for Stresemann in the following period was the hope of achieving the 'returns' on which he justified his foreign policy at home. For the moment these hardly included revision of the eastern frontier, even if for a short time the illusion was entertained in Berlin that it might be possible to exploit or even exacerbate Poland's financial difficulties and persuade it, in its economic depression, to give or sell back former German territories. Equally illusory was the hope of an agreement with Belgium on the retrocession of Eupen-Malmédy. But of greater importance were more acute questions of sovereignty, especially concerning the Rhine, and here Germany could see definite initial successes. Already at the end of 1925 the occupiers withdrew from the first (northern) Rhineland zone, and in 1927 the Inter-Allied Military Control Commission, which up till then had supervised German disarmament, ceased its work.

Economic relations too with France (as with other important trading partners) were considerably intensified. The two countries' potash and aluminium industries reached cartel agreements in 1926; in the same year their heavy industries, together with those of Belgium and Luxembourg, struck an accord on the 'International Steel Cartel'; finally, in 1927 a trade treaty advantageous for both parties was signed, which taken together seemed to point the way to an intensification and stronger association between the two countries' economic interests. Overall, amongst the Great Powers it was Germany whose foreign trade policy in the years after 1925 (especially at the World Economic Conference of 1927 in Geneva and its follow-ups) was the most strongly engaged in a liberalization of European trade that allowed even a customs union to seem a not totally impossible goal. This was an integral part of Stresemann's foreign policy, for Germany's status as a Great Power was to be regained by way of its economic power. Even if this foreign trade policy achieved only partial successes, partly because of French and British reservations, it was Franco-German relations in those years that produced further positive rapprochement. In the second half of the 1920s a network was created—admittedly a very loose one—of Franco-German contacts (e.g. in scholarship, science, cultural relations, and youth movements and exchanges). This aroused in the albeit relatively small groups involved the hope that they could move, step by step, towards mutual cooperation not only at the political and economic level, but also culturally.

At the political level Stresemann and Briand had, just after German entry into the League of Nations in August 1926, attempted the major breakthrough of a complete settlement of all outstanding questions between Germany and France. In a long-prepared-for and only ostensibly improvised tête-à-tête in the French village of Thoiry near Geneva, they agreed to resolve the pressing question of the remaining Rhineland garrison, to bring forward the restitution of the Saar region, and to end the Allied military control of Germany. In return for an early withdrawal, Germany would liquidate its obligations under the Dawes Plan in order to pay off its reparations debt to France ahead of time and thus relieve the latter's precarious financial situation. Nothing came of this plan, since not only did French public opinion resist the supposed concession of withdrawing from the Rhineland ahead of schedule, but the American banks opposed the liquidation of the loans. Nonetheless this attempt at an understanding between Stresemann and Briand shows the possibilities that had arisen since Locarno but also the limits.

The apparent continuation of a 'Concert' between Stresemann, Briand, and Chamberlain during the League sessions was something quite different from the work Woodrow Wilson had imagined the League doing. Wilson had wanted to put an end to the secret diplomacy he blamed for the outbreak of the world war. But the often completely confidential cooperation of the three statesmen and their supporting diplomats did bear fruit after 1925, not least the (mainly declaratory but by no means meaningless) Kellogg–Briand Pact, in which a total of sixty-three countries committed themselves in 1928 (including states that joined later) to outlaw war. That Germany should take part in the preliminary negotiations and exchanges between the USA and France showed how far, thanks to Stresemann's policy of entente, Germany had returned to international diplomacy. This return, however, could be achieved only by adopting a policy of moderation that aimed at compromises and excluded force to attain foreign-policy ends. Thus Stresemann's vision had itself become a factor for stabilizing peace in Europe. And even though it certainly included revisionist aims, this vision was nevertheless governed by the recognition that only a reintegrated Germany could ever achieve them and any departure from peaceful means must inevitably mean a return to isolation.

It was quite another question how far German public opinion was ready to be patient and wait for a successful outcome of Stresemann's constantly promised 'returns', which neither France nor Great Britain were ready to grant quickly. In 1928 it became clear how easily German opinion could be stirred up, when the question of reparations appeared once more on the horizon. The Dawes Plan envisaged a rise in German 'normal annuities' for 1928/9. Since this would manifestly have damaged the German economy, the French and British insisted on linking the unconditional withdrawal from the Rhineland repeatedly demanded by the Germans, and most recently in September 1928 at the League of Nations session in Geneva, with a final settlement of the reparations question. As in 1924, an international commission of experts was charged with devising a plan, which was finally accepted in August 1929 under the name of the 'Young Plan'. In brief, it fixed the total German reparations debt at a final figure of 112,000,000,000 gold Marks, laid down the time over which payments should be spread (fifty-nine years), and was particularly advantageous for Germany in that for the first years after coming into force it prescribed lower annual instalments than the Dawes Plan. Furthermore, the victors linked German acceptance of the Young Plan to the promise to withdraw from the Rhineland by the middle of 1930, five years before the date in the Versailles Treaty, thereby fulfilling the first major goal of Stresemann's revision policy.

A mere five weeks after the Young Plan had been agreed in The Hague, Stresemann, who had suffered from poor health and whose rigorous work regime had, as a consequence, worn him out, died at the age of 51 on 3 October 1929. His state funeral in Berlin became a powerful demonstration of republican forces. Some of them may well only now have realized what they had lost: as foreign minister he had dared for many years to pursue compromise with the West while minimizing dissatisfaction within Germany at the slow pace of results. In the last few months of his life he seems occasionally to have had doubts about the progress of his policy himself; and it is impossible to determine whether he could have successfully maintained his policy of incremental gains especially in the domestic and foreign circumstances of the ensuing years. Equally unanswerable is the hypothetical question whether the frequent tardiness of France and Great Britain to make counter-concessions is also partly responsible for the fact that Stresemann's great political aim of strengthening German society at home by achieving an accepted place amongst the Great Powers had been attained to only a small extent by the time of his death.

The reception of the Young Plan in Germany already showed this all too clearly: instead of its positive aspects for the country being recognized, it met with fierce resistance, systematically stoked by an invigorated nationalist right comprising the DNVP, the National Socialists under Hitler, and the veterans' organization, the Stahlhelm. They set in motion a campaign for its rejection using slogans about the lasting enslavement of the German people. The debate reached a hitherto unknown pitch of shrill demagogy. The proposed law submitted to a referendum by the radical right provided amongst other things for the unilateral repeal of Article 231 of the Treaty of Versailles and threatened all German signatories to treaties imposing burdens on Germany with jail. True, the referendum at the end of 1929, with the support of only 13.8 per cent of the electorate, was superficially a debacle for the right, and in spring 1930 the new reparations plan was accepted by the Reichstag. But the NSDAP (National Socialist German Workers' Party) had achieved a great success through its alliance with the DNVP: it had broken out of isolation and forced its way from the extreme right of the *bürgerlich* (bourgeois) camp; in addition it had brought a new tenor to the domestic debate on foreign policy that from then on would become decisive.

The end of rapprochement

Julius Curtius, who succeeded his deceased party colleague as foreign minister, may by his own account have thought of continuing the policy of compromise. But as it happened, a new approach was soon taken that de facto amounted to the first breach with Stresemann's methods. After the acceptance of the Young Plan in March 1930 the last government to enjoy parliamentary legitimacy, a grand coalition under the Social Democratic Chancellor Hermann Müller, broke up. A series of 'presidential cabinets' followed, beginning with the Centre chancellor Heinrich Brüning, that relied more on the authority of the Reich president than on a majority in the Reichstag. Brüning's cabinet quickly championed a far more active revision policy. By the time of the 'liberation of the Rhineland', that is, the withdrawal of the last Allied troops at the end of June 1930, accompanied by a massive outburst of nationalism that celebrated this as a belated victory over France, there was no mistaking the interplay between public mood and the nationalistic slogans adopted even by those politicians one would not consider as radical, and which worked off each other to create fever pitch. To this must be added the domestic consequences of the world economic crisis, namely mass unemployment that prepared further ground for radical propaganda. At the same time the depression led to attempts at autarky in all the affected countries (in Germany especially in agriculture), which again undid the healthy impact of economic cooperation of previous years.

The Reichstag elections in September 1930 with large gains for the NSDAP, not least as a result of its nationalistic propaganda in foreign policy, were a warning signal. The Brüning government saw itself—not entirely against its will—compelled to submit to these nationalistic stirrings. The brusque manner in which Germany rejected Briand's European Plan in May 1930, which (totally in French interests) sought to create European institutions, had already pointed towards a policy focused more sharply on an autonomous limiting of national states in favour of creating common-interest areas in Europe. However, the first major act in this direction, when foreign minister Curtius unexpectedly staged the coup of a customs union with Austria, turned into a fiasco because the Western Powers saw the beginning of an incorporation of Austria, prohibited by Versailles. As a result of the dilettante manner in which the union was prepared, the German initiative collapsed when brought before the International Court of Justice in The Hague in a test case. This not only cost Curtius his post, which Chancellor Brüning took on, but destroyed the international trust in the reliability of German foreign policy that Stresemann had built up.

Far more serious, however, were two other developments, namely Brüning's scheme for a solution to the reparations question and the ever-louder cry for 'equal rights' for Germany, which primarily concerned the question of armaments. It was, however, the reparations question that displayed in its most immediate form the close reciprocal connection between foreign and domestic policy that pervaded the entire Weimar Republic. Brüning's idea was that Germany could think of equal rights (and the underlying aims of dominance in Central Europe and supremacy over south-east Europe) only if it first shook off the pressing burden of reparations with all its might. To this end he wished to show

Germany's creditors that his economically prostrate country was in no way capable of bearing the burdens of the Young Plan. In order to prove this to the outside world, he gambled domestically on a policy of deflation covered by emergency orders of the president. This sharpened the economic crisis in Germany, pushed up the total of unemployed to a peak of 6,000,000, and indirectly drove more voters to the radical fringes of the KPD and NSDAP. He thus exacerbated the domestic crisis in order to achieve his foreign-policy aim of getting reparations cancelled. True, some economic historians believe that Brüning had no real alternative to his deflationary policy on economic grounds. But however that controversy may be judged,[1] the decisive fact is that Brüning deliberately introduced this policy, which led to the lowering of wages and salaries, to prolonged recession, to a massive increase in unemployment, and to mass impoverishment, in order to resolve the reparations question.

This policy was not without success. Great Britain had long ceased to be convinced of the wisdom of the Versailles Treaty; the German territorial losses in the east and in particular the intermittent oppression of the German minorities in neighbouring Poland and Czechoslovakia, which had already provoked repeated German protests in Stresemann's time, had created a feeling in London that if the occasion arose German revisionism in that region could certainly be accommodated. Meanwhile reparations had long been discredited in England, not least by the early harsh verdict of John Maynard Keynes, who had denounced them as economic nonsense. Brüning and his government could therefore certainly hope for a degree of understanding in London for their efforts. A France left alone in upholding the Treaty of Versailles could not put up any really decisive opposition. A step in this direction came with the announcement of a one-year moratorium for all debtors (including also French and British debts to the USA) by President Hoover in summer 1931. Finally, conference after conference moved ever closer towards the likely conclusion that reparations would in the long run come to an end.

In the disarmament question too, discussed from 1927 in preliminary conferences of the League of Nations and in February 1932 at the general Disarmament Conference, Germany went on the offensive. The basis of the discussions was the declaration in the Versailles Treaty that enforced German disarmament was to be only the first stage of general disarmament. But for many years none of the victorious powers had felt itself bound by this undertaking. The German demand for equal rights in the disarmament question was therefore formally justified. But the inherent threat that if the others did not disarm Germany would proceed to rearm posed the danger right from the start that there would be no room for negotiation. France, where the hopes awakened at Locarno for ongoing cooperation with Germany had disappeared, was not disposed to throw away voluntarily its remaining trump card: its military superiority. Thus the Disarmament Conference dragged along without making any real progress, and, incidentally, strengthened the idea in Germany, heavily propagated by the radical right, that the Western Powers had no interest in a Germany with truly equal rights. Here, too, the last dividends of Stresemann's policy of entente and compromise were lost.

In some ways, then, the foreign policy of Brüning's presidential cabinet meant a return to the situation before 1924 when both sides eyed each other with distrust and looked only to their own advantage, while every positive development for the other country was interpreted as a disadvantage for one's own. Foreign policy had once again become a zero-sum game.

Aggressive revisionism

Meanwhile, in 1932 polarization in domestic politics had also widened as a result of Brüning's policy of deflation, resulting that spring in Nazi large gains in regional election after regional election. There were repeated street battles between extremists of left and right, and in parts of the *bürgerlich* parties there were recurrent plans to bring the National Socialists into government. In foreign policy Brüning was moving closer stage by stage to his goal of ending reparations. But shortly before achieving success he was toppled at the end of May 1932 as result of an intrigue in circles close to the aged President Hindenburg. In these reactionaries' eyes he had not achieved his true aim of dispatching the SPD into political insignificance and bringing about the transformation of

the system in an authoritarian direction, for he had repeatedly relied on SPD tolerance for his programme.

Brüning was followed by the politically incompetent Franz von Papen at the head of the so-called 'cabinet of barons'. This cabinet was able to chalk up the success of getting the other powers at the Lausanne conference in the early summer of 1932 to agree an end to reparations. And then in July, almost as a counter-move, Germany dramatically left the sluggish Disarmament Conference in Geneva and made further participation dependent on the other powers' advance recognition of Germany's equal rights in armament matters. This was a further step towards a more brutally assertive revision policy. Whereas Brüning had made far-reaching demands, but then had been drawn into negotiations, in the few months of Papen's government German foreign policy proceeded by ultimatum and showed, for instance with the walkout from the Disarmament Conference, that it was ready to go it alone. While Brüning had sought cooperation with a receptive London, Papen basked in the illusion that he could achieve better results by a bilateral understanding with France. But Paris desisted since it quickly saw the danger of diplomatic isolation and the risk of dependence on Germany should it follow this course.

Papen did not have time to put the change of direction to the test, for the domestic stand-off now overshadowed everything else. In the elections for the Reichstag at the end of July 1932 Hitler's NSDAP for the first time became the largest party, no doubt helped in part by Papen's aggressive revisionist policy that had now become respectable. After all, why should one support a government that was still showing restraint, or other parties for that matter, when one could back a far tougher revision policy, as espoused by Hitler, which called for the definitive annulment of Versailles? True, at the new elections in early November 1932 his party suffered considerable losses, but it remained nonetheless the largest party, and the formation of a stable government was not to be expected. At the beginning of December 1932 the 'kingmaker' of the past few years, General Kurt von Schleicher, emerged from the shadows and made a last effort as chancellor to rescue the façade of constitutionality, behind which there remained only a republic long since hollowed out. Foreign policy was very much in the background during his few weeks in office. But even his planned bid for freedom in domestic policy failed when at the end of January 1933, again as a result of intrigues, Hindenburg appointed Hitler as chancellor of a new presidential cabinet.

With Hitler, foreign policy was quickly pushed into the foreground. His first great drumbeat was withdrawal from the League of Nations in October 1933, which was spectacularly confirmed by a plebiscite. To be sure the League had shown, at the latest with its ineffectual entry into the Manchurian conflict of 1931/2, how ill suited it was to handle major crises. But all the same it was a place for international negotiation, and that is precisely how Stresemann had made use of it. The German withdrawal now proved to the entire world that the country would no longer be drawn into laborious international discussions, but would proceed unilaterally—or at best bilaterally. The reintroduction of conscription and the unilateral renunciation of the military clauses of the Versailles Treaty in 1935, followed by the remilitarization of the Rhineland in early 1936 in open breach of the Locarno Treaties, were represented abroad as revisionist measures and accepted by the weakened Western Powers practically without lifting a finger. Both developments indicated the line he intended to take. In Hitler's calculation they already served to prepare for a new war whose aims would go well beyond revision of the post-war order of 1919.

The end of the First World War did not bring an ordered peace that could lead to the genuine pacification and development of Europe. This was universally felt, but above all in Germany where the unexpected defeat and even more the ensuing peace treaty were experienced as a deep humiliation. That they both coincided, moreover, with the collapse of the old regime and the establishment of the republic was a heavy burden that militated against its taking root. Thus, after initial and swiftly disappointed hopes, especially amongst Social Democrats, that with the overthrow of the old order Germany would be accepted as one of the progressive democracies, political attention was rapidly turned to attempts to revise the Treaty of Versailles. Apart from minor successes, however, it turned out that this path gave Germany little effective defence—especially in the reparations question, which above all France used as a political tool. By the time of the Ruhr occupation at the latest, with the conflicts and domestic problems that resulted from it, there was a danger that Germany might break up and revert to its condition before the foundation of the state in 1871.

Recognizing this danger, Stresemann came to the conclusion that a cautious policy of revision was to be attained only through an understanding with the Western Powers and a policy of entente. Above all, Stresemann believed Germany's economic potential, which could be thrown onto the scales only in a peaceful Europe, could be utilized to restore its former status. The middle years of the republic became the successful years in foreign policy as Germany was gradually re-accepted into the company of Great Powers and step by step moved towards full sovereignty (albeit not fast enough for Stresemann's critics).

After Stresemann's death and under internal and external pressures this approach of friendly compromises between interests was abandoned; the return to a more aggressive policy of revision brought about certain advances, in particular the end of reparations. With this shift a hardening in foreign policy occurred, while in domestic policy interaction with fiercer nationalism merely played into the hands of extremists on the right. Thus the soil was prepared for Hitler's propaganda of the humiliated German people, so that up to 1938 he enjoyed broad support for his alleged 'policy of revision'. With the subjugation of Poland in 1939 and with the victory over France in 1940, Hitler reached the height of his public esteem in Germany: now at last the 'shame' of 1918 seemed to have been wiped away. But that was merely the first step along the path that would lead to a far more catastrophic defeat and the temporary end of German statehood.

Notes

1. See the contribution by Harold James in the present volume.

The Reichswehr and the Weimar Republic

William Mulligan

The collapse of the German army in late 1918 did not mark the end of military influence in political life. Indeed, the catastrophe of 1918 was accompanied by a sense of optimism that Germany would recover, just as Prussia had done successfully after the defeat at Jena in 1806. The restoration of German military power and Great Power status was the long-term goal of the officer corps. At times, policy prescriptions and aims were radical, seeking the creation of a military utopia. Defeat and the experience of war had opened new horizons, and in terms of its production of innovative ideas, the officer corps mirrored the experimental character of German society and politics after 1918. Like social workers, engineers, and health experts, soldiers sought to remake society. At the same time, there was a hard edge of pragmatism in the military's approach to immediate issues, including cooperation with the republic. One officer compared Germany to a man caught in a treacherous marsh, who had to take one careful step after another in order to return to dry land! The tension within military policy in the 1920s was between the limited capabilities and possibilities of the present and the far-reaching aims of the future.

The army and the new regime, 1918–1920

On 6 November 1918, Wilhelm Groener, quartermaster general of the Supreme Command, informed the Kaiser, Wilhelm II, that the German army would not march on Berlin to suppress the revolution. The army now owed its loyalty to the nation, not to the Kaiser, whatever oaths officers may have sworn. This transition had occurred during the First World War. The Kaiser had become an increasingly peripheral figure since August 1914. Officers realized that in a long, industrialized conflict, it was impossible to conduct war without popular support. Groener, for example, cooperated with trade unions, a reversal of the traditional antipathy between the military and Socialist institutions. The nature of the First World War, the first large-scale, lengthy industrial conflict in history, had wrought a change in the army's relationship to society. The Prussian way of warfare, of short, decisive wars for limited aims, predicated on the separation of the military and civilian sphere, had given way to the totalizing tendencies of modern combat, sustained by industrial economies and mobilized societies.

The army's failure to deliver a quick victory made it dependent on German society. Apathy and war-weariness, increasing year by year, troubled the army. In 1914, most Germans had gone to war out of a sense of duty, rather than enthusiasm. Officers attributed defeat to the collapse of morale on the home front. The German leadership had briefly considered a *levée en masse* in October 1918, which offered a way to continue the war by mobilizing the popular will against the material superiority of the Allies. It was a hopeless recipe, a strategy of 'catastrophic nationalism'.[1] By late October 1918, German military and political leaders recognized that the nation wanted peace, rather than a pointless continuation of the war. The experience of the end of the war had important consequences for military policy in the 1920s. First, military values—discipline, sacrifice, obedience, and will-power—had to be promoted to strengthen the nation for a future war. Second, the state was responsible for the promotion of these values and had the authority to transform the nation. Third, the army acknowledged that it could not act in opposition to the general will of society. The implication of these experiences was that society had to be moulded to military aims, rather than the military adapting to German society.

The revolution, triggered by an order from naval commanders for a hopeless mission, was driven by anger at the military and a desire for peace. For officers, the birth of the republic was associated with the loss of status and identity. The revolution seemed to open a gulf between society and the officer corps. Yet optimism accompanied this apparent disaster. Before Christmas 1918, general staff officers had met in Berlin to discuss the revival of Germany as a military Great Power. Some saw the defeat as a cleansing process. They sought to emulate Prussia's recovery from defeat by Napoleonic France at Jena in 1806. This attitude recast defeat as part of a longer historical process, culminating in future victory and salvation. The year 1918 became an opportunity for renewal, which could only be achieved through cooperation with the state. Officers viewed the regime in terms of their own narrow military interests and aims, but this did not automatically translate into opposition to the republic. Indeed, the state as a monarchical or republican entity was secondary to its military effectiveness.

Instead, pragmatism and mutual interest dictated cooperation between the officer corps and the moderate Social Democrats, led by Friedrich Ebert. On 10 November 1918, Groener, in a telephone conversation with Ebert, promised to support the Provisional government, as long as it prevented a further lurch to the left. Ebert, alarmed by the development of the Russian Revolution in 1917, was prepared to forge a relationship with the officer corps. It was part of a larger coalition of a broad centre, which would direct the establishment of the republic. In return for their support, officers would retain their power of command and prevent the creation of a militia system. In theory, this was a missed opportunity to establish a military force with unquestioning loyalty to the republic. Soldiers' councils, set up at the end of the war to protect soldiers' rights, could have formed a basis for an alternative military force. In practice, however, the options were limited. Soldiers' councils were militarily ineffective. The SPD feared further risings from the extreme left, they were anxious to demobilize the army as quickly as possible, and they could not afford to alienate the powerful officer corps. The two leading officers in the German revolution, Walther Reinhardt and Wilhelm Groener, urged the Provisional government to organize elections for the National Assembly as soon as possible. These were held on 19 January. The officer corps saw the National Assembly as a bulwark against the left; the elections produced a centrist coalition, favourable to the immediate aims of the military. Moreover, officers recognized that a liberal, parliamentary republic was the only means of holding Germany together. Any other solution—from the restoration of the dynasties to the creation of an extreme left-wing Socialist republic—was fantasy politics, which would lead to chaos and civil war. Support for the republic stemmed from the considerations of power politics, rather than any ideological conviction. It subordinated the form of the state to the maintenance of German unity. From the outset, officers were *Vernunftrepublikaner* (pragmatic republicans).

In practical terms, the army protected the National Assembly and dealt ruthlessly with the left-wing opponents of the republic. Officers and moderate politicians took seriously the threat from the extreme left to the republic. In January 1919, volunteer units (the *Freikorps*) suppressed the Sparticist uprising. The rising had not been planned, but arose out of popular protests. Rosa Luxemburg and Karl Liebknecht, the two leaders of the Sparticist group, went along with the improvised rising and paid for it when they were murdered by *Freikorps* soldiers. In May 1919, the *Freikorps* suppressed the short-lived Soviet Republic in Munich. The army played an important role in restoring and maintaining order after the November revolution, though, in this context, the term 'order' could cover a multitude of sins. The restoration of order was a precondition for a functioning economy and the return to Great Power status. The army had found a new role defending the state against its internal enemies, rather than external threats, making it an indispensable factor in domestic politics, and one which, as a consequence of its perception of the national interest, consistently favoured the right over the left. Between November 1918 and the establishment of the coalition government in February 1919, events had shifted in favour of the army. In the first half of 1919, the army was able to exploit this role in domestic politics to regain complete control over military policy.

The overthrow of the monarchy allowed leading officers to reform military structures, which were now deemed to be unwieldy. Under the empire, there had been several different military institutions: the General Staff, which was in charge of planning for war, the Prussian Ministry of War, responsible for the budget and recruitment, the Military Cabinet, which advised the Kaiser on personnel matters, as well as three other ministries of war in Bavaria, Württemberg, and Saxony. This institutional chaos hampered

German military planning before and during the First World War. Officers were not so fixated on the 'stab-in-the-back' myth that they did not consider their own institutional failings. Reinhardt and Groener, in particular, wanted to use the revolution as an opportunity to centralize the military administration. This would improve military planning and decision making. In the long term a centralized state was also seen as more effective in the conduct of war. The dynasties had clung jealously to their individual ministries; the new regime, on the other hand, embarked on a course of centralization of the financial and military systems. Reinhardt was able to sweep aside the opposition of the states, especially Bavaria, to a centralized Reichswehr Ministry. The support of the coalition government and of the majority of the National Assembly enabled the officers to achieve their goals of a centralized military ministry. The officer corps did not see the republic as a threat, but as an opportunity that had to be directed towards military goals. The Reichswehr Ministry, which came into being on 1 October 1919, also integrated the planning and administrative functions, which had been previously divided between the General Staff and the Prussian Ministry of War. The friction between these two institutions had existed before the First World War and continued after it. Reinhardt wanted to integrate planning and administrative functions into one institution, subordinated to the civilian government. This policy avoided the internal military divisions of the former German empire, the *Kaiserreich*, and the separation of the civilian and military elements of the German state, factors which had hindered the development of strategic thought before the war. The Reichswehr Ministry had a head of Army Command, who oversaw all military functions. He was subordinate to the Reichswehr minister and the president. This meant that the Reichswehr had one foot in cabinet government and another in presidential government. The latter was particularly important during periods of emergency rule, when Article 48 of the Weimar Constitution was used to maintain order.

Yet the Reichswehr, an impotent instrument against external threats, was unable to exercise the same degree of influence on German foreign policy. Officers produced a number of proposals on acceptable military terms, mainly remarkable for their lack of realism. On 7 May, the Allies presented the first draft of the treaty, which included the reduction of German military power to the level of border protection and the preservation of internal order. The Reichswehr was restricted to 100,000 men, who had to serve twelve-year periods. The General Staff was abolished, a source of pride to its members and a tribute to its perceived excellence. Germany was banned from possessing any offensive weapons, such as military aircraft, tanks, and some forms of artillery. The military industrial complex, symbolized by Krupp, was to be demolished. The navy was also restricted to 15,000 sailors and a limited tonnage. The Inter-Allied Military Control Commission would enforce the terms. These terms did not change in the final version of the treaty. When Reinhardt and General Hans von Seeckt tried to put forward counter-proposals, including a 200,000-man army, the cabinet rejected them. Instead, the government pursued territorial revisions. Diplomats and politicians held fundamentally different views from the military on questions of foreign policy and the international system. For officers, military power was the vital element of national security and instrument of foreign policy, otherwise Germany would be perpetually vulnerable to the threats of other powers, especially France. Diplomats and politicians, on the other hand, believed that the revision of the treaty was dependent on economic revival. German military power had been vanquished and carried no weight in the international system. Therefore security would have to be achieved through a policy of fulfilment and the balance of power. The policy conceptions of the Foreign Office under the republic anticipated in some ways the solutions of the 1950s, with their stress on economic integration and cooperation with France as a means of reviving German influence. But the conception of the Reichswehr was more limited: it was a continuation of the *Kaiserreich*'s military security policy, but without the military power!

When the final terms were presented in June 1919, a debate broke out over whether or not Germany should accept the treaty. Terms such as the extradition of the Kaiser for war crimes, and the war guilt clause, added an emotional dimension. Some of the leading advocates of rejection were senior generals, most notably Reinhardt. The treaty, according to his view, would allow France to strangle Germany and the army would disintegrate. He argued that acceptance of the treaty would destroy national morale. And yet, if Germany rejected the treaty, the Allies would invade and occupy western Germany, leading to the collapse of the Reich. But Reinhardt believed that a new state, established in East Prussia, could become the core of a new Germany. The surrender of territory, rather than the acceptance of the treaty, would save national honour, the real basis of Germany's revival. This was the reappearance of the military strategy of 'catastrophic nationalism'. It prioritized the preservation of a set of values, amorphous though they may have been, over the preservation of territory. In a complete misreading of history, it harked back to the Wars of Liberation against Napoleon and Clausewitz's injunction that a nation should fight to the last drop of its blood. Advocated at moments of deep crisis (1918, 1919, and 1923), it was pursued by Hitler in the closing stages of the Second World War, linking an alternative Prussian military tradition from Clausewitz to Hitler, one which eschewed political calculation and made the fighting of war an end in itself.

The other Clausewitzian tradition, the subordination of the military to the political, was represented by Groener. His astute sense of political realities played an important role in saving Germany from itself in June 1919. A Württemberger, the preservation of the unity of the Reich was the lodestar of his policy. Groener argued that the surrender of territory in the event of an Allied invasion and occupation would mean the end of any prospect of Germany regaining its Great Power status. It was impossible to fight the Allies, given the absence of popular support in western Germany and the lack of material resources. Groener pointed to the patient recovery of Prussia after 1806. Only on the basis of gradual reform would Germany survive. The loss of further territory in the west would allow France to establish a permanent hegemony in Europe. On 19 June thirty generals and the Social Democrat Reichswehr minister, Gustav Noske, gathered to discuss the options. The generals based in western Germany effectively stymied any plans for military resistance when they pointed to the lack of popular support. On 22 June, the National Assembly, or, more accurately, the Social Democrats, accepted the treaty.

Following the acceptance of the treaty, a group within the officer corps, led by General Walther von Lüttwitz, began to lay plans for the overthrow of the republic, which was now seen as a precondition for the revision of the treaty. For these officers, the acceptance of terms that humiliated and weakened the military demonstrated that the republic was anti-military. Further, the demobilization of volunteer units began. Morale within the army became extremely fragile, as men faced the prospect of unemployment and thought, bitterly, that the republic had betrayed them. It was easy for Lüttwitz to find co-conspirators, such as Captain Ehrhardt, who led the Ehrhardt Brigade. Wolfgang Kapp, an East Prussian conservative, also approached Lüttwitz to support a putsch. The aims of these men were very disparate. Unlike Kapp, there is no evidence that Lüttwitz wanted to restore the Hohenzollern monarchy. Instead, it is likely that he wanted to establish a more authoritarian state, which would crush the radical left within Germany and hold the nation together against external threats. Those involved represented a broad range of discontent with the republic, and the subsequent planning for the putsch was appropriately haphazard.

The decision to dissolve the Ehrhardt Brigade, which would have deprived the conspirators of their military force, led them to act prematurely. In the early hours of 13 March, the Ehrhardt Brigade marched into Berlin, but by that time the government had fled. The decision of the government to leave Berlin owed much to the lack of support from other military units. Reinhardt had argued that the army had to, and could, support the government. A failure to do so would alienate the people from the Reichswehr, hindering the development of military policy. This policy risked splitting the nascent Reichswehr in order to preserve popular support. Reinhardt's military policy had been based on rebuilding the bonds of trust between society and the military. Seeckt opposed Reinhardt's advice, arguing that Reichswehr units would not fire on their comrades. His policy prioritized the preservation of the army. This was vital in order to suppress the radical left-wing revolts which Seeckt expected would follow the collapse of the Kapp Putsch (as it became known). Moreover, his military policy was based on the consolidation of the army, rather than its relationship with society. Ultimately, the cabinet, following Seeckt's advice, made the choice not to use military force to resist the putsch. In the event, the putsch collapsed due to a lack of popular support, civilian resistance in the form of strikes, and the failure of many bureaucrats to cooperate with the putsch leaders. Radical left-wing revolts in the Ruhr, in the aftermath of the putsch, were suppressed by volunteer units in April 1920.

The events of March and April 1920 showed the different approaches the Reichswehr took to threats from the left and right. There was a good deal of sympathy and some open support for the putsch within the officer corps. Yet relatively few officers, especially the senior ones in Berlin, joined the short-lived Kapp government. While Seeckt was unwilling to use the Reichswehr to protect the republican government, he and other officers realized that a government reliant on military power alone could not survive in the face of popular opposition. This was an important limit on the actions of the Reichswehr. There was no such compunction in dealing with the threat from the left. They did not mouth the right nationalist slogans and posed a threat to social order. If Seeckt managed to hold the army together, Reinhardt was correct in predicting the broader consequences. Distrust of the Reichswehr was much more prevalent after March 1920. Gustav Noske, the SPD army minister, was forced to resign, leaving the Reichswehr without an ally in the largest party in Germany. The new minister was Otto Geßler, of the DDP, but he had little support within the party, which also became increasingly distrustful of the Reichswehr. Reinhardt's policy, based on close cooperation with the civilian government and the broad social support for the military, now lay in tatters.

Seeckt's prescription, 1920–1923

Hans von Seeckt, head of Army Command between 1920 and 1926, had two aims: to develop closer political and military relations with the Soviet Union and to consolidate the Reichswehr, forging it into a professional force which would be the core of an enlarged future army. Often held responsible for turning the Reichswehr into a state within a state, his policies were more compatible with the republic than has been recognized.

Seeckt's immediate concern was to consolidate the Reichswehr into a professional force without political leanings. His decree to the army demanded that soldiers abstain from political activity of any kind and honour their oath to the Weimar Constitution. Yet Seeckt's support for the republic remained limited to accepting it as the only possible means of holding Germany together in its present circumstances. The army was a pillar of the state, though he was careful to differentiate between the eternal Reich and the republic, a transient form of the state. His policy of placing the army 'above parties' mirrored the right's criticisms of parliamentary politics. Seeckt's policy led him to shield the Reichswehr from parliamentary scrutiny. Geßler, another *Vernunftrepublikaner*, actively supported this policy. Doubts about the republic, the traditional deference to the military, and a respect for *Fachmänner* (experts), evident in other areas of Weimar politics, enabled the army to escape close political scrutiny.

After the Treaty of Versailles, when the structure of the force became clearer, officers began to work on the development of military doctrine. The lessons of the First World War and the limitations of the Reichswehr informed the wide variety of military doctrines and policies of the 1920s. Although the army's former quartermaster general Erich Ludendorff only coined the term 'total war' in the early 1930s, the idea was at the heart of military debate in the inter-war period. For some officers the First World War had not been sufficiently total, while for others total war was the negation of the military mission, leading to stalemate and revolution. The different stances taken on the issue of total war, and whether or not Germany should prepare for it, determined, for the most part, attitudes of officers to civil society and the state. The Reichswehr developed ideas about the use of tanks and airplanes, banned under the Treaty of Versailles, but most of their military policies and doctrines were drafted with their immediate circumstances in mind. This weakness gave rise to a wide diversity of opinion, from Seeckt's ideal of a mobile, professional army to Joachim von Stülpnagel's theories on people's war (*Volkskrieg*). While some elements of pre-war military thought remained—the advantage of the offensive for instance—the experiences of the First World War and the limitations of Versailles shattered the consensus about warfare that had developed in the pre-war officer corps.

The solution offered by Seeckt was to create a small, professional, and mobile force, which would defend Germany against Poland.

The mass armies of the First World War had led to stalemate on the western front; Seeckt's experiences on the eastern front convinced him that a well-trained army could defeat a larger force. Seeckt also saw the present Reichswehr as the core of a future 300,000-man army, once the Versailles restrictions had been lifted. A mobile force could punch holes in the enemy lines, avoid the stalemate of the trenches, and restore a decisive outcome to battle. Seeckt was the most coherent opponent of total war in the Reichswehr. Some historians have even seen him as the father of the *Blitzkrieg* ('lightning war') doctrine of 1939 and 1940.[2] Yet while Seeckt stressed mobility and the decentralization of command and authority to lower ranks, he was less clear on the role of tanks and aeroplanes. There were, in any case, many twists along the path to 1940. Seeckt's vision of a mobile, well-trained force also fitted with his conception of the professional army, isolated from society. This made him far less dangerous to the republic and civil society than other leading officers, even those seen as the most liberal, namely, Groener and Reinhardt. For Seeckt's army did not require the militarization of German society.

Still, Seeckt recognized that the 100,000-man army was not even sufficient for border defence. He sought to evade the limitations of Versailles by establishing a covert military organization. In 1919 a system of regional (*Kreis*) commissars was set up throughout Germany. Their task was to compile military information, including lists of men available to serve in case of war. There was also a network of work groups, generally composed of former soldiers and *Freikorps* members, which were to guard arms depots and liaise with the Reichswehr. This raised two important problems. First, the Reichswehr, from its birth, did not maintain a military monopoly, which undermined Seeckt's principles of a professional force, removed from the ebb and flow of civil society and political dispute. Second, these paramilitary groups were invariably opponents of the republic. The republic could either acknowledge their existence as a fact of life and try to manage them, through agreements with the Reichswehr, or they could oppose their existence, which would make it more difficult for these paramilitary groups to be an effective addition to German military power. The state governments, rather than the Reich government, were responsible for policing and the maintenance of law and order, and hence they had a major say in the regulation of the paramilitary groups. This was particularly significant in the largest state, Prussia, dominated by the SPD. Despite a number of attempts to reach agreement, the SPD and the Reichswehr failed to work out a deal in the early 1920s. This episode only served to increase the mutual distrust of both sides, as officers condemned the pacifism of the SPD, and the SPD condemned the anti-republican stance of the Reichswehr. It thus indicated the limits to civilian mobilization in the Weimar Republic.

The establishment of a mobile, professional force was supposed to make Germany *bündnisfähig* (capable of alliances), an attractive alliance partner to other Great Powers. Seeckt was determined to conduct an active foreign policy, which he saw as the characteristic of a Great Power. In 1920, he suggested that Germany should develop an alliance with Soviet Russia. Unconcerned by Communist ideology, Seeckt saw the development of relations with Russia as a return to Bismarckian foreign policy. At the core of Seeckt's policy was his loathing of Poland, a nation unworthy of being a state, and a French ally to boot. Further, an alliance between Germany and Russia, the two powers excluded from the Versailles settlement, would be a powerful force for treaty revision. France would be left isolated on the continent. The efforts of the Foreign Office to base a policy on fulfilment and German economic strength were ignored in Seeckt's unreconstructed vision of power politics. The First World War had transformed the relationship between the military and society, but the army's view of the international system was rooted in the late nineteenth century. An alliance with Soviet Russia also suited Seeckt's vision of a professional army and limited the degree of militarization of German society. Without Russian support, Germany would be much more vulnerable to French and, particularly, Polish attack. In practical terms, the Reichswehr initiated contact with the Red Army in the second half of 1920. The Reichswehr offered technological expertise and advice on military training, while the Russians offered an opportunity to test out new weapons away from the prying eyes of the Allied inspectors. Nonetheless, cooperation was troubled from the outset. German companies, invited to build factories in Russia, baulked at the financial risk; officers on both sides distrusted each other; and there was no political benefit. In April 1922, with the signature of the Rapallo Treaty, Seeckt believed Russo-German cooperation could be set on a more official footing. In reality, the treaty had little political substance, though it ignited French and British fears. It set Poincaré, the French premier, on the course towards the occupation of the Ruhr.

In January 1923, French troops marched into the Ruhr after Germany had failed to make reparation payments. This represented the decisive blow to Seeckt's policy for two reasons. First, Russia, far from supporting Germany, actively encouraged the Communist Party to overthrow the Weimar Republic. Seeckt's vision of a Russo-German partnership rang hollow. Second, Seeckt decided from the outset, correctly, that military opposition to the French occupation would be folly. He agreed with the government's policy of passive resistance. This was an admission that the Reichswehr was not capable of border defence. The passivity of the Reichswehr in 1923 sparked discontent within the officer corps, who questioned whether Seeckt's doctrines would ever work. These officers, most notably Stülpnagel, developed far more radical doctrines that threatened to subordinate civil society to the military and undermined the republic—one of the many unintended consequences of the French occupation. The Reichswehr's passivity placed the burden of national defence firmly on the civilian population in the Ruhr, who suffered deprivation and physical abuse at the hands of the French occupiers. The implication of this was that the military mission to defend Germany's borders had passed to the men, women, and children of the Ruhr.

As the state appeared to be on the verge of collapse in September 1923—sucked down by hyperinflation, French occupation, separatism, the rise of the extreme right, and the revolutionary zeal of the Communists—a state of emergency was declared by the Reich, which gave the military powers to prevent civil disorder (broadly defined). The emergency powers were exercised by Geßler and then Seeckt, though the latter was the key figure throughout the crisis. Seeckt's intentions have been the subject of debate. He was in contact with obvious opponents of the republic, he drafted a government programme, which would have created a stronger executive, and he thought about establishing a directory of three leaders, an idea taken from the ending of the French Revolution. Seeckt was clearly examining his options, including the replacement of the republic; had he gone ahead with these ideas, he might well have turned into a German Charles de Gaulle, who replaced the political fragmentation of the French Fourth Republic with the executive power of the Fifth Republic. Instead he returned his emergency executive powers to the president in February 1924, having held Germany and the republic together. This indeed was his principal goal throughout the crisis. It was also one around which most officers (with the notable exception of the Bavarians) could rally. For the dissolution of the republic could easily have led to the dissolution of Germany, marking the definite end of any Great Power ambitions. Seeckt also recognized that any army-led transformation of political structures would split the nation. The memory of the Kapp Putsch acted as a powerful deterrent to any potential military dictator.

The Reichswehr played an important role in regional crises in the central German states of Saxony and Thuringia, and Bavaria. Once again, the threats from the left and right were treated in very different ways. In the two central German states, the Communists had entered a coalition government and had formed their members into paramilitary groups known as 'proletarian hundreds'. Fearing the collapse of public order and the possibility of a Communist revolt, the Reichswehr, in both states, carried out a *Reichsexekution*—that is, the regional government was replaced by a State Commissar, appointed by the Reich government, and the army given authority for the maintenance of public order and local administration. Yet the Reichswehr approached Bavaria, arguably more of a threat to national unity and social order, with a great deal more circumspection. Here, Otto von Lossow, the commander of the 7th Division, had refused to obey Seeckt's order to ban the Nazi paper *Völkischer Beobachter* ('People's Observer'). Even worse, the 7th Division took an oath of loyalty to the Bavarian government, which had refused to acknowledge the Reich state of emergency declared on 27 September. The Bavarian units developed links with the right-wing *Verbände* (mostly veterans' associations, among them Hitler's NSDAP), who advocated a march on Berlin. As in 1920, Seeckt was not going to send Reichswehr units to shoot on their comrades. Nevertheless, the incompetence of the Nazi putsch of 8 November meant that the crisis finished abruptly, without the Reichswehr having to face the prospect of civil war.

The SPD had resigned from the Reich government in anger at the differing treatment of the left and right by the Reichswehr. While officers saw the radical left as a threat to the social order and German unity, they saw the radical right as well meaning, but misguided. The nationalist, militarist rhetoric of groups like the Nazis appealed to officers' visions of Germany as a Great Power. This apparent overlapping of interests led them to approach the right in a lenient manner. Yet, the events of 1923 also demonstrated the limits of the Reichswehr's political powers. They had been unable to impose their will on society; indeed, social and political stability was essential if Germany was to regain its Great Power status. Believing that they had saved the state in 1923, officers now sought to use the state to transform German society. As one internal report concluded, the attitude of the Reichswehr to the republic would depend on the progress of *Wehrhaftmachung* (getting fit to fight)—the militarization of society and the preparation of the state for a future war. So far, the Reichswehr had been limited by the need for social consensus. But that consensus did not accord with the Reichswehr's narrow interpretation of the national interest. Instead of accepting these limitations, the officer corps sought to use the state to transform society—a social engineering project on a grand scale.

The state and the militarization of society, 1923–1930

Even before the French occupation of the Ruhr had demonstrated the impotence of the Reichswehr in terms of external defence, Colonel Joachim von Stülpnagel of the *Truppenamt*, the successor to the General Staff, had argued for a different form of warfare, *Volkskrieg*, or people's war. Legitimizing his doctrine by drawing on the myth of an uprising of the German *Volk* against Napoleon during the Wars of Liberation, he argued that a foe with greater material resources could be defeated by the total mobilization of a nation's resources. The nature of the fighting Stülpnagel advocated was significant. The invaders, most likely French, faced with civilian resistance and guerrilla war waged by small mobile groups, would carry out atrocities against the population, including the burning of villages and the mass execution of hostages. The war would degenerate into savagery and hatred, destroying the morale of the enemy forces, slowing their advance, and enabling Germany to mobilize its greater demographic and industrial resources. The burden of fighting was to fall on the civilian population, whom Stülpnagel had transformed, in his own words, into 'the material of war and the means of war'.[3]

Needless to say, Stülpnagel's doctrine was a rejection of Seeckt's views on a professional force and limited warfare. It involved the complete collapse of the boundaries between the civilian and the military sphere, although Stülpnagel argued that the officer corps must retain control of the conduct of the people's war. This represented the subordination of civil society to the military, a development which was far more dangerous to the Weimar Republic than Seeckt's professional army. Officers expected the state to transform the values of German society, for example, by inculcating military-style discipline in schools and suppressing criticism of the army, a violation of the constitutional right to free speech. Yet the events of the five years from the end of the war had demonstrated a limited appetite on the part of German society for these types of policies, something which Seeckt had recognized during the Kapp Putsch and the emergency of 1923. As the republic failed to deliver on the expectations of the Reichswehr, officers began to seek political alternatives. Stülpnagel's ideas also represented a crisis in the military profession. The idea of military professionalism had been based on the rapid wars of the Prussian army and expertise, which limited violence, accepted political control, and spared the civilian population from the worst impact of warfare. Drawing on the experience of the Great War, Stülpnagel's extreme rejection of the nineteenth-century Prussian military tradition was born out of his belief that war had become a test of all national resources and the weakness of the Reichswehr. While many officers did not embrace the most extreme tenets of *Volkskrieg*, they did subscribe to the need to prepare German society for war. The waging of *Volkskrieg* depended on inculcating society with a set of military values so extreme that it could hardly be implemented in any sort of liberal political system.

Stülpnagel's doctrine of *Volkskrieg* was among the most radical produced in the 1920s. It never enjoyed official sanction, although it provided an intellectual link between the strategy of catastrophic nationalism put forward in 1918 and in the closing stages of the Second World War. A more limited militarization of society was an ideal widely shared within the officer corps. Its most practical exponents were Wilhelm Groener, Reichswehr minister between 1928 and 1932, and his adviser, later turned nemesis, Colonel Kurt von Schleicher. The latter was the most politically active soldier in the Weimar Republic. Like Reinhardt in 1919, he recognized the republic as a political reality with which the army needed to work, if it was to achieve its aims. His willingness to accept the republic was qualified by his belief in using the state to achieve military aims. His memorandum of December 1926 outlining his views on the republic effectively suggested a policy of conditional cooperation. Moreover, Schleicher went much further than Reinhardt. He was prepared to create political constellations to produce conditions favourable for military policy. When Groener became army minister in January 1928, the basis for his policy of cooperation with the government had already been set in motion. When an SPD-dominated coalition entered government in the summer of 1928, Groener renewed the partnership of 1919 between the moderate SPD and the officer corps in the national, and the military, interest.

The militarization of society had two distinct elements: the promotion of military values—often defined as obedience, a willingness to sacrifice oneself, and self-discipline—in society; and the formation of reserve units to circumvent the limits imposed by Versailles. The belief in Germany's eventual rebirth, an important feature of officers' expectations immediately after the war, had been replaced in many quarters, by the late 1920s, by disappointment. Officers had defined rebirth in terms of military power. Instead of nationalist and military values, the 1920s, according to many officers, had seen the progress of internationalist, pacifist, and materialistic values, an extension of the moral corruption that had destroyed the *Kaiserreich*. These latter values were associated with the SPD and DDP. The degree of militarism in German society in the late 1920s has been the subject of some debate.[4] The 'Hurrah patriotism' of veterans' organizations was very different from the willingness actually to fight a war. There was still widespread fear of war in the late 1930s and it was the relatively low casualty figures and rapid victories of 1939 and 1940 that shored up Hitler's prestige. Under the republic, officers wanted the state to play a more active role in stamping out attacks on the Reichswehr. After a series of cases against pacifist journals, attempts by the Justice Ministry to restrict the definition of treason were successfully opposed by Groener. But his attempt to criminalize the defamation of the Reichswehr was only incorporated into the Nazi decree on 'Treason against the German People' in February 1933.

The promotion of military values was a moral project, but the army had more specific ideas about institutionalizing the militarization of society. Groener realized that secret military preparations were ineffective. These had to be carried out with the active support and knowledge of the civilian government. Home and border defence units, which would treble the strength of the Reichswehr in the case of an invasion, required the participation of the ministries of transport, finance, interior, and economics, to name but a few. The limitations of Versailles meant that the army had to use the civilian administration to carry out the military mission. Groener was willing to accept some limitations in 1928 and 1929, since it was necessary to facilitate cooperation with the SPD. The establishment of border defence units had created friction between Seeckt and the Prussian government in 1923. It took over a year of negotiations before Groener reached an agreement with the Prussian government in April 1929. This agreement limited defence units to the border, although in Bavaria and Saxony the networks covered the whole region; it prohibited the use of anti-republican persons in these units. The Prussian government continued to fear the use of Nazi and Stahlhelm members in these units and abandoned the agreement in August 1929. When Groener and Schleicher had initiated the policy of cooperating with the republic, they saw it as a means of strengthening Germany's military power. They were less prepared to accept the limitations that a policy of cooperation implied.

These military preparations were oriented towards defence, rather than an offensive war. Groener accepted the basic tenets of Stresemann's foreign policy—cooperation with France and the United States, the use of German economic power to improve its international standing, and the possible revision of the eastern border with Poland at some stage in the future. The aim of a defensive war was not to defeat the enemy on the battlefield, but to delay the enemy's advance. By buying time, Groener believed that the League of Nations or another European power would step in to stop the conflict. Although he intimated in 1919 that Franco-German rivalry had not finished, he was far more concerned with immediate security needs than a future aggressive war. German security, in his view, was not solely dependent on its own military strength. The balance of power and international organizations could also play a role. This view, however, was not widely shared within the officer corps, who saw cooperation with the SPD as a tactical ploy, until a more favourable political constellation emerged, as happened in the early 1930s.

The consequences of Weimar's military vision

As the Weimar Republic headed into crisis in the early 1930s, senior officers, using their close links to Hindenburg, sought to develop Germany's military power by carrying out policies started in the late 1920s. Schleicher continued to use his links to Hindenburg to promote the Reichswehr's aims. Hindenburg, in any case, shared the concerns of senior officers. Because Brüning became ever more dependent on Hindenburg's support, the Reichswehr was able to extract concessions and pursue its goals in more favourable circumstances than those of the late 1920s. For instance, the Reichswehr's rearmament programme was exempt from the massive budget cuts of the early 1930s. On the other hand, the instability of the 1930s did not offer a permanent basis for the development of a military policy. By 1932, the question of an alternative political system loomed. Officers exploited the crisis to promote increasingly radical military policies, while at the same time seeking a stable political solution, in the form of a presidential government, a military dictatorship, or a popular right-wing government.

THE REICHSWEHR AND THE WEIMAR REPUBLIC | 97

However, there was a tension between the pursuit of military revisionism and the need for political stability. Groener continued to press for the development of a militia in the form of border and home defence units. He advocated the promotion of military sport in schools to inculcate youth with appropriate values. Criticism of the SPD continued. In 1928 Groener had been willing to utter the phrase 'healthy and responsible pacifism'. Two years later, he criticized an exhibition, 'War and Peace', opened in Breslau by the SPD *Oberpräsident* (provincial governor) Hermann Ludemann, for 'poisoning' the youth with its pacifistic tendencies.[5] Because the Reichswehr was exempt from budgetary constraints, Groener had put forward in 1928 the First Rearmament Programme, which aimed to create a sixteen-division army by 1932, about twice the size of the 100,000-man army, in violation of the Treaty of Versailles. In 1932, a Second Programme was established, which aimed to create a twenty-division army by 1938. In other words, military planning did not radically alter with the transition to presidential cabinets. But loosening itself from the necessity of cooperating with the SPD, the Reichswehr now encountered another set of problems.

The relationship between the Reichswehr and the Nazi Party was extremely complex, in large part because there were several different attitudes jostling within the officer corps. The trial of three officers at Ulm in 1930 for having spread Nazi propaganda within their barracks encapsulated the different strands. Originally Groener had seen the Nazis as a dangerous party, almost akin to the Communists. He was also aware of the appeal of Nazi propaganda to junior officers, which threatened to undermine discipline and morale in the Reichswehr. Hitler's oath of legality at the Ulm trial and the party's participation in the Thuringian regional government led Groener to rethink his views. Now that the Nazis appeared to have shed their radical image, Groener was more impressed by their views on military policy. After all, one of his aims had been to reawaken the moral forces that would sustain military power. He was also keen to include them and the Stahlhelm in border defence units. While Groener and Schleicher considered the Nazis legal due to their goals, and were willing to tolerate their tactics, the interior minister, Joseph Wirth, and the Prussian government considered them illegal due to their tactics. The Reichswehr's judgement of parties in terms of their attitude to military policy contributed to political instability in the early 1930s. Thus Groener, who had done so much to stabilize the republic in 1919, helped to destroy it, because he pursued a policy that subordinated civil society to the needs of the military mission.

Of course, political instability led to the threat of civil war in Germany by the spring of 1932, particularly as violence between the SA and the KPD's paramilitary wing, the Rotfrontkämpferband (Red Front Fighters' or Veterans' League), escalated. A civil war would set back the process of German recovery and damage the basis for military planning, which was dependent on stability. Hence the Reichswehr found itself trying to repair the damage to which it had contributed. The importance of the Reichswehr had been underlined by Groener's appointment as interior minister to replace Wirth in October 1931. While police forces were under the authority of the regional governments, the Reichswehr was supposed to strengthen the executive authority of the Reich. This would provide the internal cohesion necessary for Brüning's revisionist foreign policy. The dilemma confronting the Reichswehr reached its height in April and May 1932 with the banning of the SA. Originally Schleicher and Groener wanted to integrate the SA into a general militia system. This would tame the Nazi Party and would strengthen German military power. But the continued violence and the discovery of SA plans for the violent overthrow of the Weimar Constitution cast renewed doubts on the legality of the movement. At a meeting of police chiefs, Groener was persuaded to ban the SA. The decree was issued on 13 April 1932. However, Schleicher disagreed with the ban, believing that the SA could still be integrated into a national militia. He also realized that the Reichswehr was restless about the ban. He used his influence with Hindenburg to force Groener's resignation in May 1932.

Schleicher became Reichswehr minister in the Papen cabinet, which lasted from July to November 1932, before becoming Weimar's last chancellor. As the crisis worsened, with rising violence, two further elections to the Reichstag, and the removal of that bastion of the Republic, the Prussian government, by the Reich, Schleicher continued to try to tame the Nazis. His ideal was the formation of a broad front from the moderate wing of the Nazi

Party, represented by Gregor Strasser, to the moderate wing of the SPD and trade union movement. But by now the Reichswehr was no longer arbiter of the situation. In November, Schleicher noted, referring to the recent elections: 'Prospects for the army in this extremely unhappy: concern that we should stand in a few days in the streets against nine-tenths of the people.'[6] As in 1918 and 1923, the Reichswehr realized that its aims could not be achieved in the face of massive popular opposition or social unrest. As well as trying to create a broad centre, Schleicher examined alternative political structures. By late 1932, it was clear that the system of presidential cabinets could not continue for much longer, given that 90 per cent of the deputies elected to the Reichstag in the November election opposed the Schleicher cabinet. The Reichstag remained a political factor even in the state of emergency, since no modern state could function for long without popular support—and as the army realized, military policy was dependent on popular acceptance. Two alternatives were suggested to Schleicher by his advisers, including Carl Schmitt. One could ignore the obstructive policy of the Reichstag, arguing that it had forfeited its control over the executive. Instead, popular authority was located in the president. Alternatively, one could force the Reichstag to pass a positive vote of no confidence that would nominate an alternative government rather than simply bringing about the collapse of the existing one.

These were the final alternatives to a Hitler-led cabinet. Neither was taken, as Schleicher had become too weak. Hindenburg now distrusted him, and the Reichswehr was no longer a reliable instrument in his hands. Senior officers such as Werner von Blomberg and Walther von Reichenau had developed links with Hitler. Instead of trying to force Hitler into accepting a subordinate position in government, they were prepared to support his candidacy for the chancellorship in return for guarantees on military policy—the promotion of military values and the pursuit of a rearmament policy. Since the summer of 1932, the League of Nations had been hosting a disarmament conference. While the Foreign Office wanted to force the French to reduce their military forces, the army hoped to use the conference as a cover for their own rearmament plan. At the same time, the last elements of the Versailles settlement were collapsing, as the

French evacuated the Rhineland and the reparations payments were halted. This opened the way for a more aggressive revisionist policy, in which Blomberg's rearmament plans played an important role. The transition from the defensive military doctrines of the 1920s to the aggressive strategies of the 1930s contributed to and was facilitated by the collapse of the republic and the Versailles settlement.

Conclusion

After much wrangling, Hindenburg appointed Hitler as chancellor on 30 January 1933.[7] The reception of Hitler's appointment by the military was almost uniformly positive. This marked the moment of rebirth that officers had wanted since 1918. Blomberg, Hitler's first army minister, commented in 1935: 'A defeat is not final; it is not the day of judgment, which necessarily leads to collapse or even the beginning of the end. What is important is how a people reacts to defeat. It is clear, and the world must get used to it, that Germany did not die from its defeat.'[8] The language of catastrophe and rebirth, often coupled together, had never been far from the lips of soldiers. Yet officers also worked within the restraints of the Weimar Republic and the Versailles system. Pragmatism existed alongside the visions of military utopias. The tension between the possibilities of politics and military ideology was at the heart of the history of the Reichswehr. In 1933 officers had effectively swapped political influence and control of the military mission for military power, the reverse of Schleicher's, Stülpnagel's, Groener's, and Seeckt's vision. The acceptance of a subordinate role in the Nazi state was an acknowledgement that the Reichswehr was too weak to impose its own agenda on German society. The Nazi agenda of territorial and racial war would eventually emasculate the professional officer corps as they engaged in war crimes, plotted against the regime, and ceded control of the war effort to the Nazi Party and the SS in the final years of the war. It was, in some ways, a result of the vision of the militarization of society, with all its inherent contradictions and destabilizing consequences.

Notes

1. Michael Geyer, 'Insurrectionary warfare: the German debate about a *levée en masse* in October 1918', *Journal of Modern History*, 73/3 (2001).
2. James Corum, *The Roots of Blitzkrieg: Hans von Seeckt and German Military Reform* (Lawrence, Kan., 1992).
3. Bundesarchiv-Militärarchiv Freiburg (BA-MA) N5/11 Stülpnagel lecture, 'Wechselbeziehungen zwischen Land-, See-, und Luftkriegführung', fos. 5–6.
4. Benjamin Ziemann, 'Republikanische Kriegserinnerung in einer polarisierten Öffentlichkeit: Das Reichsbanner Schwarz-Rot-Gold als Veteranenverband der sozialistichen Arbeiterschaft', *Historische Zeitschrift*, 267 (1998), 357–98; Kurt Holl and Wolfram Wette (eds.), *Pazifismus in der Weimarer Republik* (Paderborn, 1981).
5. Johannes Hürter, *Wilhelm Groener: Reichswehrminister am Ende der Weimarer Republik* (Munich, 1993), 295.
6. Cited in Peter Hayes, ' "A question mark with epaulettes": Kurt von Schleicher and Weimar politics', *Journal of Modern History*, 52 (1980), 56–7. For a reassessment of von Schleicher's policy towards the Nazis, see Henry Ashby Turner, 'The Myth of Chancellor von Schleicher's *Querfront* Strategy', *Central European History*, 41 (2008), 673–81.
7. Henry Ashby Turner, *Hitler's Thirty Days to Power: January 1933* (London, 1997).
8. Generaloberst von Blomberg, *Der Tag der Wehrmacht* (Nuremberg, 1935), 4.

The Weimar economy

Harold James

Walther Rathenau, Weimar's most famous entrepreneur-intellectual-politician, in a speech in September 1921 claimed that Napoleon's famous slogan, that politics was destiny, was now outdated, and that it should be replaced by a new vision: 'Economics is destiny.'[1] The statement accurately reflects the obsession that gripped Weimar, a preoccupation with economic performance, economic policy, and economic constraints. 'Weimar' stands in popular parlance for three phenomena: artistic innovation, a 'perfect constitution' that collapsed, and extreme economics. There is a link at least between the second and third phenomena. Weimar politicians, pushed by very high expectations of what government should do, hoped that policy could make up for problems in performance. When they found that this was impossible, they were trapped. The whole experience demonstrated very vividly what Detlev Peukert has appropriately called the 'crisis of classical modernity'.[2] It also contributed decisively to the failure of the Weimar Republic.

Economic performance

At the beginning of the twentieth century Germany was the most powerful economy in Europe, as measured by production. In an age concerned with military capacity, in which steel played a major part as the raw material for armaments and battleships, steel output acted as a proxy for national power. In 1893, just as the new Kaiser Wilhelm II was preparing to launch his *Weltpolitik*, Germany (with over 3 million tons of crude steel) overtook British production, and in the lead-up to the First World War it continued to widen the gap.

On the other hand, in terms of income, Germany lagged behind Britain: although Germany's GDP was higher than that of the less populous United Kingdom, GDP per head of population was only 72 per cent of the British level (while in the USA, the level was 122 per cent of that in Britain). Again, though superior manpower gave Germany a military lead, Germans still looked enviously toward the richer western states. They hoped, though, that technology would allow them to make good that deficiency too.

In the course of a rapid industrialization in the second half of the nineteenth century, Germany had specialized in skilled high-technology products, in particular electrotechnical products, engineering and machine tools, and chemicals, and there were still great strengths in many traditional craft industries. All of the most dynamic German industries depended on export markets. Late nineteenth- and early twentieth-century complaints about Germany—such as those composed by the Briton E. E. Williams or the Frenchman Henri Hauser or the American Thorstein Veblen—concentrated on the unfair strategies of German competition, on an organized industrialism which used consular services as mechanisms to promote sales, and where protective tariffs offered a strategy for organized business to charge higher prices on domestic markets and engage in export dumping.

There was a widespread belief that prosperity was a national objective that could be achieved by an appropriate policy mix. Jakob Riesser of the Darmstädter Bank, the leading public spokesman for German banking before the First World War, spoke about banks having a national responsibility and fulfilling a national task. The First World War greatly strengthened this sentiment. Walther Rathenau, who had been one of the major architects of the war economy, stated that 'the reward for the trenches could not lie in a deterioration of living conditions'.[3]

In the Weimar Republic, the push to a modernization of business life continued. The state promoted economic modernization, and created new institutions such as the Reich Economics Council (or Reichswirtschaftsrat) that would draw the social actors into dialogue about overall objectives. The discussion of 'rationalization' produced great alarm from organized labour, which was frightened of the job losses and deskilling that it believed would follow from the application of Fordism, Taylorism, or other 'modern' management techniques such as the Bedaux system. Some of the most modern firms proved to be at the centre of the economic crisis: the textile producer Nordwolle, for instance, whose costly and ambitious modernization led to a default that set off the major wave of financial panic in Germany in July 1931.

While some technical advances actually occurred, they tended to be patchy and limited to a few sectors of the economy: chemicals, coal mining, and automobiles. But automobile production in Germany was restricted by a high tax regime, and only began to develop a mass market in the 1930s. There was little development in steel, where the nineteenth-century technologies still remained dominant, or in the important engineering and machine tools sector. The American author Robert Brady, whose 1933 book *The Rationalization Movement in Germany* was often cited by those who thought German industry had been transformed, concluded that in engineering rationalization 'cannot be said to have made any considerable progress in any of its many branches'.[4] Meanwhile the textile and clothing industries complained of falling productivity.

Labour productivity in the economy as a whole did not rise substantially. A recent analysis by Albrecht Ritschl of total factor productivity, which should have been rising fast in an economy with catch-up potential relative to Britain or the USA, actually showed no growth at all between 1913 and 1929, the last pre-depression year.[5]

By contrast, labour costs (wages, and social insurance provisions) increased dramatically, with the consequence that by the late 1920s, many employers thought that the cause of this surge lay in the bargaining power of trade unions, supported by the political power of the organized labour movement in the SPD and in the union wing of the Catholic Centre Party. The socialist theoretician Rudolf Hilferding in the mid-1920s told the Kiel party congress that there was a 'political wage'.[6] His argument was that state arbitration, which after 1923 could be imposed in the form of legally binding wage awards, constituted a significant improvement for the lot of the working class. Later policy reforms, such as the introduction of unemployment insurance in 1927, also looked politically attractive to workers, while employers complained that the scheme was costly and that it increased wage levels by increasing the 'reserve price' of labour. Finally, a generous round of pay settlements for the public sector in 1927 had a knock-on effect on private settlements. This discussion reached a polemical climax in the late 1920s: it arose out of the perception that Weimar politics was driving pay forward while productivity was constrained and international markets were not expanding sufficiently. In 1928, while nominal hourly wages rose by 12 per cent, productivity actually fell. Profits and investments were squeezed by high labour costs.

A similar issue to that raised by the power of organized labour was that of the agricultural sector, which was also politically organized and which pressed for state protection through subsidies, and quotas, protective tariffs, and veterinary hygienic measures to restrict imports. There were substantial agricultural interests represented in the right-wing DNVP, but also in the left-liberal German Democratic Party and in the Centre Party, and in 1927 even the Socialists, who had been primarily an urban working-class party, attempted to reach out to the farm vote. In the end, as credit conditions and indebtedness worsened during the Great Depression, many farmers migrated politically to the NSDAP.

Organizationalism spread throughout the economy, as organization in one sector encouraged other parties to follow the logic of collective action; and also as the government's approach to social regulation (often described as 'corporatism') seemed to encourage the formation of interest groups. Business in particular took up the use of cartels, which had already been widespread in the pre-war period. In 1925 there were 2,500 cartels in Germany, and by 1930 3,000. They were effective in setting prices for bulk and standardized products, such as pig iron or rails, but also for many consumer items (there were even separate cartels for crepe and non-crepe toilet paper). The idea behind the cartel was that it would stabilize the economy by avoiding 'ruinous competition'. In practice this meant the suppression of price signals, an issue critical to the Weimar story, which will be dealt with at greater length below.

The idea of organizing also spread to the interaction of the business and political worlds. Since the economic conditions for business activity were increasingly being set by political decisions, many of the most thoughtful business leaders came to the conclusion that businessmen would have to become more political in order to survive. They spent their energies in demanding subsidies from the government, or in pressing for regulatory concessions. One way of understanding the peculiarities of the Weimar economy, in fact, is as a struggle for rents in which businesses were likely to divert their attention from looking for technical innovation to pursuing innovation in rent-seeking strategies. They became political rather than technical entrepreneurs. Paul Reusch, for example, the extraordinarily powerful *Generaldirektor* (chief executive) of the steel and engineering combine Gutehoffnungshütte, had turned himself into a major political figure in the struggle against government interventions in the labour market, coining the slogan: 'Leave business alone for once!' There is an obvious paradox, in that Reusch's efforts to dismantle what he thought of as the costly and inefficient sides of organizationalism required higher levels of business organization.

The background to both the propagation of the state and corporatism as answers to an economic problem, and of the criticism of corporatism, was a rate of economic growth substantially reduced from that of imperial Germany. Ritschl's recent calculation for GNP per worker between 1913 and 1929 shows an annual growth of only 0.3 per cent, which is strikingly lower than the 1.4 per cent of the UK or 2.2 per cent in the USA.

To a substantial extent, the new weakness may be traced to demand factors, as well as to the supply side, and in particular to greater difficulties on export markets. In 1925, German exports amounted to only 87 per cent of their 1913 value, although there then followed a short-lived boom and in 1929 exports were 133 per cent of the pre-war level (in constant dollar terms). Some of the most important German patents had been confiscated by economic rivals—in particular by the United States—with the result that key technologies were no longer controlled by German companies. In the early 1920s, there was a substantial 'hate discount', in which fear and hatred of Germany (as well as discriminatory tariff legislation) excluded German products from the markets of former belligerents. But even in 1929, the German share of British and US imports was only three-fifths of the 1913

level, while German sales to neutral countries like Sweden and
Switzerland had expanded. In the late 1920s, German exports were
a significantly lower share of German GNP (14.9 per cent for
1925–9) than they had been before the First World War (17.5 per
cent). Export markets were generally weak in the 1920s, and world
trade grew less quickly in the inter-war period than before the First
World War (or than after the Second War). As a heavily exporting
country, Germany was bound to be badly affected, irrespective of
any 'hate discount'.

Knut Borchardt concluded in the late 1970s that Weimar was
a 'sick economy',[7] while Dietmar Petzina spoke of a 'Wach-
stumsstau': a blockage of growth.[8] Long before the world depression provided a final blow to German prospects, there was a
widespread consensus about the fragility of the Weimar economy.
The 1928 Annual Report of Deutsche Bank, for instance, spoke of
'the complete inner weakness of our economy. It is so overloaded
with taxes required by the excessively expensive apparatus of state,
with over-high social payments, and particularly with the reparations sum now reaching its normal level, that any healthy growth
is constricted. Development is only possible to the extent that these
restrictions are removed.'[9] There was then an expectation and a
hope that policy could remove blockages; but in practice policy
imposed new and additional obstacles.

Economic policy

The poor economic performance of Weimar resulted not just from
long-term stagnation but also from two major macro-economic
policy disasters: the Great Inflation and the Great Depression. Both
have held a fascination for students of extreme phenomena, and
both have produced major interpretative controversies, which are
worth reviewing briefly. In both cases, one influential interpretation suggests that policy makers were gripped by wrong ideas,
while an alternative current holds that the problem lies rather in a
series of structural constraints on policy.

By November 1923, the Mark had sunk to $1/10^{10}$ (or 1/1,000,000,
000,000) of its pre-war value against the dollar in what is still

(together with the post-Second World War Hungarian hyperinflation) the world's most catastrophic experience of hyperinflation.
The simplest level of explanation of the German inflation is that
it was a consequence of wrong ideas about money: in particular,
the central bank and the German authorities at least in public
seem to have thought that there was a contraction of the money
supply (which fell in real, i.e. price-deflated, terms) and that their
contribution to solving the crisis should thus lie in providing more
cash. The authorities justified this by appealing to the 'real bills
doctrine' which held that any underlying transaction could be the
basis for the creation of money: so business customers just needed
to bring trade bills to the central bank, and the government could
correspondingly present promises to pay. The last months of the
German inflation provided a dramatic picture of a central bank
believing that it needed to respond to the real fall in the value of
currency by producing more currency at faster rates. The central
bank or Reichsbank boasted of the efficiency of its 30 paper factories and 29 plate factories producing 400,000 printing plates to be
employed by the 7,500 workers in the Reichsbank's own printing
works, as well as by 132 other printing firms temporarily working
to satisfy the need for currency.

The reality, however, was not simply bad theory. Policy was
designed to meet an urgent social and political necessity. Inflation
was a policy choice that could be justified by bad economic
arguments. It was a choice that would continue to be made until
the results became so self-evidently catastrophic that some other
policy regime would be required.

The fundamental cause of the German inflation was the First
World War, and the methods with which the conflict and its
aftermath were financed. In July and August 1914, almost everyone
expected a short war, and war expenditure was paid through
the monetization of public debt at the Reichsbank. Even when
it was clear that there would be no quick military decision,
the German government—like other governments in continen-
tal Europe—rejected the possibility of financing military costs
through increased taxation. For the first two years of war, the
government successfully issued war bonds, whose purchase by the
public was widely treated as a vote of confidence in the government
and its military policy. After 1916, however, the government could

not place all the bonds with the public. The last offering, the Ninth War Loan of 1918, was undersubscribed by 39 per cent. At this stage, the public debt had to be financed increasingly by the banking system, and this meant in practice through the Reichsbank's discounts. In 1916 the reordering of the financial mobilization for war brought increases in indirect taxes, a new turnover tax, and a war profits tax; but the additional revenue was only enough to pay the debt service, so that the cost of fighting was met out of war loans but more and more through unfunded government debt. The result of the monetary expansion was that in all, by the end of 1918, there was five times as much cash in circulation as there had been at the end of 1913.

As the war dragged on, and as the costs increased, promises about the gains that would be realized at the end of the conflict became more lavish. The calculation about future public generosity that might be needed to pacify labour unrest necessitated an ever more aggressive attitude to the gains to be derived at the peace settlement; and this in itself provided a powerful obstacle to the conclusion of peace. Treasury secretary Karl Helfferich spoke of hanging the 'lead weight of the billions' around the necks of Germany's enemies.[10] In March 1918 at the Treaty of Brest Litovsk, as well as in the indemnities imposed by the supplementary treaty of August 1918, the German Empire imposed such a peace settlement on Russia. Similar promises and considerations led France in particular to insist on a similarly Carthaginian peace in Versailles in 1919.

The end of the war brought new expenditures. The German government faced a large bill for the social costs of the war—payments to the crippled of the war, and to widows and orphans. But it also became involved in paying large amounts to keep the social peace in a political situation that especially between 1919 and 1923 hovered perilously on the brink of social revolution. Food supplies were subsidized. In 1920, 12 per cent of Reich expenditure went to finance deficits in the post and railroad systems, where employment was judged a social necessity. This proportion rose in subsequent years. The government in effect adopted a full employment programme, for social policy reasons. The social explanation was given by the most famous inflation-era industrialist, Hugo Stinnes, in a dramatic conversation with the US ambassador in July 1922: 'that the inflationary weapon would need to be used in the future also, without regard to the extraordinary losses of capital, because only in this way can the population be given regular jobs, which are necessary to secure the life of the country.'[11] At the same time, similar considerations appeared in tax policy. Weak coalition governments found raising taxes politically unappealing; and there was increasingly militant opposition from business interests to the idea of paying taxes.

The Reichsbank continued to accommodate public sector debt by discounting government bills. The fall of the Mark on foreign exchange markets, which had already begun during the war, reflected the expectations about the extent to which government deficits would be financed by the central bank. In the phase of gradual or creeping inflation, which lasted until the summer of 1922, not all the debt was refinanced in this way; and foreigners in particular bought substantial numbers of German securities in the belief that there would be a recovery of the Mark. Such capital inflows, estimated at the time as between 7.6 and 8.7 billion gold Marks and more recently as highly as 15 billion gold Marks (or between 5 and 10 per cent of NDP 1919–22), helped to keep the Mark rate up. The confidence about a potential recovery was revealed by a premium for the Mark on forward markets until 1922. After July 1922, when the government and the political order were destabilized by the assassination of foreign minister Rathenau, these expectations changed. The proportion of short-term debt held by the Reichsbank now rose dramatically. The premium on forward Mark disappeared, and a dramatic fall of the Mark on the foreign exchange markets took place until the systematic attempt at stabilization and fundamental currency reform in November 1923. The result of this collapse was that the Mark, which had been undervalued in real terms for most of the time between 1919 and 1922 (i.e. the external decline in value was greater than the loss of purchasing power internally), lost that position from the second half of 1922 and by the spring of 1923 entered a period of overvaluation, in which the export advantages of the first part of the inflation process disappeared. Germany began to suffer from increased unemployment in the last stages of the hyperinflation. At the end of the year (usually a bad time for unemployment) in 1922, only 2.8 per cent of trade union members were without work, while by October 1923 the share had risen to 19.1 per cent.

Some analysts have argued that the inflation produced not inconsiderable benefits. It stabilized employment at a time when other countries were suffering from the collapse of the short-lived post-war boom that followed after the cessation of hostilities. This may have been crucial to the achievement of the precarious early political stability of the Weimar Republic. According to this interpretation, suggested at the time of the inflation by Stinnes and endorsed by analysts such as Knut Borchardt, Weimar bought consensus through the use of the printing press. Carl Holtfrerich, another leading modern interpreter of the inflation, in addition argued that German demand in the early 1920s helped to prevent a 1929-like depression on the world level. Other more culturally oriented analysts have argued that the inflation helped generate a new art, in which the imagination was unleashed and the fantastic could become everyday reality, as John Willett noted many years ago.[12]

Most contemporary commentators, however, did not share the positive view of the inflation. The most convincing analysis was that provided by Costantino Bresciani-Turroni, who emphasized the extent to which it followed from German public policy, and also argued that it was destroying German prosperity (and hence German capacity to pay reparations).[13]

The more modern economic historians shift from the macroeconomic (Keynesian) focus on big aggregates to micro-economic discussions, the more they have seen the extent of the damage done by inflation. The macro-economist used to ask: how did increased money supply affect overall demand? The micro-economist asks instead: what are the signals given as a result of inflation, and what is their effect on expectations?

Micro-economic accounts of the effects of the German inflation, such as the pioneering study of Dieter Lindenlaub in 1982,[14] show the substantial misallocation of resources that followed from wrong price signals. Industry embarked on a wave of mergers and acquisitions, in which large and diffuse vertical empires were established. They brought few efficiency gains: on the contrary, these new *Konzerne*—corporations—proved to be financially weak and vulnerable.

The legacy of the distortion of price signals in the inflation was a cult of bigness, regardless of the consequences. The leading German business economist, Eugen Schmalenbach, wrote retrospectively: 'Many expansions were carried out only for prestige reasons. Managements could not resist the drug of expansion, although their firms were operating well in the market, and did not need to fear a serious competitive battle. But they desired a monopoly position. This was enough to produce a clamour for unprofitable investments and acquisitions.'[15] The result was massive overextension of capacity, especially in the heavy industrial sector, with little technical advance.

The most perceptive and near-contemporary overall analysis of the inflation was that of the writer Elias Canetti, who vividly documented how the inflation focused people's attention on monetary transactions, to the exclusion of other values; and how the sharp fluctuations in monetary worth produced a growing sense of unreality, and at the same time a search for who was to blame.[16] With the First World War, price controls, inflation, and the evolution of a black market, large numbers of people were obliged to take up speculative, illegal, or semi-legal activities simply in order to survive. Such actions conflicted with traditional ideas of what kinds of business conduct were legitimate. One powerful argument as to why anti-Semitism flared up so poisonously during and after the First World War is that Germans widely took up activities previously defined as Jewish, hated themselves for this breach of traditional values, and reacted by transferring their hatred to the members of the ethnic group associated with the stereotype of bad behaviour. An important example of such a transition, in someone who played a crucial role in the development of the Nazi state's anti-Semitic policy, is Joseph Goebbels, who seems to have learnt Jew-hating as a bank clerk (with Dresdner Bank) during the Great Inflation of the early 1920s. Canetti actually concluded that the inflation and the hyperinflation laid the mental foundation for the Nazi Holocaust: that people became used to figures in which money was expressed with large numbers of meaningless zeroes, and then applied the same logic of meaninglessness to human life.

The end of the hyperinflation brought the end to a particular policy experiment. By late 1923, there were few social groups (apart from the radical and undemocratic political parties) who any longer saw any advantages to inflation, and as a result a consensus for stabilization emerged. The coalition government formed by Gustav Stresemann on 14 August 1923 had a broader, though fragile, support than its predecessors; and throughout the critical period to February 1924, the Reichstag tolerated emergency legislation enacted under Article 48 of the Weimar Constitution as a way of tackling the urgent financial problems. Such stabilization could only be carried out in cooperation with the foreign powers, however; and these played a crucial part not only in designing the new institutional structure of the Reichsbank, but also in promoting a change in management. Foreign bankers and central banks could be expected to play a less political and more 'expert' function, and German decision makers hoped that such outside intervention would help to depoliticize and desensitize the complicated issues that had developed as different political and social groupings in Germany had pushed their respective needs and interests. They were put on the new board of the Reichsbank, and also controlled the railway administration (Reichsbahn), where a large part of the public sector deficits had arisen. This settlement was part of a treaty negotiated in the London conference of 1924, which imposed a new reparations schedule (the Dawes Plan), and accompanied it with an 800 million Mark loan designed to re-establish German creditworthiness.

The most dramatic part of the stabilization was the introduction of a new currency, the Reichsmark, whose value was expressed in gold, and was identical with the parity of the pre-war Mark. Again, there was an international background: the currency reform was part of a general move to restore a slightly modified version of the pre-war international gold standard regime. The tie to gold was designed to represent an obstacle to budget deficits and inflationary finance: a credible commitment to a new sort of policy making. The Reichsmark was widely celebrated. The new president of the Reichsbank, Hjalmar Schacht, built a powerful political reputation on the success of the reform, and believed that his office meant that he should oppose the government, in private but also in dramatic public castigations and rebukes. The objective of the currency stabilization was to produce such confidence that foreign funds would flow in.

The stabilization did indeed produce large inflows, which were used by businesses to finance investment; but also went to public sector enterprises, municipalities, the state, and the central government (whose expenditure was much criticized by Schacht). The political artist George Grosz produced a painting in which he depicted the sun as a gilded dollar, warming the sickly Weimar economy.

Dependence on foreign money reflected a major vulnerability. The after effects of the inflation included the destruction of trust, and of long-term capital markets. In the nineteenth century, countries on the gold standard, and hence with a reputation for financial solidity, were able to develop capital markets. Weimar Germany, in the aftermath of the inflation, public sector entities, and private companies, found it hard and expensive to borrow long term in Marks, and the search for long-term capital meant using foreign capital and borrowing in sterling, dollars, or Swiss francs. The problem is a familiar one in modern 'emerging markets', and has been dubbed 'original sin' by Barry Eichengreen and Ricardo Hausmann:[17] when it is impossible to borrow long term in domestic currency, borrowers have a mismatch. They either borrow short term, in order to finance long-term investments, in which case they have a maturity mismatch; or they borrow long term, but in foreign currency, in which case there is a mismatch of assets and liabilities. Either of these vulnerabilities—both of which existed in the 1920s in Germany—set the stage for a financial and banking crisis.

A similar academic debate to that over the inflation, about the room for manoeuvre on the part of policy makers, and the appropriateness of their choices, has taken place with regard to the depression. As in the case of the inflation, one school of interpretation starts by blaming bad policy on bad theory and an incomplete understanding of economics. Why, such critics ask, did the German government not do more to stimulate demand: either, perhaps, through fiscal expansion and public work creation projects, or through a change in the exchange rate regime?

Before the depression, in the boom of the second half of the 1920s, some policy makers had a *Titanic*-style confidence about the solidity of the Weimar compromise. The optimism reflected faith in the capacity of corporatism to solve problems. To quote Rudolf Hilferding again, who was not just the major socialist economic theorist, but also finance minister at two critical turning points in Weimar history, in 1923 and then again in the Great Coalition government that ruled Germany from 1928 to 1930 as the country began the slide into depression: 'Free capitalism has undergone a transformation into organized capitalism.... The uncertainties of the capitalist mode of production are reduced, and the impact of crises, or at least the effect of these on the workers, minimized.'[18] Within a few years of this rather optimistic formulation, made in 1924, the effect of cyclical crises on the workers was evident in the over 6 million German workers registered as unemployed in 1932.

The policy environment after 1924 was rather different from that of the inflation years. Policy makers responded to the catastrophe of the inflation by trying to tie their hands, in the belief that a demonstration of their limited room for manoeuvre might promote confidence. The depression was the outcome of a particular set of policy choices, made long before the depression, but establishing a rather rigid sort of track from which policy could not deviate.

The effects of inflation on debt and on the capital market in particular constrained the government's ability to borrow. This put acutely painful limits on the ability of Weimar governments to respond to the Great Depression with fiscal stabilization measures. It was not so much that the idea of counter-cyclical fiscal policy was unknown. In fact, it had been practised by the coalition government of 1925–6, in which the finance minister Peter Reinhold had pushed tax cuts as a way of responding to recession and increasing overall levels of demand. But the failure of operations to fund the government debt in 1927, and then more dramatically in 1929, meant that the government could see no way out of its fiscal paralysis except to reduce services, cut unemployment benefits and public sector wages, and apply some tax rises. All of this reduced demand in the deflationary atmosphere of the depression, and thus worsened the economic collapse; it was also very obviously massively unpopular. By 1931, the government was engaged in a painful struggle to fund its regular expenses.

The chancellor from March 1930 to May 1932 was an austere (Catholic) Centre Party leader, Heinrich Brüning, who had at one time been close to the labour wing of the party. He was convinced that although his policies were detested, and although most of his political allies tried to shirk responsibility for the austerity decrees (which were consequently imposed by presidential decree), they were prerequisites for any sustainable economic recovery.

Deflation, like inflation, produced wrong signals, and micro-economic disincentives. In particular, it destroyed the financial and banking system. The phenomenon of the depression years was described in the case of the US economy by the economist Irving Fisher as 'debt-deflation'.[19] There was a vicious cycle. To take the example from rural America (or, indeed, rural Germany): food prices fell, so farm prices also fell; the farms were the security on which farmers borrowed, so as the value fell, banks called in loans; forced liquidations drove down farm prices further; and banks faced by bad loans called in more loans in order to maintain their liquidity. The damage done by deflation lies not simply in a macro-economic effect (the contraction of demand) but in the way many individual contracts are broken.

The result in Germany was that every aspect of debt became problematical. Small businesses and farmers were radicalized. Anti-Semitism flared up as farmers blamed moneylenders and cattle traders (who in some parts of Germany such as Franconia were largely Jewish) for their predicament. Businesses called for a systematic purging and reform of the banking system.

Unemployment surged, to reach over 6 million registered as looking for employment in early 1932. Even at the time of the occupational census in June 1933, 36 per cent of male workers and 19.5 per cent of female workers were unemployed. The census in that month gives an accurate impression of the way in which industrial Germany was being eroded, and workers were moving back into agriculture or into small-scale trading activities (such as peddling). While in 1925 13.5 million Germans had been employed in industry and crafts, in 1933 the figure had fallen to 13.1 million. In 1933, for the first time since 1882, more Germans were working in agriculture and forestry than in industry and crafts.

Brüning was obviously aware of the massive unpopularity of his regime. When he returned from the London debt conference in the summer of 1931, his staff closed the shades in his railway carriage so that he should not see the demonstrators. He was pelted by angry farmers when he visited the agrarian eastern areas of Germany. His solution to the problem of deflation was to try to make it as even-handed as possible. The culmination of the fiscal decrees came with the Emergency Decree (usually called the Fourth Decree) of 8 December 1931, in which wages were cut by 10 per cent, salaries by 9 per cent, rents by 7.5 per cent, and mortgage and interest rate payments were reduced as well. At the same time, in accordance with the fiscal necessity, taxes were raised: the transactions tax (*Umsatzsteuer*) was raised from 0.85 per cent to 2 per cent. Social security benefits were subjected to another round of cuts. The attempt to make deflation even-handed was criticized at the time as a violation of the security of contracts. It certainly did not help to stabilize business expectations. The socialist newspaper *Vorwärts* ('Forward') described it as 'the most massive and extensive intervention ever undertaken by the state in the economy in the capitalist world'.[20]

An additional consideration constrained Weimar policy making in the final phases of the republic: the reparations saga. The Versailles Treaty had imposed a large reparations bill on Germany. It was only in May 1921 that the precise amount was specified: 132 billion gold Marks, although this total was broken up into various categories, and the expert advisers certainly did not expect the part denominated as 'C' bonds to be paid. Reparations played a part in the drama of the inflation, and the moments when Mark amounts had to be transferred into foreign exchange unsurprisingly coincided with sharp falls in the exchange rate. A default on reparations deliveries in December 1922 set off the final phase of the inflation drama: the occupation of the Ruhr. As part of the stabilization package, a new reparations regime was devised, the Dawes Plan of 1924. This set an initially low figure that would rise over four years from just over 1 million Marks to 2.5 million.

Those German policy makers who wanted to reduce reparations payments saw in the accumulation of external debt a valuable instrument to force a renegotiation. If private claims, mostly in the United States, built up, the creditors would eventually see their claims in competition with reparation payments. These wealthy American individuals and institutions would then, the German calculation went, press the American government to cancel or greatly reduce inter-Allied war debt repayments from Britain and France, and the British and French governments would no longer need reparations. The problem with this calculation was that it required a sharp crisis in which the strength of the relative external claims on Germany would be tested: and the advocates of the crisis strategy were too sanguine about what effects such a crisis would have on Germany. The demonstration of credit-unworthiness could not simply be an international phenomenon, detached from any ramifications in the domestic economy.

The Allies were also weary of the German litany of complaints about reparations. Already during the immediate post-war years, in the era of the inflation and hyperinflation, German policy makers had claimed that unless Germany was treated more favourably, there was a risk that social unrest would become so pronounced that Germany might be threatened by a Russian-style revolution. When this argument was repeated, as it often was, during the Great Depression, it fell on ears dulled by the familiarity of the complaint. Germany was the boy who cried wolf in the fairy tale. Even though in retrospect it is obvious that, in the early 1930s, there was indeed a wolf at the German gate, this did not persuade outsiders, and Germany could only hope for a revision of reparations if there was a real crisis, rather than simply the threat of one.

By 1929, when a new reparations plan (the Young Plan) came into force after the international conference at The Hague, observers could calculate that Germany was massively over-indebted. There was 25 billion Marks in existing (so-called commercial) debt, and the reparations liabilities fixed at The Hague amounted to some 34 billion Marks in current value. This debt level, some 80 per cent of national income in 1929 (a prosperity year, unlike those that were to follow), is extraordinarily high even by modern comparison with over-indebted emerging market countries. The international capital markets indeed seem to have treated Germany as precarious. J. P. Morgan concluded that 'the Germans are a second-rate people'. Fresh inflows of capital, which had sustained Weimar during the boom, now dried to a very meagre trickle. What still kept the foreign capital in Germany was a dangerous game of chicken. Each creditor could realize that not all the foreign creditors could get out at once, so the best course was to stay in; if, however, there was any sign of danger, there would be a rush to withdraw money. This sign came with the May 1931 failure of the largest Austrian bank, the Creditanstalt, which although there was little direct link or exposure to Germany was held to reflect on German conditions. The Brüning government's response to the financial contagion spreading from the Creditanstalt crisis was to try to solve the reparations issue. On 5 June, it issued a fiscal austerity decree accompanied by a statement calling for a renegotiation of reparations: 'The limit to the privations which we can impose upon the German people has been reached.'[21]

The macro-economic and Keynesian tradition has tried to argue that there were real policy alternatives to the policy of fiscal deflation and attempted renegotiation of the reparation debt, since it should somehow have been possible to increase demand. In contrast to this tradition of interpretation, more modern writers starting with Knut Borchardt in 1979 have emphasized the extent to which policy was trapped. The policy makers themselves found it hard to defend what they had done, however, because they had little understanding of the process that made deflation both inevitable and harmful. Ex-Chancellor Brüning fled Germany in 1933, and eventually found a position teaching politics at Harvard. He clearly did not know how to explain why he had been so impotent politically, and sharp young economists such as John Kenneth Galbraith enjoyed teasing or provoking him about the catastrophe that in their view his economic ignorance had produced. 'At a welcoming seminar one evening I asked him if his Draconian measures at a time of general deflation had not advanced the cause of Adolf Hitler. He said they had not. When, unwisely, I pressed the point, he asked me if I disputed the word of a former Chancellor of the German Reich.'[22]

Germany was in fact in the grip of an internal and an external financial panic, which destroyed the optimism of the spring of 1931 that a recovery might set in. After May 1930, deposits in German banks contracted. The shrinking of deposits became much quicker after the Reichstag elections of September 1930 produced unexpectedly large gains for the National Socialist Party. A new panic occurred in May 1931, after the failure of the Vienna Creditanstalt. In the subsequent reports of the Reichsbank, as well as in most textbooks and historical accounts, these movements out of Mark deposits in 1930–1 have been interpreted as a withdrawal of foreign capital. But at the time, the Reichsbank, as well as many commentators in Germany, but also the crucially important foreign central banks, interpreted the losses as German capital flight. The governor of the Federal Reserve Bank of New York 'felt that the chief difficulty was a flight from the Reichsmark by German nationals and that the Reichsbank should resort to much more drastic credit control than apparently was the case'.[23] The Bank of England and the Federal Reserve Bank of New York believed in consequence that they should only help Germany if the Reichsbank were to take effective measures against capital flight. This would mean restricting banks' access to foreign exchange by denying them credit facilities. Banks could no longer rely on the Reichsbank for support; and a panic set in after big losses became evident at the DANAT bank. On 13 July, after the failure of the DANAT, a general banking holiday was needed.

The banking and financial crisis, which significantly worsened the German depression, was the outcome of the intertwining of two circumstances. First, there was the weakness and vulnerability of German banks in general, with doubts about the asset values of some major institutions (in particular the DANAT bank). Second, there were fears about the government's difficulties in balancing the budget and an interpretation that these might force Germany off the gold standard. Either of these considerations might have prompted a crisis on its own. But the Reichsbank's attempt to deal with the second difficulty (waning confidence in Germany) by internal credit restrictions made the first problem much more acute, and precipitated the final catastrophe, the final tightening of the screws on the debt deflation.

The government faced exactly the same sort of unpleasant dilemma as the central banks. Any course of action seemed only to make the crisis worse. Fiscal deflation obviously lowered demand; but fiscal expansion would have further destabilized credit and capital markets. The most knowledgeable and perceptive policy maker in the Brüning government, the state secretary (leading permanent civil servant) in the Finance Ministry, Hans Schäffer, commented frequently and despairingly about the constraint. In early 1932, he commented on the suggestions for work creation measures that were circulating widely, and which reflected the belief that the government should 'do something': 'It is impossible to pay for work creation out of the budget, which is already excessively strained; but the alternatives suggested by [finance minister] Dietrich are even more damaging: the use of central bank financing, as suggested in the drafts, is under no circumstances possible.'[24] In fact, it was illegal under the terms of the international treaties fixing the Dawes and the Young reparations plans.

But there was also an overwhelmingly depressing economic argument against the application of a Keynesian solution of fiscal expansion in the face of demand deficiency. The Keynesian option requires that the state step in to borrow in a climate when private investors are hesitating. It can do this because investors have confidence in the state, because the public sector can always be solvent as it can always tax. But while these assumptions work for some states in which there is a history of good debt management, they do not apply where capital markets for public and private debt have been destroyed by default or hyperinflation. Germany in the early 1930s was in this trap, and there was no confidence in public debt. Keynesian-style solutions were not adopted, not because no one had thought of them (indeed this was exactly the issue that state secretary Schäffer addressed in numerous memoranda); but rather because they did not represent an economic viability. The 'mistaken economic ideas' principle thus works no better in the case of explaining policy in the depression than it does for the post-war inflation. In the depression, too, policy makers were caught in the social and political constraints created by previous policies.

Economic constraints

In the first policy regime of the Weimar Republic, politicians bought social peace by a corporatist compromise. When the inflation turned into a dysfunctional hyperinflation, the political basis of that regime was destroyed. In the alternative vision of policy, realized after 1924, policy makers tried to create harmony by showing the extent to which their hands were tied, by the gold standard, the reparations treaties, and the dependence on foreign capital imports. This vision could be translated into prosperity, and political content, as long as there were capital inflows. But when these ceased, and when panic destroyed the German financial and economic system, the alternative vision was also discredited.

The depression and the fiscal dilemmas it posed created a peculiar problem in German politics that contributed greatly to the political paralysis of the democratic parties. Any measure that needed to be taken would inevitably alienate important groups of voters. Tax increases would be painful; so would cuts in social services or civil service pay. The Great Coalition government—the last fully parliamentary regime of the Weimar Republic—headed by the Socialist chancellor Hermann Müller collapsed in March 1930 because of the political pain caused by the fiscal dilemma. Labour leaders in the Socialist Party had not wanted a cut in benefits but the right-liberal German People's Party (Deutsche Volkspartei or DVP) wanted benefits cut and opposed a raise of employers' contributions. The Bavarian People's Party (BVP) objected to an increase in the tax on beer.

The obvious response was to try to avoid taking responsibility for policies during the period of the greatest economic hardship. To do this, the democratic parties in the Reichstag acquiesced in the use of the emergency provisions of the Constitution (the notorious Article 48) to bypass parliament and enact legislation in the form of decree laws.

The same calculation led many of the Weimar political elite to make the fatal calculation that Hitler and his movement could be weakened and discredited if Hitler were given some participation in political power. To this effect, Chancellor Heinrich Brüning conducted talks with Hitler immediately after the September 1930 elections, in which the NSDAP achieved its first major break-through. He believed that Hitler would have had little choice except to go along with a course broadly similar to that of Brüning, and would have thus discredited the National Socialist movement, which had committed itself to a very broad populist agenda. The strategy was to let the new and threatening movement wear itself out through government: a process described in German by the verb *abregieren* (literally: 'govern itself off'). As the crisis grew more intense, more republican politicians saw this as a possible option: they included the influential Rhineland brown coal industrialist Paul Silverberg, and the socialist theorist Rudolf Hilferding. Those political strategists who advocated this course believed that a Hitler government could not last for more than a few weeks.

Hitler was politically astute enough to see the dangers of participation in government, and refused to let himself be drawn in. Even after the major electoral success of July 1932, in which the NSDAP obtained 37 per cent of the vote, when President von Hindenburg offered a participation in government (though with non-Nazis as army and interior ministers), Hitler remained on the sidelines. The result was that the movement appeared rather powerless, and it was punished by the electors in the November 1932 Reichstag elections, when the share of the vote slid to 32 per cent. When at the end of January 1933 Franz von Papen started to negotiate again with Hitler, Papen, like many other conservatives, thought that he had trapped Hitler by getting him to agree to participate in government with some non-NSDAP ministers (including the army minister, the economics and finance ministers, and the foreign minister). Papen had stated, 'We've hired him for our act.'[25] The new economics minister, Alfred Hugenberg, stated that 'nothing much will happen . . . we'll be boxing Hitler in'.[26]

But in fact, unlike the autumn of 1930, the circumstances were not at all constraining, and the box of government no longer had any sides. In July 1932, Papen's government had at the Lausanne conference successfully negotiated the end of reparations. As a result, there were no reparations to test the new government. Before Lausanne, a German government could either pay and alienate the nationalists and populists; or not pay and face a violation of international treaties that would have legitimized French and Belgian military action against the small German army. Hitler in government before July 1932 would thus have faced an impossible dilemma: he could have backed down from the radical nationalist programme, or he would have faced a French army. After the end of reparations, a new and more radical foreign policy was possible for the first time. Secondly, the economy had reached the trough of the depression in the summer of 1932, inventories had been run down, and some kind of recovery was a possibility. A new government could easily and convincingly claim credit for such a recovery, even if it had little to do with actual government contra-cyclical policy.

Conclusion

There were two completely contrasting Weimar policy regimes. Each one produced an initial surge of confidence in the new paradigm as a way of restoring production and prosperity. The inflation paradigm (1918–23) focused on policy making by bargaining between the major collective interests. This was a 'can do' approach to policy. When it broke down, it was succeeded (1924–32) by an approach that built credibility by emphasizing restraint. This was the 'cannot do' approach to policy. The reader will wonder what happened after 1933. Most commentators have seen a major part of the Nazi success in economic policy as lying in the initiation of a new policy regime. Peter Temin attributes the new confidence after 1933 to the drama with which the Nazi government made it clear that there were new policy assumptions, and that deflation was no longer the guideline for state action. This was a definitively 'can do' approach to policy. Productions and profitability revived spectacularly. But there is no reason to think that the underlying problems of low productivity were overcome. Some commentators, notably Christoph Buchheim and the present author, have speculated that if Nazi policies were to be imagined as continuing but without the Second World War, the result would have been similar to that of the German Democratic Republic after 1949: a controlled economy, with low productivity and deteriorating quality of products.

A contemporary observer of the Weimar collapse, the Austrian economist Friedrich Hayek, used the Weimar experience as the basis on which he formulated *The Road to Serfdom*.[27] He saw a latent instability in the mix of control and market that was actually likely to produce dramatic shifts in policy and demands for more control. Hayek argued that: 'Both competition and central direction become poor and inefficient tools if they are incomplete; they are alternative principles used to solve the same problem, and a mixture of the two means that neither will really work and that the result will be worse than if either system had been consistently relied upon.'[28] Hayek tried to draw a line from the Rathenau vision of economic planning to Nazi totalitarianism. He claimed that 'Through his writings [Rathenau] has probably, more than any other man, determined the economic views of the generation which grew up in Germany during and immediately after the last war; and some of his close collaborators were later to form the backbone of the staff of Göring's Five Year Plan administration.'[29] Hayek was not right about the personal continuity; but his diagnosis about the characteristic mix of planning and market in 'classical modernity' is accurate.

Notes

1. Walther Rathenau, *Wirtschaft ist Schicksal*, ed. Uwe Grewe (Husum, 1990), 7.
2. Detlev Peukert, *The Weimar Republic* (New York, 1987), 275–6.
3. Quoted in Hartmut Pogge von Strandmann (ed.), *Walther Rathenau: Industrialist, Banker, Intellectual and Politician, Notes and Diaries 1907–1922* (Oxford, 1985), 224.
4. Robert Brady, *The Rationalization Movement in German Industry: A Study in the Evolution of Economic Planning* (Berkeley and Los Angeles, 1933).
5. Albrecht Ritschl, *Deutschlands Krise und Konjunktur 1924–1934: Binnenkonjunktur, Auslandsverschuldung und Reparationsproblem zwischen Dawes-Plan und Transfersperre* (Berlin, 2002).
6. *Protokoll über die Verhandlungen des Sozialdemokratischen Parteitages Heidelberg 1925* (Berlin, 1925), 282–3.
7. Knut Borchardt, *Perspectives on Modern German Economic History and Policy* (Cambridge, 1991), 158.
8. Dietmar Petzina, 'Zur Interpretation der wirtschaftlichen Entwicklung Deutschlands zwischen den Weltkriegen', *International Economic History Association Budapest Congress 1982*, B3: Long-Run Trends.
9. Deutsche Bank *Jahresbericht für 1928* (Berlin, 1929), 19–20.
10. Gerald D. Feldman, *The Great Disorder: Politics, Economics, and Society in the German Inflation, 1914–1924* (New York, 1993), 40.
11. Herbert Michaelis and Ernst Schraepner (eds.), *Ursachen und Folgen,* v: *Die Weimarer Republik: Das kritische Jahr 1923* (Bonn, 1960), 515.

12. John Willett, *Art and Politics in the Weimar Period: The New Sobriety, 1917–1933* (New York, 1978).
13. Costantino Bresciani-Turroni, *The Economics of Inflation: A Study of Currency Depreciation in Post-War Germany* (London, 1927).
14. Dieter Lindenlaub, *Maschinenbauunternehmen in der deutschen Inflation 1919–1923: Unternehmenshistorische Untersuchungen zu einigen Inflationstheorien* (Berlin, 1985).
15. Eugen Schmalenbach, *Finanzierungen* (6th edn., Leipzig, 1937), 309.
16. Elias Canetti, *Die Fackel im Ohr: Lebensgeschichte 1921–1931* (Munich, 1980).
17. Barry Eichengreen and Ricardo Hausman, 'Exchange Rates and Financial Fragility', in Federal Reserve Bank of Kansas City, *New Challenges for Monetary Policy* (Kansas City, 1999), 329–68.
18. Rudolf Hilferding, 'Probleme der Zeit', *Die Gesellschaft*, 1/1 (1924), 2.
19. Irving Fisher, 'The Debt-Deflation Theory of Great Depressions', *Econometrica*, 1/4 (1933), 337–57.
20. Quoted in Heinrich August Winkler, *Der Weg in die Katastrophe* (Berlin, 1987), 457.
21. Decree of 5 June 1931.
22. John Kenneth Galbraith, *Money: Whence it Came, Where it Went* (Harmondsworth, 1976), 173.
23. Federal Reserve Bank of New York Archive, Harrison Papers, 3115.2, 2 July 1931, Harrison–Norman telephone conversation.
24. Munich Institut für Zeitgeschichte Hans Schäffer papers, ED93/19, 17 January 1932 diary entry.
25. Joachim Fest, *Hitler* (New York, 1975), 362.
26. Ibid. 366.
27. Friedrich Hayete, *The Road to Serfdom* (London, 1944).
28. Ibid. 31.
29. Ibid. 129.

The 'urban republic'

John Bingham

A republic of cities

Germany's great cities of the 1920s were internationally recognized symbols of civic achievement, innovative management, urban planning, and vibrant experimentalism in the arts—fundamental characteristics of modernity and the metropolis. In crisis-ridden post-war Germany, more prosaically, municipal governments were also the primary engines, spenders, and on-site managers of the new social state. They bore the brunt of post-war demobilization, supervised emergency relief funds and work programmes, and later administered ambitious new schemes for welfare and unemployment relief, as codified in the Reich law of July 1927 governing labour exchanges and unemployment insurance. Their large-scale undertakings in public transportation, extensive housing construction, the building of spacious municipal exhibition halls, airports, roads, and a host of infrastructural and beautification projects made cities—especially the larger metropolises—barometers of the success or failure of the Weimar experiment and, not least, encouraged a close identification of the republic with municipalities that remains to the present.

Of course, all this activity was expensive. But just at the critical juncture after the First World War when cities took on tremendous new responsibilities for reconstruction and social welfare, their financial resources came under increasing pressure. The republic's tax structure, centralized in 1919–20, took away from municipal

governments their long-established right to set additional sur-
charges on local taxes according to their individual needs. Cities
now stood last in line behind the Reich and states to receive cen-
trally distributed tax revenues. Municipal coffers, in the words of
Cologne lord mayor Konrad Adenauer, were 'fed with the crumbs
left over' after the Reich and states had their fill.[1] Complicating
matters, Germany experienced extraordinary levels of inflation in
the half-dozen years after the war. The cities' desperate need for
funds drove them to continue and escalate their wartime practice
of printing massive amounts of their own emergency currency.
By early 1923, an estimated Reichsmark 2.5 billion of municipal
scrip was in circulation. Though an inadequate and short-sighted
solution to their economic problems—especially during the wild-
est and most uncontrolled phase of hyperinflation late in the
year—locally printed money nonetheless offered municipalities
immediate relief they insisted they could not do without. After
currency stabilization in 1924, local authorities turned to domestic
and foreign short-term credit to meet their new obligations. Their
high-profile borrowing and spending drew virulent criticism from
private banking and business circles. By 1930, city administrations were widely perceived as corrupt and inefficient, havens of
favour-mongering and political infighting—an impression given
credence by politically radicalized city councils and high-profile
municipal scandals, the most prominent of which brought down
Berlin's lord mayor, Gustav Böss. A much more serious challenge
to the municipalities, however, was the impact of the depression
and long-term unemployment. As workers' joblessness stretched
into months and then years, they slipped down through Weimar's
three-tiered relief scheme, ending up on the bottom where they
became wholly dependent on municipal welfare. According to the
cities, local expenditure on crisis relief and welfare more than
quintupled in the years 1929–32—from Reichsmark 0.3 billion
to 1.6 billion. In 1932, the welfare burden alone in many of the
larger cities claimed more than half their dwindling tax revenues.
Many cities, teetering on the brink of bankruptcy, were unable
to pay their employees and fell behind in their own tax and debt
payments.

The problem of urban modernity

Most histories generally accept that the end of the Weimar period saw a vehement and widespread rejection of 'the Berlin Republic' and of the metropolis and urban modernity in general. Anti-urbanism has thus become a well-known motif in narratives on the collapse of Weimar and the rise of the Nazis, whose propaganda infamously juxtaposed the hard living conditions, anonymity, and moral corruption of the big city with rural and traditional values and ways of life. Many Germans, especially in rural areas and small towns, ostensibly shared this hostility towards big cities, providing the most fertile ground for the Nazis' anti-urban propaganda. Weimar's 'revolt of the provinces' can be seen as a fundamental rejection of its specifically urban modernity: of the republic's 'foreign' (allegedly Allied-imposed) and Socialist (urban) origins, of its democratic and urban working-class politics, of its experimental art, municipal big government, reputed widespread corruption, and cosmopolitanism. Yet despite recent valuable contributions on many aspects of Weimar's modernity (and lack of it), literature addressing the critical problem of the larger role of the metropolis continues to be predominantly impressionistic, resting heavily on the thought of contemporary intellectuals and writers such as Oswald Spengler and Werner Hegemann, both of whom were critical of the modern city.[2]

If, as most historians agree, modernity's richest and most significant complexities are found in its inherent contradictions, then Weimar's surface tensions need to be traced back to deeper structural fissures in society and economy. As historian Detlev Peukert noted, German society enthusiastically embraced certain aspects of modernity while vehemently rejecting others. Peukert argued that uneven economic growth created 'sectoral imbalances' that the weak republic had neither the political nor economic resources to resolve, bringing on what he dubbed a 'crisis of classical modernity'. He speculated that if 'the crucial factor governing a society's stability and survival is going to be the way in which that society deals with these broadly inevitable tensions', then such tensions offer potential insight into the specific causes, as well as the deeper determinants, of the republic's failure.[3] Although Peukert's work has been a starting point for much subsequent Weimar research, historians have had difficulty both locating clearly articulated points of such tensions and applying them to his larger structural and paradigmatic themes. Much of this work has centred very sensibly on the urban environment: where time, space, and work are rationalized and old communal ties severed, where aesthetic experimentation, mass housing, urban functionalist architecture, and other 'modern' factors are concentrated. As usual, the problem lies in the transition from the particular to the general: the contained singularities that make case studies such promising sites for understanding Peukert's crises also make them resistant to broader generalization. The extent to which the urban experience and its responses differed markedly between cities and across regions cautions against easy generalizations about the ways Peukert's 'broadly inevitable' social, economic, and cultural tensions accompanied the advent of modernity in a specific locale.

Nevertheless, following Peukert's broad perspectives, this chapter retains the emphasis on cities and the urban setting. Its underlying premiss is that Peukert's 'crisis of classical modernity', difficult to discern from individual experience or within the borders of individual cities, may be more easily seen in the economic, cultural, administrative, and political disjunctures that accompanied urban growth across Germany as a whole. The stresses that attended urbanization created structural, supra-local strains as cities and towns competed for resources and, via internal migration and tax policies favourable to business, absorbed capital and attracted labour from the surrounding countryside.

Reform pressures

The field of enquiry here is national, but the point of departure is local, focused particularly on situating the cities' reform campaign within a larger frame of activity on the part of the Reich and state governments, as well as numerous lobby organizations, to rethink and reshape Weimar in the later 1920s. The new post-war republic was in reality an inherited patchwork of nineteenth-century state and local jurisdictions that covered the Reich in such byzantine intricacy that even experts were pessimistic about achieving 'a really objective overview of the whole administration'.[4] A deputy in the Saxon parliament, for instance, complained that opening a 30-kilometre railway line from Merseburg to Leipzig involved consulting such an array of authorities—including offices of the Reich, two state governments, and multiple county, district, and local officials—that it would be easier to travel from Berlin to Siberia. The police, too, argued that centralizing state and municipal records would help control crime. Efforts to improve the republic's efficiency and, ultimately, its viability thus turned to reform of the Reich's constitution and territory, often in bewildering variety. By the late 1920s, Germans could read on a given day reports and analyses of official reform projects at every level and activity of government, proposals, committee proceedings and more, all of it of more or less daunting legal and economic complexity. If producing reports could have done the job, so the joke went, the Reich would have been reformed long since.

The relatively few histories of the knotty reform problem have followed the official line at the time, treating it largely as a matter of high politics between the Reich and states that aimed first to resolve the duality of the powerful Reich and Prussian governments, and second to establish uniform standards of national administrative practice, particularly for tax collection and distribution of revenue. The lack of attention to local governments and their potential role in the reform debate has historical roots. Prior to the mid-1920s, German municipalities evinced little practical interest in high politics and their fledgling associations said little about state or federal matters. In some ways the lack of interest was reciprocated: by the end of the First World War, the states had not revised in half a century the constitutional and legal bases of local government, the principal resource for managing urban change. Yet this was precisely the period of the cities' most explosive growth. A host of new problems associated with urban crowding—housing regulation, water sanitation, policing, large-scale planning and provision of public transport, to name a few—required quick and effective resolution by local authorities. Nor did the Weimar Constitution of 1919 address the problem: the ostensible 'guarantee of self-government' in Article 127 simply continued the tradition of leaving the affairs and management of local governments under the supervision of the states. Finally, although numerous social, economic, and governmental experiments were posited during the year or so after the revolution of 1918–19, the fiscal chaos of the early post-war years kept municipal authorities busy scrambling to fund and manage welfare and emergency works. Too pragmatic and preoccupied to intervene systematically in theoretical reform debates as this point, the cities continued to rely on local self-administration in its traditional sense and saw little sense in trying to redefine their rights and responsibilities on a larger scale.

It was not until the arrival of what historians have agreed to call 'relative stability' in the mid-1920s that the inadequacies of the Reich's new financial environment became clear to urban administrators, forcing them to recognize that out-of-date bureaucracies and financial practices needed to be revised to fit more effectively the cities' new roles and growing burdens. Although local authorities remained nominally subordinate to the states, the Reich now imposed many onerous new social responsibilities directly on them, and interfered increasingly in communal finance, welfare provision, and the regulation of local taxes. The decisive power determining the cities' fate lay in Berlin, not the state capitals. Adenauer summed up the problem succinctly: 'The cities belong to the states, while the Reich has the money'.[5] From the mid-1920s, the cities increasingly interpreted the disadvantages of their position as a constitutional problem.

Some peculiarities of the German case should be noted at this point. First, urban-driven efforts to reshape the administrative and financial environment were not unique to Germany. Intensive urbanization brought tremendous new social and economic responsibilities to large cities throughout Europe. The need to muster resources and to focus managerial expertise drove local authorities to join together in supra-local governments, both as single-purpose collaborations as well as more permanent consolidations of cities, towns, and neighbouring lands into large central metropolises. In scale, however, the reform projects of German cities were considerably more ambitious, in that they shifted these aspirations from the local and regional to the national level.

The Städtetag

Secondly, nowhere else were cities and other local authorities joined together in such close-knit and influential collective associations. Through the Deutsche Städtetag (German Congress of Cities, or DST), Germany's large municipalities campaigned energetically in the late 1920s for their own 'new order', insisting that growing urban centres and powerful modern metropolises required equally modern administrative structures and practices.[6] The Congress comprised some 300 regular member cities, of which Berlin was the most prominent, and slightly over 900 additional towns that belonged indirectly through their provincial and state associations. A central Berlin office at Alsenstrasse 7 was dubbed the 'Städtehaus' or 'City House'. Over 1,000 delegates from municipalities across the country convened every three years in a different host city for a full members' congress. The agenda and tone were determined by the DST Council, comprising some forty mayors and councillors, and the even smaller Executive Committee; both met more frequently, usually in Berlin.

Municipal activity of every kind increased rapidly in the mid-1920s, and the Städtetag's influence and public profile rose accordingly. The Congress expanded its organization and office staff in Berlin, and hired high-profile experts in municipal affairs to take over its top offices. In 1926, the DST Council appointed as its executive president Oskar Mulert, a former director of communal affairs in the Prussian Ministry of the Interior (1920–5). Mulert came with a record of an almost indefatigable capacity for work, formidable negotiating skills, and a penetrating expertise in all areas of city finance, planning, and management. His energy, acuity, forceful personality, and close connections with ministerial and political figures in the Prussian and Reich administrations made for a powerful combination. In every area of Städtetag activity and policy making, his influence was quickly manifest. In the first months of his presidency, for example, he pushed for the appointment of a new press representative to help raise public awareness of 'the extent and importance of the work of the cities and of the Städtetag', and insisted that the DST intensify its efforts to bring city problems before the nation through closer relations with the press: 'Publicity is the life-element of German cities, the sole atmosphere in which they can really live'.[7] A new DST press office disseminated information about municipal affairs, promoted commentary on communal issues—especially by mayors and their staffs, many of them experts in their respective fields—and set up large press conferences after DST Council meetings. The DST also began coordinating the activities of municipal press services and created special press offices in Kassel, Frankfurt am Main, Mainz, and Saarbrücken.

For the next half-decade, Mulert's formulations of the cities' problems and the solutions he proposed drove their reform efforts. A keen sense of the shifting balance between local, state, and federal governments predisposed him to look for long-term solutions to the cities' problems at the national rather than state or local levels, focusing particularly on the creation of central ministerial and parliamentary agencies that would allow the cities to bypass the states and connect directly with the Reich government. In December 1926, the Städtetag launched a comprehensive new programme entitled 'The Protection of City Interests', whose ultimate goal was the creation of institutional connections between municipalities and central authorities. Strategy and tactics of the campaign dominated the cities' deliberations over the next three years at the Städtetag's annual congresses in Magdeburg (1927), Breslau (1928), and Frankfurt am Main (1929). The all-member Magdeburg congress was certainly the most visible and widely publicized demonstration of the cities' collective power during the entire Weimar period. Over 1,000 delegates from DST member cities and organizations from all over the Reich attended, along with a great many key figures in politics and administration, including for the first time a Reich chancellor, Wilhelm Marx, and the finance minister, Heinrich Köhler.

The cities' 'new order'

Mulert's keynote address at Magdeburg announced clearly the DST's intention to raise the profile of cities in national and state policy making. His central demands were for enhanced municipal participation on the Reich Economic Council, the establishment of a communal policy office in the Reich Ministry of the Interior, and the creation of an inter-party committee for communal affairs in the Reichstag. Most ambitiously, he also urged that cities be given seats on the Reichsrat, the upper chamber of state and federal representatives responsible for national legislation, so that their practical expertise and knowledge of specific conditions would balance more generalized federal initiatives. The cities, for their part, would be able to ensure that central legislation reflected more realistically the immediate requirements and long-term plans of the German population, especially in tax matters.

Mulert's proposals together formed a 'unified whole' whose scope was considerable. Tighter links between a larger and more interventionist central government, on the one hand, and urban authorities with increased social burdens, on the other, would have altered perforce the Reich's constitutional structure. If the states ended up both yielding their jurisdiction over local affairs to the Reich and losing seats on the Reichsrat to the communes, they stood potentially to become the weakest part of the triad. The danger of a defensive counter-campaign by the states was thus very real, and Mulert chose his words carefully. He avoided referring directly in his subsequent speeches and articles to the sensitive issue of constitutional reform, downplayed those sections of the programme most threatening to state power, and stressed the 'interdependence' of state and locality.

The response both from official circles and the press was encouraging. Open support came in 1928 from Prussian interior minister Albert Grzesinski, a Social Democrat whose government was itself engaged in a tremendous and much-publicized revision of administrative boundaries in the highly urbanized Ruhr region, implemented finally in July 1929. Reich interior minister Carl Severing also responded positively, promising DST delegates a communal affairs bureau by April 1929. Press reports and editorials sympathetically compared the cities' financial difficulties with their lack of national influence and argued that reform was necessary in a modern state. Negative notices, principally in the conservative, agrarian, and regional press (particularly in Bavaria), were in the minority. They rejected the cities' 'dangerous' plans and condemned the Städtetag for leaving 'the banal paths of communal politics and raising itself proudly to the higher spheres of Reich and state policy'.[8] But across the spectrum of opinion about city-based problems was a pervasive awareness of the larger significance of the cities' arrival on the national stage, of the increasing tempo of reform, and of the cities' central role in it. Looking ahead, Berlin city councillor Paul Michaelis commented that 'connections between the Reich and communes propel [us] towards a new order'.[9]

In mid-1928 reform was in the air. 'Unified state and administrative reform', exclaimed the *Frankfurter Zeitung*, 'the whole year 1927 was filled with public discussion of these two problems!'[10] The Prussian government was engaged in ten major territorial reform projects. Former chancellor Hans Luther's high-profile reform association, the Association for the Renewal of the Reich, in 1928 published its manifesto, *Reich und Länder* ('Reich and regional states'). As was not unusual in Weimar, domestic politics in this case had a strong foreign component. In October 1927, the Allied agent for reparations, S. Parker Gilbert, had submitted a much-noticed report in which he argued that German administrative inefficiency was hurting the national economy and (his main point) endangering Germany's ability to fulfil its post-war reparations obligations. By borrowing and spending irresponsibly, he argued, the cities were burdening an already unstable economy and undermining Germany's ability to pay reparations. One month later, in a much-noted speech in Bochum, Reichsbank president Hjalmar Schacht sharply criticized what he alleged was the cities' irresponsible borrowing abroad to pay for 'luxuries'—construction and development projects such as sports stadiums, swimming pools and parks, libraries, exhibition halls, museums, and airports.[11]

Taken together, the cities' Magdeburg proposals and the two public attacks by Gilbert and Schacht pushed the reform issue into the limelight. Ministerial staff and officials were instructed to survey public opinion and provide strategic analyses of the problem, while a flurry of discussions and hearings in the Reich Chancellery—in which Schacht played a leading role—prepared the ground for a national constitutional conference. Prominent personalities from across the spectrum of Weimar politics took up the problem, falling into a loose pattern of support for a

strong central government or 'unified state' on the left and for a
more traditional federal association of strong states on the right.
The pattern contained a fluid variety of motives and positions,
however: the right-wing German National People's Party (DNVP)
made the federated state part of its demand for reinstitution of
the monarchy; Social Democrats, though nationally in favour of a
unified state, in the south supported a federal solution that would
preserve Bavaria's favoured status amongst the other states.

In January 1928, Reich and *Land* delegates convened in Berlin
to begin working on reasonable and practicable plans for a comprehensive national reform (*Reichsreform*). In his opening speech,
Reich Chancellor Wilhelm Marx declared that the objective of the
conference was to discuss relations between the Reich and states:
no other authorities would participate. The cities immediately
protested: 'Communal interests must receive due consideration
in its deliberations if the decisions of the States Conference are
to be moulded into a positive outcome'.[12] But as long as the
states were suspicious of the cities and of Mulert, whom they
viewed as an 'impassioned unitarian' unconditionally hostile to
Länder interests, the cities were forced to watch the proceedings
as 'outside petitioners'. The DST had no alternative but to submit
its proposals and demands in writing, a strategy that held little
promise of success with over ninety different *Reichsreform* reports
and programmes competing for the conference's consideration.

At irregular intervals over the next two years, experts and representatives prepared reports on administrative, territorial, and
financial issues. The DST's final *Reichsreform* proposal, submitted
in June 1929 both to Reich interior minister Severing and to the
conference itself, summarizes the cities' overall reform programme
as a simple and, again, 'unified whole'. Local affairs would remain
the business of local governments exclusively. Reich authorities
would set principles and guidelines, but practical implementation
of national laws would revert to local governments. Future territorial reforms and urban consolidations were to be undertaken
solely to ensure the continued health, productivity, and efficiency
of local communities. Moreover, if Reich lawmakers were to make
informed decisions about local legislation, they needed information about local conditions and experience that could come only
from firm institutional contact with local authorities.

The regulation of communal affairs would be standardized across the country, as codified in a new national municipal charter (*Reichsstädteordnung*). At this point, twenty-five different charters were in effect across the Reich, with considerable variation between the states; a standardized charter had been high on the cities' list of priorities ever since the founding of the republic. But while their previous charter proposals had shown a pluralist willingness to accommodate the several forms of communal government then in Germany, the mayors in the DST by 1929 had come to prefer a unicameral system with strong mayoral powers. The vociferous campaigns of the banking and private sectors against public spending in the cities took as their starting point municipal irresponsibility and corruption. The infamous 1929 Sklarek scandal in Berlin brought accusations of corruption and bribery against long-standing lord mayor (and Städtetag chairman) Gustav Böss, and cast a pall of distrust and suspicion over big-city politics and administration. As a result, 'self-responsibility' became a much-quoted credo for local leaders, invoking diligence and sobriety in conducting the affairs of their cities. Equally significant, crippled municipal finances and the increasing prominence of radical, obstructionist politics in municipal councils combined to paralyse local governments, raising the danger that the states would intervene in the cities' affairs in order to re-establish financial and political stability. Once this happened, warned the DST executive, the damage to local authorities' right of self-government would be permanent. Extending and strengthening mayoral powers was thus a step toward obviating this threat, since streamlining and simplifying municipal authority would bring a stronger public awareness of governmental responsibility. Both power and accountability would be vested in a central figure, the mayor (*Bürgermeister*), who would have the power to cut through political and bureaucratic entanglements and get things done.

While the charter proposal found general support from the cities and the press, the agrarian and conservative right objected that federal interference in the states' regulation of communal law would set a constitutional precedent leading to further erosion of state power. Small towns, through their own association, the Reichsstädtebund, also complained that the proposed charter made no distinction between the metropolis and the middling or smaller city. A 'unified' charter would lump together all cities and towns regardless of size and character, thereby failing to allow for regional variation and specific circumstance. Naturally, these objections to some extent were reflexively aimed at the big cities and the DST itself, which came under attack from writers hostile to the idea of dictatorial mayors dominating the cities. The critics of the 'Oberbürgermeister-Städtetag' (city congress of lord mayors), claimed in a telling phrase that it would be the principal beneficiary of the law, which would create a Germany of 'city republics with presidents elected to long terms, whom no one, but no one, would be able to gainsay'.[13]

The DST's final programme, when eventually submitted to the States Conference in July 1929, received little attention. The conference's Constitution Committee instead focused on Reich–state relations, drawing up a 'differentiated general solution' proposing the establishment of two different types of states, 'old' and 'new'. The 'old' southern states would remain largely unchanged. After the dissolution of Prussia, 'new' states in the north would be built on the old provinces; the lesser of these would be enlarged by absorbing their poorer small neighbouring states, many of which by 1928 had been forced to conclude agreements with Prussia to manage their administration of justice, commerce, police, and welfare. Preparation of the 'general solution' by the Reich Ministry of the Interior took an additional year. By the time it reached the cabinet in 1931, the German economy was in a dire state and the government of Chancellor Heinrich Brüning was too preoccupied with domestic emergencies and foreign policy issues to give the bill consideration; the attention of officials and the public was directed elsewhere. Prussian delegate Arnold Brecht, a staunch and optimistic advocate of reform, remembered: 'During the tumultuous events of those days, Germany's reorganization was considered of secondary importance'.[14]

Of the various reform proposals to address the republic's urban deficit, Mulert's proposal for city representation on the Reichsrat (Reich Council of Ministers) implied the clearest and most radical relocation of power from the centre to the local. Cities, Mulert insisted, were precisely the proper agents of such a reform. In private DST council sessions, lord mayor Ludwig Landmann of Frankfurt am Main put it more bluntly. The states themselves had become anachronisms, too weak to justify their current levels of power and influence: 'politically, the division of strength is such that the communes [will] sink helplessly into insignificance if they don't have the opportunity to make their wishes known in the Reich's central agencies'. But this was also the critical point on which even some Städtetag mayors parted ways with Mulert's grand vision. If cities could get the power they needed only at the expense of regional diversity and strong state governments, then demanding Reichsrat representation essentially required establishing a strong central state. Foremost among those uneasy with the idea and its complex politics, unsurprisingly, were the southern lord mayors (*Oberbürgermeister*) Karl Scharnagl (Munich) and Hermann Luppe (Nuremberg), who feared its careful phrases were too subtle. The German public would simply see the cities demanding a unified state. Other members present argued that the state should be both apolitical and above interest politics and they protested that the cities and their associations represented 'other interests' that had no business mixing in high politics.[15]

The majority of delegates gathered at Magdeburg apparently agreed with one or both of these objections. The Reichsrat resolution was dropped from the list of proposals to be ratified by the members. Even so, Mulert went ahead and mentioned it in his speech. In the end, the reservations of his conservative colleagues were justified to an extent: press reporters and even Congress delegates came away with the general impression that Magdeburg had been a clear 'demonstration in favour of a unified state'. His speech, in particular, made such a strong impact on his audience that although the Reichsrat proposal never became part of the DST's official platform, it was widely viewed as such by the public and even by Städtetag members, a fact that speaks eloquently for the entire programme's unity of conception. It also indicates something of the cities' already evolved understanding of their own roles and interests. It was clearly no great leap for Mulert's listeners to make the connection between the proposal's specific aim to strengthen the cities' collective voice in German administration and law-making, with which they were long familiar by now, and its more general implications, whether formally included or not. While historians of urban Weimar have undoubtedly been correct to view Mulert as a formative influence on the cities' sense of collective identity as agents of modernity within the Reich, they may have underestimated the extent to which municipal leaders themselves were already sensitized to the larger economic and political realities of the cities' situation. Many, such as Brecht and observers in the press, recognized the problem of urban power as the real engine driving *Reichsreform*. It was no accident 'that the cities push ever more strongly from the idea of self-government toward the concept of the German unified state'.[16]

'Reform born out of catastrophe'

The depression and political crisis in 1929–30 ended the cities' hope for a negotiated reform. Early in 1930, Reich officials informed the DST in no uncertain terms that all reform plans were on hold for the foreseeable future. As the depression settled in with a vengeance, the cities' efforts to situate themselves more favourably within Germany's constitutional and financial structure ran out of steam or—as in the case of their earlier exclusion from the States Conference—encountered stiff resistance from conservatives convinced that 'Reich institutions are becoming representatives of interests, and all of these interests want to become independent holders of power'.[17]

As in the crisis years of the First World War, the depression again forced the state to rely on the cooperation of communal associations as mediators to manage the crisis at the local level. Ironically, this desperate time marked the peak of Mulert's influence. He and Städtetag staff worked frantically to stabilize municipal finances, meeting frequently with senior officials to strategize how best to manage skyrocketing unemployment and welfare relief costs. In equal measure, however, his meetings with ministerial and cabinet staff gave him the opportunity to register stinging protests against the incursions of the Brüning government's emergency decrees. He was keenly aware of the fragility of the cities' new-found position: whatever benefits they enjoyed now were more than offset by the self-serving fiscal policies of federal and state authorities who balanced their own budgets with little regard for the municipalities' heavy load of unemployment and crisis relief payments.

State intervention, Mulert warned presciently, posed a grave and permanent danger to local autonomy. In 1931, as a way of bypassing paralysed local governments and forcibly re-establishing stability, Prussia installed hundreds of state commissioners empowered to pass municipal budgets and impose unpopular austerity measures (including new taxes). The record shows that National Socialists in 1933 cited such precedents as marking a useful erosion of the institutions of local governance.

The impetus for reform in these and other cases came from above in the early 1930s, driven by the centralizing agendas of conservative officials who held the purse-strings. Significantly, the Reich's two central financial officers, Hans Luther (Reichsbank president, 1930–3) and Hermann Dietrich (Reich finance minister, 1930–2), both hoped to realize 'a reform born out of catastrophe' by consolidating control of finance in Berlin and further undermining the autonomy of the states and municipalities alike. Luther, for one, 'did not believe it right always to start from the premise that cities should not be allowed to go bankrupt', and thought 'it would be most beneficial for the cities if some of them should go to the wall', since 'it was dangerous if communes always had the feeling that they would be helped'.[18] As for Dietrich, Mulert recalled with particular venom in 1933 the finance minister's continued insensitivity to the cities' plight, concluding that he 'had fully [and] intentionally put the interests of the communes behind all other interests'.[19] Luther's and Dietrich's obvious lack of sympathy for local governments is all the more remarkable when it is remembered that both men began their public careers in municipal administration and were formerly lord mayors.

It has been argued with some force by Weimar historians— prominent among them Knut Borchardt and, to a lesser extent, Detlev Peukert—that powerful conservative forces and structural constraints from the outset seriously undermined the potential for viable reform in the republic; once the depression started, any chance of a negotiated reform disappeared. Yet negative judgements after the fact leave unexplained the intensity of reform activity across Germany at every level of government and politics from late 1927. Even more, they are not reflected in the memories of those most intimately connected with it. Arnold Brecht, for one, continued to believe even in retrospect that Prussian minister-president Otto Braun intended to follow through with a meaningful reform once one was available.

The deeper significance of the cities' reform campaign can most instructively be seen in its creation of new potentials for constructive change. The Städtetag's campaigns of course cut a wide public swath, but even more fundamentally the cities were the cause of the debate simply by the fact of their existence or, to put it more exactly, by the continued systemic disruption of Germany's economic and administrative structures wrought by sustained urban growth. In closed Städtetag strategy sessions, mayors and city councillors expressed their conviction that urbanization, combined with foreign demands that Germany restructure in order to meet its reparation obligations, posed an 'unanswerable argument' that the days of the states and of federalism were numbered; and that cities were uniquely positioned to help bring the unified state into existence. Civil servants and legal experts alike agreed that relations between the Reich and states could not return to those of the pre-war imperial days; nor could they remain in their present vague, undetermined state. There was 'only one way to go . . . forward!'—a much-quoted phrase of Mulert's reflecting two deep-seated convictions in the minds of both the experts and the lay public: that cities were defining features of modern life; and that a modern state should be based on principles of scientific planning and rational management.[20]

The main issue of reform in Weimar—to distribute the republic's scarce resources more equitably and efficiently from centre to local—was driven by the problem of structural urban change. That the reforms failed to come to fruition should not obscure the equally important point that they were widely perceived in post-war Germany as appropriate, even inevitable, or that the details of the various proposals, though technically arcane and difficult to understand, appeared frequently in the popular press. In these years, German participants in the republican experiment appear to have exhibited a healthy interest in acknowledging and adapting to a new environment. It should be no surprise that Weimar's cities failed to solve the intractable problem posed by large, powerful urban centres in a centralized modern state or, to put it more specifically, to find feasible ways to assimilate a specifically urban modernity into the constitutional and economic fabric of the Reich after 1918—a fundamental tension that remains currently unresolved in Germany as elsewhere. Many of the republic's institutions failed, but for the reasons discussed here, the cities' failure appears more significant than most. Their efforts to shape a republic that would sustain them economically and politically describe with special force missed opportunities of the short-lived republic.

Notes

1. Quoted in Otto Ziebill, *Geschichte des Deutschen Städtetages: Fünfzig Jahre deutsche Kommunalpolitik*, 2nd edn. (Stuttgart, 1956), 231.
2. Oswald Spengler, *Der Untergang des Abendlandes* ('The Decline of the West'), 2 vols. (Berlin, 1922–3); Werner Hegemann, *Steinerne Berlin* (Berlin, 1930).
3. Detlev J. K. Peukert, *The Weimar Republic: The Crisis of Classical Modernity* (New York, 1992), 82.
4. Arnold Brecht, quoted in Harold James, *The German Slump: Politics and Economics, 1924–1931* (Oxford, 1986), 46.
5. Deutscher Städtetag (hereafter DST) Council, 10 Dec. 1926, Landesarchiv Berlin (LAB), Repositur 142/1, St.A 315, published in shortened form in *Mitteilungen des deutschen Städtetages* (*Mitt. DST*), 21 (1927), cols. 1–4. Adenauer quotation from meeting of 24 Aug. 1931, LAB 142/1, St.B 3612.
6. *Berliner Tageblatt*, 27 Sept. 1927.
7. Mulert's speech to the Reichsverband der Deutschen Presse, 17 Jan. 1928, *Mitt. DST*, 22 (1928), col. 51.
8. *Mitt. DST* 22 (1928), Sonderheft 'Reichsaufbau und Selbstverwaltung': press clippings, cols. 114–29.
9. *Berliner Tageblatt*, 27 Sept. 1927.
10. *Frankfurter Zeitung*, 19 May 1928 (morning edn.).
11. Ben Lieberman, *From Recovery to Catastrophe: Municipal Stabilization and Political Crisis in Weimar Germany* (New York, 1998), 122–37.
12. DST Council, 23 Jan. 1928, LAB 142/1, St.A 751.
13. *Deutsche Selbstverwaltung*, Aug. 1930, and *Magdeburgische Zeitung*, 13 May 1930, both in *Mitt. DST*, 24 (1930), press clippings, 309, 314.
14. Arnold Brecht, *The Political Education of Arnold Brecht: An Autobiography, 1884–1970* (Princeton, 1970), 301.
15. DST Council, 22 Sept. 1927, LAB 142/1, St.A 541/I.

16. Heinrich Scharp, 'Die Städte in der Republik', *Deutsche Republik*, 26 Oct. 1928.

17. Reich finance minister Hermann Dietrich, quoted in Gerhard Schulz, *Zwischen Demokratie und Diktatur*, iii: *Von Brüning zu Hitler: Der Wandel des politischen Systems in Deutschland, 1930–1933* (Berlin, 1992), 265.

18. Reich Finance Ministry meeting, 1930, quoted in James, *German Slump*, 103.

19. DST Council meeting of 3 Feb. 1933, LAB 142/1, St.A 340 and 734.

20. '. . . nur ein Vorwärts', Deutscher Städtetag, *Jahresversammlung des deutschen Städtetages, 1928 in Breslau* (Berlin, 1928), 30.

Women and the politics of gender

Kathleen Canning

The history of women and gender in the Weimar Republic was profoundly shaped by the four years of the First World War and its revolutionary end. The wartime transformations of women's place in German society, and the anxieties they generated, were formative of gender relations in the Weimar Republic, from the figure of the 'new woman' who became representative of both the crisis and promise of modernity in the 1920s, to that of the 'new man', whose idealization of war and fantasies of revenge became a hallmark of nationalist politics in the mid-1920s. The politics of gender in the Weimar Republic were profoundly shaped by the war and the widely shared sense that the transformations it wrought were in need of thorough and urgent reversal. Thus underpinning the fragility of the Weimar economy and state, its political party landscape and welfare system, was the drive to return to the pre-war notions of family and gender as the foundation of social stability.

Women, war, and transformations of gender, 1914–1918

If the mass mobilization of Germans into war welded the once disparate *Volk* (race) into a nation for the first time in 1914, German women enthusiastically claimed their place in the nation at war. Educated and skilled women of the upper middle and middle classes filled the ranks of the National Women's Service

(Nationaler Frauendienst), which had a visible and influential role in organizing the war efforts on the home front. Upper- and middle-class women who had long sought an active role for women in German public life, whether through social work, educational, or moral reform, were entrusted with authority over wartime welfare of children and mothers, job placement for women and youth, and the rationing of food and coal. The war proved a transformative experience for poor and working-class women as well, as they moved into skilled and higher-waged jobs usually reserved for men and formed a new civic consciousness in the bread lines that became a symbol of civilian hardship and hunger on the home front.

Women of all social classes enjoyed a new independence from men during the war in both the family and the public sphere and gained unprecedented recognition from the state for their contributions to Germany's war effort, leading some to conclude that the war had an emancipatory effect on German women. The absence of fathers, husbands, sons, and brothers may have forced women to acquire new skills and responsibilities, but the anguish in awaiting news from the front, the grief and horror at the mounting death toll, mitigated against any sense of liberation, fuelling instead intensifying protests of women against the war. By the time of the 'turnip winter' of 1916–17 the chronic shortages of food and coal had created sharp social divides between poor and working-class women's experiences of the war—the so-called 'women of lesser means'—and those of the middle- and upper-class women whose devotion to the fatherland remained unshaken.[1] Food shortages during the last year of the war meant, for example, that adult women on the home front consumed less than 1,000 calories per day on average, as many staples, such as meat, milk, and eggs, virtually disappeared from the market. The death rate for adult women rose 67 per cent between 1914 and 1918, even before the onset of the influenza epidemic, which killed some 400,000 Germans.[2]

Even if emancipation is not an apt term to describe women's wartime experiences, the war did provide German women with crucial lessons in citizenship that would shape their participation in the early years of Weimar politics. The militarization of industrial production drew thousands of women into new sectors of work and into posts in unions and labour councils formerly held exclusively by men. The militarization of reproduction—the work of feeding, clothing, and nurturing the family—as well as the reproduction of the nation—through pregnancy, childbirth, and infant and childcare—came increasingly under the purview of state and military authorities. The proliferation of new military agencies, censorship, rationing, and the regulation of all aspects of civilian life erased the purported boundary between the public and the private. In the lines for bread, coal, and ration cards, or in encounters with state welfare offices, women entered into direct relationships with the state. Not only did their expectations and claims upon the state grow as the hardships of war intensified, but their consciousness of themselves as actors, in possession of both duties and rights, grew as well.

By the time the German government sought an armistice from the Allies in October 1918, the desire for political reform, for a democratic republic to replace the rule of Kaiser and military, was already widespread. In the forefront of the question of political reform was the issue of suffrage reform, not least the vote for women, which was broadly viewed as a reward that German women had earned for their active support of the war efforts. Although radical, liberal, and Socialist women's organizations had campaigned for female suffrage since the turn of the century, conservative and religious women's groups had considered suffrage unnecessary during the pre-war years. Women's most significant contribution to society would come through social and moral reform and the exercise of the principles of 'social motherhood' rather than through their participation in politics. The war indisputably transformed women's views of their own potential to contribute to their national, civic, and local communities: by 1917 German women, across political, social, and religious divides, considered themselves worthy of the right to vote based on their contributions to the war efforts.

Yet the languages of citizenship and the place of suffrage within them differed markedly across these milieux. For patriotic and religious women citizenship was cast in terms of rebuilding the nation. They imagined their votes as merely the first step in restoring its moral, social, and cultural foundations in the aftermath of war, followed by the mobilization of female experts and 'social mothers' into the realms of family, child, and workers' welfare, health and hygiene, and education reform, areas of acute need during the immediate post-war years. The Socialist and radical pacifist women's movement, by contrast, sought the vote as part of a broader vision of political reform, encompassing democratization of suffrage and parliamentary governance among moderates, and among independent Socialists and Communists more radical visions of socialization of industry and rule by workers' councils, inspired by the Russian Revolution. Left and Socialist female activists had a crucial role in the mass protests for bread, peace, and suffrage during the last two years of the war, helping to undermine the military state and to prepare the way for the revolution of November 1918. Inherent in the visions of political reform were the principles of political, civic, and economic equality between women and men.

The visible place of women in the social economy of the home front, and the obvious reliance of military authorities' upon them, suggested to some observers that the war had indeed unleashed a process of emancipation. Others perceived the changing gender relations of wartime as a 'sexual crisis' or even a 'Geschlechterkrieg' (gender war). Whether 'emancipation', 'sexual crisis', or 'gender war', conservatives and nationalists agreed that the looming 'feminization' of German society would be extremely difficult to reverse once the war had ended, especially if women were granted citizenship rights. These anxieties only intensified as the prospect for a German victory waned and calls grew louder for the abdication of the Kaiser in favour of a democratic republic. The rhetoric of feminization took stock of the numerical shifts in the German population resulting from the loss of 2 million men at the front, leaving women a distinct majority in the adult population. Apprehension about the anticipated *Frauenüberschuss* (excess of women) also encompassed more general fears of female dominance in male sectors of public, politics, and labour. Specific concerns included the urgent task of demobilization that Germany would face at the war's end, enforcing a removal of women from 'men's positions' in favour of the returning soldiers. Another site of reversal and restoration was families and households, led by women during the war, in which men should be returned to positions of authority. Finally, worry about the 'female excess' also stood in for the growing panic in the later war years about the urgent need to replenish Germany's birth rate in the face of mass death. Images of sexually licentious war wives and single women prompted calls for stricter policing of sexual behaviour and frivolous consumption and for the enforcement of bans on birth control and abortion and measures to encourage marriage and child-bearing.[3]

In the early days of November 1918 the German war effort ground to a halt and the Wilhelmine empire crumbled amidst sailors' mutinies and the founding of workers' and soldiers' councils from Kiel to Munich. Although women had comprised 40 to 60 per cent of the protesters in the mass strikes of April 1917 and January 1918, the revolutionary councils were almost exclusively male, although reports of the formation of housewives' councils circulated through northern Germany. One of the first acts of the national Council of People's Representatives, which formed between 9 and 12 November, was the proclamation of republican citizenship, abolishing the Prussian three-class suffrage system and giving women and men over the age of 20 the right to vote. Up to the very eve of the revolution civilian and military authorities had refused to grant women's demands for the vote, so the revolutionary proclamation stunned middle-class feminists. Indeed it seemed to them as if suffrage rights had fallen 'overnight from a storm cloud' on 12 November, turning German women into citizens 'with a dash of a pen, with a mere announcement in the daily paper'.[4] This act sparked an extraordinary campaign of political agitation and mobilization of women, as each of the new or reconstituted political parties sought to win their loyalties. Women also streamed into both the Social Democratic and Catholic labour unions, which gained a new political role in shaping the conditions of labour in the emerging democracy. The Social Democratic textile union, for example, saw its female membership increase 450 per cent between 1918 and 1920.[5]

Once women's voting rights had been declared, the meanings of the 'female excess' shaped the strategies of the political parties, which engaged in vigorous contests for the female vote. Between the revolution and Germany's first democratic election on 19 January 1919, 'voters were showered with leaflets and every fence, empty shop windows, and street corners were covered with fliers'. Each party had the instinctive sense that this was a decisive moment in the future of the German state, in which women, now the majority of voters, 'held Germany's future in their hands'.[6] At the same time women voters quickly became a puzzling and unpredictable political force, prompting the various parties to initiate improvised courses to school women in matters of state and in meaningful exercise of their new rights.

Uncertain of women's political inclinations, the campaigns of 1919 and 1920 generated mixed images of the new female voters with newly defined interests of their own, as members of families, social classes, religious or regional communities.[7] The colourful posters and fliers of the Social Democratic Party portrayed women as political actors, joining hands with men to hoist the red flag, while the Democratic Party showed women bursting through locked gates to reach the voting urns. Conservative and nationalist propaganda appealed to women as mothers and protectors of their families against the material hardships of the post-war years or more dramatically as Germania poised to defend the nation from the rapacious Allies.[8] The parties generated contradictory appeals to women as individuals who now enjoyed a new equality with men and as members of families, social classes, religious or regional communities, as voters concerned with public matters of state, economy, and society and as voters whose primary interests were family, morality, and social reform. In fact, the election campaign of January 1919 became a concentrated site of discourse on women and family, in which both the transformations of wartime and the urgent need for a new system of governance converged. As such, it marked a formative moment in the history of women and gender in what would become the Weimar Republic.

Women and gender in the founding of the republic

The revolutionary councils had named women citizens in November 1918, but the work of writing citizenship into law began only when the delegates were seated in the National Theater of Weimar in February 1919.[9] Between the months of February and August

1919 forty-one female delegates, comprising almost 10 per cent of the Assembly, took an active part in defining the terms of women's citizenship.[10] In the view of female activists the presence of elected female delegates in the republican National Assembly was monumental. Noting that 'This is the first time that a woman has been permitted to speak to a parliament in Germany as a free and equal person,' Social Democratic representative Marie Juchacz also noted that 'it was the revolution that allowed the old prejudices to be overcome in Germany'. Spurning the notion of the vote as a gift to women, she asserted: 'We German women do not need to express our gratitude to this government, which introduced female suffrage . . . Instead, what this government did is the most obvious thing in granting women that which has been unjustly withheld from them until now.'[11]

Not only was every aspect of women's citizenship contested among and between the parties, but the newly acquired right to vote stood in stark contrast with the mass displacement of women from their jobs that took place as soldiers returned from the front and the process of demobilization began. The demobilization decrees, drafted by the state and supported and enforced by unions and factory labour councils, sought to restore social stability by returning newly discharged veterans to their jobs as quickly as possible. The decrees stigmatized thousands of women as 'double earners' (those whose husbands, fathers, or brothers were employed and could presumably provide for them) and forced them to relinquish their jobs in favour of men.[12] The success of demobilization was swift: most women who had entered new sectors of employment during the war had already lost their jobs before the delegates convened in Weimar.[13] Even as deliberations began over the terms of their citizenship, a parallel political demobilization removed women from the posts they had held in unions and factory councils.

The citizenship the National Assembly ascribed to women, like the Constitution of which it was a part, represented a compromise between the forces of change—in this case left-liberal and Socialist female delegates, who sought full equality between the sexes—and the pressures to reorder society, family, and gender. Female citizenship was both qualified and gender specific, assigned to persons with specific male and female qualities. Article 109 in the

'Basic Rights and Basic Duties of Germans' deemed all Germans equal before the law. Yet men and women were assigned 'the same rights and duties as citizens' merely 'in principle', rather than fundamentally.[14] Thus the realization of women's citizenship rights would depend upon the 'natural limits' of sexual difference, and the qualifying phrase 'in principle' left open the possibility that local, provincial, or state laws might choose to interpret the law differently, as its critics pointed out.[15] The Independent and Majority Social Democratic delegations fought vigorously to strike the term 'in principle' from the Constitution, pointing to the equally valuable obligations that men and women bore in relation to the state, equating women's crucial role in bearing and raising children as parallel to soldiers' sacrifices for the fatherland. The Assembly voted, however, in July 1919 in favour of the formulation 'in principle' by a vote of 149 to 119. According to Article 119, marriage formed 'the foundation of family life and the reproduction of the nation' and thus enjoyed the special protection of the Constitution, which also held state and local governments as responsible for the health, integrity, and social welfare of the family unit.[16] Yet the Constitution also envisioned marriage as based on the equality of both sexes. At the same time, however, the Assembly chose to leave in place the Civil Code of 1900 (*Bürgerliches Gesetzbuch*), which favoured husbands' dominance over wives with respect to property, employment, and child rearing. The attempts of left-liberal and Socialist legislators to amend the outdated code and to bring it in line with the new Constitution also failed in a vote of 144 to 128.[17] The Assembly's vote to approve the Constitution in August 1919 confirmed women's citizenship, even if it did not fulfil the hopes of many for political and social equality. The citizenship rights which the Weimar Constitution accorded to women upheld and reinforced their significance as mothers and wives, while seeking to reorder that which the war had disrupted—the relationship between the sexes and between family and state.

The impetus of reordering relations between civil society and state, women and men, was evident, not only in the writing of the Constitution, which left restrictions on women's civil rights in marriage and family in place, thus privileging protection of family and reproduction of nation over women's civil rights, but also in the policy arenas of labour, welfare, and family. The rapid implementation of the demobilization decrees in 1919, for example, literally stripped women both of their actual jobs and their right to work. The female social reformers who envisioned and staffed many branches of the Weimar welfare state were barred from key positions in crucial arenas of social policy where the 'vital interests of state' were defined and negotiated.[18]

The efforts to restore familiar gender ideologies and hierarchies remained incomplete or unfulfilled in many respects. The idea that women, or, for that matter, men, could effectively 'return' to their former place in families and households, for example, rests upon the assumption that those families and households had somehow managed to remain unscathed by the drastic transformations of civil society during the war and could actually provide escape or solace from the chaos and change of post-war society. Moreover, the transformations of masculinity during the war, the proliferation of shell shock, newly recognized as a form of male hysteria, and other forms of bodily and psychic trauma, maiming, and dismemberment, were deepened by the German defeat and inscribed into the founding of the republic by those who sought blame through the 'stab-in-the-back' theory or revenge through the mobilization of nationalists against a republic willing to negotiate with the Allies. The fact that neither masculinity nor femininity could simply be restored or returned to an idealized pre-war era is confirmed by the current of crisis that ran through the republic regarding matters of gender and sexuality, especially surrounding attempts to revitalize the family's reproductive function, to restrain and regulate sex, pleasure, birth control, and abortion.

Gender and the party-political arena

The National Assembly's task of writing Germany's first democratic constitution created a crucially important framework for women's rights during the Weimar Republic. The struggle to define and then to exercise women's new rights in 1918–19 had unquestionably inspired and energized female activists, many of whom had campaigned for suffrage since the turn of the century.

The wave of politicization following the German defeat, revolution, and convening of the National Assembly also drew new female actors into the political process, including many whose wartime experiences had been decisive. Yet by the next election of February 1920, which took place under the shadow of the punitive peace of Versailles, the spaces for women's active citizenship in the realms of party and parliamentary politics had narrowed, as women's interests were subsumed under the pressing crises the fledgling republic faced. The impetus towards overcoming the disorder of wartime by restoring the family, gender relations, and birth rate became vital to Germany's recovery, which had barely begun before it was encumbered by spiralling inflation and the escalation of political violence in the wake of the Versailles Treaty. Nationalist and right-wing women, in fact, embraced their new political rights in order to mobilize on behalf of reinvigorated gender differences, appealing to their female constituents to activate the feminine capacities for compassion, moral fortitude, and self-sacrifice in order to repair the broken nation.[19] In the face of these crisis conditions, the space for reinventing politics or pursuing greater equality was curtailed by these crises and the republic's struggle for legitimacy. The political parties expected women to fall into line with their programmes rather than pursuing their own special interests. In fact, women did not appear to vote on the basis of the parties' policies towards women, but supported those parties whose standpoints on social, religious, and cultural issues matched their own. Catholic women, for example, adhered closely to the Catholic Centre Party, while the Socialist Party, as the most vociferous advocate of women's suffrage rights, continued to draw most of its voters from the ranks of workers and left-leaning intellectuals. Jewish women experienced the dichotomy between their status as citizens in the new republic and the denial of the vote to women in Jewish communal elections.[20] After the imposition of the Versailles Treaty nationalist women and those organized in the pre-war colonial women's movement mobilized new identities of citizenship centred on the nation rather than the republic, fostering a politics of colonial revisionism and advocating on behalf of the rights of ethnic Germans 'trapped' within the redrawn boundaries of Eastern Europe.[21]

While the declaration of female suffrage compelled the political parties to compete fiercely in the elections of 1919 and 1920 for women's loyalties, it proved more difficult to build stable constituencies of female voters in the longer term. In the face of the crippling political and economic crises of the years 1919–24, the issues that had propelled women into politics were soon overshadowed by the more immediate matters of governance and insurrection, both Communist and nationalist, and by the looming economic crisis represented by the devaluation of the currency and reparations owed to the Allies. While some feminists continued to pursue the idea of a 'women's party' during the early years of the republic, in fact most women activists remained affiliated with one or the other of the established political parties. The German Democratic Party, for example, counted in its ranks the prominent activists Marie Baum, Gertrud Bäumer, and Marie-Elisabeth Lüders, while Käthe Schirmacher and Paula Müller represented women's interests in the German Nationalist People's Party (DNVP). The ranks of Socialist female activists split along the lines of the party's divide during the war: Marie Juchacz was the female face of the Majority Socialists in the Reichstag, while Luise Zietz represented the Independent Socialists until her death in 1922 and Clara Zetkin became the female icon of the Communist Party and remained a Reichstag delegate until 1933.[22] Having won the vote many middle-class and politically active women turned from the explicitly political arenas of parties and parliaments to the realms of social reform and social welfare, where their feminine and motherly expertise, honed during the war in the arenas of hygiene, maternal, infant, and child welfare, was in demand.[23] This apparent turn from the political to the social has led many historians to conclude that the vote itself, as the centrepiece of citizenship, was without broader consequences for Weimar politics. In fact, historians have interpreted women's lower rates of voter participation and general disenchantment with party politics after 1920 not only as a rejection of politics but as a 'willing return to traditional gender roles'.[24] Yet the core of female political activists who left their imprint on the republic's *Frauenpolitik* (policies towards women) regarded parliamentary politics and the arenas of welfare and social reform as not only compatible but inextricably intertwined: Marie Juchacz, for example, served as the head of the Social Democratic workers' welfare organization Arbeiterwohlfahrt (Workers' Welfare) from its founding to 1933, while continuing to represent the SPD in the Reichstag during the same period.[25]

Although the founding of the Weimar Republic—and its ultimate fate—were decided in the political arena of the Reichstag and its constituent political parties, gender mattered to other arenas of politics as well, whether local or communal or in institutions such as trade unions and consumer co-ops. The organized women's movement remained a formidable force during the 1920s, despite the fact that an array of political, confessional, and social divisions cut through its rank and file. The Bund deutscher Frauenvereine (League of German Women's Associations or BdF), an umbrella organization encompassing some forty-seven different women's groups, had close to 1 million members in 1920. Professional associations, from rural housewives to white-collar workers, formed the largest constituencies within the BdF and tended towards conservative, even nationalist political views, advocating economic interests for women in professions that were consistent with women's nature and inherently feminine qualities. At the same time radical feminist activists and pacifists of the Women's International League for Peace and Freedom (IFFF), expelled from the BdF during the war for their internationalism and peace activism, remained separate from the BdF, as did the advocates of free love and reproductive rights who belonged to Helene Stöcker's Bund für Mutterschutz (League for the Protection of Mothers).[26] Also outside of the BdF were the over 200,000 members of the German Evangelical Women's Federation, who broke with the BdF over the issue of women's suffrage and remained closely tied to the German People's Party (DVP), as well as the Catholic Women's Federation with some 250,000 members, which sought a close affiliation with the Catholic Centre Party.[27] By contrast, the Jüdischer Frauenbund (League of Jewish Women or JFB), comprised of 485 locals and 20 provincial associations, belonged to the BdF until 1933, and JFB leader Bertha Pappenheim served on the BdF's governing board from 1914 until 1924. While the JFB shared many of the BdF's standpoints and goals, including the embrace of sexual difference and elevation of women's maternal principles, it also sought to improve both the 'position of women in Judaism' and 'the situation of Jews and women in Germany'.[28] Yet the JFB diverged sharply from the BdF on some issues of reproductive politics, including eugenics, and in its commitment to peace and its ties to the feminist peace movement. Furthermore the JFB had to contend with anti-Semitism within the BdF, which took an official policy of solidarity with the JFB against anti-Semitism throughout most of the republic, but which nonetheless encompassed many groups whose members were virulent anti-Semites.[29]

Women's political inclinations are only one measure of their place in the new democracy. The fact that their voting rates and participation in party and parliamentary politics shifted after 1920 and that most female political figures harnessed their visions of change to the established parties by no means suggests that women fled politics or the public sphere. Some 530,000 women left widowed by the war, for example, constituted a highly visible public of welfare clients, whose status as war victims lent credibility to their recurrent and often enraged protests about pensions and state provisions.[30] In fact, the most visible female citizens of the republic may well have been the mobilized and politicized war widows, whose party affiliation was less definitive than their membership in war victims' associations. War widows, representing themselves and the 1.9 million children left fatherless by the war, not only staked claims to state social benefits, but became the most prominent symbols of mourning and memory of the war, along with the maimed veterans who haunted the streets of post-war German cities.

Labour, consumption, and sexual politics in the era of rationalization

The very meanings of both publics and politics changed with the expansion of consumption, mass culture, and the mass media during the 1920s. Women participated in an array of widening public arenas, including those of cinemagoers, reading publics, consumer cooperatives, and advocates of a new body culture or mass sports. At the same time the number of female university students increased steadily between 1919 and 1932, from 9.5 per cent to 19 per cent of students, including the numbers of women pursuing doctorates.[31] In the last years of the republic women in both the Socialist and Communist milieux led vigorous campaigns for reproductive rights and against restrictions on birth control and abortion. Sexuality was not only more openly debated in the democratic republic, but it was also disciplined and redefined by sexual reformers who criss-crossed the professions of medicine, social work, and scientific research. Their particular social activism centred on the reform of sexual relationships and practices with the aim of advocating enjoyable and productive sex for both women and men. A different type of sexual reform activism took place during the Weimar Republic among homosexuals, who sought legal rights, in particular the abolition of paragraph 175 of the German penal code banning sex between men, but also to redefine the terms of sexuality and gender to include the 'third sex'. During the 1920s a new public sphere, visible to those who sought it, emerged in Germany's metropolises, especially Berlin, of lesbian and gay nightlife, which became sites of both sexual socialization and sexual politics. While neither the new democracy nor the legacy of the war dismantled patriarchy entirely, the landscape of the republic was one traversed by women who were increasingly at home in the public of the new democracy.

The workplace constitutes yet another public in which women were increasingly visible, not only in their journeys from home to the factory gates, but also in their participation in work communities, unions, and labour councils, or their role as clients of factory or municipal welfare agencies for working women, from childcare facilities to maternity and paediatric clinics. Despite the mass expulsion of women from their wartime jobs in the early months of the republic, women's employment in industry increased in the early 1920s, before the inflation crisis of 1923–4, and again during the era of stabilization and rationalization of industry.

Rationalization of the industrial labour process created new semi-skilled positions for women in the expanding metal, chemical, and electronics sectors, while they continued to comprise the majority in industries such as textiles and garments. Taylorized assembly-line production placed new emphasis on skills that had been long heralded as 'female', such as manual dexterity. From the standpoint of employers women were particularly attractive assembly-line workers in the newly expanding industries because of their lower wages and presumed docility. Thus despite the attempts to restore the pre-war division of labour at the end of the war, the modernization of industry fostered new sectors of female employment amidst the outcry of unionized and skilled male workers against 'deskilling' and 'feminization' of the factory workplace. Rationalization redefined the division of labour in both the factory and white-collar workplace, maintaining sharply gendered notions of skill, wage, and work ethic while fuelling an expansion in women's work outside the home. At the same time, however, women's unskilled and semi-skilled jobs were far from crisis proof: women workers, often decried as 'double earners' if their husbands, fathers, sons, or brothers had employment, were the first workers who lost their jobs or were laid off during economic downturns, especially during the late 1920s.

The growing sector of white-collar employment relied on a young and versatile workforce of mainly single women, who both worked the counters in offices, bureaucracies, and department stores and constituted a new force of consumers after hours. While many of the new positions as *Angestellten* (sales or office clerks) paid less than factory jobs, the social status of clerks was markedly higher, not least because in department stores or offices their customers or clients were largely from the middle or upper classes. One phenomenon of the 1920s was the emergence of a subculture of the salaried workers, known as *Angestelltenkultur*, which fascinated social and cultural critics like Siegfried Kracauer. Eschewing the rhetoric of class identity and solidarity in the labour movement, along with its elevation of manual skill, salaried workers were identified as a *Stand* (estate), which sought its place, socially and politically, in a society increasingly polarized between unions and capital.[32] Emphasizing individualism and membership in a profession, salaried workers often aspired to an upward social mobility that increasingly became unattainable amidst the recurrent crises of the Weimar economy and state. The desires of salaried female workers to distinguish themselves from workers in factories or domestic shops prompted new attention to clothing, fashion, and make-up, as a vital part of the new consumer culture of the 1920s. Salaried workers stimulated consumption in another respect as well: they comprised an important part of the mass audience of avid filmgoers and book club members, of those who flooded into the dance halls and jazz clubs in Germany's urban metropolises.

Rationalization became a motto of much more than the organization of labour during the second half of the Weimar Republic. Rationalization signalled a new social consciousness about the human economy that subtly displaced the notion of 'natural' differences between the sexes with new norms of rationality, scientification, and efficiency that conjoined men and women in the task of reorganizing labour, households, reproduction, and sexuality, with the goal of rendering their outcomes both more predictable and more productive. Factory managers and office supervisors, as well as housewives and mothers, were to learn to avoid 'wasteful expenditure of energy, time and materials' as the codes of rationalization penetrated the most intimate spheres of daily life.[33] The debates about rationalization formed one site of envisioning the future in Weimar Germany, an optimistic embrace of modernity that emphasized Germans' capacity for innovation and improvisation. 'Machbarkeit' (feasibility) became a keyword of rationalization, encompassing the confidence that reorganization of labour, consumption, national and individual reproduction with the goal of higher levels of efficiency and predictability was both imperative and 'doable' (machbar).[34] Social reforms on both the left and the right shared this 'heady sense of the possible', which extended to the assumption that human material, the Volkskörper—the national or social body—could be 'remolded' and society fundamentally renovated and re-energized—despite or precisely because of the recurrent crises of governance and economy that beset the republic.[35] The debates about rationalization advanced new thinking about the roles and capacities of the two sexes, not only in the sense of remaking individual and national bodies. Rationalization became a code word for efficiency, productivity, and modernity, one that was even applied to the sphere of sexuality in the later years of the republic. So the sexual reform movement of the late 1920s, representing a coalition of Socialists, democrats, and Communists, sought to rationalize sexuality by encouraging healthy couples to have sex that was both productive and pleasurable, with the aim of producing a higher birth rate and higher quality of offspring in a Germany that was still contending with the population loss of wartime.[36]

The particular fascination with America that was a hallmark of the German rationalization debates prompted new attention to consumption as a vital part of the reorganization of both middle-class and working-class household economies.[37] The capacity of women to manage the double or triple burdens of waged labour, household, and child rearing depended increasingly upon an array of new household appliances and technologies that cultivated a 'scientific and rational organization of home and family', idealized in images of Taylorized American households. Rationalized housework, as Mary Nolan notes in her study *Visions of Modernity*, should combine American techniques with a German *Geist* or work ethic, a goal that was viewed as central to Germany's economic vitality while constituting a crucial part of women's 'cultural duty' as mothers and citizens.[38]

In fact, with the expansion of both consumption and mass culture during the Weimar Republic, the spheres of citizenship widened, politicizing the everyday activities of shopping, joining book clubs, or going to the movies. The rapid growth of advertising and the increasing sophistication of visual culture helped to mediate and mobilize female consumption, both on behalf of family and household and as individuals whose definitions of the self were increasingly bound up with fashion and public display. As Julia Sneeringer has argued, producers and advertisers both acknowledged 'women's power over the household purse' and assigned consumption 'a deeper significance for the stability of the nation', especially in the aftermath of the inflation and currency devaluation of 1923–4.[39] If Bernd Widdig's study of *Culture and Inflation* is correct in its assertion that the rampant inflation of 1922–3 became associated in the popular mindset with female excesses, then the everyday acts of a frugal female shopper could be viewed as vital to economic recovery.[40]

While the consumer economy was a defining feature of Germany's modernity during the 1920s, it was also constituted by the many innovations it unleashed, from the visionary architects and artists of the Bauhaus, whose 'containers for living' sought to provide affordable housing for those of modest means, to the films of Fritz Lang and the growing audiences at the cinema, cabaret, and jazz clubs; and the improvisations of political theatre from Bertolt Brecht and Erwin Piscator to the left-wing agitprop theatre troupes.

The proliferation of mass media and entertainment culture, from dance halls, to gramophone and radio, to penny novels and the popular press, photography, and advertising, marked the widening of the public into the spheres of work and home. Also modern was Weimar's corporatist economy, which conjoined capital and unions in a shared commitment to economic efficiency and social peace; its modern and expansive welfare state that committed the resources of the state to fostering high standards of health and hygiene for German families and public assistance for vulnerable citizens, such as war victims, the elderly, pregnant women. Yet the crisis of modernity always lurked inside its promise—the eugenicist vision underpinning the notions of health and hygiene, the sexual excesses that seemed to abound in the metropolis of Germany, Berlin, where young women moved about freely and popular culture transgressed the moral codes of the past. Another dark side of modernity was represented by the virulent anti-modernism of nationalists and anti-Semites who waged increasingly vehement campaigns against all that modernity encompassed—democracy, a rational economy, political compromise, and the rights of women and minorities, especially Jews.

The figure of the new woman became iconic for the Weimar Republic as a symbol of both Weimar's modernity and its endemic crisis. Representing single young working women in their twenties, the figure of the new woman helped to define the culture of the salaried female workers: its hallmarks were short, modern haircuts, fashionable clothing, and the use of cosmetics. New women were represented at both work and play, traversing Germany's expanding public spheres—cinema, dance halls, sports—or roaming the streets as female *flâneurs*. Implicit in this figure was the ability to purchase, which suggested employment and earnings: new women appeared as agents whose choices about consumption, adornment, and self-representation defined their place in society and visual culture. Yet another aspect of new womanhood was the capacity to manage the challenges of modernity, including the dual demands of earning a living and running a household. In their depictions of modern women ironing or vacuuming in high heels and fashionable clothes, advertisements for new consumer and household goods made clear that young housewives could also count as new women.

The youth of the new woman, her implied economic independence, and her ability to articulate her needs formed the basis of that which seemed the most threatening about this figure: the embrace of change, motion, and freedom of movement through Germany's expanding urban metropolises. The capacity to represent the self was transformed and complicated by the explosive expansion of visual culture during the Weimar Republic, leading some historians to conclude that the new woman was merely an image, even a male fantasy, produced by advertising. The image of the 'glamour girl', who worked 'by day in a typing pool or at the sales counter in some dreamland of consumerism, frittering away the night dancing the Charleston or watching Hollywood and UFA films', constituted a myth, promoted by the media, that 'bore little resemblance' to the lives of most young female workers, argued Detlev J. K. Peukert some years ago.[41] Yet this dismissal of the evocative power of the new woman overlooks the power of images to inspire desire, identifications, subjectivities that embody these images. The new women represented on the covers of books, magazines, or in the ads for facial creams and lipstick represented shifting views of femininity, as well as the social practices and lived social realities of Weimar's young women. But the images themselves, endlessly reproducible and circulating widely through Weimar's consumer culture, also had the power to shape and inform habits and desires. The anxiety and fantasies surrounding the sexual agency of 'new women' stemmed in part from the dissemination of this figure across an enormously diverse and variable media that itself reconstituted notions of public, consumption, and pleasure in the course of the 1920s.

The permeable boundary between social reality and image—the sense of not knowing if those who dressed like new women also lived like or really 'were' new women—rendered this figure ungovernable and contingent, formed by the sense that characterized much of the republic itself that 'nothing was certain and everything possible'.[42] Moreover, in some representations, especially in fashion and cosmetic advertising, the new woman had an uncertain relationship to the strained and struggling nation: she was not unambiguously German. As the recent transnational exploration of the 'modern girl around the world' shows, what made this figure distinctive in any one setting 'was her continual incorporation of elements drawn from elsewhere', her occupation of 'the liminal space conjoining the national and the international'.[43] This apparent denationalization of the modern girl made this figure more volatile during the 1920s when Germany had lost its colonies and seen its national borders curtailed.

New modes of artistic expression, particularly within the cultural movement known as 'New Objectivity', also fostered new notions of gender and sexuality. For example, the photomontage works of Dada artist Hannah Höch and Marianne Brandt, a member of the Bauhaus, contended with the transformed landscape of gender relations during the 1920s, juxtaposing familiar and transgressive images of women that made women both the symbols and agents of change.[44] At the centre of Brandt's montages, for example, was often an unmistakably new woman, distinguished by her short hair, lipstick, and cigarette, and by her detached and discerning gaze that suggested her capacity to assemble her own world view out of the fragments surrounding her. The rapid growth of *Unterhaltungsliteratur* ('entertainment literature') popularized both visual and textual images of new women. The expansion of print culture, an often overlooked aspect of both Weimar democracy and popular culture, saw the founding of new publishing houses, new magazines, and journals, including illustrated weeklies and dailies. Increasingly popular among female readers was the new genre of women's novels in which the plots turned around the conflicts and dilemmas facing modern young women. At the centre of novels like Irmgard Keun's *Gilgi—eine von uns* ('Gilgi—One of Us') or *Das kunstseidene Mädchen* ('The Artificial Silk Girl') and Vicki Baum's *Stud. Chem. Helene Willfüer* were different types of new women, whose unconventional choices regarding love, marriage and pregnancy, and economic dependence/independence preoccupied female readers and became the subject of newspaper serials and debates among women in the new informal public arena of women's book clubs.[45] The female reading clubs, along with the cinemagoing female public, came into view in the course of the mid-1920s as their reading and viewing tastes stoked a new sphere of consumption—that of entertainment. The attempts of both Social Democrats and bourgeois feminists to guide and prescribe young women's tastes for literature and to warn of the dangers of film offer evidence of the unease in both movements about the unpredictability and ungovernability of young women's habits of consumption, whether of fashion, entertainment, or literature. The 'new interpretive communities' of female readers and moviegoers were viewed with suspicion as potential sites of female agency, pleasure, and self-representation.[46]

This examination of the figure of the new woman suggests that the public of leisure, pleasure, and consumption was at least as important as the democratic republic in lending femininity its newness during the Weimar Republic. Although women had gained the right to vote in 1918, the volatility of the new woman did not appear to stem primarily from her engagement in party or parliamentary politics, but from the articulation of a sense of self, the freedom to define, adorn, and represent the self—in an array of expanding publics. Recent accounts of the new woman note that her capacity to stylize herself as the embodiment of an entirely new and generationally specific *Lebensgefühl* ('life feeling') was, in fact, contingent upon her disavowal of political claims.[47] Indeed the identification of new womanhood as explicitly sexualized has led to the presumption that new women were inherently apolitical or had chosen the pursuit of pleasure over politics. Yet the fact that sexuality and consumption were both deeply political arenas became starkly evident in the last years of the republic when battles over reproductive rights became a major dividing line through party politics and the ranks of social, medical, and sexual reformers. The anxiety surrounding the figure of the uncontainable 'new woman' which continued to trouble Weimar political culture until its end was focused on a generation of women who were perceived as cut loose from the moorings of marriage and family, yet relentlessly present, as both pleasure seekers and citizens, in the expanding publics of the new democracy. The fact that new women were both real and symbolic, as Atina Grossmann argued some years ago, is revealed not only in the spheres of leisure and pleasure, or by the discursive obsession with the excess female population, but also in the tangible anxieties that periodically beset the republic over gender and sexuality.[48]

Sexual crisis and the crisis of the republic

An undercurrent of sexual crisis percolated through politics and culture during the Weimar Republic, adding to the visibility and volatility of the figure of the new woman. As an icon of both modernity and crisis, the sexualized figure of the new woman seemed a continued reminder of the urgent task of harnessing female sexuality to the reproductive needs of the nation if the social or familial order was to be restored. The figure of the new woman became the most readily available symbol of gender disorder, whether involving issues of labour and wage earning, birth rates and body politics, the practices of consumption and popular culture, even the wide-ranging issues of republic and nation, citizenship and national boundaries. One revealing case that has garnered scholarly attention in recent years is that of the 'black horror on the Rhine'. The French and Belgian occupation of the Rhine in the early 1920s, particularly French deployment of African soldiers, appeared to violate not only Germany's fragile national boundaries, but also the sexual purity of German women.[49] Lurking in the often hysterical propaganda about the unbridled sexuality of African soldiers and their perpetration of rape across the Ruhr and Rhineland was the fear of German women's sexual agency and the suspicion that they had actively pursued sexual liaisons with the occupation troops.

If the years of so-called stabilization were the high point of cultural achievement and visionary experimentation, also of a certain openness regarding gender and sexuality, political crisis increasingly tore at the seams of the republic during the late 1920s. Facing spiralling unemployment, labour unrest, and industrialists' determination to undermine the 'trade-union state', democrats and 'reasonable republicans' found it increasingly difficult to defend the republic after 1928. The coincidence of the stock market and banking collapse with the Nazis' huge electoral success in the fall of 1930 fundamentally crippled Weimar democracy, changing the terms of citizenship and foreclosing the visions of modern women in the republic. While it is easy to argue that gender and women simply fade from the scene of the republic's last and highest-stake battles, fought most dramatically by armed bands of men—Nazis, Communists, and Social Democrats—in the streets of German cities, these years were marked by a remarkable campaign for reproductive rights, which widened the scope of the citizenship claims that women had articulated in the founding years of the republic.

The stakes of body politics sharpened in the face of widespread economic misery and desperation: as Atina Grossmann has argued, amidst 'parliamentary paralysis and political polarization' during the last years of the republic 'questions about women and reproduction moved to the centre of a national debate on social priorities and entitlements' that turned on the viability of both the German welfare state and the national body politic.[50] As unemployment soared and discrepancies between classes sharpened after 1930, a broad coalition of left-wing sexual and social reformers, including many female activists, took up the struggle against paragraph 218 of the German penal code, which punished both women seeking or undergoing abortions and the doctors who performed them. The campaign to legalize medical abortions, to make birth control available through the health insurance or communal welfare systems, and to improve state support for mothers placed reproductive politics at the heart of a struggle to widen citizenship rights on the eve of the republic's collapse. They also railed against a system of class injustice that condemned working-class women to 'quacks and hazardous, potentially deadly "self-help"', while bourgeois women were able to procure therapeutic abortions which doctors more readily 'justified as "medically necessary"'.[51] The campaign against paragraph 218 fomented wider opposition to the social policies of Heinrich Brüning, the 'hunger chancellor' of the Catholic Centre Party, which included the controversial attempt to ban female 'Doppelverdiener' ('double earners') from paid employment outside the home and thus from access to social insurance. By this time the numbers of abortions had risen to over 1 million per year, with tens of thousands of deaths or permanent injury. The issuance of the papal encyclical 'On Christian marriage' in December 1930, in particular its denunciation of birth control and abortion, buttressed Brüning's conservative social policies and galvanized the movement against both the state and the Catholic Church.[52]

The campaign against paragraph 218 reached its high point in the winter of 1931 with the arrest and imprisonment of two doctors in Stuttgart for performing abortions, which not only unleashed wide social protest, but drew public intellectuals, playwrights, filmmakers, and artists into the movement to free the doctors and repeal the law.[53] While some have contended that amidst this turmoil the phenomenon of the new woman disappeared from the landscape of culture and consumption as quickly as she had arisen, the campaign against paragraph 218, according to Atina Grossmann, addressed women as both mothers and new women, thus revitalizing new womanhood at the republic's end.[54] Although the movement against paragraph 218 cast women's reproductive rights as fundamental human rights under the conditions of extreme social and economic distress of the early 1930s, the largest women's organization, the League of German Women's Associations (BdF), with over 750,000 members, refused to become involved, focusing its policies instead on the protection of mothers and advocacy on behalf of its many professional associations. By 1932 the leadership of the BdF had shed any remaining vestiges of its liberal heritage, turning now to embrace the notion of a corporate state, modelled best by Mussolini's Italy, in which women were to constitute a crucial corporate body.[55]

In the last elections of the Weimar Republic, while battles raged over women's reproductive rights and legislation against 'double earners' was debated in the Reichstag in 1932–3, women voters, still a majority of the electorate, were courted 'with an ardour not seen since the first days of female suffrage'.[56] Interestingly, each of the parties appealed to women to consider the implications of a Nazi victory for the future of women's rights. Assuring women of their vital role in national renewal, the Nazis promised to free women from the detrimental 'emancipation' of the Weimar Republic.[57] While the Nazis campaigned vigorously as the liberators of the nation from the republic, they also envisioned the reordering of gender relations which the Weimar Republic had never achieved: not only would the individualism and sexual identifications of new women be expunged from German culture, but the elevation of mothers would have a definitive place in the Nazi notions of the racial *Volksgemeinschaft* (people's community), and in their visions of war, resettlement, and the genocidal remaking of Europe.

Notes

1. Belinda Davis, *Home Fires Burning: Food, Politics, and Everyday Life in World War I Berlin* (Chapel Hill, NC, 2000).
2. Robert Weldon Whalen, *Bitter Wounds: German Victims of the Great War, 1914–39* (Ithaca, NY, 1984), 73–4.
3. Birthe Kundrus, 'The First World War and the construction of gender relations in the Weimar Republic', in Karen Hagemann and Stefanie Schüler-Springorum (eds.), *Home/Front: The Military, War and Gender in Twentieth-Century Germany* (Oxford, 2002) and Ute Planert, *Antifeminismus im Kaiserreich: Diskurs, soziale Formation und politische Mentalität* (Göttingen, 1998).
4. Marie Bunsen, 'Wir Wählerinnen', *Vossische Zeitung*, 624/286 (Ausgabe A), 6. Dezember 1918, 2 and Helene Lange Archiv, Berlin, Aktenzeichen 1062: Dr Agnes von Harnack, *Die Frauen und das Wahlrecht*, ed. Ausschuß der Frauenverbände Deutschlands (Vorbereitung der Frauen für die Nationalversammlung. Deutscher Staatsbürgerinnen-Verband e.V.) (no date of publication, but mostly likely Jan. or Feb. 1919).
5. Deutscher Textilarbeiterverband (DTAV), 1928 *Jahrbuch 1927* (Berlin, 1928), 147.
6. Bundesarchiv Berlin-Lichterfelde, Nachlass Anna Blos 2026/3, 32–60 for a selection of these congratulatory letters. There are also several from male acquaintances of Wilhelm and Anna Blos, including possibly other members of the Stuttgart SPD chapter. It is interesting that the women who wrote to Blos did not know her personally but were moved to write by her visibility as a female representative.
7. Wilhelm Ziegler, *Die deutsche Nationalversammlung 1919/1920 und ihr Verfassungswerk* (Berlin, 1932), 29–30.
8. Julia Sneeringer, *Winning Women's Votes: Propaganda in Weimar Germany* (Chapel Hill, NC, 2002).
9. Ziegler, *Die deutsche Nationalversammlung*, 30.
10. Christel Wickert, *Unsere Erwählten: Sozialdemokratische Frauen im Deutschen Reichstag und im Preussischen Landtag 1919 bis 1933*, vol. 2 (Göttingen, 1986), 64.

11. Antje Dertinger, 'Marie Juchacz', in Dieter Schneider (ed.), *Sie waren die Ersten: Frauen in der Arbeiterbewegung* (Büchergilde Gutenberg, 1988), 214.

12. Richard Bessel, ' "Eine nicht allzu große Beunruhigung des Arbeitsmarktes": Frauenarbeit und Demobilmachung in Deutschland nach dem Ersten Weltkrieg', *Geschichte und Gesellschaft*, 9 (1983), 211–29 and Susanne Rouette, *Sozialpolitik als Geschlechterpolitik: Die Regulierung der Frauenarbeit nach dem Ersten Weltkrieg* (Frankfurt am Main, 1993).

13. Richard Bessel, *Germany after the First World War* (Oxford, 1993), 140–1.

14. Article 109 reads: 'Alle Deutsche sind vor dem Gesetz gleich. Männer und Frauen haben *grundsätzlich* dieselben staatsbürgerlichen Rechte und Pflichten.' It is worth noting that Hugo Preuss's draft of part I, 'Die Einzelperson', reads: 'Alle Deutschen sind vor dem Gesetze gleichberechtigt', without mention of women or men. See *Die Verfassung des Deutschen Reichs vom 11. August 1919* (Stuttgart, n.d.), 36–7. For a comparison of Preuss's draft and the final version of the Constitution, see Ziegler, *Die deutsche Nationalversammlung*. Also see the new collection, Deutsche Nationalstiftung (ed.), *Weimar und die deutsche Verfassung: Geschichte und Aktualität von 1919* (Stuttgart, 1999).

15. Willibalt Apelt, *Geschichte der Weimarer Verfassung* (Munich, 1946), 306–7 and Fritz Stier-Stomlo, 'Artikel 109: Gleichheit vor dem Gesetz', in Hans-Carl Nipperdey (ed.), *Die Grundrechte und Grundpflichten der Reichsverfassung: Kommentar zum zweiten Teil der Reichsverfassung* (Berlin, 1929), 201–3.

16. Dr h.c. Alfred Wieruszowski, 'Artikel 119: Ehe, Familie, Mutterschaft', in Nipperdey (ed.), *Grundrechte und Grundpflichten*, 72–9.

17. Geh. Justizrat Prof. Dr Eduard Heilfron (ed.), *Die deutsche Nationalversammlung im Jahre 1919 [und 1920] in ihrer Arbeit für den Aufbau des neuen deutschen Volksstaates* (Berlin, 1919–20), vi. 3825.

18. Christiane Eifert, 'Coming to terms with the state: maternalist politics and the development of the welfare state in Germany', *Central European History*, 30/1 (1997), 45–6. Also see the path-breaking work of Young-Sun Hong, 'The contradictions of modernization in the German welfare state: gender and the politics of welfare reform in First World War Germany', *Social History*, 17 (1992), 251–70 and her *Welfare, Modernity and the Weimar State, 1919–1933* (Princeton, 1998).

19. See, for example, Raffael Scheck, *Mothers of the Nation: Right-Wing Women in Weimar Germany* (Oxford, 2004).

20. Marion Kaplan, 'Sisterhood under siege: feminism and anti-Semitism in Germany, 1904–1938', in *When Biology Became Destiny: Women in Weimar and Nazi Germany* (New York, 1984), 175–6.

21. Raffael Scheck, 'Women against Versailles: maternalism and nationalism of female bourgeois politicians in the early Weimar Republic', *German Studies Review*, 22 (1999), 21–42; Lora Wildenthal, *German Women for Empire, 1884–1945* (Durham, NC, 2001), chapter 5; Elizabeth Harvey, *Women and the Nazi East: Agents and Witnesses of Germanization* (New Haven, 2005), chapters 1–2.

22. Heidemarie Lauterer, *Parlamentarierinnen in Deutschland 1918/19–1949* (Königstein im Taunus, 2002). Also see Richard J. Evans, *Comrades and Sisters: Feminism, Socialism and Pacifism in Europe, 1870–1945* (Hove, Sussex, 1987).

23. See Young-sun Hong's chapter in this volume.

24. Katharina von Ankum (ed.), *Women in the Metropolis: Gender and Modernity in Weimar Culture* (Berkeley, 1997), 6.

25. Christiane Eifert, 'Marie Juchacz', in Henrike Hülsberger (ed.), *Stadtbild und Frauenleben: Berlin im Spiegel von 16 Frauenporträts* (Berlin, 1997), 105–22; also see Eifert's *Frauenpolitik und Wohlfahrtspflege: Zur Geschichte der sozialdemokratischen Arbeiterwohlfahrt* (Frankfurt, 1993).

26. Ute Gerhard, *Unerhört: Die Geschichte der deutschen Frauenbewegung* (Reinbek bei Hamburg, 1990); Richard J. Evans, *The Feminist Movement in Germany 1894–1933* (Oxford, 1976).

27. Ute Frevert, *Women in German History: From Bourgeois Emancipation to Sexual Liberation* (Oxford, 1989), 173–4.

28. Kaplan, 'Sisterhood under siege', 176–8.

29. Ibid. 180–8.

30. Whalen, *Bitter Wounds*, 95–9.

31. Gerhard, *Unerhört*, 370–2.

32. Frevert, *Women in German History*, 180–2; Siegfried Kracauer, *The Salaried Masses: Duty and Distraction in Weimar Germany*, trans. Quintin Hoare (London, 1998) (1st pub. as *Die Angestellten: Aus dem neuen Deutschland*, serialized in the *Frankfurter Zeitung*, 1929). Also see Patrice Petro, *Joyless Streets: Women and Melodramatic Representation in Weimar Germany* (Princeton, 1989).

33. Dagmar Reese, Eve Rosenhaft, Carola Sachse, and Tilla Siegel (eds.), *Rationale Beziehungen? Geschlechterverhältnisse im Rationalisierungsprozeß* (Frankfurt am Main, 1993), 'Einleitung', 7–8. See also the contribution by Adelheid von Saldern in this volume.

34. Peter Fritzsche, 'Did Weimar fail?', *Journal of Modern History*, 68/3 (Sept. 1996), 653–4. Here Fritzsche references the views of the late

Detlev J. K. Peukert in his study *Max Webers Diagnose der Moderne* (Göttingen, 1989).

35. Fritzsche, 'Did Weimar fail?', 652–4.

36. Atina Grossmann, *Reforming Sex: The German Movement for Birth Control and Abortion Reform, 1920–1950* (New York, 1995).

37. Mary Nolan, *Visions of Modernity: American Business and the Modernization of Germany* (New York, 1994).

38. Ibid., chapter 10 'Housework made easy', 206–35, especially here 207, 221.

39. Julia Sneeringer, 'The shopper as voter: women, advertising, and politics in post-inflation Germany', *German Studies Review*, 27/3 (Oct. 2004), 478–9, 486–7.

40. Bernd Widdig, *Culture and Inflation in Weimar Germany* (Berkeley, 2001), 200–3.

41. Detlev J. K. Peukert, *The Weimar Republic: The Crisis of Classical Modernity* (New York, 1987), 99–100. Mary Fulbook argues in a similar vein in her *Twentieth-Century Germany: Politics, Culture and Society, 1918–1990* (New York, 2001), 61–2. Also see Paul Bookbinder, *Weimar Germany: The Republic of the Reasonable* (Manchester, 1996), 187, and Frank Tipton, *A History of Modern Germany since 1815* (Berkeley, 2003), 354–5.

42. Fritzsche, 'Did Weimar fail?', 633.

43. Tani Barlow, Madeleine Yue Dong, Uta Poiger, Priti Ramamurthy, Lynn Thomas, and Alys Eve Weinbaum, 'The modern girl around the world: a research agenda and preliminary findings', *Gender & History*, 17/2 (Aug. 2005), 246.

44. Elizabeth Otto, *Tempo! Tempo! The Bauhaus Photomontages of Marianne Brandt* (Berlin, 2005), 9–10. Also see Maud Lavin, *Cut with the Kitchen Knife: The Weimar Photomontages of Hannah Höch* (New Haven, 1993).

45. Kerstin Barndt, *Sentiment und Sachlichkeit: Der Roman der neuen Frau in der Weimarer Republik* (Cologne, 2003). Also see Vibeke Rützou Petersen, *Women and Modernity in Weimar Germany: Reality and Representation in Popular Fiction* (New York, 2001).

46. Kerstin Barndt, 'Mothers, citizens and consumers: female readers in Weimar Germany', in Kathleen Canning, Kerstin Barndt, and Kristin McGuire (eds.), *Weimar Publics, Weimar Subjects: Rethinking the Political Culture of Germany in the 1920s* (New York, forthcoming 2009). Also see Richard W. McCormick, *Gender and Sexuality in Weimar Modernity: Film, Literature, and 'New Objectivity'* (New York, 2001).

47. Christiane Eifert, 'Die neue Frau: Bewegung und Alltag', in Manfred Görtemaker (ed.), *Weimar in Berlin: Porträt einer Epoche* (Berlin, 2002), 82–3.

48. Atina Grossmann, '*Girlkultur* or thoroughly rationalized female: a new woman in Weimar Germany?', in Judith Friedlander, Blanche W. Cook, Alice Kessler-Harris, and Carroll Smith-Rosenberg (eds.), *Women in Culture and Politics: A Century of Change* (Bloomington, Ind., 1986), 62–80.

49. Tina Campt, *Other Germans: Black Germans and the Politics of Race, Gender and Memory in the Third Reich* (Ann Arbor, 2005), especially chapter 1: 'Resonant echoes: the Rhineland campaign and converging specters of racial mixture', 31–62. Also see Christian Koller, '*Von Wilden aller Rassen niedergemetzelt': Die Diskussion um die Verwendung von Kolonialtruppen in Europa zwischen Rassismus, Kolonial- und Militärpolitik (1914–1930)* (Stuttgart, 2001).

50. Grossmann, *Reforming Sex*, 79–80; Cornelie Usborne, *The Politics of the Body in Weimar Germany* (Ann Arbor, 1992) and Cornelie Usborne, *Cultures of Abortion in Weimar Germany* (Oxford, 2007).

51. Grossmann, *Reforming Sex*, 20–1.

52. Sneeringer, *Winning Women's Votes*, 221–2; Grossmann, *Reforming Sex*, 78–9.

53. Grossmann, *Reforming Sex*, 79–92.

54. See, for example, the entry 'Die neue Frau', Deutsches Historisches Museum On-Line: <http://www.dhm.de/lemo/html/weimar/alltag/frau>, which contends: '[The image of the self-contained and independent "New Woman"] as a cultural and consumer-oriented phenomenon disappeared from everyday life as quickly as it had appeared.' On the place of the new woman in the campaign against paragraph 218, see Grossmann, *Reforming Sex*, 88, 94.

55. Evans, *The Feminist Movement*, 245–7.

56. Sneeringer, *Winning Women's Votes*, 223.

57. Ibid. 231–2.

The Weimar welfare system

Young-Sun Hong

Introduction

The Weimar Republic was the first polity to stake its legitimacy on its claim to be a social state that was responsible for actively promoting the well-being of its citizens. This commitment was written into the Weimar Constitution itself. Article 7 gave the Reich authority to legislate in the areas of welfare for the poor, veterans, and survivors; population policy; maternity, infant, and youth welfare; and labour legislation, worker protection, and social insurance. Marriage, the family, motherhood, children (especially the children of single mothers), and labour were singled out as objects of special solicitude (Arts. 119–22, 157). The economy was to be based on the principles of justice and individual dignity; the right to unionize was recognized; and citizens were guaranteed a nebulous right to work in exchange for an equally nebulous obligation to employ their energies for the common good (Arts. 151, 159, 163).

It is important to distinguish at the outset between social policy and social welfare. The purpose of social policy programmes, such as social insurance and labour legislation, was to alter the rules of the capitalist game in favour of the traditionally disadvantaged labouring classes in order to expand their rights and opportunities, ensure that as many of them as possible could provide for themselves and their families through their own industry, and thus strike a more stable balance between capitalism and democracy.

I would like to thank Larry Frohman for his helpful comments.

Welfare was something different. In contemporary terms, welfare was individualized help in the form of monetary aid was that to be combined with guidance, assistance, and often moral edification on the part of social professionals in order to educate and strengthen the character of precisely those people who could not satisfy their own basic needs without outside help—ostensibly because they could not live up to basic social norms regarding such things as work, hygiene, child raising, and household management.

The distinction between social policy and social welfare was drawn to a large degree along gender lines. German social legislation reflected and reinforced the prevailing norm of the male breadwinner family and the gender hierarchies and sexual division of labour on which it rested. The basic idea here was that women were essentially nurturing, caring beings whose natural maternal calling could be most fully realized within the private space of the home, and women's economic and political dependence on men was the correlate to their ostensible entitlement to protection and support from the male breadwinner, who would also be responsible for representing the 'private' family in the public domain. This was, of course, an ideological construct that had never corresponded to the realities of working-class life, but it nevertheless served to justify both the discriminatory treatment of women with regard to working conditions and the need for 'protection' to which these cultural and legal disabilities gave rise. While social policy legislation focused largely upon the needs of the male breadwinner, women's dependency made them the privileged object of individualizing welfare.

Although the war and the revolution marked a seismic shift in the parameters of social policy legislation, this chapter will focus on social welfare programmes, where wartime and post-war changes were no less dramatic. Not only did the social provisions of the Weimar Constitution expand the scope of direct state authority into areas that had previously been the domain of local, voluntary initiative. They also marked the breakthrough of a new kind of welfare whose underlying assumptions, methods, and political rationality differed in systematic ways from poor relief and charity in the nineteenth century.

The development of these new programmes, which consummated a development reaching back to the 1890s, was made possible by the emergence of a new form of social knowledge, a social perspective on poverty. This social perspective was based on the belief that the various manifestations of need—material destitution, disease, delinquency, and so on—were more the product of the social environment than of sin, sloth, or improvidence. The acceptance of these ideas marked the birth of a new, distinctly Progressive approach to social assistance known as 'social relief' or 'social welfare' (*soziale Fürsorge* and, after the First World War, *Wohlfahrtspflege*). Social welfare was qualitatively different from nineteenth-century poor relief and charity, which attributed need to individual moral failing and provided assistance in a deterrent, minimalist, and subsidiary manner in order to promote self-reliance. It was based upon a new understanding of the rights and duties of citizenship, new strategies for tackling the social problem, and new methods of social work. In an age of intensified imperialist rivalries, the health, productivity, culture, and political integration of the population became the key to national strength. As a result, the working population was increasingly seen more as a scarce resource that had to be rationally managed than as a source of political danger, while dependency, illness, delinquency, and crime represented costs to the nation that could no longer be tolerated. These concerns made the social problem into a matter of overriding national importance, provided a compelling rationale for the expansion of public (both state and voluntary) programmes to rationalize the reproductive culture of the working classes, and justified the shift from deterrence to prevention.

The recognition of the social or structural causes of need also implied the existence of new forms of interdependency which gave new rights to both the individual and society—and which imposed new obligations upon them. Since the failure of any single individual to maximize his or her potential posed a risk to or a burden on society, the fortunes and well-being of this individual could not be a matter of indifference to the community, which found itself individually and collectively obligated—in ways which were unimaginable for classical liberalism—to take positive steps to promote the development of all individual members of the nation. On the one hand, this implied that the needy had a social right to the assistance that would equip them to discharge the duties that society imposed upon them as fathers, mothers, workers, soldiers, and citizens. Moreover, since every individual was potentially needy, the emergence of welfare as a positive obligation for the state also entailed the generalization of welfare from the poor to all citizens as it became the central mechanism for the rational and efficient production of a population of physically fit and culturally competent citizens, who quite literally embodied the economic, demographic, and military potential of the nation. On the other hand, this expansion of social rights also entailed a concomitant expansion of both individual obligations towards the community and the rights of the community to compel the individual to anticipate, prevent, and treat need in all its diverse forms in order to secure the 'risk-free existence' ('der risikofreie Mensch') which represented the perfection of this secularized utopia. Although the social work profession only came into its own during the First World War, during the Weimar Republic social workers were the technicians of social modernity and the apostles of social reconciliation. Social workers sought to gain influence and leverage over their clients by appealing alternately to the authority of science, the authority of the state, and the ideology of helping and selfless service. However, their own experience of the resistance of the needy to their guidance and their inability to alleviate the structural causes of need through individualizing casework ensured that social workers would be as much critics of the welfare state as its agents.

Historiographical parameters

The most important study of the German welfare system in the period of classical modernity is Detlev Peukert's *Limits of Social Discipline*, published in 1986. Drawing on the work of the social theorist Jürgen Habermas, Peukert argued that the development of youth welfare in Germany from the 1880s into the Third Reich was driven by the efforts of Progressives to combat what they perceived as social disorder and juvenile delinquency by rationalizing the life-world of working-class urban youth in accordance with norms of family life, domestic culture, hygiene, and industry that were drawn from the middle classes. In so arguing, Peukert cut the ground out from under the *Sonderweg* literature, which had sought to explain how a backwards-looking, authoritarian state could have developed one of the most modern welfare systems in the world, and provided an alternative framework that enabled historians to see the new preventive social welfare programmes as a quintessential expression of modernity.

However, Peukert also recast the terms of the debate in a second, unexpected direction that called into question the positive connection between modernity and welfare. According to Peukert, the first generation of youth welfare reformers developed new forms of scientific knowledge to define and diagnose this deviance and new programmes and institutions in order to monitor wayward and endangered youth, control them, and re-educate them in accordance with these social scientific norms. The problem was that there always remained a core group of delinquent youth whose behaviour could not be reformed through pedagogical means alone, and the resulting frustration with this group led social workers to seek ways of disciplining those incorrigibles whose open rebellion threatened to bring the entire pedagogical project into disrepute. When the depression hit, it began to appear more reasonable to many to repress these asocial delinquents and concentrate on helping those who allowed themselves to be helped, rather than investing even more resources in a seemingly quixotic and wasteful attempt to reform the incorrigible. In turn, the growing influence of eugenics on social policy and the subsequent equation of incorrigibility with hereditary inferiority provided a rationale for the permanent exclusion of these marginal youths from the body politic. This authoritarian unravelling of the scientific optimism of the youth welfare movement led Peukert to conclude that liberal modernity was not, in fact, intrinsically emancipatory, but rather politically contradictory, and that the peculiar combination of fascist authoritarianism and racist social policies characteristic of National Socialism represented a pathological possibility latent in the Progressive project that could be—and was—realized under specific circumstances.[1]

All of the subsequent literature has been forced to engage with Peukert's interpretation and the broader conclusions that he drew from this study, even if subsequent work has been critical of his explanation of the birth of the Holocaust out of the spirit of Progressive social engineering.[2] The legacies of the war forced the Weimar welfare system to take on tasks that overtaxed its political and economic resources. But more important than this in explaining the failure of Weimar Progressivism were the political dynamics unleashed by the war and the expansion of the welfare state itself.

On the one hand, the massive expansion of social services that began in the second half of the war led first to the growth of a number of centralized, nationwide umbrella organizations: the Catholic Caritasverband, the Lutheran Inner Mission, the Social Democratic Workers' Welfare, the conservative German Red Cross, and the Fifth Welfare League (a moderately conservative organization that focused primarily on hospitals and hygiene), as well as minor players such as the Central Welfare Bureau for German Jewry and various Communist self-help organizations. Progressives, municipal officials, and the women's movement (all of whom overlapped with one another in varying degrees) were represented by the German Association for Public and Private Welfare, the most influential expert group in the field during the Weimar Republic. The political and ideological cleavages among these organizations mirrored those of the polity itself. The expansion of the public welfare bureaucracy unleashed an intense struggle among these organizations for control over the system in order to ensure that the efforts of social workers to influence the needy reflected their own specific values and world-view. The authoritarian proclivities of many social institutions during the Weimar years were due as much to the successful resistance of these conservative organizations to Progressive social pedagogy as to the contradictions within Progressivism itself.[3]

On the other hand, the poor themselves began to mobilize to assert their rights.[4] The overwhelming majority of the persons assisted by the Weimar welfare system were people whose need was a direct (military) or indirect (economic) consequence of the war, not the traditional recipients of municipal poor relief. These persons were in a position to make demands upon the state by virtue of their wartime sacrifices or their status as victims of state policies, and these were moral and political debts that could not be paid off in the currency of poor relief. At the same time that these groups were competing with one another for scarce public resources, their demands for financial compensation and moral recognition clashed with the insistence by the professionals who staffed the new social bureaucracy that their claims would have to be determined individually on the basis of medical, legal, and welfare expertise.

As a result, the everyday encounters of the new poor with welfare officials and social workers increasingly alienated these persons from the very institutions that had been created to meet their material needs, rather than integrating them politically into the new republic. All of these problems combined to set in motion a politically corrosive circle: the increasingly well-organized and mobilized groups of the new poor campaigned for a statutory pension system that would take the determination of social services out of the hands of these experts or, failing this, to secure greater representation within the public welfare system in order to protect their own interests, while the new social professionals relied on the rhetoric of expertise, political neutrality, and selfless helping to limit the influence of the new poor on welfare policy and practice, with public officials at both the local and the national level striving vainly to satisfy competing political demands with the limited financial resources available to them. The outcome of this clash between competing modernities—of scientific expertise and democratic participation—was a hybrid between a pension plan and individualized welfare services. This arrangement satisfied no one, and these conflicts dragged on throughout the 1920s before the specific point of contention was submerged in the rising tide of misery during the depression.

Unemployment relief

The precipitous end of the war and the hasty demobilization of the army unleashed a flood of nearly 6 million soldiers back onto the labour market that was itself caught in the throes of the transition from wartime to peacetime production. There was no way that all of these men—and the women whom they displaced from wartime industries—could expect to find immediate employment. Assistance to the able-bodied unemployed had largely been anathema in the pre-war years. However, the impending reality of mass distress and the fear that this could further radicalize the revolution that was under way led to the creation of the first systematic unemployment relief programme on 13 November 1918, only four days after the proclamation of the republic. Eligibility was predicated on ability and willingness to work; women enjoyed only limited rights under the law, while their subordinate status was reflected in the graduation of relief according to the number of persons dependent upon the normatively male family head and breadwinner. Although unemployment relief was means tested and administered by welfare committees to be established by local government, it was to be separate from poor relief and to entail none of the stigma associated with public assistance.

This unemployment relief programme was important for two reasons. First, in addition to its perpetuation of the breadwinner model, it marked the recognition that the inability to find work was a structural risk of the capitalist labour market, not a sign of sloth or weakness of character. Second, the establishment of the unemployment relief programme set a precedent that could not easily be reversed. While the system had to be continuously adapted to external contingencies and its own internal inadequacies, the proposed solutions were by turns unsatisfactory to every major stakeholder. The idea of an unemployment insurance system, which had been largely confined to the realm of social policy speculation before the war, gradually emerged—under the changed political parameters of the republic—as the most viable solution to the problem of assistance to the unemployed.

One of the most important reforms of the unemployment relief system was effected by the July 1922 Labour Exchange Law. The Law institutionalized what until that point had been viewed as a temporary expedient while placing its administration in the hands of the municipal labour exchanges that were to be established under the law. Before the war, this integration of unemployment assistance and labour exchanges had been one of the most important demands of social reformers, who regarded this as the precondition for further progress towards an unemployment insurance system. There was an intrinsic tension within the system between the desire to provide adequate assistance to those without work and the need to limit benefits, restrict eligibility, and impose work tests in order to give the unemployed an incentive to find work on their own. Part of the problem was that, if assistance were set high enough to ensure adequate support, then these rates would approximate, if not equal, the local wage for unskilled labour, thus diminishing the incentive to find work. However, every attempt to more finely calibrate assistance rates and eligibility conditions was thoroughly thwarted by the hyperinflation and the collapse of the economy, which sent the unemployment rate through the roof.

The 15 October 1923 Enabling Law fundamentally restructured the unemployment relief system. It introduced contributions (with workers and employers each paying 40 per cent of the cost of the programme with local government picking up the remaining 20 per cent) and limited eligibility to persons who had paid contributions to the sickness insurance funds for at least twenty-six weeks during the previous year. Benefits were still means tested, and there was no right to benefits that corresponded to the mandatory contributions. But once contributions had been introduced as a means of reducing the burden on Reich finances, workers began to demand the guarantee of a right to benefits commensurate with their earnings and contributions, and both workers and employers sought a role in the administration of the system that was proportional to their share of the cost of the programme. From this point on, it was only a matter of time until the relief system was transformed into a formal insurance system.

The July 1927 Labour Exchange and Unemployment Insurance Law was perhaps the most important piece of social policy legislation passed during the Weimar Republic. It was also one of the most fateful ones. While the law embodied the social aspirations of the Weimar coalition, it immediately became the focus of the intense conflict between organized labour and organized capital that played a major role in undermining the parliamentary system. While the unemployment insurance system was never designed to support millions of unemployed through an extended structural crisis like the depression that engulfed Germany after 1929 (thus forcing millions of unemployed back onto unemployment relief and general welfare), the fact that the Reich government was obligated to cover the deficits of the system meant that the unemployment insurance system directly transformed debates over labour market policy and the cost of unemployment insurance into constitutional issues that led many conservative and business circles to the conclusion that the only way to successfully reform the Weimar welfare state was to overturn the parliamentary system itself.

Veterans, dependants, survivors, and the other new poor

German programmes for assisting disabled veterans, their families, and their survivors exemplify both the forced modernization of social welfare under the influence of total war and the contradictions of the welfare system that emerged out of this process. While other belligerent countries granted pensions to disabled veterans primarily in recognition of their service and sacrifice, the German military pension system was based on the principle that the welfare of disabled veterans, and that of the nation as a whole, could best be guaranteed by reintegrating these men back into the productive life of the nation, where they could reassert their dignity by again fulfilling their roles as productive citizens and fathers.

On the one hand, this meant that military disability pensions were graduated according to the degree of disability and set at such a level that in the absence of other property and income only completely disabled veterans could survive without working. On the other hand, this financial stick was coupled with extensive regenerative treatment, social services, and social policy measures to facilitate the occupational rehabilitation of these men. While these programmes prefigured the therapeutic principles of the Weimar welfare system, they also institutionalized the systemic conflict between the new poor, who based their demands on a discourse of sacrifice and service, and the new social experts, who condemned the new social politics as an illegitimate politicization of helping while at the same time deploying a productivist discourse that in practice subordinated the rights demanded by the new poor to the imperatives of national reconstruction. This conflict proved to be irreconcilable, and it remained a sore on the body politic until the end of the republic.[5]

Medical treatment and rehabilitative therapy for disabled veterans was provided by the military, which could draw on advances in orthopaedics and surgery and the expertise of the disability insurance funds in the area of therapeutic assistance to help wounded veterans regain the fullest possible use of their injured bodies. However, already during the war a new form of social welfare had grown up around this kernel of medical and rehabilitative treatment. This included such services as occupational counselling and retraining, assistance in finding work, and a variety of other measures designed to ease the transition back into former occupations, or into new ones. These programmes were known as social welfare for the 'war-damaged' or *Kriegsbeschädigtenfürsorge*. This was a new term, which early on in the war supplanted the traditional language of war cripples, and it reflected the more modern therapeutic and productivist principles underlying the German approach to the welfare of disabled veterans.

These wartime programmes were codified soon after the war and formed the basis of veterans' welfare throughout the Weimar Republic. In February 1919, the Reich finally assumed responsibility for the welfare of disabled veterans, an idea that had been broached as early as autumn 1914, but that had been left in legal and political limbo pending the end of the war. Meanwhile, the programmes developed during the war were formally codified by the May 1920 Reich Pension Law, which regulated pensions and individualized medical and social services for the estimated 1,537,000 disabled veterans and 1,945,000 survivors. One of the basic principles of wartime welfare—one that contrasted sharply with traditional poor relief and charity—was that it should be sufficient to maintain dependants and survivors in their social position. This principle was carried over in attenuated form into the Pension Law, though its preamble noted that even the claims of veterans and survivors—the most privileged groups of welfare recipients—would have to take account of the general decline in the standard of living due to the war.

While pensions were graduated according to the degree of disability, the law provided for supplements of 25 per cent for persons who had worked in occupations requiring substantial knowledge and skills and 50 per cent for those who had occupied what were called positions of special responsibility. The Pension Law also codified the practice of guaranteeing veterans and survivors representation in the national and local bodies that set policy for these programmes. This law was itself supplemented by the April 1920 law requiring that public employers and firms meeting certain criteria reserve a specified percentage of their positions for severely disabled veterans and workers who had been disabled by industrial accidents. This grouping of the disabled veterans of war and work reflected the Progressive vision of a unitary welfare system that would be based not on group distinctions, but on the individualizing determination of need by trained professionals and the graduation of assistance according to the expected contribution of the beneficiary to the productive life of the nation.

The welfare programmes for widows and orphans that were codified in the Reich Pension Law had also grown out of wartime practice, and they, too, broke with traditional poor relief and charity in important ways. The Reich government was obligated to pay separation allowances to the families of men serving in the military, though this concept was steadily expanded through the war years to include virtually any person who had actually been supported by the soldier, including illegitimate children, whom all other legislation regarded as not related to the father. In addition, the delivery agencies responsible for administering these separation allowances were also required to make supplementary payments to these allowances (often as much again as the separation allowances themselves). These payments, in turn, could be supplemented by assistance by voluntary organizations, which were increasingly drawn into the administration of these public programmes, especially in terms of house visiting to determine the needs of mothers and children, something for which those women who performed most of this work were believed to be peculiarly well suited. All of this voluntary assistance (including monetary assistance and individualized social services) beyond the statutory separation allowances was known as 'wartime welfare' or *Kriegswohlfahrtspflege*.

In earlier wars, the welfare of soldiers' families had been regarded primarily as a matter for local charities. However, the First World War was fought by an entire nation mobilized for war, with nearly half of all men of military age serving in the armed forces between

1914 and 1918. The goal of wartime welfare had been to maintain the spirit of the men fighting at the front by ensuring the welfare of the home front. In contrast to municipal poor relief, which provided only an existence minimum (and provided this only under harshly deterrent terms and burdened with political disabilities and social stigma), wartime welfare was legally separate from poor relief and aimed at securing for these women and children a *social* existence minimum that would allow them to maintain their pre-war income and living standard.

The extension of such benefits to millions of women and children during the war represented a serious challenge to the principles of deterrent poor relief. Moreover, separation allowances and wartime welfare were also deeply paternalist and were designed to maintain the breadwinner family. The order of the home, and, by extension, the very foundations of society, were believed to be endangered by the temporary or permanent absence of so many family fathers, and the purpose of the new social welfare programmes for dependants and survivors was to provide the guidance and support needed to fill this void. In the words of one leading welfare reformer, 'families must be provided [with] what they lack: this is not, in the first instance, money, but rather the direction and leadership of the family head.'[6] If these *Kriegerfrauen* (war wives) enjoyed an entitlement to welfare programmes by virtue of the military service of their breadwinner, this was not an unlimited or unconditional right: these women were expected to adhere to certain social norms and devote their energies to their domestic and maternal duties or, in certain instances, productive labour, and these obligations created an opening through which social workers could monitor and discipline these women and children and promote more modern, rational approaches to the entire spectrum of maternal tasks. However, wartime welfare programmes also had the potential to unsettle this gender order because the transformation of mothering from a private into a public concern made it possible to at least raise the question of women's citizenship.

The Reich Pension Law established pensions for women, children, and dependent parents whose husbands or breadwinner had been killed in the war. Since survivors' pensions were determined as a percentage of the pension to which these men would have been entitled in case of complete disability, they too were pegged to civilian income and social status, rather than military rank, as had been the case with the pre-war military pension system. This was an important change that reflected the changing relations between military and society in the age of total war. The base pension for war widows was 30 per cent of the amount to which a fully disabled husband would have been entitled; this was raised to 50 per cent if the woman was unable to work because of physical condition, childcare obligations, or advanced age (50 or older); and dependent children were entitled to an additional 15 per cent. These pension rates were in part set so low in order to encourage these women to remarry, and about 40 per cent of these war widows did so in the immediate post-war years, though approximately 360,000 women continued to receive pensions until the end of the 1920s and beyond. The Pension Law also provided for medical assistance and individualized social services to help war widows maintain their household and provide a proper upbringing and education so that their children could attain the social position that they could have been expected to occupy were it not for the war. In contrast to poor relief, the social dimension of both the pension system and these individualized services lay in this concern for the maintenance of the income, lifestyle, and expectations of the family and for the impact of family life upon the quality of the population and the strength of the nation.

There were two other important components of the new, post-war poor who found themselves dependent on state assistance. On the one hand, wartime and post-war inflation reduced the real value of financial assets (i.e. savings, bonds, annuities, and insurance policies) to such a degree that many members of the middle classes saw themselves effectively impoverished. These déclassé pensioners, or *Kleinrentner*, were joined by other members of the commercial and professional middle classes who saw their standard of living and social status decimated by inflation, the forced closure of their businesses due to the death or absence of the male and/or wartime shortages. On the other hand, the pensioners of the social insurance system, or *Sozialrentner*, also saw the real value of their benefits decline at the same time that high post-war unemployment rates effectively shut them out from the kinds of work that they had traditionally relied on to make ends meet. The continued rise in prices across the early 1920s, and the subsequent hyperinflation, forced the Reich government to grant across-the-board increases in veterans' and survivors' pensions, and many cities improvised welfare programmes for the impoverished middle classes.

The Reich Social Welfare Law

These developments brought to the fore another issue that had been simmering since the early war years: what would be the impact of wartime welfare on the poor relief system? Municipal relief officials had long claimed that generous separation allowances and wartime welfare programmes were weakening the work ethic and encouraging the dangerous notion that the poor had a right to assistance. They regarded across-the-board increases as wasteful and corrosive, and they argued that the public good would be much better served by the individualized determination of need based on the careful investigation of family, character, and circumstances. There was also a strong affinity between this fiscal interest in the individualized determination of need and the Progressive idea that social rights should be based on the expert determination of the future contribution of the needy individual to the productive life of the nation, rather than on either past sacrifice or service to the nation or past moral failings. Many Progressives argued that the individualized determination of need was more just than schematic pension programmes and that the extension of this approach to all groups of the needy could serve as a powerful lever for modernizing all forms of public assistance in accordance with the preventive, therapeutic principles pioneered since the war. On the other hand, the poor themselves feared that fiscal interests would win out over progressive ideals and that individualization would instead be used to level benefits downwards and ultimately lump together the respectable groups of the new poor with those disreputable persons who had been traditionally assisted by municipal poor relief. What the new poor wanted were special welfare programmes that spelled out their entitlement to certain levels and kinds of benefits and committed the Reich government to funding these programmes and policing the fiscal machinations of local government. These conflicts intensified as the Mark spiralled down into the abyss of the hyperinflation, dragging the real economy down with it.

The February 1924 Reich Social Welfare Law (*Reichsverordnung über die Fürsorgepflicht*) and the subsequent guidelines for its implementation were an attempt to bring order to the delivery and financing of the sprawling social welfare system during this period of chaos and economic collapse, while at the same time responding to these demands for entitlements and systematically reforming the poor laws. This law, which was pushed through as part of the post-inflation stabilization package, was the most important piece of legislation in the field since the creation of the Prussian relief residence system in the 1840s. It consolidated all of the separate social welfare programmes created since the war, as well as poor relief, maternity benefits, and other programmes, in the hands of municipal welfare offices in hopes of achieving greater economy and effectiveness, while the 1931 Third Emergency Tax Decree restored to the cities the fiscal autonomy and resources needed to fund these programmes. It abolished the relief residence system, which for more than eighty years had been the basic mechanism for redistributing the total cost of poor relief nationwide between rural areas of outmigration and industrializing cities, in favour of the principle that the locale where a person lived at the onset of need should be responsible for the necessary assistance. The law also allowed the states to regulate the rights of welfare recipients to participate in setting welfare policy, though it stipulated that these rights had to be at least as extensive as those guaranteed by the Reich Pension Law. But the Reich Social Welfare Law focused primarily on organizational matters, and rules governing the actual provision of assistance were contained in the supplementary guidelines, which were issued in December 1924, after nearly a year of bitter conflict among all stakeholders.

Over the strenuous opposition of all of the groups represented in the German Association for Public and Private Welfare, who wanted to make prevention and rehabilitation on the basis of the individualized determination of need and benefits into the basis of a unitary welfare system, the Labour Ministry reaffirmed the right of specific groups of the new poor—veterans, survivors, *Kleinrentner*, and *Sozialrentner*— to monetary assistance and social services that were to be qualitatively superior to those available to persons who did not belong to these enumerated groups. Though this decision was made (in the words of a Labour Ministry official) less to positively discriminate in favour of these groups than to protect them from the fiscal interests of local government, it reflected the irreconcilable opposition between two competing modernities. This decision meant that two people whose personal circumstances and needs were identical could be treated differently simply because one of the persons belonged to one of these groups and the other did not. While this may have reflected the modernity of democratic politics, in the eyes of Progressives it offended grievously against the modernity of science and the norms of equity in ways that could only further encourage the subordination of expert knowledge to interest group politics. As Wilhelm Polligkeit, the chair of the German Association for Public and Private Welfare and the most influential welfare expert during the republic, warned, any violation of the principle of individualization and the establishment of special rights for any group of persons would unleash 'orgies of group egoism'.[7]

These guidelines, however, did not bring the issue to an end. The problem was that, in view of the financial constraints that followed upon the currency stabilization, assistance rates for all groups of welfare beneficiaries, including the unemployed, had been set artificially low. While the various groups of the new poor called on the national government to raise assistance rates across the board and to strengthen their legal claims to minimum benefits, municipal officials argued in an equally predictable manner that such 'schematic' increases were wasteful and expensive and should be abandoned in favour of supplemental payments for particularly needy families based on the individualizing investigation of their circumstances. The outcome of this renewed cycle was a hybrid between a state pension system and individualizing system of social services. This satisfied no one, and across the second half of the decade this unresolved problem alienated everyone from the state and the parliamentary system until the depression, when the distress of these groups lost its distinct political contours among the general impoverishment of the depression.

Welfare, corporatism, and the Weimar state

The 1922 Reich Youth Welfare Law was one of the most important and controversial laws passed during the republic, but not so much for its topic (to which we shall later return) as for the questions it raised about the nature of the Weimar state and the commitment of broad sectors of the population to the parliamentary system. The conflicts here prefigured, and contributed substantially to, the ultimate crisis of the republic, and they showed how the rhetoric and reality of the democratic process could be used to legitimize illiberal, exclusionist, and ultimately authoritarian politics. The basic question here was the extent to which state agencies, i.e. the proposed municipal welfare offices, should be directly involved in providing social services to the needy population. This was such a sensitive issue because most charity or welfare organizations, but especially the confessional organizations, believed that social work was primarily a pedagogical undertaking since what the needy most often needed was education, friendly guidance, and a stronger moral centre rather than material assistance. Without this guidance, they insisted, material assistance would be at best ineffective and at worst positively harmful.

Religion was the key here. While the doctrine of brotherly love drew people into charitable work, the belief in such selfless service enabled social workers to gain the trust of the needy, which was the precondition for helping them, while religious doctrine itself provided the basis for their pedagogical labours. However, not only did this view of the nature of need and the mission of social work imply that the social worker had to be of the same confession as the needy. It also meant that such activity had to fall under the purview of the Church, not secular authorities, because only the Church was competent to guide such work and judge whether it reflected a proper understanding of religious dogma. In this matter, confessional welfare was often supported by a substantial segment of the Progressives, who generally advocated a more humanistic or inter-confessional basis for social pedagogy, but whose belief in the importance of voluntary social engagement led them to support the churches in their opposition to the direct provision of social services by public employees.

To a large degree, this controversy over public youth welfare paralleled the debate over secular public schooling. The issue had come up during the war with regard to the state regulation of charitable fund-raising and the proposed Prussian youth welfare law that had been discussed in the last few months before the end of the war. But the revolution raised the stakes because one of the major goals of the Social Democrats was to nationalize (or communalize) the welfare system and bring it under the control of properly constituted democratic authorities in order to eliminate traditional paternalism and discrimination against the working classes. They were especially hostile towards the church charities, whom they regarded as the worst offenders in this regard. For their part, the confessional welfare organizations equated public control of youth welfare, especially in those areas where local government was dominated by Social Democracy, with the victory of a materialistic, atheistic world-view. It was the proposed Reich youth welfare law, which was to give substance to the constitutional pronouncements regarding the welfare of the nation's youth, that brought the matter to a head.

The law that was passed in 1922 represented a clear triumph for the confessional welfare organizations that was to have a huge short- and long-term impact on the shape of the German welfare system. Instead of laying the foundation for the public supplementary education of needy youth, as the original advocates of public youth welfare had desired, the law actually served to shield voluntary welfare from the encroachment of public agencies. The law, whose passage owed much to the pivotal position of the Catholic Centre Party in the Weimar coalition, permitted the new youth welfare offices to delegate their statutory responsibilities to voluntary organizations (a provision that was sharpened during the currency crisis), and it guaranteed voluntary welfare representation within the welfare offices to ensure that they would not be frozen out by public officials. These provisions effectively codified the principle of the subsidiarity of public welfare in relation to voluntary initiative (and, incidentally, thus laid the foundation for the current 'pillarized' or corporatist organization of the welfare sector in which these voluntary yet quasi-public organizations bear

194 | YOUNG-SUN HONG

primary responsibility for delivering social services to those needy
persons who share the basic world-view of these providers—based
on public subsidies and under only the loose supervision of public
authorities).

Although this corporatist organization of the welfare sector was
supposed to diminish conflict among the various organizations by
removing their internal affairs from external oversight and control,
such conflicts could not be repressed forever. Just as the confessional organizations claimed the right to care for those persons
who had been born into one of the churches, so Workers' Welfare
(Arbeiterwohlfahrt) claimed to be the natural representative of the
working classes. Given the degree of overlap between these groups,
this was an important question, and it gave rise to a bitter cultural
struggle in the second half of the decade that revealed nothing so
much as the shallowness of the commitment to democracy on the
part of the religious welfare organizations and the churches. In the
end, the stabilization of the corporatist system of welfare required
the exclusion of Social Democracy and a break with parliamentary
government, but the support of the confessional charities for the
Nazi campaign to overthrow the republic moved them out of the
republican frying pan and into the totalitarian fire.[8]

Social hygiene, social discipline, and the question of continuities between Weimar welfare and Nazi racism

I want to turn now to specific programmes developed under
the republic, especially in the areas of social hygiene and youth
welfare, because these programmes reflected most clearly the liberal
optimism concerning the ability to prevent or cure the manifold
forms of need that had once been regarded as natural or God
ordained. Scientific discourses constituted these new forms of
need as objects of knowledge, spelled out through their definition
of these problems the strategies to be followed in combating them,
and provided a rationale for doing so. In turn, this biopolitical
concern with a healthy, productive population as the foundation

of national existence provided the foil for the construction of social rights, such as the 'right to education', the right to health, and other social rights that corresponded to the obligations imposed upon them as citizens. The question, though, is not only how did these programmes work, but also what did they mean to their ostensible beneficiaries?

For two decades, now, the history of welfare state formation has been theorized as a process of social discipline. The concepts of social discipline and medicalization are used to describe, on the one hand, the process by which ostensibly universal, scientific norms of public and private comportment with regard to such matters as labour, hygiene, procreation, time economy, bodily self-control, and so on are internalized to produce 'normal' subjects and citizens who embody the virtues on which the social order is believed to rest. The institutions and social practices in which these norms are embodied act in an economical, continuous, and all-pervasive manner to govern everyday comportment, both public and private, and the meaning that we attribute to these actions, and in this way they produce normal subjects and citizens whose field of strategic rationality is determined by these internalized norms.

On the other hand, social discipline also means the process by which the behaviour of social deviants is corrected and brought into accordance with these social norms. It is this possibility of deviance that creates the space for social intervention, and within this space welfare can operate in different ways: to integrate normal subjects tightly into the community through ever-vigilant efforts to keep them from deviating from the social norm; to reintegrate those persons or groups who are deemed to have the potential to become fully-fledged members of the community, but who have failed to do so due to inadequate socialization; or to protect the social body from two groups—reprobates who, although potentially members, have proven themselves to be hopelessly irredeemable, and those persons who, by their very nature, are regarded as incapable of integration into the community and whose difference makes them into real or imaginary threats to its very existence. Although the social discipline paradigm clearly captures the logical connections between the constitution of need, surveillance of the needy and the endangered, and the measures to normalize and regulate this population, in its stronger versions (such as Peukert's) it ignores the fact that people both welcomed and resented welfarist intervention because these programmes both enhanced the welfare of the needy in some ways while restricting it in others, often at the same time. Consequently, in looking at social hygiene and youth welfare programmes we need to be more sensitive to their contradictions and ambiguities.

The two most important preventive social hygiene programmes were those designed to combat tuberculosis and infant mortality. These programmes were inspired by the social hygiene tradition and its insistence that the higher incidence of these diseases among the working classes was due to their living and working conditions, in the broadest sense, rather than to morality or heredity, and their goal was less to treat individuals than to prevent disease by breaking the circle of contagion and infection. The success of these programmes was predicated on the ability to do three things: seek out the sources of infection and systematically monitor endangered populations, secure timely medical treatment for affected individuals, and explain to the untutored working classes the bacterial causes of tuberculosis and infant mortality and the principles of personal and domestic hygiene that they had to follow to protect themselves, their families, and the general public from these threats.

The cornerstones of these programmes, and the institutional embodiment of this preventive project, were the tuberculosis and infant welfare centres or dispensaries (*Fürsorgestellen*).[9] These centres relied on a variety of incentives (including free medical consultations, though not treatment, and monetary payments to encourage mothers to breastfeed their children) to draw potential clientele into them. The physicians employed there would then have the opportunity to examine these visitors and enlighten them concerning the relevant hygienic principles. In turn, social workers would be dispatched to visit these people in their homes to assess the need for social services, advise the family on how best to put medical advice into practice, monitor compliance with this advice, and reproach those who did not comply.

The first of these welfare centres had been established already in 1899, and they spread steadily in the pre-war years before expanding explosively during the war. By the mid-1920s, the nation was covered by a network of such centres. In 1924, there were 4,781 infant welfare centres, 2,608 welfare centres for pre-school-age children, and 2,144 counselling centres for pregnant women, and in 1926 there were over 3,000 tuberculosis centres. These centres and their associated programmes were pillars of the Weimar welfare system. The maternity assistance programme that was established in December 1914 helped to accelerate the spread of the maternal advice and infant welfare centres under the republic. This programme offered a number of benefits to the needy wives of men who were serving in the military, and it was a sign of the *populationist* concerns of the time that these benefits were also extended—against the opposition of religious conservatives—to unmarried women.[10] The programme was carried over into peace-time under different eligibility conditions, and it was revised several times during the 1920s.

But this concern for infant welfare also pointed in two other directions. On the one hand, it led towards a greater focus on counselling and social services for pregnant women within an expanded mission of the infant welfare centres. This was an issue that could either be conceptualized in narrowly medical, obstetrical terms or seen as part of a broader complex of social, sexual, and reproductive distress, which was the approach favoured by the sexual or marital advising centres established during the republic.[11] On the other hand, there was little use in devoting so much energy to saving infants if these gains were dissipated by a lack of concern for their health and welfare as they grew older. This led to new initiatives in the field of 'early childhood welfare' (*Kleinkinderfürsorge*) and school hygiene.

The capstone of these Weimar social hygiene programmes was the activities of the German Hygiene Museum in Dresden and the 1926 GESOLEI exhibition, whose title was a condensation of the terms health, social welfare, and physical fitness. Both of these highlighted the importance of hygiene enlightenment in bridging the gap between medical expertise and the broader lay public. The underlying assumption here was that the success of preventive social hygiene depended on the informed collaboration of the people themselves, not coercion or mute obedience to the authority of science or the state. The organizers of these and other exhibitions sought creative ways to make complex processes comprehensible to the uneducated, and to do so in ways that would ensure that the viewers drew the proper conclusions from what they saw. These exhibitions reflected both a broader concern with physical culture and the rational, economic management of the human body and the biological resources of the nation and a confidence in the ability to use the latest advances in medical science to solve the social problem.[12]

The success of these social hygiene programmes depended more on hygiene enlightenment and convincing endangered groups to collaborate in the preventive project than it did on either material incentives or repression. The social discipline literature has underestimated both the degree to which the labouring classes valued these programmes and their positive impact on the health and well-being of these groups. Much of the recent literature on Weimar social hygiene has been written in the shadow of the Holocaust, and it has been concerned with uncovering the discursive origins of Nazi racial and social policies in seemingly Progressive policies of the Wilhelmine and Weimar years. Eugenic ideas did, in fact, permeate the social language of the Weimar Republic, especially within the medical community, and it was easy to view preventive social hygiene measures as positive eugenics. However, it needs to be emphasized that the architects of these preventive social hygiene programmes came out of a different intellectual tradition and that their understanding of prevention was based on educating rather than physically eliminating the unfit and the asocial.[13]

Youth welfare

Many of these points also hold true for the other innovative field of social engagement: youth welfare.[14] Here, as in so many other areas, the critical innovations had already been made before the war, and they were simply codified by the 1922 National Youth Welfare Law, though they assumed a new importance as part of a plan to reconstruct the nation in the aftermath of the Great War. While the law recognized that parents had primary responsibility for raising their children, it also followed the pre-war youth welfare movement in insisting that, since the state had a legitimate interest in the physical, intellectual, and spiritual development of its future citizens, it had the obligation to step in to secure the rights of the child whenever parents were unable to fulfil their duties. The scope of public responsibility for needy youth was expanded by the law and transformed from the provision of a minimal level of material assistance to destitute children to the prevention of all forms of juvenile need. The law required the creation of separate youth welfare offices, though this mandate was later weakened during the currency collapse. In much the same way as the tuberculosis and infant welfare centres, the youth welfare offices were to be the organizational focus for these efforts to prevent juvenile delinquency and criminality by seeking out and monitoring endangered youth so as to correct their incipient waywardness through timely pedagogical interventions. Though the law was intended to assist parents and strengthen the family, this expansion of the rights of the child and the duties of the state inevitably altered the relation between the child, the family, and the state.

To achieve this expanded mission, the law brought a broad spectrum of programmes, ranging from infant protection to correctional education, within the competence of the youth welfare offices, though (as noted above) the law was written in such a way as to encourage the delegation of the actual provision of these services to voluntary organizations. The law also regulated foster care, guardianship (and innovations here had been the key to extending public supervision over endangered youth in the pre-war years), and assistance for poor children (which was thereby removed from the scope of the poor laws and integrated into pedagogical tasks of the youth welfare system). It contained the first national regulations on probation for juvenile offenders, which had been introduced before the war on an ad hoc local basis, and correctional education (*Fürsorgeerziehung*, or reform schooling), where it extended Prussian legislation to the entire nation with only minor modifications. These latter sections of the law must be viewed in conjunction with the Juvenile Court Law, which was passed that same year.[15]

The expansion of juvenile courts and the broader use of conditional probation for juvenile offenders had long been a goal of Progressives, who favoured using pedagogical means to transform endangered and wayward youth into productive citizens, rather than confirming them in their marginality through punishment. The juvenile court system also expanded the scope of social work in investigating the family circumstances of juvenile offenders, providing the presiding judge with expert opinion on the matter, and in maintaining protective supervision over those offenders released on probation. It also opened the way to the more scientific study of delinquency and to the growing influence of such disciplines as psychiatry, psychology, criminology, criminal biology, and eugenics within the youth welfare system. But it was the correctional education system that most clearly illuminated the edges of Progressive youth welfare.

Before the revolution in 1918, reform schooling had been dominated by established religious organizations that alone could afford to maintain juvenile correctional institutions. These groups generally equated delinquency with sin, and their pedagogical practice was a combination of labour, religious education, and corporal punishment that was intended to reclaim the endangered souls of their charges and—quite literally—drum into them a respect for God and the principle of authority. As Peukert argued, the revolution created a space for a more Progressive pedagogy around the margins of a correctional education system that was still dominated by these conservative groups. This Progressive pedagogy, however, was murky. While the new degree of respect for the dignity, freedom, and personality of reform school inmates stood out with relative clarity against the authoritarian pedagogy of the religious institutions, Progressive youth welfare reformers were troubled by the problem of what to do with those incorrigibles who did not respond to this pedagogical opening and by their inability to alter the milieu that had contributed to the delinquency of these children in the first place.

At the end of the decade, dramatic revolts took place within a number of correctional education institutions, and the position of youth themselves within these institutions, and their alienated and hostile attitudes towards their ostensible benefactors, was publicized with dramatic effect in Peter Martin Lampel's 1929 play *Revolt in the House of Correction*. Conservatives argued that these revolts were caused by the lack of discipline on the part of reformers, who failed to recognize the flaws in their own humanistic belief in the natural goodness and infinite malleability of the human character. But, by force of example, these revolts indirectly weakened the strict authoritarian regime that was the basis for the success of the religious institutions. According to Peukert, these revolts unleashed a legitimization crisis of correctional education and of the entire youth welfare system whose linchpin it was.[16] Not only did this attack on the humanist foundations of the Weimar welfare system draw correctional education into the culture wars that were part of the general crisis of the republic. These revolts also led to a growing awareness of the limits of social pedagogy and to a desire to save what could be saved of the Progressive project by excluding those incorrigibles whose refusal to let themselves be helped had brought the entire undertaking into disrepute. For Peukert, it was precisely at this point that Progressivism revealed its authoritarian, illiberal face and established a dialectical continuity between it and the authoritarianism of the Nazis.

The law that wasn't: correctional custody and the ambiguities of social citizenship

While reform schooling for convicted juvenile offenders presented few problems, correctional education rubbed against the limits of liberal jurisprudence in two respects. On the one hand, progressive reformers considered it to be unfair to the child and wasteful to society to wait until an endangered child had actually committed an offence in order to act, and they argued that it was important to identify endangered youth and intervene in their lives before they had actually committed a punishable act in order to protect them from themselves and prevent their waywardness from degenerating into criminality. This was especially so in the case of young children, where the prospects of successful intervention declined as the children grew older. The 1900 Prussian Correctional Education Law and other state legislation had permitted such preventive intervention under specified conditions, and these provisions were taken over into the 1922 youth welfare law. The question, though, was how could such intervention be justified, and how far could it be pushed? On the other hand, older, unreformed delinquents presented a different problem. Youth welfare officials were reluctant to release into the freedoms of adulthood delinquents who had reached the age of legal majority, and who would thus leave the correctional education system without having internalized the norms and self-control necessary to protect society from their depredations. The question was how far could the preventive detention of adults be justified?

This was a practical problem for youth welfare officials, especially when the depression made it increasingly difficult to justify investments in such persons. But it also had a much broader significance because welfare officials and social workers working with vagrants, prostitutes, and other asocial groups had long called for a law that would permit them to detain those persons whose weakness of character and intellect made them a permanent danger to themselves and to society. Although the idea of such a correctional custody (*Bewahrung*) law, which sought at once to protect both the endangered individual and the public that was endangered by the individual, was a topic of recurring interest within the welfare community, it faced serious problems. One practical obstacle was the fact that any law that would have given welfare officials leverage over these problem groups would have also been prohibitively expensive. But differences of opinion concerning the scope of such a law also reflected differences of opinion concerning its purpose. While such a law could only be justified as a pedagogical measure designed to enhance the welfare of the individual, rather than as a penal measure to protect society, the basic question was how such a proposed correctional custody law could be reconciled with legitimate concerns for the personal freedom of these wayward adults. The answer to this riddle was that the idea of correctional education for both adolescents and adults rested on a belief in the infinite malleability of the human mind and a faith in the power of Progressive social technology, maternal nurturing, Christian love, and/or Christian authority to effect such change. Whether such faith was justified is, of course, another question. In any case, the combination of financial concerns and the inability to craft a law that would give welfare officials meaningful control over these marginal groups while adequately safeguarding their rights blocked the passage of a correctional custody law during the republic.[17]

Conclusion

There were clearly continuities between the Weimar welfare system and the Nazi regime in terms of institutions, personnel, and techniques. But the discontinuities are more important.

As the decade came to an end, Progressives became increasingly alienated from a republic whose democratic system enabled the needy to convert their numbers into (quasi) entitlements that these Progressives felt corroded the personal responsibility of these persons. Social workers turned against a welfare bureaucracy that offered them positions of public influence while confining them within a bureaucratic apparatus that paid little heed to those maternalist principles that had inspired the development of social work as a women's vocation. The new poor, whose primary point of contact with the welfare state was the local welfare office, turned against social workers, the bureaucracy that they represented, and elected officials at both the local and national levels all of whom appeared unable or unwilling to respond to the voice of the people. The working classes turned against both a welfare system and an unemployment insurance programme that was unable to protect them against unemployment—or to shield itself against political forces that viewed such programmes as the problem, rather than the solution. And the confessional welfare organizations, together with the churches and the parties that stood behind them, seized the opportunity presented by the depression to strike back against a republican political system based on a view of human nature that they did not share and a pluralistic welfare system that threatened their control over the reproduction of their own socio-cultural milieu; they rallied against all those whose demands for greater rights reflected a pathological weakness of character and offended against the principles of charity and authority, the two poles of Christian piety. Ultimately, the republican welfare system failed because so many wanted to overthrow it.

Thus the relationship between the Weimar welfare system and the social policies of the Nazi regime is more one of rejection than one of continuity, even of the kind of dialectical continuity identified by Peukert. While Peukert suggests that the retreat of the

Progressives from their earlier pedagogical optimism represents an important line of authoritarian, exclusionist continuity in the welfare systems of the Weimar Republic and the Third Reich, the Nazis had a much grander plan for reshaping German society along racial lines, and they were concerned with these marginal and asocial groups precisely because they occupied a key position in this larger vision.

Nazi social and racial policies flowed to a large degree from their understanding of eugenics and racial hygiene. As we have seen with regard to the correctional custody debate, Weimar social reformers argued that the greatest efforts should be made to help those who were in the greatest need, and they were sustained in this vision by their optimistic estimation of their chances of success. However, the experience of the limits of educability and the shortage of resources during the depression began to call into question the wisdom of these social investments and the meaning of the social rights that underlay them. Eugenics provided a means of theorizing this reversal of priorities and a blueprint for the use of differential welfare programmes to construct a new society based on the biological inequality of individuals, the subordination of the specific individual to the welfare of the transgenerational racial community, and the graduation of social services (both positive and negative) according to the perceived racial quality of the individual and his or her value to the community. In this way, the Nazis turned eugenic principles into the foundation for social policies that rhetorically dispatched preventive social welfare, which had been the cornerstone of the Weimar welfare system, as 'welfare for the worthless', and justified the repressive exclusion, and ultimately the physical annihilation, of these marginal, asocial groups as racially unfit.

Notes

1. Detlev Peukert, *Grenzen der Sozialdisziplinierung: Aufstieg und Krise der deutschen Jugendfürsorge 1878 bis 1932* (Essen, 1986), *Max Webers Diagnose der Moderne* (Göttingen, 1989), and in English 'The genesis of the "Final Solution" from the spirit of science', in David Crew

(ed.), *Nazism and German Society, 1933–1945* (London, 1994). For two analyses of the issues raised by Peukert, see Young-Sun Hong, 'Neither singular nor alternative: narratives of welfare and modernity in Germany, 1870–1945', *Social History*, 30/2 (May 2005) and Edward Ross Dickinson, 'Biopolitics, fascism, democracy: some reflections on our discourse about "modernity" ', *Central European History*, 37/1 (Mar. 2004), 1–48.

2. Young-Sun Hong, 'Neither singular nor alternative: narratives of welfare and modernity in Germany, 1870–1945', *Social History*, 30/2 (May 2005), 133–53 and Edward Ross Dickinson, 'Biopolitics, fascism, democracy: some reflections on our discourse about "modernity" ', *Central European History*, 37/1 (Mar. 2004), 1–48.

3. This dynamic is the topic of my own study *Welfare, Modernity, and the Weimar State, 1919–1933* (Princeton, 1998).

4. David Crew, *Germans on Welfare: From Weimar to Hitler* (Oxford, 1998) applies the principles of the history of everyday life (*Alltagsgeschichte*) to recover and theorize the experiences of welfare clientele in their encounters with the new social bureaucracy.

5. There is only limited English-language literature dealing with veterans or the other new poor: Robert Whalen, *Bitter Wounds: German Victims of the Great War 1914–1919* (Ithaca, NY, 1984), Greg Eghigian, *Making Security Social: Disability, Insurance, and the Birth of the Social Entitlement State in Germany* (Ann Arbor, 2000), chapters in Hong, *Welfare, Modernity, and the Weimar State* and Crew, *Nazism and German Society*, and Deborah Cohen, *The War Come Home: Disabled Veterans in Britain and Germany, 1914–1939* (Berkeley, 2001).

6. Christian Jasper Klumker in Sitzung des Zentralausschusses [des Deutschen Vereins für Armenpflege und Wohltätigkeit] am 22. und 23 Januar 1915, Institut für Gemeinwohl 226 (2).

7. Cited in Hong, *Welfare, Modernity, and the Weimar State*, 123–4.

8. Ibid., and Edward Ross Dickinson, *The Politics of German Child Welfare from the Empire to the Federal Republic* (Cambridge, Mass., 1996).

9. Larry Frohman, 'Prevention, welfare, and citizenship: the war on tuberculosis and infant mortality in Germany, 1900–1930', *Central European History*, 39/3 (Sept. 2006), 431–81. Welfare programmes for alcoholics and people suffering from venereal disease also set up similar dispensaries.

10. The population question had already been a point of concern before the war, and one of the first major post-war welfare conferences was devoted to the 'Preservation and increase of the nation's strength'.

11. Atina Grossmann, *Reforming Sex: The German Movement for Birth Control and Abortion Reform, 1920–1950* (Oxford, 1995).

12. Michael Hau, *The Cult of Health and Beauty in Germany: A Social History, 1890–1930* (Chicago, 2003). The holdings of the German Hygiene Museum can be accessed at <http://www.dhmd.de/neu/>.

13. The most important English-language account of the impact of authoritarian eugenics on German social welfare is Paul Weindling, *Health, Race and German Politics between National Unification and Nazism, 1870–1945* (Cambridge, 1989).

14. While Dickinson focuses on policy debates, the best English-language account of the changing fortunes of Progressive youth welfare practice is Elizabeth Harvey, *Youth and the Welfare State in Weimar Germany* (Oxford, 1993).

15. While youth welfare was a system of supplementary public education for endangered and wayward youth, there was also a broad spectrum of programmes (*Jugendpflege* rather than *Jugendfürsorge*) directed at the edification, protection, and social integration of 'normal' youth. See Derek Linton, *'Who Has the Youth, Has the Future': The Campaign to Save Youth Workers in Imperial Germany* (Cambridge, 1991).

16. Peukert, *Grenzen der Sozialdisziplinierung*, 247 ff.

17. In English, the debate over the proposed correctional custody law is dealt with most systematically in Hong, *Welfare, Modernity and the Weimar State*, 243–50, 267–71. In German, see Peukert, *Grenzen der Sozialdisziplinierung*, 263 ff., and Matthias Willing, *Das Bewahrungsgesetz (1918–1967)* (Mohr Siebeck, 2003). Correctional custody provisions for 'endangered' persons were built into the 1962 Federal Social Assistance Law, but were declared unconstitutional in 1967 as unreasonable restrictions on personal freedom.

'Neues Wohnen'

Housing and reform

Adelheid von Saldern

Introduction

Walter Gropius, who founded the Bauhaus in 1919, believed that 'from a biological perspective a healthy human needs above all else air and light but only a small living space'. This view required new kinds of dwellings and a new way of living: rationalization was the order of the day and technology was to be the key to this. The associated reformist ideas for society aimed at emancipating humanity from want and misery. Capitalist class society was to be overcome with the help of a comprehensive rationalization, planning, and functionalization of all areas of production and society, of people, and even products; 'true reality' created through art and human society as a collective-rational nature finally brought into harmony with the world and the cosmos. The new housing of the 1920s symbolized the model of the future development of the private sphere, and fed the hope of reformers that the reorganization of the private sphere would match up with a corresponding reorganization at a work level and in the public area of the cities. In short, house building at the time sent out loud social policy signals and even roused visions of social utopias.[1] For this reason the new construction of housing at that time represents a particularly fruitful area of research. It can be compared with a prism through which social renewal, including its limits, can be viewed.

Visible evidence of social reform

Not only the lost war but also the revolution of 1918–19 shook German society to its very core. Social reforms, such as new housing, were intended to prevent a continuation of the revolution. Moreover the goal 'Every German a healthy dwelling' was even embedded in the Weimar Constitution of 1919 in the form of Article 155.

During the Wilhelmine era the state had generally kept out of the house-building sector, and municipal authorities as well as building societies did not get much beyond the initial plans of a building policy. Similar to England after 1918, the new German government helped war veterans with the building of small housing settlements geared towards a domestic subsistence economy. But this was mostly piecemeal, for the economic parameters were missing for a large-scale house-building programme to fill the big lack of dwellings. Only after the currency stabilization at the end of 1923 could such a programme be extended. The main source of finance was the so-called house interest tax (*Hauszinssteuer*), by which the state levied a compensation tax on rents on pre-1913 buildings whose mortgages had been wiped out by the hyperinflation of 1923. Within a few years approximately 2.5 million dwellings were built. By 1930 around every seventh dwelling in Germany was new.[2] Between 1919 and 1932, roughly 7.7 million people profited from the republic's new housing programme. Even if de facto individual buildings accounted for the greater part of construction volume, nevertheless many cities laid great importance on constructing relatively uniform large-scale housing estates.

It soon became clear once the construction programme was under way that the housing situation could not be solved, in spite of the subsidies for new buildings. There were two principal reasons for this. On the one hand, this was because there were only a few years in which house building was fully under steam, before the economic crisis from 1930 caused substantial downturn; on the other hand high interest rates led to a rent level that most working-class families found too high, even though these were meant to 'only' cover costs. For this reason, not the broad strata of the working class, but predominantly married couples and families from the lower and middle ranks of white-collar employees and civil service, as well as the skilled 'labour aristocracy', moved into the new dwellings.

Functionalist-oriented architects hoped to get to grips with the financial problem by means of the rationalization and industrialization of construction. Individual parts were to be standardized, serial manufacturing of product types privileged, assembly method accelerated, new building materials employed, and certain building designs favoured. Everywhere in the cities were seen building lifts, concrete mixing machines, and cranes in operation. And when all these measures still failed to solve the financial problem, the final option was the reduction of floor space. If until then small and medium dwellings usually covered between 55 to 75 square metres, then the 'dwelling for the subsistence level' amounted to barely 40 square metres. Walter Gropius maintained, however, that these small apartments were not so much the product of an emergency but represented a progressive development in lifestyle.

The concepts of the reformers and the profiles of the housing estates

Through its espousal of uncompromising functionalism and the accompanying mantra of efficiency, the Bauhaus was *per se* a permanent challenge to the hitherto dominant building conventions and values of cultural conservatives.[3] Inevitably this led to a polarization within the architect profession, whereby the struggle over 'correct' building styles on a symbolic level was politically loaded.[4] While pitched roof and window shutters stood for the traditional-vernacular architectural style, the flat roof and smooth external façades were considered as recognizable characteristics of the new style. The new spatial arrangements and the generous employment of glass were intended to counteract the separation of space, to allow its fusion with people, and to signal transparency to the outer world. Accordingly, the standards of building aesthetics were radically changed. Beauty was equated with simplicity and functionality and called 'New Objectivity'.

Generally, reformist ideas concentrated on three spheres: production, the public domain, and private life. In the workplace many employers themselves provided for a certain measure of transformation. In factories production methods also moved towards Fordism, although assembly lines were not often introduced at that time. The order of the city was likewise completely cast against the backdrop of the functionalism of time and space. Thus work, living, leisure, and commerce were to be assigned to different zones of the city, and all confusion and uncertainties were to disappear. These hierarchical principles were later written down in the Charter of Athens (1933). Among the difficult projects of city planners was that of clearing the old urban quarters of their slums, a process that had been occurring in Germany on an ad hoc basis since before the First World War, as in Hamburg, but which was put on a back burner in the 1920s in favour of the construction of estates on the periphery of towns and cities. After 1933 the Nazis took up slum clearances in a number of cities and connected this with the purpose of 'cleaning' the old quarters of Communists and so-called 'asocials'.

The decision of numerous municipalities to allow the construction of compact new housing estates provided unique opportunities for architects to promote themselves through the social-spatial reorganization of whole areas. City planners were able to exercise a massive influence over the large contracts because they had the opportunity to preside over the flow of subsidies. Therefore, much of the end product depended on the respective planners. Similar to Martin Wagner in Berlin, Ernst May in Frankfurt represented the clearest functionalist line. Paradoxically, as much as the new functionalist estates stood in the glare of public and media attention, they in fact did not predominate in quantitative terms. Indeed, only roughly 5 per cent of the new housing estates were built in the purely functionalist style. Moreover, considerable differences existed between the functionalist architecture of, for example, the Berlin Britz Estate, where functionalism was cushioned by the impact of a generous and communicative circular park (the *Rondellanlage*), and the functionalist architecture which characterized the settlements of the Dammerstock Estate in Karlsruhe or that of Westhausen in Frankfurt, where, in spite of the various footpaths designed to encourage sociability, a more technocratic functionalism dominated that lent a sense of serial monotonousness. The bulk of the new estates, however, were not designed along strictly functionalist criteria, but according to a rich variety of conceptions aligned to a 'moderate modernity', as in Hanover, Munich, and Hamburg. In these examples the architects responsible for the estates used partly rationalized building methods and ground plans without rejecting some traditional designs, such as steeply pitched roofs and brick walls. But even where concessions to traditional building methods were made and an architectural hybrid form resulted, certain principles were obeyed: air, light, and sun were to be the order of the day more or less everywhere. In addition a relatively low building density and a comparatively strong greening of the estates were likewise the rule.

The new housing estates consisted usually of two- to four-floor blocks. Whilst one of the largest estates to be built in the functionalist style, that of Westhausen in Frankfurt, numbered approximately 1,500 dwellings, most estates accounted for between 500 and 1,000 dwellings. Contractors were often non-profit corporations and to a lesser extent cooperatives. By the mid-1920s, however, the zenith in the history of cooperatives as housing contractor had already passed, because large building projects could be managed more easily by non-profit corporations, which were better able to raise the needed finance.

The estates were usually built on the outskirts of town where land was cheaper and more easily available than within the inner city. In keeping with functionalist principles in city planning, the estates were conceived as pure suburbs for families to live—separated from all commercial districts.[5] In addition the advantages of town and country were to be combined according to the ideas of Ebenezer Howard's garden city. The location of estates on the urban periphery allowed for a closeness to nature, and this increased the residential value particularly for those families oriented towards life reform. It corresponded, moreover, to the ideals of conservative reformers, who were realistic enough to see that the big cities could not be abolished, but at least could be partly redeveloped. Conservatives saw in the new estates the possibility that people could gain more rootedness and closeness to the soil. In their eyes the big city appeared as chaotic and as a quagmire of immorality, whereas housing estates on the edge of towns embodied the healthy counter-model to the existing old quarters of tenement housing in the inner city.

Independently of construction methods, most estates exhibited a generous degree of comfort relative to conditions at that time. The dwellings were generally equipped with a lockable front door, running cold and hot water (usually a gas boiler), a shower or bath, own toilet, partially with a modern central heating system, and a lit stairway. The Frankfurt estates and some other residential complexes had besides these amenities a complete system of electricity. Beyond that could be found tenants' gardens, roof terraces, loggias, or balconies; very often there were also children's playgrounds, as well as some shops or businesses, and some estates even had small libraries and launderettes.

The obligation to the modern lifestyle

The new housing estates of the 1920s were considered as prototypes and models for the development of a new domestic culture and a new lifestyle in the sense of social rational behaviour. The reformer Hildegard Grünbaum-Sachs reminded her readers in *Soziale Praxis*: 'The estate is a place for well-maintained and orderly households; the new dwelling obligates!'[6] A disciplined and purposeful-rational appearance guided by the principles of quiet, cleanliness, and order was generally demanded of an estate's residents. But the new lifestyle forms were by no means just connected to functionalism. For example, in Switzerland where there were few estates in the new style, the model of social-rationalist living likewise dominated.[7] A look at so-called 'Red Vienna' as well as at new housing estates in England or in Sweden shows that everywhere similar educative concepts were being discussed and converted into housing policy, not least by Social Democrats.[8] A new living style and lifestyle had to be found, in which people could develop Socialist personalities as a precursor to establishing a Socialist society.[9] Thus within the framework of this so-called 'cultural Socialism' it was necessary to create 'new people'.

Typical of social rationalization was that it exhibited a polyvalent character and so accordingly could be connected with various objectives and ideologies (*Weltanschauungen*). For example, efforts at rationalizing behaviour in the home could be supported by the rather conservative Reich Federation of German Housewife Associations. Similar to bourgeois social reformers the Housewife Associations hoped for an easing of the burden of housework, an awareness of a healthier and moral lifestyle, a strengthening of the family, a faster regeneration of the worker, a better public health, and much more besides.[10] The mechanization of the household was thus not to be a purpose in itself, but a means to an end: to facilitate a new way of living.[11] Many of these reformers, who hailed from bourgeois families, wanted to actively advance the now necessary transformation of the private sphere, including the household, even if they did not have anything in common with the radical-functionalist principles of the Bauhaus. Their main goal was to connect the modernization of life and housekeeping with what they saw in each case as the fundamental ideas of society and gender.

The USA was the unsurpassed outrider when it came to the modernization of the household. Developments there were taken into account with both a selective and critical eye. The mechanization of American society, which was often regarded as soulless, was to be countered in Germany by re-actualizing appeals to the 'German soul' and a 'German nature' in the context of modernity. In particular those reformers who favoured a 'moderate modernity' strove to transfer so-called German 'cosiness' as a lifestyle value to the modern way of living.

Behind the housing reforms stood new norms of living based on scientific knowledge. These new norms had such a broad impact not least because they were communicated to large parts of the population via old and new media to a hitherto unprecedented extent. In tune with the emerging media age, weekly newspaper supplements, as well as magazines and pictorials, radio, film, and advertising, all advanced to become important conduits for the new living norms, above all the German Werkbund, and their colleagues in Dresden and Munich. Advice was often given without a 'raised finger' in contrast to the conventional improvement manuals that also continued to flourish. To be sure, media alone would not have been sufficient for the popularization of the new living forms: opinion leaders were also necessary—on the one hand the architects, on the other hand the scientists, in particular the medical profession and public health specialists. Finally, some exhibitions, such as the Weissenhof Exhibition, organized by the German Werkbund in Stuttgart in 1927, had great impact on public opinion.[12]

The administrative offices of the large housing estates regulated the collective behaviour of tenants through leases, house rules, and partly through obligatory notices published in the estate newsletters, all monitored by so-called housing inspectors, who were usually female. These inspectors were to provide good advice to households and control the dwellings. However, there was a lack of necessary funds during the Weimar Republic to facilitate their employment in large numbers. Nevertheless such controls increased during the last years of the Weimar Republic, especially after the Prussian welfare minister issued a decree (*Erlass*) in 1929 to that effect. Since the purpose was to prevent deplorable conditions from developing in the first place, new housing developments were also to be subject to examination. The minister's decree demanded regular control. If no money was available then volunteers would have to substitute for inspectors. Thus the line between advice and control became ever more blurred. One should 'allow oneself to be willingly advised and not regard a well-meant instruction as an interference' into personal rights, wrote the Frankfurt estate newsletter soothingly.[13] Interference in the private sphere of tenants was justified by the fact that all dwellings and their furnishings were considered as valuable elements of the national wealth, a point made in the Prussian decree.[14]

To create 'a clean and comfortable home' was considered to be the highest obligation.[15] Thus 'cleanliness is the foundation of all housing culture. Hygiene and a sense of order ordain it. The simple purity of things creates the purity of mind, the order of things gives also to the soul its equilibrium.'[16] Moreover, housing hygiene standards were to be maintained for health reasons. The standards for cleanliness were increased considerably and popularized in various ways. But the new normalizing of whatever was to be understood by modern hygiene exhibited a polyvalent character: that is to say, it could be aligned with various political and ideological positions and contexts. Weimar's conservatives considered cleanliness as a weapon against the allegedly dirty—i.e. immoral—masses of the revolution of 1918–19, the dirty workers' neighbourhoods in inner cities, and the dirty new mass culture. Eventually, the National Socialists tapped into the already well-established hygiene discourse to connect this with their fanatical conception of racial cleansing.[17]

Hygiene required social rationalized behaviour. As in factories, it was necessary to rationalize the uses of space and flows of motion. Following the Ford model people had to behave functionally in their dwellings, thus enabling them to get by with as little space as possible.[18] The rationalized floor plans as well as the functional purpose and equipping of rooms were intended to contribute to the inhabitants being educated in a 'muted way'. Indeed, the technical equipment was deployed in such a way as to ensure the 'mute education' of residents, as can be seen in the case of the Frankfurt Praunheim Estate. Here the hot-water boilers were installed in such a manner that they provided for only one full bath each day, whereas the custom was for all family members to take a bath on Saturday afternoon. In Praunheim this was no longer possible, unless they all shared the same bath water.[19]

This 'mute education' applied particularly to housekeeping. In a professionally and rationally organized household the process of housework itself would correspond to the new principles of Fordism. Thus it was necessary to apply scientific methods to housekeeping, to view the household as a business concern in its own right, and correspondingly to keep an accounts ledger and to create index card boxes in which household activities and needs were easily to hand.[20] The famous Frankfurt kitchen, a 6 m² modular kitchen based on the American model, was completely designed so as to allow the maximization of efficiency of the averagely tall woman.

The nuclear family and the
well-maintained neighbourhood

Whilst there were moves to publicize collectivized living forms, for example on the part of some younger female Social Democrats,[21] whilst left-wing avant-garde architects prophesied that the future belonged to communal forms of living, in fact it was de facto the nuclear family with its autonomous housekeeping behind its own locked door that dominated as a contemporary and in future feasible model. This did not, however, exclude maintaining friendly and disciplined relations with the neighbours. The new estates, conceived of as communicative-friendly settlements, facilitated easy contact with other inhabitants. There were places designed for contact, such as the tenants' gardens and, where they existed, the communal laundries, as well as children's playgrounds. And these good communicative opportunities were actually used by the tenants. Former inhabitants of the estates recalled in discussions how one knew many neighbours, and that neighbourhood assistance was very much in demand. Of course there were conflicts, this was only natural, but allegedly nothing was ever stolen.[22] The ideal that was propagated was that of harmonious neighbourhood relations and the creation of a kind of micro 'people's community' (*Volksgemeinschaft*[23]) without a direct connection between politics and living. The hanging of flags, for example, was frowned upon, not to say demonstrations and political propaganda. Thus the new estates differed radically from what bourgeois circles saw as the chaotic, threatening, and politicized milieux of the old working-class quarters.[24] Part of the idea that the estates were depoliticized zones was that newsletters steered clear of controversial topics, such as the high level of rents, or social protection for tenants, or paragraph 218 of the criminal code (abortion), or alternative living forms, among other things, not to mention political events of the day.[25] Thus a sharper separation of private and public spheres took place as an indication of modernity in the new housing estates—while simultaneously both spheres were more interlinked by the new medium of radio.

The traditional gender order in modern guise

Most of the pedagogical initiatives in the private sphere were directed primarily at women because these were considered responsible for the organization of everyday life in the home.[26] They were presented with a particular image of housewife and, above all, mother, who did not work, unless the family unexpectedly fell into straitened circumstances. And indeed most of the women living on the Frankfurt estates did not work outside the home.[27] The model of the non-working wife and mother corresponded to the views of many trade unionists. One of the key goals of social policy, according to the trade unionist Heinz Potthoff, was to 'keep the wife and mother out of the factory and office and return her to the home'.[28]

The advocacy of a home-centred life for wives and mothers functioned as a counterweight to the signs of the dissolution of the old gender relations visible in cities in the 1920s and popularized in the media. One need only mention in this regard the increased numbers of women working outside the home, more possibilities of activities for women in the public and semi-public spheres of cities, a greater media consumption that appeared both difficult to control and to manipulate, a new type of heavily sexualized body language in the shape of dance, fashion, hairstyle, and make-up, and finally, the perceived sexually uninhibited musical form of jazz, as well as media images of greater sexual freedom. This image of a 'new woman' was challenged by an alternative image of a 'new woman' in the context of the new housing estates, an image that focused on the modernized new home and that was supported not only by social reformers and architects but also by women's associations, as we can also see from Kathleen Canning's contribution to this volume.

Negative types indirectly defined the projected image of housewives. A blot on the landscape of all reformers was, as ever, the so-called 'lazy housewives'. These should be finally made 'to keep their dwelling clean and maintained and in addition to educate their children to respect the floors, walls and doors as somebody else's property'.[29] Among the group of 'lazy housewives' probably ranked those women who preferred to read novels or 'penny stories' or who went to the cinema instead of taking care of their family and household. Another negative image referred to the worn housewife, who neglected herself as a consequence of too much work. In order to distance themselves from such negative types, women should not let the perennial efforts of everyday life take their toll on their outward appearances, instead dressing smartly after housework was done in order to create a groomed look and thus keep their spouses at home. The idea that this could be accomplished in a playful way also belonged to the modern image of housekeeping. Signs of hard manual labour, for instance, calloused hands, were to be a thing of the past. The fact that adverts for the detergent Persil showed women and girls dressed in white was not accidental.[30] Advertisements also showed well-dressed women using a vacuum cleaner easily with only one hand. In fact the mechanization of the household, in particular the electrification of the kitchen, remained during the entire inter-war period more a picture of the future than one of contemporary reality, because most people had too little money to afford such items. Nevertheless, it should not be forgotten that futuristic plans could influence existing modes of feeling and interpretation, as well as the behaviour of people.

Finally the tenants of the new housing estates were expected to pay heed to the secular trend of rationalized procreation. The number of children had to fit spatial and financial conditions. On Frankfurt's estates, for example, only families with up to two children were desirable,[31] whilst 'large families' were supposed to be accommodated in special housing estates as far as they were considered 'worthy' and not 'asocial' families.

The peripheral location of most estates, with their poor transport connections, made most non-working women dependent on their immediate neighbourhood. On the one hand, the lack of transport was surely down to public cost, but reformers also saw a great benefit in this isolation. Nanny Kurfürst, a delegate to the Social Democratic Party Women's Congress in 1927, believed that such estates offered families the opportunity to once again do more together, in contrast to the living conditions in the inner cities with their many cinemas and other superficial attractions.[32] Of the new media, only moderate radio listening was valued, which, because of state influence, broadcast many educational and other 'worthy' programmes. Thus they would become acquainted with new nutritional standards, as well as with baby care and childcare, learn about contemporary hygiene, and get to know economic views. The aim was to make housework attractive to housewives and mothers by 'professionalizing' it, and to attach housewives to the private sphere by allowing them to participate in the public sphere via the media.

From the point of view of reformers, the education of housewives not only served to transform them into citizens, but it also served to stabilize the family. For the women it meant being able to meet the intellectual demands of their husbands, and so make them good partners in this respect also. Here likewise traditional education goals for women were transferred into the modern spirit of the times. A wife was expected to happily serve her husband after a day's work. Even on the progressive Frankfurt estates an image dominated whereby women's roles were defined through the relationship to their husbands and continued in traditional form, albeit in modern guise.[33] It is no surprise, therefore, to find in a bourgeois newspaper in Hanover that most housewives were interested in 'doing the necessary housework with a minimum expenditure of time and energy in order to be fresh and able to take on the other demands which life makes on them—such as showing an interest in their husband's hobbies, the children's education, and sociability'.[34] Here, the woman's role was still focused on husband and children; not even her civic obligations were mentioned, let alone any professional ambition that lay outside the home. The housewife had to know 'that *her* occupation was also an occupation'. The aim was to 'keep abreast with the times, and to adopt all that which exemplifies the modern woman'.[35] The modernization of the household served as a new legitimization for upholding the traditional gendered division of labour in that now housekeeping allegedly no longer meant a special physical exertion or burden. The split of responsibilities and work between the sexes corresponded with the spirit of Fordism in the workplace and of urban functionalism.

Modern taste as hygienic obligation

The prevailing mood that arose from hygiene and functionalism also rejected the housing tradition of the old ornate living style of the labour aristocracy and the middle classes. On the agenda was a complete transformation of the home, as Bruno Taut, the Bauhaus architect, demanded in his book *The New Dwelling: Woman as Creator*:

except for the actual curtains, everything shall be removed from the windows; to prevent obscuring the view only a sleek net curtain (*Mullvorhang*) is necessary; redundant cushions, covers, knick-knacks, vases, pictures, box-shelves, embroidered house blessings and sayings and every such are consigned to the grave. Just as redundant are rugs, furs laid over carpets . . . sea-shell ornaments, superstructures over sofas, tassels, shawls etc. are easy to remove; finally, the excesses of the joiner are also to be sawn off.[36]

Such advice mirrored the spirit of the age, the new era of modernity which wanted to put an end to historicism and which called ornamentation a crime (Loos). Whoever could not afford this new furniture or wanted it, he or she was advised to 'shave' the existing furniture: that is, to remove scrolling and ornamentation and so smooth its surface. Suitable household items, such as the so-called 'estate net curtains', underpinned the modernizing efforts. Model exhibitions and model dwellings likewise served to reorient taste.

Furthermore, in the fight against dust, the advice was not to pack dwellings with too many furnishings. Photographs, knick-knacks, and pictures were considered needless gatherers of dust. In the spirit of the New Objectivity there was no longer a place for visual mementoes, nor for cherished collectibles. In one estate periodical, closely associated with a trade union, could be read: 'I am a person of today therefore my housing should not exhale the dust of dead times.'[37] The spirit of rationalized progress meant that neither cultural uncontemporaneity nor contradictions in everyday life were to be tolerated. 'One surely could not live in the previous century' was the general tenor.[38] Frau Elise, who had apparently modernized her entire apartment according to functionalist principles, told her readers in a Hanover newspaper that the 'deeply embedded riches of memory' were not to be found in pieces of furniture 'that no longer corresponded to contemporary aesthetics'.[39] The postulate to live exclusively in the present and to dematerialize memories may have corresponded to enlightened, rational thinking, but it did not take into account the function of mementoes for individual and collective memory—not to speak of the *longue durée* of mentalities of many individuals shaped by uncontemporaneity.[40]

Complex ways of appropriation

Whoever studies the processes of adaptation to the new functionalist skills has constantly to be aware that living on the estates was highly valued by the residents. This led to a positive attitude among them whereby most residents simply accepted the functionalist architectural language of the houses as a given, and as not so important for their well-being. When interviewed, a number of former residents stated that families happily lived on the estates, particularly since there were at that time no better alternatives for them.[41]

Regardless of the efforts by reformers to also modernize the taste of residents according to hygiene knowledge and aesthetic changes in norms, success remained by and large quite limited. Housing reformers were probably irritated by furniture that was 'mostly far too large for the small apartment and far too pompous for a simple life-style. One does not buy furniture according to one's needs—a medium size sideboard or a bookcase and one or two comfortable seats—but a complete dining or living room suite.' The only large room, according to one disapproving reformer, is often used as a bedroom. 'And because of the oversized furniture the family huddled together during the day in the kitchen, so as to have at night a petit bourgeois bedroom with a coquettish orange light and a picture of dancing fairies over the marriage bed.'[42] Such observations suggest that much of the advice was still being ignored.

Obviously people did not automatically change with their move to new housing, bringing instead some of their old habits with them. And yet they more or less were drawn into what was at the time considered as a modern lifestyle. Thus the inhabitants did not see the many good pieces of advice as prescriptive, but rather were grateful for the helpful guidance. Also the housing companies selected their future tenants not only on the basis of ability to pay the rents but also sought out those who were receptive to the new living style. This selection rule applied above all to the working-class families. In their cases it was said that they were people who 'were generally above average in terms of rationally organized living'.[43] Furthermore it should be borne in mind that young married couples generally were more amenable towards modern trends than the older generation, and it was they who had the best chance to move to the new estates.

Four typical forms of behaviour, although in reality they were often mixed together, crystallized among the residents: acceptance, adaptation, evasion, and participation. Those families which stood fully behind the new way of life were probably those that ensured neighbours likewise adapted to the regimen of the new lifestyle. Whoever did not accept the communal rules and the modern conduct of life probably undermined these charily, for instance by drying laundry on Sundays when it was forbidden to do so. The housing management had to repeatedly publish reminders in the estate bulletin to keep these and similar rules. In addition not all housewives approved of the technical innovations, for instance the central wash kitchens or the hot-water tanks.[44] Most frequently the demands to purchase new furniture were ignored, particularly since money for this was lacking. Nonetheless, it appeared incomprehensible to housing reformers that even with a shortage of money the dwellings were not at least emptied. One can draw from the complaints about 'unbelievable junk', that is to say complaints about inappropriate and superfluous furniture, wall decoration, and thick curtains, that families on the new estates ignored the calls to adopt the 'good' taste of modernity.[45]

The situation was different with regard to responsibility for the household, attributed solely to women. Many women at that time may have regarded this (today) discriminatory claim as self-evident. In the opinion of numerous women, this 'women's realm' should remain a field of activity for the female sex, which—in spite of the constant grind—nevertheless provided certain creative possibilities. The call to be a good housewife meant a lot to them. But some women began to question the 'self-evident' nature of the sexual division of labour in the home. Thus Social Democratic women attending the Women's Conferences held during the party congresses complained that their men did not bother with the household and behaved in a petit bourgeois way, which was why a Socialist way of life based on comradeship between the sexes could not be carried into families.[46] Especially younger Social Democratic and Communist women questioned and criticized the sex-specific division of labour, without being able to change for their part the strongly masculine culture of their parties.

But it was not just a case of acceptance, adaptation, and evasion. In some estates tenant associations were even established. To be sure these were primarily identity-based organizations that promoted communication among them, but they also served to articulate particular interests. In those housing developments belonging to a cooperative, the members' meetings offered possibilities for participation, albeit primarily for the usually male heads of household. In addition on estates that belonged to larger housing companies there were occasionally tenant committees that had certain consultative rights with the housing administration. But remarkably this—for living areas—new form of participation was not publicly promoted as a future social model. Not even the trade unions were particularly pleased, since they often appeared indirectly as landlords and hence regarded such bodies uncomfortably. Indeed, as we know from the experience of the Frankfurt estates, there were differences of opinion and tensions, among other things, over rents, high additional expenses, and the condition of the dwellings. In order to avoid the creation of such tenant committees the relationship between the housing associations and their tenants was characterized as allegedly conflict free; indeed the argument was made that the housing societies were non-profit-making organizations and as such there could be no clashes of interests. But the actual reason for snubbing the committees was the fear that Communist-inclined tenants could, together with other 'awkward' residents, take the opportunity to disrupt what was seen as a harmonious relationship between housing management and tenants.[47]

The 'new feeling of life' in society

The question remains open as to what extent the functionalist principles of modern living, of which the new estates were
exemplars, influenced society *per se*. Contemporary observations
and inferences can offer at least a rough orientation. The cultural and social scientist Alfred Weber at Heidelberg University,
a supporter of Weimar democracy, placed the New Objectivity (*Neue Sachlichkeit*) in direct relationship to a 'new feeling
of life, which is most obviously [expressed] in the new architecture'. At a Werkbund conference held in Munich in 1928 he
stated, 'not the technical aids of our time, but a consciously
new mental attitude is the crucial factor. Today's youth rejects
emotion and each falsehood; they thereby reject traditional dec-
orative forms (*Zierformen*) and would like to confine themselves
to spatial arrangement and colour.' Weber held such an architecture to be 'infinitely fruitful'. The architectural scholar Emil
Pretorius, although he doubted the size of the group receptive
to the new living culture, supported Weber. According to Pretorius, 'The new feeling of life and its expression are up to now
with certainty only the affair of an intellectual minority, which
senses the new life form. It is doubtful how far in truth it is also
the idiom of an estranged working-class. The traditional middle
class rejects it.' This appraisal elicited a prompt rebuttal from
the editors of the journal *Bauwelt* ('World of Construction'), in
which the report on the conference was published: 'The new feeling of life appears nonetheless to be spreading rapidly under the
current generation and even more among the next generation
(*Heranwachsenden*).'[48]

By also consulting other sources, we can discern three groups
which, it can be assumed, were very much amenable to the Bauhaus
model when it came to furnishing their own apartments. First there
were the architects who represented modernity, secondly, the 3,000
members of the Werkbund,[49] and thirdly, the 'avant-garde artists of
the younger generation', among them 'remarkably many painters',
who espoused 'colour and broken surface (*flächenzerlegenden*)
painting'.[50]

Pretorius rightly referred to the cultural resistance among the broad section of workers, particularly since the majority of these workers did not come into direct contact with the new living norms for financial reasons; whilst the everyday cultural habits of many semi- and unskilled workers followed a social logic that stemmed from a 'culture of necessity and poverty'. While the unskilled and those workers in casual employment were mainly engrossed in pure survival, and thus fixated on the day-to-day and 'instant gratification', those working-class families living in materially stable households continued to decorate their homes in order to express cultural capability in their ways. This included kitsch objects which served as mementoes or decoration. Framed family photographs, including important events such as confirmation and weddings, were displayed or hung with pleasure in the 'good parlour', and thus happy moments of life in the past were captured in the picture, expressing the personalization of life experiences and feelings. Part of this experience included the crowding of the family in the kitchen, while the 'good parlour' was used only on special occasions.

In contrast to the new housing estates, so-called 'half-open' family households, the result of sub-letting and taking in overnight lodgers (*Schlafgänger*), were still widespread in the older working-class neighbourhoods during the 1920s, in spite of overcrowding; and these conditions gave the impression to the middle class that the morality of the family was endangered. Moreover, the middle class and government agencies thought of these working-class neighbourhoods as disorderly and chaotic, not least because neighbourhood social relations followed rules that were difficult for reformers to comprehend.[51] They appeared as old-fashioned, irrational, and unhealthy, so that the impression developed that the necessary speedy regeneration of productive capacity of these groups of workers was no longer ensured. It is no surprise, therefore, that reformers included also older housing in their modernization concept, for 'as long as people do not change their ways in the existing dwellings, the new architecture will not progress one step further'.[52] But in spite of all their educational lessons, reformers always quickly came up against the limits of their influence to change the lifestyles of these groups.

The reference by Pretorius to the cultural resistance of the 'traditional middle class' is surely apposite, but a little imprecise, since the 'middle class' consisted of many sub-strata, ranging from the handicrafts-based petite bourgeoisie to the academically trained employees and officials. While the former in the maintenance, reactivation, and invention of traditions and in cultural residualism discovered for itself a valuable symbolic capital that could be converted under favourable circumstances into social and economic capital (Bourdieu), another part of the middle class was receptive to the principles of the new lifestyle. These families voluntarily moved into the new housing estates, and as such can be regarded as the outriders of modernity.

The upper middle class was also partially receptive to the values of light, air, and sun, and the associated concepts of purity, health, and hygiene, publicized by scientific experts. The customary gloomy dwellings of earlier decades were the first to be changed. With regard to furnishings, the impression prevailed that the heretofore extreme overfilling of rooms decreased. Thus a new spatial sense and a new spatial arrangement developed, even if old furniture was neither 'shaved' (i.e. its decoration removed) nor exchanged. Often—not least under pressure from the younger generation—there was a coexistence of old and new pieces of furniture. Generally, a broader differentiation of domestic taste and domestic lifestyles among upper-class families can be discerned in the Weimar society of the 1920s.[53] Envisioning the challenges and chances of modernity, taste pluralism, although limited, was emerging among well-to-do families. This did not, however, mean that the very different world-views and political attitudes of bourgeois groups and strata in the Weimar society were directly mirrored in the type of their living arrangements.

Transnational communication

Germany's new housing estates were viewed as model settlements and as such attracted much international recognition. At an exhibition held in Warsaw in 1926, examples of the new architecture from Germany, the Netherlands, Belgium, France, and

Czechoslovakia were presented. The following year in Stuttgart an exemplary housing exhibition was held at the Weissenhof Estate, at which the Dutch architects J. J. P. Oud and M. Stam, the Belgian V. Bourgeois, and Le Corbusier were given the opportunity to present new architectural designs. Likewise at the Frankfurt House-Building Congress in 1929 numerous foreigners participated, among them a considerably large Hungarian delegation.[54] The well-known architect Richard I. Neutra from the USA joined representatives from fifteen European countries at the II CIAM Congress (Congrès Internationaux d'Architecture Moderne) in 1930, which, incidentally, also took place in Frankfurt, and which took as its theme 'The minimum existence dwelling'.[55]

In 1925, for the first time, Walter Gropius called for the programmatic internationalization of construction methods and styles, to which a number of people allied themselves. Le Corbusier—the doctrinaire emissary of a functional division between industrial and residential areas—had already attained international notoriety with his city plan ideas. Moreover, from 1923 the Bauhaus operated at an international level where it represented universal ideas, and thus came into a fierce conflict with the Germanic regionalist and nationalist architects gathered around Paul Schmitthenner and Paul Bonatz (the so-called Stuttgart School). Bauhaus teachers and pupils originated from different countries. The Hungarian architect Farkas Molnar, for example, developed his concept of the KURI city in 1925 from models that he had tried out before as a student of the KURI Group at the Bauhaus.[56] In Brünn (today, Brno), owing to the commitment of young town planners and architects, above all Josef Polaseks, the new international style was implemented to such a considerable extent that the city is comparable with Frankfurt, Rotterdam, and Tel Aviv.[57] In Warsaw, a modernist architect group also managed to establish themselves.[58] And Ernst May, the renowned city planner of Frankfurt, left Germany in 1930 for the Soviet Union when he saw no more possibility of carrying out his ideas for modern residential areas. Even as a non-Communist he received, albeit briefly, wide-ranging opportunities as a city planner. The foregoing are examples that suggest an intensification of the exchange of experience and information, as well as of the international interlinking of avant-garde city planners and architects in Europe, whereby Germany formed one of the centres. In 1928 the Congrès Internationaux d'Architecture Moderne (CIAM) was founded in Switzerland; it stabilized the transnational connectedness among modern architects.

Conclusion

The New Architecture and New Living (*Neues Wohnen*) were on the one hand both an expression and result of modernity, while on the other hand they contributed to shaping it. Because of the considerable influence of the Bauhaus and the international reputation of the Frankfurt estates, Germany can be considered in the European context as being in the vanguard of modernity. Thus the German example serves well for working out the ambivalence inherent in modernity.[59] On the positive side there is the high number of newly built, healthy dwellings and their high living value. The problems lie in the increased exclusion of non-compliant residents, in the trend towards absolutes in architecture and living standards, in the maintenance of the old gendered division of labour, as well as in the tendencies to social disciplining. The separation of the upper echelons of the working class from the broad mass of workers, and their spatial incorporation with the families of lower and even partly with middling white-collar employees and public officials, pointed to the future. This socio-spatial fusion was followed by a cultural convergence as a result of the uniform education in living styles. Certainly one should guard against giving too much weight to such socio-spatial and everyday-life changes, especially in Germany where employees and public officials still cultivated a class-based habitus at that time that differentiated them from the skilled worker. Nevertheless, the typically crude status symbols of the old class society were to disappear in and because of the new estates, to be replaced by new, nuanced distinctions tailored to the modern 'mass age'. Taken together, the new housing estates and the new living style expressed in an exemplary way and symbolically the contours of a socially rational-ordered post-class society. At the same time the socio-spatial and socio-cultural separation of skilled workers from the broad mass of workers meant that the latter's culture and way of life was further marginalized and seen as primitive and untamed.

Housing reform gave momentum to the modernization of family everyday culture. The new models and norms of 'Neues Wohnen' concerning cleanliness and order, as well as the various strategies for the revaluation of the family and the housewife's role, had spread to the public via the media and had become accepted by many people regardless of party affiliation. At the same time conventional ideas regarding gender roles within the private sphere continued to hold sway. This deliberate intertwining of old and new norms led to a modern 'culture of domesticity', a paradigm that was typical for the period and which could also be found elsewhere.[60] One should, however, always differentiate between ideals and the much more complex reality.

Finally, an analysis of inter-war ideas for the reorganization of the domestic sphere makes clear that different reform groups regarded modernity as a challenge and felt obliged to participate in shaping it. As certain components of reform, such as rationalized and clean lifestyles, bore polyvalent characteristics, these were not only valued as socially ordering concepts in the Weimar Republic but also in other periods of the twentieth century.

Notes

1. This chapter is based largely on original research. Some results can be found in Adelheid von Saldern, *Häuserleben: Zur Geschichte städtischen Arbeiterwohnens vom Kaiserreich bis heute* (Bonn, 1995).

2. *Blätter für Wohnungswesen*, ed. Bau- und Sparverein Solingen, 10 (1930), 8: 12. Dan Silverman, 'A pledge unredeemed: the housing crisis in Weimar Germany', *Central European History*, 3 (1970), 112–39.

3. Magdalena Droste, *Bauhaus 1919–1933* (Cologne, 1993).

4. Werner Durth, *Deutsche Architekten: Biographische Verflechtungen 1900–1970* (Braunschweig, 1986), 55–6.

5. On Frankfurt, for example, see Günther Uhlig, 'Sozialräumliche Konzeption der Frankfurter Siedlung', in Dezernat für Kultur und Freizeit, Amt für Wissenschaft und Kunst der Stadt Frankfurt (ed.), *Ernst May und das Neue Frankfurt 1925–1930* (Frankfurt am Main, 1986), 93–101.

6. Hildegard Grünbaum-Sachs, 'Neue Aufgaben einer zeitgemäßen Wohnungspflege', *Soziale Praxis*, 39 (1930), 6: 143–9, here 147.

7. Daniel Kurz, ' "Den Arbeiter zum Bürger machen": Gemeinnütziger Wohnungsbau in der Schweiz 1918–1949', in Günther Schulz, *Wohnungspolitik im Sozialstaat* (Düsseldorf, 1993), 285–305, here 292.

8. One thinks, for example, of the Octavia Hill Society at the turn of the century, whose educative concepts in approaching its tenants represent the transition from Victorian morality to a modern social-rationalist norm. For Austria see Helmut Gruber, *Red Vienna: Experiment in Working-Class Culture 1919–1934* (New York, 1991). For a good general description of housing in inter-war Europe, see Elizabeth Denby, *Europe Re-housed* (London, 1938).

9. Maria Juchacz; see *Protokoll über die Verhandlungen des Parteitages der Sozialdemokratischen Partei Deutschlands, Reichsfrauenkonferenz* (Berlin, 1927), 367–8, 363–4.

10. Martina Heßler, '*Mrs. Modern Woman*': Zur Sozial- und Kulturgeschichte der Haushaltsrationalisierung* (Frankfurt, 2001), 210–62.

11. Ibid. 262.

12. Jürgen Joedicke and Christine Plath, *Die Weissenhofsiedlung* (Stuttgart, 1977); Richard Pommer and Christian F. Otto, *Weissenhof 1927 and the Modern Movement in Architecture* (Chicago, 1991).

13. *Die Siedlung*, 3 (1931), 6: 88.

14. Erlass II B 226, 24 Jan. 1929, in *Die Siedlung*, 1 (1929), 6: 11.

15. *Blätter für Wohnungswesen*, 5 (1925), 12: 6.

16. *Einfa: Nachrichtenblatt der Einfa* (June 1932), 6: 2.

17. Detlev J. K. Peukert, 'The genesis of the "final solution" from the spirit of science', in Thomas Childers and Jane Caplan (eds.), *Reevaluating the Third Reich* (New York, 1993), 234–52.

18. *Hannover Anzeiger, Illustrierte*, 24 Mar. 1929.

19. Heßler, '*Mrs. Modern Woman*', 300.

20. *Die Frau von Heute: Sonderblatt des Hannoverschen Anzeigers für alle Frauen-Interessen*, 8 May 1930.

21. For instance *Hannoversche Volkswille*, 29 Feb. 1928 (supplement); see also the edition of the same paper from 8 Feb. 1928 (supplement).

22. Interviews with former residents of Frankfurt-Westhausen, Hamburg-Dulsberg, Berlin-Britz, and of some residential areas in Hanover were carried out by the author in the late 1980s.

23. *Die Siedlung* (1932), 12: 157. For more see Michael Wildt, ' "Volksgemeinschaft" als politischer Topos in der Weimarer Republik', in Alfred Gottwaldt, Norbert Kampe, and Peter Klein (eds.), *NS-Gewaltherrschaft: Beiträge zur historischen Forschung und juristischen Aufarbeitung* (Berlin, 2005), 23–39.

24. Anthony McElligott, 'Street politics in Hamburg 1932/33', *History Workshop Journal*, 16 (Autumn 1983), 83–90.

25. See for example *Die Siedlung* (1932), 4: 43; and 8: 105.

26. For the different models of the New Women see Adelheid von Saldern, 'Gesellschaft und Lebensgestaltung: Sozialkulturelle Streiflichter', in Gerd Kähler (ed.), *Geschichte des Wohnens*, iv: *1918–1945: Reform, Reaktion, Zerstörung* (Stuttgart, 1996), 45–183, here 138–46; Katharina Sykora et al., *Die Neue Frau: Herausforderung für die Bildmedien der Zwanziger Jahre* (Marburg, 1993).

27. See for instance *Soziale Praxis*, 39 (1930), 6; *Wohnungswirtschaft*, 7 (1930), 6.

28. *Blätter für Wohnungswesen*, 5 (1925), 12: 6.

29. In the words of Dr Brandt, a housing officer from Hamburg. *Zeitschrift für Wohnungswesen*, 22 (1922), 18: 219.

30. Ute Daniel, 'Der unaufhaltsame Aufstieg des sauberen Individuums: Seifen und Waschmittelwerbung im historischen Kontext', in Imke Behnken (ed.), *Stadtgesellschaft und Kindheit im Prozeß der Zivilisation: Konfigurationen städtischer Lebensweise zu Beginn des 20. Jahrhunderts* (Opladen, 1990), 43–77. The image can be found on p. 52.

31. Demographers believed that at least three children per family was necessary for maintaining population levels.

32. *Protokoll über die Verhandlungen des Parteitages der Sozialdemokratischen Partei Deutschlands, Reichsfrauenkonferenz* (Berlin, 1927), 358.

33. In this respect see the journal *Die Siedlung*, which appeared from 1929.

34. *Hannoverscher Kurier im Bild* (1927), 37.

35. *Hannoverscher Anzeiger*, 30 Apr. 1930.

36. Bruno Taut, *Die neue Wohnung: Die Frau als Schöpferin* (Leipzig, 1924), 61.

37. *Einfa*, 2 (1931), 10: 2.

38. Ibid.

39. 'Alte Einrichtung auf neu. Verbesserungen ohne große Ausgaben', *Die Frau von heute: Sonderblatt des Hannoverschen Anzeigers für alle Frauen-Interessen*, 8 May 1930.

40. See above all, Ernst Bloch, *Erbschaft dieser Zeit* (Frankfurt am Main 1973; 1st edn. 1935); Peter Gorsen, 'Zur Dialektik des Funktionalismus heute: Das Beispiel des kommunalen Wohnungsbaus im Wien der zwanziger Jahre', in Jürgen Habermas (ed.), *Stichworte zur 'geistigen Situation der Zeit'*, ii: *Politik und Kultur* (Frankfurt am Main, 1979), 688–706.

41. Besides my interviews see Heike Lauer, ' "Die neue Baukunst als Erzieher"? Eine empirische Untersuchung der Siedlung Römerstadt

in Frankfurt am Main', in Wolfgang Hofmann and Gerd Kuhn (eds.), *Wohnungspolitik und Städtebau 1900–1930* (Berlin, 1993), 265–84, here 275.

42. *Wohnungswirtschaft*, 7 (1930), 383–4.

43. Hildegard Grünbaum-Sachs, 'Neue Aufgaben einer zeitgemäßen Wohnungspflege', *Soziale Praxis*, 39 (1930), 6: 143–9, here 143–4.

44. See, in particular, Heßler, '*Mrs. Modern Woman*', 294–302.

45. *Die Siedlung*, 3 (1931), 6: 89.

46. *Protokoll über die Verhandlungen des Parteitages der Sozialdemokratischen Partei Deutschlands, Reichsfrauenkonferenz* (Berlin, 1927), 359; ibid. (Berlin, 1925), 345. For more on this see Adelheid von Saldern, 'Modernization as challenge: perceptions and reactions of German Social Democratic women', in Helmut Gruber and Pamela Graves (eds.), *Women and Socialism/Socialism and Women in Interwar Europe* (New York, 1998), 95–135.

47. *GEHAG-Nachrichten* (1930), 3: 3.

48. 'Bericht über die Münchner Werkbundtagung am 9. Juli 1928', *Bauwelt* (1928), 28: 660.

49. The figure represents membership for 1928: Paul Betts, *The Authority of Everyday Objects: A Cultural History of West German Industrial Design* (Berkeley and Los Angeles, 2004), 28.

50. Max Schoen, 'Du musst Dir neue Möbel anschaffen', *Das schöne Heim: Illustrierte Zeitschrift für angewandte Kunst*, 3 (1932), 222–31, here 231.

51. See the account by Anthony P. McElligott, 'Das "Abruzzenviertel"': Arbeiter in Altona 1918–1931', in Arno Herzig, Dieter Langewiesche, and Arnold Sywottek (eds.), *Arbeiter in Hamburg: Unterschichten, Arbeiter und Arbeiterbewegung seit dem ausgehenden 18. Jahrhundert* (Hamburg, 1983), 493–507.

52. Taut, *Die neue Wohnung*, 58.

53. For more see Adelheid von Saldern, 'Rauminszenierungen: Bürgerliche Selbstrepräsentationen im Zeitenumbruch (1880–1930)', in Werner Plumpe and Jörg Lesczenski (eds.), *Bürgertum und Bürgerlichkeit zwischen Kaiserreich und Nationalsozialismus* (Mainz, 2009).

54. Monika Platzer, 'Die CIAM und ihre Verbindungen nach Zentraleuropa', in Eve Blau and Monika Platzer (eds.), *Mythos Großstadt: Architektur und Stadtbaukunst in Zentraleuropa 1900–1937* (Munich, 1999), 227–32, here 227.

55. Internationaler Kongress für Neues Bauen und Städtisches Hochbauamt in Frankfurt am Main (ed.), *Die Wohnung für das Existenzminimum* (Frankfurt am Main, 1930), 39–40.

56. KURI = constructive, utilitarian, rational, international. Molnar conceived his city plan as a counter-conception to Le Corbusier's city, which he understood as capitalist. Renate Banik-Schweitzer, 'Städtebauliche Visionen Pläne und Projekte 1890–1937', in Blau and Platzer (eds.), *Mythos Großstadt*, 58–73, here 58, 69. Many Hungarian architects, like Molnar, studied abroad.

57. Rostislav Švácha, 'Prag, Brno und Zlin 1918–1937', in Blau and Platzer (eds.), *Mythos Großstadt*, 215–26, here 217; Jane Pavitt, 'From the garden to the factory: urban visions in Czechoslovakia between the wars', in Malcolm Gee, Tim Kirk, and Jill Steward (eds.), *The City in Central Europe: Culture and Society from 1800 to the Present* (Cambridge, 1999), 27–45, here 38.

58. Beate Störtkuhl, 'Wohnungsbau der Zwischenkriegszeit in Breslau im ostmitteleuropäischen Kontext', in Alena Janatková and Hanna Kozinska-Witt (eds.), *Wohnen in der Großstadt 1900–1939: Wohnsituation und Modernisierung im europäischen Vergleich* (Stuttgart, 2006), 337–59.

59. Peukert, 'The genesis of the "final solution"', 239 ff.; idem, *Max Webers Diagnose der Moderne* (Göttingen, 1989); Zygmunt Bauman, *Moderne und Ambivalenz: Das Ende der Eindeutigkeit* (Hamburg, 2005).

60. Martin Pugh, *Women and the Women's Movement in Britain 1914–1959* (Houndmills, 1992), 209 ff.; Steven Mintz and Susan Kellogg, *Domestic Revolutions: A Social History of American Family Life* (New York, 1988), 113 ff.

Weimar Jewry

Anthony D. Kauders

Why include a chapter on the Jewish community, which comprised less than 1 per cent of Germany's population, if at the same time the more numerous Catholics and Protestants are not treated separately? We can detect at least three reasons that have led historians of Weimar to include the Jews in their surveys of the period: the Jews were important not because of their denomination but because of their ethnicity. Inasmuch as they were made out to be different, their role as a minority—perhaps *the* ethnic minority—allows us to understand better the way in which the majority imagined 'German identity' in this period.

The Jews were important because members of the community occupied prominent positions in public life. From Walther Rathenau, foreign minister in the early 1920s, to Walter Bensemann, founder and editor of the soccer magazine *Kicker*, Jews were visible in politics and culture, disproportionately represented in medicine and law, and widely identified with the Weimar 'spirit'. This conspicuousness allows us to understand better the way in which the majority perceived the character of the Weimar Republic.

The Jews were also important because they became the victims of genocide. In order to grasp the phenomenon of National Socialism, it is imperative that we appreciate whom the extreme right vilified. And since this vilification led to the mass murder of millions, we must know how prejudice was transformed into persecution. Investigating the Jewish minority in the Weimar years allows us to understand better both the rise of Hitler and the causes of the Holocaust.

In each of these accounts, the Jews figure as the objects rather than the subjects of history. The Jews are of interest insofar as they explain the visions and obsessions of the majority; furnish reasons for the demise of the first German democracy; and delineate the origins of National Socialist racialism. While these concerns remain essential, they are reminiscent of earlier histories that sought to study Weimar as the prelude to the Third Reich. They are problematic on other grounds, too. For one, it is suggested that someone like Walther Rathenau pursued German foreign policy in his capacity as a Jew, which is patently false. Jewish revolutionaries envisaged utopian societies, Jewish doctors alleviated pains, but they did so as revolutionaries and doctors, not in the name of the Jewish people. For another, it is implied that in order to comprehend 'German identity' or the phenomenon of anti-Semitism, we require a history of the Jews. In this case, however, we had better focus on popular conceptions of 'Germanness' or anti-Semitic stereotypes—and on the forces that conjured up a 'Jewish question' in the first place—than undertake to establish connections between who the Jews were and why they were despised.

If we endeavour to move beyond teleological considerations, the initial question—Why include the Jews in a book on Weimar?—becomes pertinent again. The question can be put more forcefully: What was it about the Jews that would justify our special engagement where other religions (Catholics, Protestants) or ethnic groups (Poles) might merit similar attention? The argument that will be put forward in the following pages is threefold: First, the Jewish minority in the Weimar Republic was unique in that many of the conflicts emblematic of the time, conflicts between visionaries and pragmatists, between reformers and traditionalists, between fundamentalists and pluralists, existed here in magnified form. It is not only that a history of the Jews resembles a 'micro'-history of the period, it is that the Jews were Weimar Germans with all their problems—and on top of that Jews whose status within society was being increasingly questioned. Their lot, in other words, was symptomatic of what Detlev Peukert has called the 'signature of the epoch', insecurity—only doubly so.

Second, the Jewish minority was unique in that, the above-mentioned divisions notwithstanding, it was overwhelmingly concerned with the survival of the republic. Other groups whose ideological resemblance suggested some agreement on the nature of Weimar's problems often clashed violently in their assessment of the republic's future. This disagreement led Social Democrats to fight for and Communists to fight against the 'system'. In their deliberations as to whom to elect, the Jews behaved differently from a great many Germans. Not only did they hold fast, for the longest time, to one creed in particular, left-liberalism, they were also willing to opt for the SPD or the Catholic Centre Party in an effort to save the republic. Neither social background nor ideological preference determined the voting patterns of German Jews in Weimar's final years, when the rise of Hitler seemed inexorable and political liberalism diminished to the point of non-existence. In this sense the Jews represented the most conservative factor amongst the electorate. In this sense, too, they refused to share the 'conviction that these emergency conditions could be managed to Germany's advantage'.[1]

Third, these particularities—the magnified sense of crisis, the continued support for Weimar—gave rise to a dualism that was in many ways singular. For while most German Jews engaged in the doctrinal disputes of the time, this engagement rarely if ever affected their stance on the republic. Jewish nationalists may have envisioned a future in Palestine, Jewish intellectuals may have contemplated a renaissance of Jewish culture, but they still wholeheartedly welcomed the democratic polity. Jews in Jewish politics, then, engaged in divisive controversy, whereas Jews in German politics preferred republican unity. This view qualifies two arguments that have informed Jewish and German historiography respectively. In the former case, scholars have come to hold that German Jews were Jews in private and Germans in public, 'men and women on the street and Jews at home'.[2] Yet it is possible to argue that the ideological ('private') disputes within German Jewry predominantly reflected 'German' hopes and fears at the same time as ('public') electoral behaviour predominantly mirrored 'Jewish' hopes and fears. To put it differently, Jewish ideological discourse (mysticism versus rationalism, for example, or communitarianism versus liberalism) paralleled the discourse within German cultural life as a whole, whereas Jewish conduct at the polls, both in its predictability and in its outcome, had no equivalent.

In the latter case, scholars have contended that 'neither liberalism nor illiberalism provides a helpful benchmark' for addressing the subject of Weimar Germany.[3] If we take the Jews, however, the contrast—renamed pluralism versus anti-pluralism—remains relevant. Jews in the Weimar Republic partook of debates that bespoke pluralism. This pluralism existed within both Jewish communities and society at large. It was to be underwritten, most Jews hoped, by a constitution that guaranteed the free exchange of ideas. It was also to be underwritten by a pervasive ethos that subsumed ideological strife under the general framework of liberal democratic solidarity. For a majority of Jews, the dilemma of Weimar Germany consisted in the discrepancy between the existence of pluralism on the one hand, and popular opposition to the concept of pluralism on the other. The rise of radical anti-Semitism, unrelenting and oblivious to reason, as well as the ever-increasing calls for a *Volksgemeinschaft* (people's community) devoid of Jewish influence made the struggle for pluralism a very important one indeed. Insisting on this point does not imply that the Weimar Republic be judged according to liberal standards, reanimating a *Sonderweg* (special path) thesis that has few followers in the field. Rather, it means that the 'life worlds' of Weimar's Jews were very much influenced by the fact that the number of people who not only lived pluralism but subscribed to it was dwindling rapidly. For most Jews in the Weimar Republic, liberal democracy in German public life assumed normative status.

Who were the Jews?

Much has been written on the subject of 'German-Jewish identity'. On the whole, the debate has focused on three related questions: whether the Jews were German; whether they were Jewish; and whether there existed a German-Jewish 'symbiosis'. The first question was especially urgent for non-Jews in the Weimar Republic. The second question is especially compelling for Jewish historians today. The third question defined the research in the three or so decades after the Holocaust.

Many Germans in the Weimar period refused to accept that Jews were Germans. To be sure, social intercourse in the form of intermarriage, economic ties, public debate, or recreational activity was visible, but the frequent Jewish protestations of fealty to the nation indicate the precariousness of the situation. Indeed, had it not been for the hostility they encountered, many Jews would have had to reflect much less on their 'Germanness'; it would have become more of a habit than an exercise in public cerebration. What many of them envisaged, though, and what their detractors could not stomach, was a combination of German and Jewish (and Wormser or *Rheinländer*, for that matter), something approaching multiculturalism as we know it today. According to this ideal, the state guarantees the freedom of ethnic minorities to maintain their customs, while the hegemonic power or majority population—if such a majority is to be found—accepts or even endorses that freedom. The Jews of Weimar, then, with the exception of those who had recently emigrated from Eastern Europe and those whose ideological propensities (uncompromising Zionism) precluded appeals to two or more loyalties, *felt* German, which is all we need to know.

A majority felt Jewish, too. It has become somewhat of a pastime for Jewish historians to embark on studies that aim to disclose the 'Jewishness' of their protagonists. This 'search for identity' may be attributed to at least two developments. First, in the case of German Jewry, the desire to counter earlier verdicts whereby Germany's Jews had succumbed to 'assimilationism'. This reproach, usually advanced by contemporary and later Zionists, denies that a large part of German Jewry lived *substantially* Jewish lives. That is, their 'Jewishness' had been superseded by an altogether more prevalent 'Germanness'. Present-day historians, by contrast, are less adamant in demanding allegiance one way or the other. They are therefore able to detect forms of Jewish existence that did not entail faithfulness to Jewish law (*Halakha*), the espousal of a return to Zion, or cultural participation.

The second and more controversial factor is the desire to vindicate late twentieth-century multiculturalism. Once it had become clear that Jewish life in the Diaspora was not only possible but, in North America and Western Europe, devoid of serious threats to life and property, Jewish historians could embrace the idea that being American (or British, or French) and being Jewish need not be a contradiction. This realization in turn permitted many of them to expand the definition of 'Jewish identity' so as to make it more inclusive and less exacting. This essay will endorse their view that most German Jews led lives that contained enough elements to make them *feel* Jewish too.

The debate surrounding a German-Jewish 'symbiosis', finally, proceeds from the premiss that there were two clearly demarcated groups in the Weimar Republic, *the* Germans and *the* Jews; that these groups could but in the end failed to have a mutually advantageous relationship; and that post-Holocaust attempts on the part of rueful Germans and nostalgic Jews to claim that such a kinship had existed are at best naive and at worst reckless. The debate has usually been associated with Gershom Scholem, the eminent historian of Jewish mysticism. In a famous piece published in 1964, Scholem disputed that a 'conversation' between 'Germans' and 'Jews' had ever taken place, since any conversation required two parties 'who listen to each other, who are ready to take note of and respond to the other in his otherness'.[4] Instead, only the 'Jews' had tried to converse with the 'Germans', 'from all possible angles and points of view, demanding, pleading, and imploring, grovelling and defiant, in all tones of moving dignity and godforsaken lack of dignity'.[5] An early convert to Zionism, Scholem had emigrated to Palestine in the early 1920s. His stance was reinforced, moreover, in the aftermath of Auschwitz.

Yet by and large, current research has moved away from his sweeping judgement, based as it is on hindsight as well as on the mistaken notion that 'Germans' and 'Jews' were mutually exclusive entities that could engage in dialogue—resembling as it were two sides whose only common denominator was the instrumental use of language. Besides, Scholem's focus—Jewish intellectual exclusion from German-Christian thought and consideration—ignores the everyday existence of those who did not envision dialogue of an abstract kind. As outlined above, Weimar's Jews felt German and Jewish (and local), and many would have found it amusing to be asked to join the Jewish side in such a debate. In the oft-quoted words of the novelist Jakob Wassermann: 'I am a German, and I am a Jew, one as intensely and as completely as the other, inextricably bound together.'[6]

Even so, Scholem's bitter assessment does point towards one aspect of German-Jewish identity in the Weimar Republic that affected the lives of Jews from all walks of life, namely the overall lack of interest amongst Gentiles to come to terms with an ever-growing anti-Semitism. It is in this respect that Scholem's Zionist premises coincide with the more 'postmodern' position adopted here. Whereas non-Jewish Germans faced repeated periods of insecurity, Jewish Germans faced anti-Semitism even in times of security. Thus, although we ought to reject teleological readings of the German-Jewish past, the following passages do reveal the extent to which Gentile indifference as well as Gentile enmity influenced Jewish lives in no uncertain terms. In order to make sense of German Jewry in the Weimar Republic, however, we need first to adumbrate its prehistory.

The origins of Weimar Jewry

Following the implementation of full legal equality in 1871, Jewish integration into German society gained momentum. Jews joined, and sometimes founded, local clubs and associations; studied and taught at universities; befriended, sometimes married, non-Jews; and debated in municipal councils and parliaments. Although scholars have demonstrated that, based on their incomes, even better-off Jews did not always belong to the *Bürgertum* (bourgeoisie), their upward mobility had nonetheless been astonishing. In many towns across the country, Jews were visibly affluent. At the beginning of the twentieth century, Frankfurt's Jews paid, relative to their numbers, four times as much taxes as the city's Protestants, and eight times as much as the Catholics. In Berlin, Jews made up 4 per cent of the population and 15 per cent of all taxpayers, but contributed 30 per cent to direct tax revenues.

Still, the 'Empire's record, for all the emancipatory legislation, for all the guarantees of legal equality, was one of half-fulfilled promise'.[7] This was not only so because Jews were refused entry to the imperial civil service and barred from the army officer corps, both institutions that in many respects defined the self-image of imperial Germany. It was so, more importantly, because prominent figures such as the historian Heinrich von Treitschke or the court preacher Adolf Stoecker advanced ideas, often clothed in respectable language, which threatened to undo emancipation. Anti-Semitism also emerged in the Conservative Party, and became an important element in mass organizations such as the Agrarian League, special interest groups such as the German National League of Commercial Employees, and nationalist pressure groups such as the Pan-German League.

Jews reacted to the anti-Semitic menace in several ways. University students established fraternities that figured as alternatives to the clubs from which they had been excluded. In Jewish communities throughout the country, rabbis and teachers defended German Jewry in meetings, articles, and manifestos. Beyond reaction, Jews during this time regained interest in their heritage, founding 'Societies for Jewish History and Culture' under whose auspices lecture series, reading rooms, and libraries came into being. This 'organizational renaissance'[8] had the unintended consequence of strengthening Jewish identity without simultaneously loosening Jewish ties to Germany. In early 1893, coinciding with the spread of Jew-hatred in the Conservative Party and elsewhere, a group of Jews in Berlin founded the Central-Verein deutscher Staatsbürger jüdischen Glaubens (Central Association of German Citizens of the Jewish Faith or CV), an association of 'German citizens of the Jewish faith' whose express goal it was, first, to emphasize the Jews' German patriotism and, second, to defend Jewish honour openly. Instead of traditional behind-the-scenes appeals to the seat of power for protection, the CV waged its battle against anti-Semitism before the eyes of the German public. The CV was to prove to be the most popular German-Jewish organization before and after the First World War.

Four years later, Jews in Cologne set up the first Zionist organization (Vereinigung) in Germany, whose initial leadership consisted of men who wished to combine Jewish 'clan' (*Stamm*) sentiment with German self-understanding. A radical faction, less concerned with bourgeois mores, gained ground just before the war, resolving to persuade as many Jews as possible to leave Germany behind in favour of Jewish national self-consciousness in Palestine. Where the

CV was a legal-oriented organization that fought anti-Semitism, the Zionist Vereinigung was an ideological-educational movement that fought assimilation. Although liberal-minded activists within the CV acknowledged that Zionism had promoted Jewish pride and confidence, they continued to criticize its attempt to 'denationalize' the Jews from Germany. Zionists, in turn, reproached the CV for what they described as its 'deracinated', purely faith-based understanding of Judaism.

In Jewish intellectual life, the years before and after 1914 were marked by calls for change, appeals to reform, and evocations of authenticity not dissimilar to protests against bourgeois culture found amongst non-Jews. Frequently these demands accorded with the Zionist postulate that assimilation had run its course. Beyond the rejection of liberal Judaism, however, Jewish reformers aimed at bringing about a new sense of Jewishness, culling elements from neo-mysticism, Nietzscheanism, and *Lebensphilosophie* (philosophy of life). Martin Buber, to take the best-known example, claimed that Judaism's life force had been spent—and that it could only be restored if Jews regained access to the non-materialist, non-intellectual, non-rational realities of existence, all of which could be discovered in Eastern European Jewry. 'Young Germans talked about the "new German"', George Mosse writes, 'young Jews spoke of the "new Jew" in exactly the same terms'.[9] Indeed, it is possible to define the period between 1890 and 1930 as a second *Sattelzeit* in German intellectual life, one during which 'numerous traditional theological and religious terms . . . lost their meaning'. In the process, theologians, philosophers, and religious thinkers, often exemplars of a new generation, renounced 'genuine religious discourse' for 'political and aesthetic language worlds'.[10]

On the eve of the First World War, then, the parameters that would determine Jewish debates in Weimar Germany had been all but set: cultural-religious debate revolved around the question of Jewish authenticity. For a growing number of young Jewish intellectuals, the rational promises of yesteryear, epitomized in the neo-Kantian philosophy of Hermann Cohen, were to be replaced by communal action and spirituality, by regeneration and a 'new Jewish sensitivity'.[11] For them, the Eastern Jew embodied everything the Western Jew lacked, particularly 'real' Jewish *völkisch* consciousness—and thereby came to figure as a foil upon which their fears and aspirations could be projected. Jewish thinkers in the Enlightenment tradition were forced to respond to this challenge.

Political debate centred on Jewish belonging. To be sure, Zionists displayed German patriotism during the war and congratulated Jewish soldiers on their military prowess. They had also welcomed Wilhelm II's call for a *Burgfrieden* (social peace) as they would later welcome the establishment of the republic, appreciating each as an opportunity to prove Jewish loyalty towards Germany. Yet to all intents and purposes, the question as to whether Jews should further acculturate to, as opposed to dissimilate from, German society remained acute. In light of an ever-growing anti-Semitism, it was again the liberal camp that was obliged to respond to the Zionist challenge.

Gentile–Jewish relations hinged on the question of acceptance. The basic features of racism had been formulated in the last two decades of the nineteenth century. Unlike 'traditional' Judeophobia, which focused on the 'proper' place of the Jew in society and perpetuated Christian stereotypes of Judaism and the Jews, racialist thinking undertook to ascertain the essential differences between 'German' and 'Jew', differences that could not be eliminated through assimilation or conversion. Soon after the outbreak of war, the subject of acceptance resurfaced with even greater urgency, as radical anti-Semites began to intensify their campaign against the Jewish 'other'. This agitation culminated in the infamous *Judenzählung* or census of Jews of 1916, when the army, yielding to the fabrication that Jews were shirkers and war profiteers, set out to determine their number in the trenches. Although all Jews faced the racist peril, the threat to liberal Jewry, whose *raison d'être* stood or fell with the success of integration, was by far the gravest.

That being the case, the most novel aspect of Weimar Jewry was not a change in personnel: the generational conflict had already erupted before. It was not a change in style either: 'new' Jews had already dismissed the antics of bourgeois respectability. Content and quality, too, remained the same: liberals vied against nationalists, rationalists against spiritualists, racists against Jews. What was novel, rather, was the 'context of cultural production and consumption'.[12] The context was such that Jews carried on the above debates in an atmosphere of heightened tension, one that followed from the economic and political turmoil of the time, but that was exacerbated by growing hostility towards them. Jews eagerly consumed the various 'products' on offer, but they did so with an eye to Jewish welfare and survival in a liberal democratic state. However much they embraced cultural, religious, and political change, therefore, the end result would distinguish them from many of their Gentile contemporaries.

Liberalism ante mortem? Jewish politics

Even where they differed, Jews in the Weimar Republic had a number of things in common. Demographically, the Jewish population would have declined well before the war had it not been for Eastern Jewish immigration. In 1925, foreign-born Jews, most of who had fled from persecution or whom the wartime military government had enlisted, comprised about 19 per cent of the Jewish population. Ninety per cent of these non-nationals came from Eastern Europe. From the mid-1920s on, however, stagnation gave way to decline, mainly as a result of low birth rates and Jewish urbanization. By 1933, nearly 55 per cent of Germany's half a million Jews lived in cities with a population of 100,000 or more, 32 per cent of whom resided in Berlin. While the number of Jews in Germany amounted to 535,200 or 0.93 per cent of the population in 1910, twenty-three years later this figure had dropped to 499,700 and 0.77 per cent respectively.

Although most Jews lived in large towns, there were important exceptions. Particularly in southern Germany, so-called *Land-juden* (rural Jews) made up a large percentage of the Jewish population: in Bavaria, Baden, and Hesse, about one-third lived in rural areas. In some towns, such as Rhina near Kassel, 10 to 15 per cent of the population was Jewish. A majority of these Jews engaged in trade, specializing in wine, cattle, and grain. Despite the fact that traditional mores retained a greater hold here than elsewhere, rural Jews 'were at best selective in their religious observance and hardly scrupulous about refraining from work on the Sabbath'.[13] They were also affected by the impact of urbanization, as many communities confronted an ageing populace that had difficulties paying for religious, cultural, and welfare services.

Most Jews chose jobs in commerce and the free professions, where approximately 70 per cent found employment. In the latter sector, the figures for 1933 show a slight increase from 1907, with 16 per cent of all lawyers and 11 per cent of all doctors being Jewish. Amongst the 24 per cent who worked in industry and trade, many owned small shops and firms. These statistics indicate that Jews retained their preference for occupations that had always been their domain, not the least because Christian impositions of an earlier age had precluded Jews from owning land or joining guilds. More important, Jews would have manifested unusual behaviour had they moved into agriculture and industry at a time when the tertiary sector was expanding rapidly.

These peculiarities notwithstanding, Jews suffered considerably from the effects of economic dislocation. During the period of hyperinflation, small shopkeepers lost their savings, while pensioners, already disproportionately represented within the Jewish population, were forced to re-enter the job market. Real income declined in absolute terms. Jews were equally hard hit during the depression. Demand for clothing and consumer goods, areas in which Jewish employment was high, decreased dramatically, so that Jewish workers and employees often experienced joblessness earlier than their Gentile counterparts. Jewish merchants, moreover, faced growing competition from those who sought to make a living in areas that seemed more promising than crisis-ridden agriculture or large-scale industry. Finally, members of the Jewish bourgeoisie found it ever more taxing to send their children to university. While total enrolment in Prussia witnessed a moderate increase between 1911 and 1925, the number of Jewish students fell from 2,212 to 1,675.

As outlined above, Jewish politics before the war had been characterized by two contrary positions. The first, embodied in the liberal Central-Verein, stressed that German and Jewish commitments were compatible. The second, embodied in the Zionist movement, dismissed such professed mutuality as illusive. Although the CV had been moving away from its erstwhile definition of Jewry as solely confessional, the differences with Zionism persisted, especially in light of the institutional changes that would occur after 1918.

These changes came about because the country had adopted a new constitution, because anti-Semitism was raising its ugly head, and because the Jews were transforming the meaning of 'community'. The new democratic order of Weimar forced the Jewish communities to introduce universal suffrage on the basis of proportional representation. This expansion, in turn, gave voice to groups that had been marginalized in the past. Anti-Semitism, before 1914 confined to vanguards with a racist *Weltanschauung* (ideology) or part of a cultural code that demanded Jewish social and economic subordination, now influenced wider circles within the population. And the new meaning of 'community' entailed an altogether more encompassing role for the Jewish *Gemeinde* (community). In the nineteenth century, communities had defined themselves in terms of religious practice (*Religions-* or *Kultusgemeinde*), debate usually accentuating issues of synagogue decorum or the status of particular rabbis. At the end of the century, Zionists had demanded that this status be converted into a national-oriented *Volksgemeinde*, a community that dealt with culture and learning, education and instruction, welfare and legal protection. But it was only in the Weimar Republic that their vision assumed relevance.

In post-war Jewish politics, the main points of contention hardly changed. Community elections saw the Liberal Party, supported by members of the CV, pitted against the Jewish People's Party (JVP), supported by members of the Zionist Vereinigung. The former group, long established and often of an elitist bent, stood for the continuation of the *Kultusgemeinde*, without thereby ignoring the need for communal solidarity. The latter group, an alliance of Zionists, Eastern Jews, and nationalist Orthodox Jews, propagated the *Volksgemeinde*. Both parties dominated Jewish politics in the Weimar period, relegating religious factions or extreme 'national-German' Jews to the sidelines. Apart from its natural electorate, the JVP attracted the support of young German Jews who resented the liberal establishment. It also managed to channel hostility against 'assimilationists' who purportedly underestimated the impact of anti-Semitism. The JVP's greatest triumph came in 1926, when it managed to overthrow the liberal majority in Berlin, forming a coalition with the Orthodox that was first contested in court and ended in the JVP's electoral defeat four years later.

Conflict over the ideological composition of the *Gemeinden* was a permanent feature of Jewish political life. From a liberal perspective, Eastern Jews continued to pose a threat to the self-understanding of German Jewry. True, German Jews assisted their co-religionists in numerous ways, placing welfare facilities at their disposal or helping them find employment. In the name of unity, they also provided for religious needs, maintaining Orthodox synagogues and allowing for traditional dietary laws in communal settings. What is more, the liberal CV, representing some 300,000 people, declared that Jews comprised a 'community of destiny' (*Schicksalsgemeinschaft*) and that they should therefore discard the quest for 'anaemic' assimilation.

But often enough Jewish liberals feared that Eastern Jews would vitiate German Jewry's image, giving rise to the idea that Jews in fact did not belong to the German 'nation'. The propensity of *Ostjuden* (Eastern European Jews) to support the Zionist cause in community elections and elsewhere did not improve their standing in liberal eyes. In towns where native-born Jews confronted a sizeable Eastern Jewish population or even numerical preponderance, German Jews regularly upheld their political hegemony by limiting or proscribing Eastern Jewish rights. In Leipzig and Dresden, for example, separate voting lists for *Ostjuden* guaranteed comfortable liberal majorities. When the Prussian state intervened on behalf of Eastern Jewish rights, some communities introduced laws which stipulated that only members who paid community taxes—those Jews, in other words, who could afford to do so—would be eligible to vote. In other communities, enfranchisement was dependent on extended periods of legal residency.

Even so, historians have recently averred that, far from merely assuming relevance, the JVP paradigm of a Jewish *Volksgemeinde* became a matter of fact. That is, the community of faith no longer commanded enough support at a time when the principle of *Gemeinschaft* (society) gained considerable ground. Several developments tend to underscore this view. Most communities, for example, took on responsibilities normally reserved for the state, including the administration of hospitals and old-age homes, schools and adult education programmes, or unemployment benefit. Where synagogue attendance dwindled, participation in community elections increased, so that in Berlin some 60 per cent of the *Gemeinde* electorate went to the polls in 1930. Likewise, many communities began to publish their own newspapers and became centres of cultural life at the expense of private clubs and associations. The number of pupils attending Jewish schools also rose in several cities.

Why did this transformation take place and what did it mean for most Jews? Looking at the school system, it is clear that the growing numbers owed much to Eastern European, Orthodox, and Zionist interests. A minority of children from liberal backgrounds notwithstanding, Jewish schools catered primarily to the stalwart adherents of Jewish *Gemeinschaft*. Resistance to the idea of educational separatism did not subside either. On the contrary, liberal majorities on community councils repeatedly denied funds and the use of community buildings to Jewish schools. Similarly, most of the newly founded associations provided for leisure-time activities. Unlike Socialists or Catholics who created veritable subcultures, Jews did not found trade unions and only rarely established professional organizations, preferring instead to be members of local societies that represented special interests regardless of denomination.

Turning to community elections, it is evident that the Jews in Germany were as politicized as their Gentile counterparts. This politicization was the result of the Zionist challenge, of the proliferation of different ideologies, and of liberal efforts to preserve their dominance. The democratization of political life gave Zionists the opportunity to defy the status quo openly. Not surprisingly, their rivals fought tooth and nail to defend the liberal conception of German-Jewish existence. The clash between liberals and Zionists took on such an importance in the 1920s that at times Zionism seemed to be 'the main problem of German Jewry'[14] —and vice versa. But whether this clash typified *Gemeinschaft* is another matter. It could be argued with equal force that the *absence* of political controversy would have been truly remarkable. Furthermore, Moritz Goldstein's lamentation of 1912, that it was impossible 'to speak to all Jews as Jews',[15] still held true, for a Jewish public in terms of a clearly defined subculture had not materialized. Jews therefore did what most other Germans did, albeit with a difference. They continued to vote Liberal, both in their communities and in local, state, or national elections.

As for communal life, *Gemeinschaft* clearly emerged in the wake of economic disruption. Like Protestant and Catholic welfare, Jewish help for the destitute compensated for the absence of state assistance. Collapsing institutions, whether private societies or municipal establishments, engendered alternative initiatives. It is here that we find one principal source for the growing significance of Jewish communities in the Weimar Republic. The other source is anti-Semitism. Not only did pupils from liberal homes attend Jewish schools because of Jew-hatred. Many other Jews, too, faced with a form of hostility that was non-negotiable, retreated from mainstream social life. Students who would have otherwise fenced alongside non-Jews looked to Jewish clubs instead. And hikers who would have otherwise enjoyed the company of Catholics or Protestants preferred fellow Jews who did not continuously question their integrity, loyalty, and probity.

This argument, anathema as it is to the idea that extreme assimilation bred Jewish nationalism, entails a prediction of the future. It suggests that, had the republic stabilized, had the quest for order given way to felt order, and had anti-Semitism worn off, the ideal of a Jewish *Gemeinschaft* would have been short-lived and German Jewry might have eventually resembled a highly acculturated community with varying degrees of allegiance to Judaism. To be sure, the Jewish pursuit of community demonstrates that Jews, too, 'strove for contingency'.[16] But it does not imply that this pursuit would have become as distinct as it did had the rest of the population seriously included the Jews in its 'semantics of unity'.[17] The argument also assumes a rereading of Jewish *Gemeinschaft*. In fact, the 'search for Jewish community' was often no search at all, but rather a consequence of circumstances beyond the Jews' control. Those who pursued Jewish *Gemeinschaft* without simultaneously reacting to Gentile malevolence belonged to a minority. Finally, it serves as a reminder of Jewish liberal tenacity. Most Jews in Germany retained their predilection for liberalism, and did so at a time when the pressure to abandon this creed emanated from both within and without. It is this liberal continuity that is perhaps the most characteristic aspect of German Jewry in the Weimar Republic.

In a liberal key: religious-cultural debate

We can detect this resolve in religious and cultural discourse as well. At first sight such a statement may sound strange. After all, current scholarship has gone a long way to disclose the impact of irrationalism, holism, and nationalism on these areas. In the words of Michael Brenner, 'Whereas rationalist thought and individual faith had been the principal characteristics of nineteenth-century liberal Jewish ideology, in the Weimar period mysticism, Romanticism, and the collective experience became increasingly significant.'[18] Indeed, as we shall see below, Weimar's Jews espoused ideologies that approximated the ambitions of their contemporaries, seeking alternatives to what many believed was outmoded—especially 'the complacency of the German-Jewish bourgeoisie'.[19] But even here, hidden in the language of 'resurrection' and 'renewal', the search for order did not necessarily exclude the 'conservative' liberal paradigm.

Like their Protestant and Catholic equivalents, Jewish theologians discovered the forces of the irrational at a time when appeals to the unconscious and mystical pervaded intellectual debate. Within Jewish Orthodoxy, for instance, 'cultural pessimism, lack of trust in authorities, uncertainty about the merits of the present condition, the expectation of an approaching new world, [and] a shift toward the irrational' became familiar at this time.[20] This change did not mean, however, that religious fervour increased during the Weimar period. In fact, the 'signs of religious decline were more numerous than those of revival'.[21] Low attendance at religious services was a frequent matter of complaint; the number of rabbinical students declined steadily; and synagogues were usually filled during the performances of oratorios and concerts only. Liberal Jews, representing the overwhelming majority of the community, responded to this religious indifference by attaching greater importance to the worshippers themselves—they were to become participants rather than mere listeners—by introducing communal evenings, or by holding youth services.

In the cultural fold, numerous efforts were under way to expand the notion of Judaism as well as to discover new forms of attachment. Thus, Jewish popular learning expanded in the form of adult education institutes. Publishing houses came into being, editing multi-volume encyclopedias, translating Hebrew classics, and putting out poetry and novels on Jewish themes. Reappropriating Jewish knowledge also involved the transmission of Yiddish culture, which was usually limited to East European and Zionist circles. As is true for the religious realm, care must be taken not to overestimate the impact of these attempts at 'regeneration', sidelining as they do the lives of acculturated Jews, who, numerically speaking, 'hardly represented a quantité négligeable'.[22] In a reversal of Scholem's verdict, one might also warn against idealizing a purported renaissance at the expense of more mundane German-Jewish existence. The famous Frankfurt Freies Jüdisches Lehrhaus, for example, where luminaries and laypeople delivered courses in various fields of Judaism, never attracted more than about 4 per cent of the local Jewish population. Its lifespan of six years did not betoken colossal success either. Still, the attempt to revive Jewish cultural life was recognized everywhere, even if this awareness, at least for the majority of German Jews, did not occasion more than passing interest.

Let us take three prominent examples, two from within liberal Jewish theology and one from the world of culture and philosophy, to trace the shifts in focus as well as to illustrate continued attachment to seemingly dated values.

Leo Baeck was the most important liberal rabbi in Germany. In his famous book *The Essence of Judaism* (1905) he had contradicted the traditional Christian polemics against Pharisaic Judaism as propounded by Adolf Harnack in his *Essence of Christianity*. In doing so, Baeck portrayed Judaism along the lines of a rational, humanistic, and ethical enterprise. Yet in the second edition of his work, published in 1922, the prominent theologian introduced a new tone, prompting the historian Michael A. Meyer to write that Baeck's rationalist and universalistic approaches were 'increasingly balanced by their polar counterparts, which achieve[d] equivalent importance'.[23] Baeck now incorporated mystical elements, accepted the Kabbalah as a source of inspiration, and acknowledged the unfathomable aspects of religious belief. But even in this case we find the objective to embrace irrational moments *in order* to highlight ethical precepts. Baeck remained adamant that real piety only existed where ethical life prevailed, adding that for Jewish mysticism, too, the 'meaning of life is manifested in the deed'.[24]

In the 1920s, Leo Baeck was busy writing another book, this time on 'Classical and Romantic Religion'. The first section of the work—and the only one to be published—appeared in the Festschrift for the Hochschule für die Wissenschaft des Judentums (College for the Science of Jewry) in 1922, but was later revised and expanded. Here Baeck distinguished between classical and romantic appreciations of the irrational. According to his reading, in classical religion (i.e. Judaism) 'the irrational is not an ocean in which the ego, swelled with feeling, drowns'. Whereas in classical religion 'longing strives ever again for the goal which is to unify all men and impels them to follow the commandment of God', in romanticism (i.e. Christianity) 'longing always in the end returns to the self and remains at the level of a mere mood'.[25] Despite Baeck's new emphasis on the inscrutable and mysterious, he felt obliged to insist that Judaism did not belong to the romantic tradition; that in fact Judaism differed from Christianity in its ethical impulse, which was pitted against the latter's 'self-congratulation' on the state of grace.[26] However much the eminent rabbi may have supported the popular turn to spirituality, then, reason was never spurned altogether and Jewish mysticism remained tied to the overall objective that was ethical in nature. Jewish irrationalism, while gaining ground, did not supersede rationalism.

The second example is Max Wiener, a young liberal rabbi who served under Baeck in Düsseldorf and later joined him in Berlin. Wiener was one of the most important Jewish theologians in the Weimar Republic and has been associated with the call for a 'religious renewal based on the integration of nonrational elements—the feeling of belonging to the Jewish people and the self-consciousness of the particularity of the Jews as a chosen people—into modern Judaism'.[27] Indeed, Wiener is often cited as the prime example of a liberal rabbi who came to endorse nationalism, irrationalism, and supernatural revelation.

Like other liberal rabbis of his day, Wiener distanced himself from philosophical interpretations of Judaism that he regarded as too abstract, as too far removed from life. Wiener repeatedly avowed that philosophy and religion were inimical to each other, holding that the former led to an uncalled-for intellectualization of the latter. This line of reasoning often went in hand in hand with anti-Christian polemics whose thrust derived from the contention that Christianity was a religion of thought as well as dogma. But Wiener also faulted Jewish thinkers, including Maimonides and Spinoza, for falling into the philosophical trap. His theology was equally particularistic in nature. He believed in the blood bonds of the Jewish *Volk*. And he maintained that revelation had been confined to this *Volk* only.

Nevertheless, in criticizing the rational sides of earlier liberal theology, Wiener continued to insist on the humanist bases of the Jewish religion. In his magnum opus, *Judaism in the Age of Emancipation* (1933), the espousal of particularistic ritual fell together with the espousal of *Sittlichkeit* (ethical life). In fact, only through religious practice in the shape of Jewish law could the 'humane idea of religion'[28] be expressed and perpetuated. In the final section of his work, he again returned to the theme of Jewish 'feeling' and Jewish 'soul', concentrating on the poet Heinrich Heine, the Socialist thinker Moses Hess, and the liberal politician Gabriel Riesser. According to Wiener, Heine was that strange poet who differed from his fellow Romantics in castigating cultural and political reaction. Hess, on the other hand, combined 'social-humanistic' and 'national-Jewish enthusiasm',[29] declaring that the Jewish nation—safe, sound, and on its own piece of land—would disseminate universalistic values to the world. Riesser, finally, united the belief in Jewish ethical teachings with the emphatic struggle for emancipation. Although highlighting the emotive ties linking all three figures to their Jewish heritage, Wiener at the same time lauded their moral stands, ascribing them in large measure to Jewish sources. What we have here, in short, is one of the more radical representatives of German liberal Jewry refusing to make concessions on the issue of ethics while concurrently discarding both 'narrow' rationalism and 'one-sided' universalism. In this respect he resembled Baeck and other liberal thinkers such as Max Dienemann or Caesar Seligmann who tried to fuse contemporary thought with an undiminished liberal persuasion.

No other figure symbolizes the 'new' Jewish culture in Weimar better than Franz Rosenzweig, the founder of the Frankfurt Lehrhaus, the author of the *Star of Redemption*, and the co-translator of the Bible into German. As head of the Lehrhaus from 1920 on, Rosenzweig resolved to broaden and spread Jewish knowledge in the Diaspora as against supporting national 'homecoming' in Palestine. He insisted, furthermore, that Jewish learning would have to concentrate on the 'alienated' and 'assimilated' members of the community, smuggling as it were 'Jewish knowledge into the general Bildung [learning] so dear to German Jews'.[30]

For Rosenzweig, the First World War 'caused the collapse of the central idea of the whole Western philosophical tradition, namely, that of a reasonable universe regulated by the logos'.[31] Like many other contemporary Jewish thinkers, he felt that Hermann Cohen's rational religion had to be supplanted by immediate, unconstrained access to faith and tradition. Along with the philosopher Leo Strauss, he felt that the 'liberal proclivity for Enlightenment rationalism crowded out traditional theological concerns'.[32] And similarly to his fellow German philosophers, he welcomed the turn to intuition and metaphysics as set forth in various derivations of *Lebensphilosophie*. Accordingly, he identified Judaism neither with ethical precepts nor with the rational idea of God, but rather with a way of life. From this idea two further concepts followed. The first, in line with Heideggerian existential ontology, stressed authentic modes of being. The second, in line with the likes of Max Wiener, placed authentic experience in a holistic, communal setting. Jews differed from other peoples, Rosenzweig asserted, in that their existence was future oriented. Unlike other nations, whose specificity originated in claims to states and territories, the Jews refused to adhere to the present, thereby anticipating, in the act of choosing temporality over permanence, the experience of redemption. These were complicated ideas, but they summarized what for Rosenzweig came to take on particular significance: the authentic experience of Jewish community outside 'regular', secular history. This concern was also evident elsewhere.

When Buber and Rosenzweig embarked on their translation of the Hebrew Bible in the mid-1920s, their main concern was to lead the German-Jewish reader back to the original, so as to retrieve the 'genuine' spirit of the ancient book. By Hebraizing the German language, then, they sought to manifest the essence and life force of Judaism as it existed at the time of the Tanakh. Yet unlike other translations in the tradition of Romantic 'linguistic nationalism',[33] their enterprise was to focus on the original language and its 'national' dimension rather than on the target language. Thus, Buber and Rosenzweig chose German words that best fitted what they took to be the oral character of the Bible, rendering the Hebrew *tohu va'vohu* (without form and void), for example, into *Irrsal und Wirrsal* as opposed to the earlier and less aural *wüst und leer* or *öd und wüst* (denoting desolate and empty). Many of the favourable reviewers welcomed this emphasis on 'authenticity', claiming that it enabled Jews to repossess the ancient roots of Judaism. What is more, numerous Jewish schools had recourse to the Buber–Rosenzweig translation in their religious education, while reading circles gathered to recite sections of the newly interpreted work and newspaper editors recommended the Bible as an ideal Hanukkah or birthday gift. By contrast, less forthcoming responses, such as the one by the famous cultural theorist Siegfried Kracauer, castigated Buber and Rosenzweig for resorting to archaic and reactionary language in the tradition of 'Bayreuth and Valhalla', as well as for employing a vocabulary of this-worldly presence that did not in fact reflect 'this world' but tried to echo a distant 'Urtext' (original text). Orthodox critics, meanwhile, could not accept the fact that Buber and Rosenzweig relied on Grimm's German dictionary and Herder's interpretation of ancient Hebrew rather than on established and time-honoured Bible commentaries.

Recently Peter Gordon has contended that Rosenzweig's indifference to politics had the unintended consequence of immunizing him against extremist positions à la Heidegger. 'This "liberal" commitment to the separation of religion and state, while not actually argued from liberal premises, may have shielded Rosenzweig from some of the possibly illiberal consequences of his own philosophy.'[34] One could go a step further, however. Analysing the literature on the 'Jewish cultural renaissance' in Weimar, it is not unusual to encounter silence on the question of whether Jewish holism, irrationalism, and mysticism had wider ramifications. Although scholars insist on contextualizing these belief systems in order to demonstrate that Jewish discourse was 'German' too, there are few references to the similarities with right-wing thought. The impact of irrationalism, in other words, is taken to be sign of a Jewish renaissance, but not as a potential threat to Jewish existence. We may attribute this oversight to an unspoken assumption, according to which Jews had to remain at least in part liberal despite their rejection of both *Bildung* and bourgeoisie. If we want to move beyond assumptions, however, the possible reasons for this Jewish liberal reticence need to be addressed.

One immediate reason relates to the fact that the rupture of 1914–18 was much less complete than has previously been suggested, so that the 'overlap of languages and approaches between the old and the new, the "traditional" and the "modern", the conservative and the iconoclastic, was apparent both during and after the war'.[35] That is, while Jews participated in the discourse on reform and revolution, they also held fast, like their Gentile contemporaries, to more 'conventional' ideas.

Nevertheless, the 'context of cultural production and consumption' had changed after 1918, and under the altered circumstances the overall fate of liberalism was not a happy one. In the Jewish case, its fate, as has been argued throughout, was much less dismal. In this regard Steven Aschheim has shown that even such critics of 'Liberal-Bourgeois Modernity' and instrumental rationality as Leo Strauss, Hannah Arendt, or Max Horkheimer 'held on however grimly to the universal emancipatory promise', whether 'out of a sense of their own perceived vulnerability, or a commitment to older Enlightenment humanizing traditions, or even because of their own Jewish ideals'.[36]

If we take the above-mentioned discussions and controversies, it is apparent that 'Jewish ideals' did not preclude Jews from championing *völkisch* mysticism or neo-romantic holism. Some Jews also had no compunctions censuring 'humanizing traditions' that smacked of nineteenth-century rationalism. But whether Buber appealed to ties of blood, Baeck invoked spirituality, or Rosenzweig called for authentic community, Jewish predilections for liberalism persisted. And they did so not because Jews were better Germans, but because of the historical connection between Jewish emancipation on the one hand, and the quest for a liberal (national) state, on the other. In the Weimar Republic, this connection became all the more important, leading many Jews to display 'Jewish' peculiarity in their public defence of the liberal cause and 'German' peculiarity in their personal and communal espousal of new ideas, fashions, and creeds. In this sense, Thomas Mann, perhaps predictably, got it wrong in his novel *The Magic Mountain*, when he identified irrationalism, anarchism, mysticism, and communism with the Jewish convert Leo Naphta. Although contrary to his authorial intentions, the famous writer might have added to his portrayal of Naphta the image of someone who, while indulging in prophecy and proclaiming various truths, remained a secret liberal in his appreciation of the Weimar-Jewish predicament.

Notes

1. Peter Fritzsche, 'Landscape of danger, landscape of design: crisis and modernism in Weimar Germany', in Thomas W. Kniesche and Stephen Brockmann (eds.), *Dancing on the Volcano: Essays on the Culture of the Weimar Republic* (Columbia, SC, 1994), 37.
2. Marion Kaplan, *The Making of the Jewish Middle Class: Women, Family, and Identity in Imperial Germany* (Oxford, 1991), 33.
3. Peter Fritzsche, 'Did Weimar fail?', *Journal of Modern History*, 68 (Sept. 1996), 630.
4. Gershom Scholem, 'Wider den Mythos vom deutsch-jüdischen Gespräch', in idem, *Judaica 2* (Frankfurt am Main, 1995), 7.
5. Ibid. 8.
6. Jakob Wassermann, *Mein Weg als Deutscher und Jude* (Berlin, 1921), 126.
7. Peter Pulzer, 'Between hope and fear: Jews and the Weimar Republic', in Wolfgang Benz, Arnold Paucker, and Peter Pulzer (eds.), *Jüdisches Leben in der Weimarer Republik: Jews in the Weimar Republic* (Tübingen, 1998), 271.
8. Peter Pulzer, *Jews and the German State: The Political History of a Minority, 1848–1933* (Oxford, 1992), 13.
9. George L. Mosse, *Germans and Jews: The Right, the Left, and the Search for a 'Third Force' in Pre-Nazi Germany* (Detroit, 1987), 81.
10. Friedrich Wilhelm Graf, *Die Wiederkehr der Götter: Religionen in der modernen Kultur* (Munich, 2004), 171.
11. Anson Rabinbach, 'Between Apocalypse and Enlightenment: Benjamin, Bloch, and modern Jewish Messianism', in idem, *In the Shadow of Catastrophe: German Intellectuals between Apocalypse and Enlightenment* (Berkeley and Los Angeles, 1997), 27.

12. Matthew Jeffries, *Imperial Culture in Germany, 1871–1918* (London, 2003), 264–5.
13. Michael A. Meyer, '*Gemeinschaft* within *Gemeinde*: religious ferment in Weimar Liberal Judaism', in Michael Brenner and Derek J. Penslar (eds.), *In Search of Jewish Community: Jewish Identities in Germany and Austria 1918–1933* (Bloomington, Ind., 1998), 16.
14. Martin Liepach, *Das Wahlverhalten der jüdischen Bevölkerung: Zur politischen Orientierung der Juden in der Weimarer Republik* (Tübingen, 1996), 56.
15. Moritz Goldstein, 'Deutsch-jüdischer Parnaß', *Kunstwart*, 11/25 (1912), 282.
16. Martin H. Geyer, *Verkehrte Welt: Revolution, Inflation und Moderne: München 1914–1924* (Göttingen, 1998), 399.
17. Paul Nolte, *Die Ordnung der Gesellschaft: Selbstentwurf und Selbstbeschreibung im 20. Jahrhundert* (Munich, 2000), 92.
18. Michael Brenner, *The Renaissance of Jewish Culture in Weimar Germany* (New Haven, 1996), 7.
19. Noah Isenberg, *Between Redemption and Doom: The Strains of German-Jewish Modernism* (Lincoln, 1999), 108.
20. Mordechai Breuer, *Modernity within Tradition: The Social History of Orthodox Jewry in Imperial Germany* (New York, 1992), 355.
21. Donald L. Niewyk, *The Jews in Weimar Germany* (New Brunswick, NJ, 2001), 102.
22. Ulrich Sieg, *Jüdische Intellektuelle im Ersten Weltkrieg: Kriegserfahrungen, weltanschauliche Debatten und kulturelle Neuentwürfe* (Berlin, 2001), 319.
23. Michael A. Meyer, *Response to Modernity: A History of the Reform Movement in Judaism* (Oxford, 1988), 208.
24. Leo Baeck, *Das Wesen des Judentums* (Darmstadt, 1966; 1st pub. 1922), 54.
25. Leo Baeck, *Aus drei Jahrtausenden: Wissenschaftliche Untersuchungen und Abhandlungen zur Geschichte des jüdischen Glaubens* (Tübingen, 1958), 120. The translation is taken from Leo Baeck, *Judaism and Christianity* (Philadelphia, 1958), 291–2.
26. Baeck, *Jahrtausenden*, 58.
27. Brenner, *Renaissance*, 45.
28. Max Wiener, *Jüdische Religion im Zeitalter der Emanzipation* (Berlin, 2002; 1st pub. 1933), 22.
29. Ibid. 262.
30. *Bildung* refers to self-formation through culture and education; Brenner, *Renaissance*, 89.

31. Stéphane Mosès, *System and Revelation: The Philosophy of Franz Rosenzweig* (Detroit, 1992), 24–5.
32. David N. Myers, *Resisting History: Historicism and its Discontents in German-Jewish Thought* (Princeton, 2003), 121.
33. George Steiner, *After Babel: Aspects of Language and Translation* (Oxford, 1976), 324.
34. Peter Eli Gordon, *Rosenzweig and Heidegger: Between Judaism and German Philosophy* (Berkeley and Los Angeles, 2003), 311.
35. Jay Winter, *Sites of Memory, Sites of Mourning: The Great War in European Cultural History* (Cambridge, 1995), 3.
36. Steven E. Aschheim, 'Against social science. Jewish intellectuals, the critique of liberal-bourgeois morality, and the (ambiguous) legacy of radical Weimar theory', in idem, *In Times of Crisis: Essay on European Culture, Germans, and Jews* (Madison, 2001), 26–7.

High brow and low brow culture

Karl Christian Führer

The memory of the Weimar Republic is strongly shaped by its various art forms. Some would see the 'expressionist film' epitomizing the culture of the 1920s, with the vampire Nosferatu from F. W. Murnau's film of the same name or the female robot in Fritz Lang's film *Metropolis* having become part of the iconography of the twentieth century. Others would cite literary monuments like Thomas Mann's *The Magic Mountain* or Alfred Döblin's *Berlin Alexanderplatz*, the works of Brecht or those of the composers Kurt Weill and Paul Hindemith, as aesthetic high points of the era. The pioneering quality of the epoch is also commonly evoked in other spheres: in the cool, elegant designs of the Bauhaus or in the cultural criticism of Walter Benjamin and Siegfried Kracauer.

Many accounts of Weimar culture have understandably focused on these pinnacles of aesthetic and intellectual achievement. This chapter, however, will take a different tack. Our understanding of Weimar culture is incomplete without a grasp of broader patterns of cultural production and consumption, and skewed if it does not take into account the conservative tastes and the forces of tradition which also characterized it. Seen from this broader perspective, the cultural life of the republic emerges as less spectacular and less experimental than it appears in many accounts. This chapter begins by describing the system of public support for cultural activities as a central element of the cultural history of the Weimar Republic. There follows an examination of the relationship between art and leisure, since this illustrates particularly well the connection between tradition and innovation in German cultural life during the 1920s. Finally, it will consider some data that shed light on how frequently and in what ways ordinary citizens of the Weimar Republic participated in its cultural life.

The public promotion of art and culture

One major cultural innovation of the Weimar era has gone virtually unnoticed: the assumption that the state should use taxpayers' money to subsidize the arts and ensure the broadest possible spread of cultural provision. To this day, this assumption remains a distinctive feature of German life that marks it out from many other countries. Although the beginnings of such cultural subsidies can be traced back to the era of the German empire, it was only after 1918 that they became a crucial factor in German cultural life. Subsidies provided vital financial support to the majority of theatres, opera houses, and orchestras, many museums and public libraries. There was even a national fund—the 'German Arts Community' (*Deutsche Kunstgemeinschaft*)—that provided interest-free loans to individuals to enable them to purchase paintings and sculptures: thanks to this initiative, artists such as Otto Dix, Käthe Kollwitz, Max Pechstein, and Emil Nolde could sell paintings that might not otherwise have found buyers.[1] Given that Germany had just lost a war and was struggling to meet the new social and welfare responsibilities that were among the war's consequences, it is doubly surprising to see how widespread official promotion of art and culture was after 1918.

There were admittedly broad areas of the republic's cultural life that had to manage without public subsidies. For instance, the production and showing of films were left to private commercial initiative; the law of supply and demand also applied to the book market; and finally, broadcasting, which was introduced in 1923, was financed exclusively from the revenue it received from listeners.[2] Cinema fared particularly badly when compared with theatres and museums, not only because it did not receive public subsidies, but because it had itself to support the state in the form of a leisure tax, the *Lustbarkeitssteuer*, which increased the price of each cinema ticket. With this levy, to the great annoyance of film producers and the owners of cinemas, the state placed cinema attendance on a par with public dances and varieté shows, and the German cinemagoer was forced to make an indirect contribution to the public subsidy of theatres, opera houses, orchestras, and museums.

Cultural subsidies under the republic were collected and distributed through the municipal authorities and the federal states (*Länder*). The Reich government was not involved in the promotion of the arts: under the republic's federal system neither the Reichstag nor the Reich cabinet had any say over cultural matters. And even though these subsidies were only a small part of municipal and *Land* budgets (usually they constituted barely 3 per cent or even less of the budget), they were of paramount importance for the viability of cultural life.

The best example of this is the theatre. In the mid-1920s there were approximately 160 publicly subsidized theatres in Germany, with on average more than 50 per cent of their revenue provided by public authorities. As a result of this subsidization, theatre flourished even in small towns. The smallest German town with its own theatre was probably Neustrelitz in Mecklenburg with a population of only 14,000 inhabitants. There was a publicly subsidized theatre in Bunzlau in Silesia, a town with 18,000 citizens; Coburg in Bavaria was a little larger with 25,000 inhabitants, but its theatre was already in a different league, being of the 'three-strand' type (*Drei-Sparten-Haus*). This meant it not only had theatre productions, but also a chorus and soloists, an orchestra, and a ballet troupe for its own regular productions of operas, operettas, and ballets. 'Three-strand' provision was the norm for the great majority of publicly subsidized theatres, enabling a full repertoire that ensured a different programme every evening.

Germany was the only country in the world to have such a dense network of repertory theatres. Italy's provision in terms of premises was comparable, but its many provincial theatres had only irregular performances provided at short notice by travelling opera companies, and the number of theatre productions in Italy came nowhere near that of Germany. In other countries such as France or Great Britain, theatre life was organized completely differently and concentrated in the respective capitals, where a rich abundance of productions contrasted sharply with the dearth of provision in the provinces. The opposite was the case in Germany, where thanks to public subsidies the majority of the population could relatively easily go to the theatre, and where even the smaller theatres put on a diverse and elaborate programme. For example, in 1929 the municipal theatre of the industrial town of Duisburg staged 49 different operas, 29 plays, as well as 5 ballet productions; meanwhile in Aachen during the same year the municipal theatre staged 30 premières within six months. Neither theatre was particularly unusual in this respect. Even in those towns that did not maintain their own theatre troupe, there were often regular theatre performances: twenty-five publicly subsidized regional touring ensembles (*Landesbühnen*) took performances even to the remotest corners of provincial Germany.[3]

Germany's self-image as a nation of culture (*Kulturnation*) was thus not unfounded in this era. Nowhere else in the world during the 1920s were there so many theatre performances, so many opera houses, and so many classical concerts. In some places one could even talk of a glut. In Mainz and Wiesbaden, for example, two medium-sized cities directly facing each other on the Rhine with a combined population of 250,000, inhabitants had the choice between performances of two independent opera companies, two theatre ensembles, and three symphony orchestras. Similarly, in the Ruhr area most cities maintained their own theatres, even though these urban centres lay extremely close together and were already in this period connected to one another through an extensive public transport system.

This densely woven cultural scene had already existed in the nineteenth century (its origins lay in part even earlier), but only under the Weimar Republic did the state become its indispensable patron. Extensive subsidies that balanced perennial deficits had existed during the period of the empire, but only for a small group of theatres, primarily for the court theatres of the German monarchs. Bequeathed by the absolutist rulers of the baroque period to later generations, such court theatres existed not only in Prussia, Bavaria, and Saxony but in nearly all the twenty-two states that made up the empire from 1871. When the revolution in November 1918 terminated the rule of the princes, the new governments in most states decided without hesitation to maintain the court theatres as state theatres (*Landestheater*) and to settle their deficits from the budgets. This decision was supported by near-universal consensus in the individual parliaments of the *Länder*, usually with all parties from right to left voting for the bill after only brief discussions.[4]

There had already been numerous municipal theatres alongside the court theatres during the period of the empire. However, these were run by private companies which leased the premises from the city and received only very modest public subsidies, if any. This pre-1918 system operated according to a general pattern whereby the city owned the theatre building, stage props, and scenery and paid the wages of the technical staff, who were municipal employees on permanent contracts; this 'basic outfit' of the theatre was then leased to a private investor and manager, who put on shows at his own risk, made his own artistic decisions, and who in addition employed and paid the actors, singers, and musicians. He had to cover the running costs and also the often not inconsiderable lease fee from his cash income. If the theatre director received any further financial support, this was often only in indirect form, for instance through a reduction in the price of the electricity or gas supply.

This leasing system broke down after 1918. Although the reasons for this have not been fully researched, some overall trends are clear. First, the costs of the directors rose sharply because—probably for the first time in the history of German theatre—they could no longer get away with paying starvation wages to their artistic personnel. While a few 'stars' had always been well paid, low wages had been the rule for the numerous less prominent actors and singers but above all for the members of the chorus and orchestra. Now, those who worked in the theatre could benefit from the republic's social legislation, with collectively negotiated wage agreements regulating conditions of work and securing appropriate remuneration. Another reason for private theatre companies struggling financially after 1918 was that theatre takings declined, probably due to the worsening inflation that impoverished the middle classes who constituted the bulk of theatre audiences. The widening scissors effect of rising costs and falling income during the inflation years threatened municipal theatres almost everywhere in Germany with bankruptcy. The prospect of theatres going dark induced most municipal administrations to take the theatre into public ownership: deficits were settled from the city coffers and the theatre manager was henceforward transformed into a municipal employee.

The change did not occur as smoothly as the transfer of the court theatre into a *Landestheater*. Financially weaker than the federal states, the municipalities were more fearful about taking on new financial burdens.[5] In the final analysis, however, the municipal theatres became exactly the same type of 'non-profit theatre' as the former court theatres and for the same reason: prestige was at stake. In much the same way that *Länder* governments made money available for theatres and opera houses because they wanted to use them to promote themselves as vital constituent parts of the new republic, municipal administrations took over the 'lease' theatres after 1918 as urban enterprises because they viewed a flourishing theatre as an integral part of urban life. A city without a theatre—so local politicians in the Weimar Republic believed—lacked will-power and dynamism: the lack of a theatre undermined the local pride of its citizens and signalled a reluctance to challenge neighbouring or equally large municipalities in the civic image stakes—and, more concretely, to secure its share of tourists. Because of this central importance of the theatre for local identity and the image it presented to the outside world, subsidies found support in unexpected quarters. Even associations of retailers and craftsmen as representatives of the petite bourgeoisie frequently voted overwhelmingly for the generous support of the local theatre because they too saw it as an 'advertisement for our city' that would in the end benefit all inhabitants.[6]

The theatre subsidies that the federal states and municipalities had taken on after 1918 rapidly became a necessity and were accepted as essential if theatres were to survive. Even the end of the inflation in November 1923 and the improvement of the economic situation after the stabilization crisis of 1924 did not bring a return to the old system of the 'lease' theatre. In fact, the opposite was the case. Public subsidies rocketed during the short 'golden years' of the Weimar Republic, rising in only three years between 1925/6 and 1928/9 by 39 per cent. Contemporaries commented half ironically, half appreciatively, on the scramble by cities to outbid one another in prestige and cultural standing and even talked of a municipal 'arms race in the sphere of the theatre'.[7]

Only in some large cities in the mid-1920s were there theatres that did not survive on public funds. Berlin was in this—as in many other aspects of cultural life—an absolute exception. Here, and only here, a wide range of commercial theatres existed exclusively on their ticket sales and thus operated according to the same laws of the market as theatres in London's West End or on Broadway in New York. The performance runs of new productions were determined by theatre attendances; actors only received contracts per show; a 'flop' meant unemployment, left losses, and could push the producers into financial ruin. Depending upon the expenditure—which was determined by the size of the show—a new production had to play no less than between 25 and 50 times in order to cover at least the costs and make first profits.[8] Berlin had thirty such commercial theatres in the mid-1920s. The only enterprises to receive public funds were the City Opera in Charlottenburg (subsidized by Berlin), and the *Schauspielhaus* (Theatre) at Gendarmenmarkt and the State Opera Unter den Linden (both subsidized by Prussia).[9]

There were also large and small commercial theatres in Hamburg, Munich, and Düsseldorf (indeed, in Hamburg all theatres had to get along without public funds, because the city-state subsidized only its opera house). But even in these large cities the local theatre scene was much less lively and diverse than Berlin with its constant flood of new productions. The writer Erich Kästner, who essentially earned his keep as a theatre critic in Berlin during the 1920s before his children's book *Emil and the Detectives* made his name and fortune, reviewed during 1928 alone a hundred theatre premières in Berlin and saw 'another dozen dramas' without reviewing them. And since he did not review operas but only plays, even he caught only a portion of Berlin's theatrical life despite being at the theatre every other evening.[10] What kept all this going was partly the sheer size of the city, which with its 4 million inhabitants was more than twice as big as Germany's second city Hamburg, and partly the constant flow of tourists from elsewhere in Germany and from abroad.

Outside the capital, theatre provision was nearly everywhere secured by subsidies and correspondingly subject to the conditions and expectations that went with public funding. One of these was social inclusiveness. In this period, 'art for the people' was not simply a slogan of the left but an aspiration shared by the conservative-bourgeois parties, who saw public subsidies for cultural facilities as only being justified if the whole population had access to them.[11] An anti-elitist attitude was therefore one basic element of the cultural debates in Weimar Germany.

The other expectation linked to public subsidies was that the theatre should be a place of edification and uplift: shallow commercial theatre would give way to a new 'cultural theatre' (*Kulturtheater*). Germany after 1918 experienced a high point of the cultural idealism that had featured in its intellectual history since the eighteenth century. In the words of one commentator in 1919: 'Whoever recognizes in the theatre its ethical, aesthetic, popular pedagogical (*volksbildnerisch*) significance—only the low brow and philistines do not—suffers bitterly under its deplorable distorted mirror image: the barren spiritually empty amusement hall to which capitalist exploitation has reduced it'. Another critic, also writing in 1919, wrote of 'the moment of redemption of the theatre' thanks to the introduction of public funding: now, the 'amusement hall' would become that which it was destined to be: a mechanism for the moral and aesthetic education of the audience, who, through contact with 'great art', would become better human beings.[12]

If writers and theatre directors were particularly prone to this hyperbole, politicians on occasion also expressed similar sentiments. In 1927, the conservative mayor of Hanover, Arthur Menges, made a speech on the occasion of the 75th anniversary of the Hanoverian Opera House in which he declared that

[t]he point [of artistic endeavour] is that the divine spark which rests in each person's heart is awakened and maintained, that a liberating uplifting feeling is given to the people, which in the festive evening mood transforms an individual whose life during the day is determined by his work (*Arbeitsmenschen*) into a person of culture (*Kulturmenschen*). The soul of the people (*Volksseele*) is thus deepened, and the community comprising all members of the nation (*Volksgenossen*) is strengthened as the basis of our art and spiritual life. If one keeps these ambitious goals in mind and takes into consideration that the impact of the theatre is more profound than that of any other artistic endeavour, only then can one estimate its great importance for the spiritual and cultural life . . . and thus for the recovery of our nation.[13]

The exaggerated hopes placed in art as an instrument of moral education as well as a remedy for social ills that were expressed in many contemporary comments reflected a host of contemporary anxieties. The moral power of art seemed to offer Germany in these years a solution to internal conflicts between hostile political camps and social milieux. It might even heal the wounded pride of a defeated nation. Comparable perhaps to the achievements of scientists, art seemed to be a potential vehicle for restoring Germany's damaged international reputation and providing Germans with a new feeling of self-worth.

Particularly among the educated middle classes, national pride in the Weimar Republic was to a large extent identical with pride in the richness of German cultural life. In 1930 Thomas Mann, Nobel laureate and prominent voice of the cultured bourgeoisie, praised civic competitiveness over theatre provision and presented the way cities sought to out-compete their rivals as a badge of national cultural distinction. 'Germany is my fatherland lastly, perhaps above all as a country of the theatre ... as a country of cultural competition among cities', and hence he felt in the theatre more than anywhere else 'proudly secure as a German among Germans in national tradition and civilization'.[14] The 'cultural discipline' which Mann experienced in municipal and state theatres among actors and audiences was for him 'that which is most native, most German'.[15] Social Democrats were somewhat more reserved where the role of art in Germany's 'national rebirth' was concerned, but they shared with liberals the hope for its politically reconciling and socially healing effects. Adolf Grimme, Prussia's Social Democrat minister of cultural affairs, saw in art a 'character forming and national-shaping force' and a means to the 'intellectual forging of the nation' (geistige Volkwerdung).[16]

This consensus on what theatre should achieve did not prevent considerable battles over the actual programme of the publicly subsidized theatre. This is hardly surprising: the demands placed on 'art' and artists by the art idealism of the 1920s were on closer examination contradictory and even incompatible. Theatres were to open themselves up to the widest possible audiences, but at the same time preserve a commitment to 'high art' as a pedagogical tool. This ignored the question of the public's actual preferences and the extent of its demand for works of high artistic and moral value, however these were defined. As will be seen below, the tension between the commitment to accessibility and the belief in the pedagogical mission of high art was often resolved in favour of what the public wanted—which often tended to be entertainment rather than challenging or demanding works.

A second axis of conflict over the content of theatre programmes arose because the system of public subsidy intensified the 'culture wars' around what were seen as provocative and offensive works. 'Scandals' of this sort were nothing new—one only has to think of the scandals that accompanied the premières of Gerhard Hauptmann's naturalist dramas *Die Weber* ('Weavers') and *Die Ratten* ('Rats') in Berlin in 1894 and 1911. But if taxpayers' money had been spent on an 'offensive' production the potential for public indignation was greatly amplified, and the way was open for politically charged conflicts to be played out in the cultural sphere. Contrary to the hopes expressed by idealistic politicians and cultural commentators, the republic's cultural scene contributed little to the internal reconciliation of Germans.

Art as leisure

The normative distinction between art and entertainment has a long tradition in Germany, summed up in pronouncements such as that of Goethe that art occupied itself with 'the profound and good'. Implicit in this definition was that anything 'light' was the opposite of art. Entertainment was regarded at best as a pleasant matter of minor importance; at worst it was viewed as superfluous or even as a dangerous diversion from the really important works and topics. The distinction between art and entertainment also shaped contemporary discussions over Weimar culture. However, the divisions ran along very different lines from those often presented in the literature. A common but mistaken assumption is to equate publicly subsidized municipal and state theatres exclusively with traditional highbrow culture and bold artistic experiments, and then to contrast this with cinema and radio, which as new forms of mass media allegedly stood for a new entertainment-oriented mass culture. This notion is wrong for a number of reasons.

On the one hand, entertainment played an immensely important role in theatre programmes; on the other hand, there were also films in German cinemas during the 1920s that represented a new form of 'highbrow culture' alongside more undemanding fare. Finally, because of political decisions that determined its special ownership and production structures, radio can be seen as an instrument for the defence of traditional cultural hierarchies, even though the new medium certainly offered entertainment as well. Thus the boundary between art and entertainment did not run between publicly promoted artistic institutions on the one hand and privately financed cultural offerings on the other, but in a more complex way within the individual art forms and media.

For all the demands for a 'cultural theatre' that had been linked to public theatre subsidies, the programmes of municipal and state theatres during the 1920s differed little from those of the 'commercial theatres' under the empire. They were neither sites of avant-garde experimentation nor temples dedicated to the great classics of the dramatic genre. The 'classics' did feature, but within a carefully arranged selection of easily accessible pieces which could be relied on to draw an audience. Looking back on the 1920s, a long-serving theatre critic described the repertoire of Germany's theatres as follows: '75 to 25 per cent, or sometimes also 60 to 40 per cent was a good selection of family entertainment mixed with tried and tested classics. Occasionally two to five per cent would be given to interesting modern experiments.'[17] A recent statistical study comprising all theatre programmes confirms the dominance of entertainment on the Weimar stage. During the 1929/30 season 58.9 per cent of all productions belonged in the category 'light fare' (comedies and farces); in 1930/1 the proportion even rose to around 63 per cent.[18]

The predominance of entertainment was particularly pronounced in Germany's theatre capital Berlin because the private theatres that dominated the scene here were in the majority extremely risk averse. Erich Kästner wrote in 1930, 'light theatre stands to the fore. ... Operettas, revues, musicals, comedies, farce—such fare is more than ever in demand and accordingly is also supplied.'[19] Likewise, in 1931 Herbert Jhering, one of the leading theatre critics of the Weimar Republic, noted the prevailing characteristics of Berlin's theatre scene as 'middle of the road, conciliatory, obliging, levelling, disguising contradictions'.[20]

The situation looked hardly different in the publicly subsidized theatres, only here the cautious policy of avoiding provocation not only resulted from adjustment to public taste, but also frequently stemmed from political pressure (particularly that of the right-wing parties). This applied to Berlin as much as it did to the non-profit theatres in other German cities. Kästner discovered in 1928 at the Berlin State Theatre only 'a decent middling programme—despite the public subsidy—or one could also say—just because of it'.[21] In Munich an expressly conservative mood had prevailed in the theatres ever since the victory of the Catholic Bavarian People's Party in the municipal elections at the end of 1924. Here even the 'middle line', which occasionally and only to a modest extent included controversial 'contemporary pieces' and artistic experiments, was vigorously contested.[22] In 1929 a theatre critic dismissed the municipal theatres of the Ruhr as 'mixed goods trade' (*Gemischtwarenhandlung*). The chief characteristic of their programmes was the 'simultaneous inclination towards all sides'.[23]

Public subsidies, rather than emancipating the theatre artistically, had thus forced it into a new dependence. The political parties which voted annually on cultural grants in town councils and state parliaments were also able to exert influence, at least indirectly, on the repertoire of the theatres by threatening budget cuts in case of displeasure. Sometimes interference took a more direct form. Thus in 1921, the newly appointed theatre director of Hanover was explicitly instructed by the theatre committee of the town to keep to a 'tasteful middling line' in the programme.[24] At the same time, however, subsidized theatres still depended as before on takings at the box office because the subsidies only covered a part of their costs. Thus even without (political) pressure each director of a city theatre was compelled to give consideration to public taste. Artistic experiments remained therefore a carefully calculated exception. The theatres were particularly cautious with regard to politically controversial pieces. Often they were aired only in special shows, as a matinée or also in the afternoon, only then to quickly disappear completely from the programme. As a rule, and particularly in Berlin, new German plays were performed in this manner. In other cities theatres resorted to even greater precautions. For example, the Hamburg Opera was particularly concerned about the performance in 1925 of Paul Hindemith's opera *Sancta Susanna*. Since the work was considered by some as scandalous—it portrays a young nun who harbours erotic feelings for the sculpture of the crucified Christ—it was subjected to a sort of double quarantine: *Sancta Susanna* was performed in only one special show on a Sunday afternoon; at the same time all visitors had to pledge themselves first in writing to refrain 'from [making] any embarrassing expression of disapproval'.[25]

For most German theatres, innovation was restricted to 'classics in modern dress', a strategy that became so common that 'Hamlet in coat tails' became a cliché. For example, Mozart's *The Magic Flute* was produced with expressionist stage scenes and with costumes loaned from contemporary revues; Schiller's *The Robbers* was staged as a revolutionary drama with many red flags and an actor made up as Leon Trotsky. Audiences and critics were often lukewarm in their reception of such experiments, and by the end of the decade they were considered a fad that had already had its day. Herbert Jhering, one of the few theatre critics with a nationwide impact, called in 1930 for an end to 'whimsical' and 'tyrannical' directing (*Regiewillkür* and *Regieterror*); later that year he noted with satisfaction that 'the very concept of directing' was being 'reined in', and that the theatre of the coming decades would see the director becoming a 'helper' to the actor and a 'monitoring colleague' to the dramatist.[26]

In general German theatre life in the 1920s was thus far more conservative than it appears in most cultural histories of the Weimar Republic. The traditions of the empire lived on because the public's desire for entertainment determined the programmes, and because most directors shied away from controversial pieces. Theatre in Weimar Germany, far from being bold and innovative, was more often concerned not to cause offence.

The image of Weimar culture as a laboratory of modernity becomes even more doubtful if one looks at film. Of course there were the expressionist films at the beginning of the 1920s (of which *The Cabinet of Dr Caligari* is the most famous example), and later cinematic masterpieces such as *Secrets of a Soul*, *Pandora's Box* (both directed by G. W. Pabst), or *The Last Man*, *Tartüff*, and *Faust* (all three produced by F. W. Murnau). These films, which use all the possibilities of the silent screen in order to create visual works of art, are, however, about as typical of Weimar cinema as Orson Welles's *Citizen Kane* is of the Hollywood film of the 1940s: they were high points in a sea of undistinguished and undemanding work.

That said, these films have an important place in the social history of film. They marked the completion of a process begun in Germany before the First World War in which film gained public acknowledgement as an independent art form and became thereby part of bourgeois high culture. The première of Murnau's *Faust* in 1926 in Berlin demonstrates how far the medium had left behind its origins as a cheap fairground attraction or as a barely ten-minute varieté show: it attracted not only artists (including from the theatre world) and the whole of Berlin's high society, but also members of the Reich government. The trend towards taking film seriously as an art form was reflected in the building of opulent new cinemas targeting an affluent public and seeking to compete with the established theatres. For example, in 1927 a luxurious cinema was opened in Hamburg, leading one of the local daily papers to comment, impressed: 'if this film theatre delivers what it promises, then the Hamburg stage and our opera have a serious competitor'.[27]

Notwithstanding these developments, the cinema also remained what it had always been: namely an entertainment medium that placed few, if any, demands on its public. Overall, films without artistic merit and cinemas that packed in the maximum number of screenings were more typical of cinema under the Weimar Republic than the socially exclusive luxurious film theatres that showed the latest high-budget productions. Films that were aesthetically demanding never attracted more than a small audience.[28] Nostalgic stories set in the nineteenth century which told 'bitter-sweet' love stories were particularly well liked by Weimar cinemagoers. Germans gladly did without a happy ending because this final triumph of love against all odds was considered typically American and therefore regarded as a foreign cultural import (significantly, the very term, abridged into 'happy end', became colloquial German during the 1920s). Featuring attractive landscapes as backdrop, many of these films were set in regions by the Rhine or the Neckar and in particular in Heidelberg, the epitome of 'romantic Germany'.

By 1927 it was impossible to escape these sentimental films, even in Berlin where, in Kästner's words:

at present the Heidelberg epidemic prevails in the cinemas. One can wander every night for hours through the lit-up streets of Berlin and keep seeing the film adverts: 'I Lost My Heart in Heidelberg', or 'My Heidelberg, I Cannot Forget You', or 'I was a Student in Heidelberg', and so on. If there is competition . . . then it is propaganda for the Rhine, for its landladies, wine and girls: 'The Lime Tree Landlady of the Rhine', and 'A Rhineland Girl with Rhineland Wine', enjoy particular popularity. The Rhine and Neckar rivers flow through Berlin's cinemas as if it could not be otherwise, and the couples hold their hands in the dark and borrow each other's handkerchiefs and shed a tear.[29]

One film critic observed how the 'pining disease of "Heidelberg-itis"' had struck the Germans collectively.[30]

But 1927 was also the year when Universum Film Aktiengesell-schaft (Universal Film Company—Ufa) brought Fritz Lang's monumental film *Metropolis* to the German screen. The temporal proximity between this film and the wave of 'Heidelberg' films demonstrates in particular the selectivity of cultural memory, especially where the Weimar Republic is concerned. *Metropolis* with its (undoubtedly impressive) images of the city of the future has become one of the icons of the 1920s, indeed even of modernity itself, and it is one of the films that immediately come to the fore when Weimar cinema or even the republic *per se* is considered. Nobody, however, would associate the 1920s with the images of Heidelberg's old district, although contemporaries preferred these pictures to the bold skyscrapers and the dark 'underground city' which the architect Otto Hunte designed for Lang's fantasy metropolis. Indeed, in contrast to the nostalgic Heidelberg and Rhine films, *Metropolis* was a box office flop that proved costly to Ufa. Thus old traditions lived on not only in the theatres but also in the cinemas of the Weimar Republic where the empire and the nineteenth century were much more a presence than is usually remembered today.

Finally, we turn to broadcasting in order to complete this picture of a cultural landscape that was strongly shaped by tradition and nostalgia. The organizational form into which the new medium was forced at the time of its introduction into Germany in 1923–4 made it the instrument of an attempted defensive modernization. Radio, the most modern mass medium at that time, was to serve the aesthetic education of its listeners through key elements of programming. In this regard entertainment was only the means to an end, because the 'real' task of radio was the popularization of traditional highbrow culture that filled the greater part of the early evening programme when most listeners sat around their sets. To be sure, there was a clear trend toward the end of the decade to provide more entertainment (particularly through 'light' music) because radio dealers repeatedly demanded such programmes in order to increase sales figures, and because ever larger parts of the day were now filled by radio programmes. Nonetheless, the fundamental conception of German radio remained unchanged. Those responsible in the radio broadcasting companies for the type of programmes saw their listeners above all as objects of an aesthetic education.[31]

Thus the tension between art and entertainment influenced theatre, film, and broadcasting in different ways. Film was unquestioningly shaped most strongly by the public's demand for entertainment since it functioned wholly according to the laws of the market; but the need for prestige among the big production companies (above all Ufa) ensured nevertheless that films were made which also appealed to a culturally demanding bourgeoisie. In theory, artistic considerations in the theatre should have clearly predominated, but in practice Germany's municipal theatres were far more frequently places of harmless entertainment than noble sites of aesthetic and moral education. With such light programmes theatre directors were responding to the tastes of the petite bourgeoisie which regularly attended the theatre. The critics might complain, but theatre audiences welcomed plays that sought nothing more than to entertain. In broadcasting the concept of 'educating' the public ruled supreme, especially during the evening programme, because the broadcasting companies in each case possessed a regional monopoly on the production of radio programmes. This excluded any 'squalid competition' for the attention of the public.

Arts and the public

In 1926/7 municipal theatres in Germany registered attendance figures of nearly 12 million. For a nation of approximately 60 million that is an impressive number, and appears to bear out the Weimar Republic's claim to be a 'cultural nation'. But closer scrutiny provides a different picture, for in reality the great majority of Germans in the 1920s never went to the theatre. Apart from this completely 'agnostic' majority there were two groups: a small minority of dedicated theatregoers and a somewhat larger group that went occasionally and irregularly.

Striking confirmation of the social exclusivity of the theatre is provided by a survey carried out among more than 42,000 manual and white-collar workers in Berlin at the beginning of 1934. Two-thirds of them had never seen a play on the stage; more than 80 per cent had never set foot in an opera house; hardly 10 per cent were regular theatregoers (this proportion was even less than 4 per cent for the opera).[32] These numbers are, moreover, remarkable in several respects. Those questioned were all employed by the giant electrical concern Siemens; that is, they enjoyed higher wages and more stable conditions of employment than was otherwise typical for most workers in German industry. As noted, Siemens's white-collar workers were also included in the survey, and that certainly meant people who could not be defined as proletarians but as members of the middle class. Finally—and this is perhaps the most extraordinary—all of those questioned lived in Berlin, Europe's glamorous and exciting theatre metropolis, renowned above all for first-class entertainment. But even the many stars of the Berlin stage could not lure the majority of the Siemens workforce out of the house after the end of the working day.

Other data also show that only a small section of the population participated in the theatre during the 1920s. Whether or not entertainment or the classics was playing on the stage, the audience comprised primarily members of the traditional middle class: higher officials, lawyers, doctors, owners of small businesses, together with their wives.[33] Often they had a subscription, which brought them into the theatre each week or at least fortnightly during the course of a season. It was simply the 'done thing' in such circles to have a theatre subscription, and it was often essential for maintaining social standing that one had 'one's own particular seat at the theatre'.[34]

For most Germans, however, regular theatre attendance during the years of the Weimar Republic was simply too expensive. An extremely tight household budget tended to exclude even the families of average wage earners from cultural activities. This fact also explains the slack attendance at theatres. On average only 50 to 60 per cent of tickets were sold and even the existence of two 'visitor clubs', which offered their members substantially reduced theatre tickets for a modest monthly contribution, did little to change this.[35]

The number of cinemagoers by far outstripped the number of those who went to the theatre. In 1926, 332 million cinema tickets were sold in Germany compared to 12 million theatregoers. Even when we look at the number of cinemas and theatres, there is a vast discrepancy. In the mid-1920s there were 3,900 cinemas in Germany; at the end of the decade this number had increased to 5,000. Meanwhile there were barely 230 theatres and opera houses in the entire Reich. They offered at best usually only one show daily, whereas the cinemas played at least two to three times daily, particularly in the larger cities. Going to the cinema was a lot simpler than attending a stage performance—and that was not only a result of the greater popularity of cinema, but also a consequence of the particular attractiveness of this sphere of cultural life.

Film was unquestioningly a massively popular medium during the years of the Weimar Republic. That does not mean, however, that cinema was also a 'mass medium' in the sense that it transcended class: on the contrary, cinema audiences were marked by patterns of social difference and social exclusion. The study quoted above of the leisure habits of the 42,000 Siemens employees also gives some indication of this. Over 50 per cent of those surveyed did not attend a cinema, even though in Berlin they would have had the opportunity to visit one of the many 'neighbourhood cinemas' located around almost any corner; a further 30 per cent only went to the cinema infrequently or occasionally; and only a minority of around 20 per cent actually watched new films regularly. Taken together with the results of visits to the theatre, these numbers point to a life focused very much on the home. Thus it appears that the majority of working-class and white-collar employee families in Berlin during the 1920s usually remained at home in the evening and, at best, read in the newspapers about the legendary cultural life of the Weimar Republic.

As in the case of the theatre, other data confirm the results of the Berlin study. Contemporaries estimated that during the 1920s and 1930s approximately half of all Germans never went to the cinema at all. Also the number of film enthusiasts seems to have been substantially smaller for economic reasons than in other industrial nations. The number of cinemagoers per head and per year was at any rate substantially lower in Germany than in Great Britain or France, not even to speak of the USA. Statistically, each US citizen went to the cinema 67 times in 1926, compared with a figure of less than 7 cinema visits per head for Germany in the same year.[36] This enormous gap should be borne in mind when we speak about cultural life in the Weimar Republic.

Cultural consumption is luxury consumption. In Weimar Germany, which suffered first from the consequences of the war and the inflation, and was then hit massively by the world economic crisis from 1929 after a short phase of stabilization, such luxury consumption could develop only to a modest extent. This fact, it seems to me, has hardly ever been taken into consideration in the available literature on the history of 'Weimar culture'.

Perhaps, then, it is time to bring the town of Weimar back into our mental picture of Weimar Germany. This small town in Thuringia, haunted by memories of its former cultural grandeur and dominated by a theatre that was not only much too large for the size of its population, but also burdened with the pompous name *Nationaltheater* (National Theatre), this town that experienced not only the first flowering of the Bauhaus, but also in 1930–1 the first cultural purge carried out by its Nazi interior and cultural minister Wilhelm Frick, may well be a much more fitting representation of Germany during the 1920s than the images of Berlin (not to speak of *Metropolis*) that have come to dominate our perception of this troubled period of modern German history.

Notes

1. H. Schulz, 'Die Deutsche Kunstgemeinschaft und die deutschen Städte', *Der Städtetag*, 23 (1929), cols. 679–86. A loan was only made available to a purchaser of a work of art by a living artist.
2. However, the new medium was constrained in a particular way by public guidelines that excluded competition between programme providers. See in general Karl-Christian Führer, 'A medium of modernity? Broadcasting in Weimar Germany, 1923–1932', *Journal of Modern History*, 69 (Dec. 1997), 722–53,
3. See also Albert Brodbeck and Thias Brünker, *Wanderbühnen in Preußen* (Berlin, 1932).
4. Hans Lebede, 'Zur Umwandlung der Hoftheater in Staatstheater', *Der Neue Weg*, 48 (1919), 5–6; Ludwig Seelig, 'Zur Verstaatlichung der Hoftheater', ibid. 438–9.
5. For details see Wolfgang Lenk, 'Das kommunale Theater' (Ph.D. Universität Berlin, 1930); Thomas Höpel, 'Städtische Kulturpolitik in Deutschland und Frankreich 1918–1940', *Historische Zeitschrift*, 284 (2007), 623–58.
6. See for example 'S.O.S.', *Der Neue Weg*, 60 (1931), 561–2 (resolution of the Association of Duisburg Retailers). See also F. Schwede, 'Die wirtschaftliche Bedeutung des Coburger Landestheaters für die Stadt Coburg', *Der Neue Weg*, 61 (1932), 7; 'Für die Erhaltung der Breslauer Oper', *Frankfurter Zeitung*, 89 (3 Feb. 1930).
7. Hans Heinsheimer, 'Zur Situation der deutschen Bühnen', *Frankfurter Zeitung*, 892/893 (1 Dec. 1931).
8. See Erich Kästner, 'Ein Jahr Berliner Theater', in idem, *Gemischte Gefühle: Literarische Publizistik 1923–1933*, 2 vols. (Zurich, 1989), ii. 114–18.
9. In fact, both the *Schauspielhaus* and the State Opera played on two stages: the Schiller-Theatre served as the second house for theatrical productions while the *Kroll-Oper* was a branch of the Linden-Opera. In 1927, the *Kroll-Oper* was transformed into an independent company. Due to cuts in Prussia's cultural subsidies, it was closed in 1931; in the following year also the Schiller-Theatre was closed down.
10. Kästner, 'Ein Jahr Berliner Theater', 114.
11. See for example 'Kunst und Parlament', *Der Neue Weg*, 48 (1919), 703–6, and *Der neue Weg*, 49 (1920), 34–8, 78–80.
12. Max Alberty, 'Gegen den Schund auf der Bühne', *Der Neue Weg*, 48 (1919), 61–2, and Ernst Stern, 'Kunst für's Volk', ibid. 226–8.

13. Cited in Ines Katenhusen, *Kunst und Politik: Hannovers Ausein-andersetzungen mit der Moderne in der Weimarer Republik* (Hanover, 1998), 101.

14. 'Thomas Mann über Theater und Film', *Der neue Weg*, 59 (1930), 319.

15. Thomas Mann, 'Kultur und Sozialismus', in idem, *Das essayistische Werk*, ed. Peter Bürgin, v: *Politische Schriften und Reden*, ii (Frankfurt am Main, 1968), 165–73, here 170.

16. 'Kunstpflege im Massenelend?', *Der Abend*, 1 Oct. 1930. See also 'Germany celebrates a museum centenary', *New York Times*, 19 Oct. 1930.

17. Thomas Kore, 'Hamburger Theatereindrücke', *Die Neue Zeitung*, 14 Feb. 1947.

18. Thomas Eicher, Barbara Panse, and Henning Rischbieter, *Theater im 'Dritten Reich': Theaterpolitik, Spielplanstruktur, NS-Dramatik* (Seelze-Velber, 2000), 595. If this statistic gave us the number of performances instead of productions (*Inszenierungen*), the predominance of light theatre would be more pronounced.

19. Erich Kästner, '1913 und "1914"', in idem, *Gemischte Gefühle*, ii. 248–50, here 248.

20. Herbert Jhering, 'Theaterkrise? Geistige Krise!', in idem, *Der Kampf ums Theater und andere Streitschriften 1918 bis 1933* (East Berlin, 1974), 380–5, here 384.

21. Erich Kästner, 'Ein Jahr Berliner Theater', in idem, *Gemischte Gefühle*, ii. 114–18, here 114, 116.

22. Jürgen Gimmel, *Die politische Organisation kulturellen Ressentiments: Der 'Kampfbund für deutsche Kultur' und das bildungsbürgerliche Unbehagen an der Moderne* (Münster, 2001), 306 ff.

23. Cited after Dörte Schmidt and Brigitte Weber (eds.), *Keine Experimentierkunst: Musikleben an Städtischen Theatern in der Weimarer Republik. Mit Beiträgen v. Markus Bruderreck u.a.* (Stuttgart, 1995), 3.

24. Katenhusen, *Kunst und Politik*, 695.

25. Compare *Stenographische Berichte über die Sitzungen der Bürgerschaft zu Hamburg im Jahre 1925* (Hamburg, 1926), 123–31, citation 126.

26. Herbert Jhering, 'Staatstheater oder—?', in idem, *Der Kampf ums Theater*, 327–30, here 328.

27. 'Die neue Ecke', *Hamburger Anzeiger*, 23 Feb. 1927.

28. Compare for example 'Das Ergebnis der Abstimmung', *Film-Kurier*, 9 (1927), 85; Georg Herzberg, 'Der schlechte Geschmack des Publikums ist schuld!', *Film-Kurier*, 10 (1928), 131.

29. Erich Kästner, 'Berliner Kleinkunst', in idem, *Gemischte Gefühl*, ii. 7–10, here 7.

30. 'Filmkritik', *Film-Kurier*, 9 (1929), 183.

31. See Führer, 'A medium of modernity?'

32. 'Eine Analyse der Freizeit des schaffenden Berliners', *Scherls Informationen*, 106 (June 1934), 11–12.

33. Karl Christian Führer, 'German cultural life and the crisis of national identity during the depression, 1929–1933', *German Studies Review*, 24 (2001), 461–86, here 465.

34. A. Winds, 'Theatergemeinden', *Deutsche Bühne*, 15 (1923), H. 14, cited after Heinz Rahlfs, *Die Städtischen Bühnen zu Hannover und ihre Vorläufer in wirtschaftlicher und sozialer Hinsicht* (Hanover, 1928), 109.

35. Führer, 'German cultural life', 466.

36. Curt Andersen, *Die deutsche Filmindustrie: Aufbau, Gliederung und volkswirtschaftliche Bedeutung* (Munich, 1930), 49.

Further Reading

General works

The starting point for most of the contributions to this volume is Detlev J. K. Peukert, *The Weimar Republic: The Crisis of Classical Modernity*, translated by Richard Deveson (London, 1991), which challenges the student to consider the larger structural transformation underlying the republic. The English version is now out of print; however the German edition is still going strong. A succinct synopsis of Peukert's thesis can be found in his essay Detlev J. K. Peukert, 'The Weimar Republic: old and new perspectives', *German History*, 6/2 (1988), 133–44. The Weimar Republic has no shortage of histories but many of these were originally published many years ago and—in spite of some revision in reissued editions—are now seriously dated in terms of their focus and methodological approach (comments here are restricted to textbooks in the English language). Erich Eyck's elegantly written two-volume *A History of the Weimar Republic*, translated by Harlan P. Hanson and Robert G. L. Waite (New York, 1970), was first published in German in 1954 and is now more of historiographical interest than an up-to-date account, as too is Arthur Rosenberg, *A History of the German Republic*, translated by Ian F. D. Morrow and L. Marie Sieveking (London, 1936). Two standard short textbooks, Anthony J. Nicholls, *Weimar and the Rise of Hitler* (Palgrave, 2001) and John Hiden, *The Weimar Republic* (Longman, 1996), are useful for those with little or no knowledge of the subject, but do not incorporate any recent scholarly work and ignore the social and cultural spheres entirely. Gordon Craig's *Germany 1866–1945* (Oxford, 1981) is still a valuable read, but its chapters dealing with the republic are severely limited by their exclusive focus on 'high' politics and 'high' culture; Edgar J. Feuchtwanger, *From Weimar to Hitler, 1918–1933*, 2nd edn. (Basingstoke, 1995), and Helmut Heiber, *The Weimar Republic*, translated by W. E. Yuill (Oxford, 1993), are good on detail (albeit with some errors), but again concentrate mostly on 'high politics' with some concession to social history, but with little or no engagement with more recent directions in scholarly treatments of the republic, while Paul Bookbinder, *Weimar Germany: The Republic of the Reasonable* (Manchester, 1996) purports to be a 'corrective' to the doomed republic thesis but relies almost entirely on the London *Times* as a source. Probably the best introduction is that by one of the leading scholars of the period, Eberhard Kolb, *The Weimar Republic* (London, 1988, 2nd edn., 2005). It is also a pity that its extensive bibliography is mainly of use to those with a grasp of German. Richard Bessel, *Germany after the First World War* (Oxford, 1993) is an important study. Richard J. Evans, *The Coming of the Third Reich* (Harmondsworth, 2003) is a gripping narrative account of Weimar Germany and as such is a good starting point; but readers beware: the republic is presented as prequel to the Third Reich. Jeffrey Herf, *Reactionary Modernism: Technology, Culture and Politics in Weimar and the Third Reich* (Cambridge, 1984) is an important and provocative account of conservative modernity; Bernd Widdig, *Culture and Inflation in Weimar Germany* (Berkeley, 2001) looks at that episode through the lens of the cultural historian. Eric D. Weitz, *Weimar Germany: Promise and Tragedy* (Princeton, 2007) is the most recent account of the republic and provides a highly readable account of Weimar's social and cultural history interwoven with political developments.

Two volumes of essays in English that are still worth consulting are: E. J. Feuchtwanger and Richard Bessel (eds.), *Social Change and Political Development in the Weimar Republic* (London, 1981) and Ian Kershaw (ed.), *Weimar: Why did German Democracy Fail?* (London, 1990). At the time of their publication these volumes represented important contributions to the student's arsenal of Weimar studies by focusing on problems of economy and society in a way that had been largely ignored in earlier literature. Two further collections of essays that incorporate chapters on the Weimar Republic are: Mary Fulbrook (ed.), *Germany since 1918* (London, 1997) and Panikos Panayi (ed.), *Weimar and Nazi Germany: Continuities and Discontinuities* (Harlow, 2001). Neither edition specifically focuses on the republic, though Fulbrook's book contains two useful discussions on the economy and cultural trends. Not much has appeared in English in recent years in the way of insightful review essays: we rely therefore on Peter Fritzsche, 'Did Weimar fail?', *Journal of Modern History*, 68/3 (Sept. 1996), 69–656, an important essay; less substantial but delightfully iconoclastic is John Hiden, 'Hard times: from Weimar to Hitler', *Historical Journal*, 32/4 (Dec. 1989), 947–62; Gerald D. Feldman, 'The Weimar Republic: a problem of modernization?', *Archiv fur Sozialgeschichte*, 26 (1986), 1–26, is still a good introduction to some of the problems raised in this volume. For students with German under their belt: two excellent overviews can be found in Eberhard Kolb, 'Literaturbericht: Weimarer Republik', *Geschichte im Wissenschaft und Unterricht*, Part 1: 43/5 (1992), 311–21; Part 2: 43/10 (1992), 636–51; Part 3: 43/11 (1992), 699–721; Part 4: 45/1 (1994), 49–64; Part 5: 45/8 (1994), 523–43 and Wolfram Pyta, 'Literaturbericht: Weimarer Republik', *Geschichte im Wissenschaft und Unterricht*, Part 1: 53/7–8 (2003), 473–81; Part 2: 53/11 (2003), 688–702. Older, but nevertheless important, is the essay by the conservative historian Michael Stürmer, 'Weimar oder die

Last der Vergangenheit: Aufstieg und Fall der ersten Republik als Problem
der Forschung', in idem (ed.), *Die Weimarer Republik. Belagerte Civitas*
(Königstein im Taunus, 1980).

First-hand accounts can be found in: Stephen Spender, *The Temple*
(London, 1988), *The Harold Nicolson Diaries 1907–1963*, paperback edition
edited by Nigel Nicolson (London, 2004), and Christopher Isherwood,
Berlin Stories: The Last of Mr Norris and Goodbye to Berlin (New York,
1963); a critical if somewhat pessimistic left-wing view of the republic
in its early days is Morgan Philips Price, *Dispatches from the Weimar
Republic: Versailles and German Fascism* (London, 1999), edited and
introduced by his daughter, Tania Rose. The diaries of the socialite
and one-time member of the Berlin Workers' and Soldiers' Council
Harry Graf Kessler are also an indispensable source and are published
in a shortened form in English as *The Diaries of a Cosmopolitan: Count
Harry Kessler, 1918–1937*, translated and edited by Charles Kessler (London, 1991). Important documents are gathered in Herbert Michaelis and
Ernst Schraepler (eds.), *Ursachen und Folgen: Vom deutschen Zusammenbruch 1918 und 1945 bis zur staatlichen Neuordnung Deutschlands
in der Gegenwart*, 26 vols. (Berlin, 1958–79) and in the twenty-two
volumes of official minutes of cabinet meetings *Akten der Reichskanzlei: Weimarer Republik* (Boppard, 1968–90), now available online at
http://www.bundesarchiv.de/aktenreichskanzlei/1919–1933/0000/index.
html. Meanwhile Anton Kaes, Martin Jay, and Edward Dimenberg (eds.),
The Weimar Republik Sourcebook (Berkeley, 1994) is ever popular with
students of Weimar's social history.

Geoff Eley offers valuable aid in navigating the now voluminous literature on 'modernity' in his essay 'German history and the contradictions
of modernity: the bourgeoisie, the state, and the mastery of reform', in
idem (ed.), *Society, Culture, and the State in Germany, 1870–1930* (Ann
Arbor, 1996). And for those who like a rewarding challenge: Modris
Ecksteins, *Rites of Spring: The Great War and the Birth of the Modern Age*
(London, 1989).

Chapter 1

As well as consulting some of the works cited above, a key work in
English translation on Weimar's political history is Hans Mommsen,
From Weimar to Auschwitz: Essays in German History, translated by Philip
O'Connor (Oxford, 1990) and his influential *The Rise and Fall of Weimar
Democracy*, translated by Elborg Forster and Larry Eugene Jones (Chapel
Hill, NC, 1996). Elmar M. Hucko (ed.), *The Democratic Tradition: Four
German Constitutions* (Oxford, 1987) provides a useful edition of the

Constitution (as well as those of the Bismarckian Reich and the Federal Republic), while Martin Needler, 'The theory of the Weimar presidency', *Review of Politics*, 21/4 (Oct. 1959), 692–8, gives a brief exposition on the role of the presidency. On the revolution and the council movement, Reinhard Rurüp, 'Problems of the German revolution 1918–19', in *Journal of Contemporary History*, 3/4 (Oct. 1968), 109–35; Richard Bessel, *Germany after the First World War* (Oxford, 1993) looks at demolition.

G. Best, 'Elite structure and regime (dis)continuity in Germany 1867–1933: the case of the parliamentary leadership groups', *German History*, 7 (1990) and Peter D. Stachura, *Political Leaders in Weimar Germany: A Biographical Study* (Hemel Hempstead, 1992) provide background information on some of Weimar's political leaders; Martin Broszat, *Hitler and the Collapse of Weimar Germany*, translated and with a foreword by V. R. Berghahn (Leamington Spa, 1987), is stimulating reading. On the bourgeois 'middle' see: Robert A. Pois, *The Bourgeois Democrats of Weimar Germany* (Philadelphia, 1976); Bruce B. Frye, *Liberal Democrats in the Weimar Republic: The History of the German Democratic Party and the German State Party* (Carbondale, Ill., 1985); Larry Eugene Jones, *German Liberalism and the Dissolution of the Weimar Party System, 1918–1933* (Chapel Hill, NC, 1988). William J. Patch, *Heinrich Brüning and the Dissolution of the Weimar Republic* (Cambridge, 1998) provides a sympathetic antidote to Mommsen's scathing account of the 'hunger chancellor'. Richard Breitman, *German Socialism and Weimar Democracy* (Chapel Hill, NC, 1981) is a more up-to-date account of the Social Democrats than Richard N. Hunt, *German Social Democracy 1918–1933* (New Haven, 1964), which nonetheless can be read with profit. Heinrich August Winkler, 'Choosing the lesser evil: the German Social Democrats and the fall of the Weimar Republic', *Journal of Contemporary History*, 25/2–3 (May–June 1990), 205–27, looks at the constraints facing SPD in choosing their policy of toleration 1930–3. Dietrich Orlow, *Weimar Prussia 1918–1925: The Unlikely Rock of Democracy* (Pittsburgh, 1986) and *Weimar Prussia, 1925–1933: The Illusion of Strength* (Pittsburgh, 1991) remains the best account in English of the Socialist-led government of Prussia. For the right, Roger Woods, *The Conservative Revolution in the Weimar Republic* (London, 1996) is a good introduction; D. P. Walker, 'The German Nationalist People's Party: the conservative dilemma in the Weimar Republic', *Journal of Contemporary History*, 14/4 (Oct. 1979), 627–47, Shelley Baranowski, 'Conservative elite anti-Semitism from the Weimar Republic to the Third Reich', *German Studies Review*, 19/3 (Oct. 1996), 525–37, William L. Patch, Jr., 'Class prejudice and the failure of the Weimar Republic', *German Studies Review*, 12/1 (Feb. 1989), 35–54, and Raffael Scheck, 'Women against Versailles: maternalism and nationalism of female bourgeois politicians in the early Weimar Republic', *German Studies Review*, 22/1 (Feb. 1999), 21–42, are excellent essays that delve into the organization, milieu, and mentality of bourgeois conservatives. Robert Gerwarth *The Bismarck Myth: Weimar Germany and the Legacy of the Iron Chancellor* (Oxford, 2005) and Richard E. Fraenkel, *Bismarck's Shadow: The Cult of Leadership and the Transformation of the German Right, 1898–1945* (Oxford, 2005) look more broadly at the quest for a 'strong leader' after 1918; while Theodor Eschenburg, 'The role of the personality in the crisis of the Weimar Republic: Hindenburg, Brüning, Groener, Schleicher', in Hajo Holborn (ed.), *Republic to Reich: The Making of the Nazi Revolution* (New York, 1972), is a classic account of the failings of those 'strong leaders'; Henry Ashby Turner, *Hitler's Thirty Days to Power: January 1933* (London, 1996) picks up where Eschenburg stops and deals with Papen's role in bringing Hitler to power. The importance of discourse and political vocabularies are dealt with by Dennis E. Showalter, 'Letters to "Der Sturmer": the mobilization of hostility in the Weimar Republic', *Modern Judaism*, 3/2 (May 1983), 173–87, Thomas Childers, 'The social language of politics in Germany: the sociology of political discourse in the Weimar Republic', *American Historical Review*, 95/2 (Apr. 1990), 331–58, and Ben Lieberman, 'The meanings and function of anti-system ideology in the Weimar Republic', *Journal of the History of Ideas*, 59/2 (Apr. 1998), 355–75, are lucid accounts of political language.

Chapter 2

Sources on the foreign policy of the Weimar Republic have been published in abundance. Of prime importance are the documents made available from the archive of the Berlin Foreign Office (Auswärtiges Amt) by an international consortium of publishers, the many thousands of pages of *Akten zur deutschen auswärtigen Politik [ADAP] 1918–1945*: series A, covering the years 1918–25, is in 14 volumes (Göttingen, 1982–95), series B, for 1925–33, in 21 volumes in 23 parts (Göttingen, 1967–83). Important too for understanding German foreign policy and its relations with internal politics are the volumes of the *Akten der Reichskanzlei: Weimarer Republik*, noted above. The most important view from the outside is offered by the published documents on foreign policy of the other Great Powers, the most significant being those from Great Britain in the *Documents on British Foreign Policy 1919–1939*, series I and IA and series II, vols. i–iv (London, 1947–86) and, taken from the 'Confidential Prints' of the Foreign Office, *British Documents on Foreign Affairs*, part II: *From the First to the Second World War*, especially series F, *Europe 1919–1939*, I, *The Paris Peace Conference of 1919*, and J, *The League of Nations, 1918–1941*

(Frederick, Md., 1990–4); F. L. Carsten, *Britain and the Weimar Republic: The British Documents* (London, 1984).

A concise survey of details relating to these texts, and to numerous other sources on the foreign and domestic policies of the Weimar Republic, is afforded by *Quellenkunde zur deutschen Geschichte der Neuzeit*, ed. Winfried Baumgart, vi: *Weimarer Republik, Nationalsozialismus, Zweiter Weltkrieg (1919–1945)*, part 1: *Akten and Urkunden*, ed. Hans Günter Hockerts; part 2: *Persönliche Quellen*, ed. Wolfgang Elz (Darmstadt, 1996–2003); the entire work is now available in a second, revised edition on a CD-ROM (Darmstadt, 2005). There are also many useful references to sources for German foreign policy in Christoph M. Kimmich, *German Foreign Policy, 1919–1945: A Guide to Research and Research Materials*, rev. edn. (Wilmington, Del., 1991).

Research and publications on the history of the Weimar Republic are by now almost impossible to monitor even for the specialist. The standard survey of its foreign policy is Peter Krüger, *Die Außenpolitik der Republik von Weimar* (Darmstadt, 1985; 2nd edn. 1993), a more concise summary in handbook form is Gottfried Niedhart, *Die Außenpolitik der Weimarer Republik* (Enzyklopädie deutscher Geschichte, 53; Munich, 1999, 2nd edn., 2006). A good overview of the boundless literature and the state of research on the Paris peace negotiations and the Treaty of Versailles is the concise summary by Alan Sharp, *The Versailles Settlement: Peacemaking in Paris, 1919* (The Making of the 20th Century; Basingstoke, 1991); Manfred F. Boemeke, Gerald D. Feldman, and Elisabeth Glaser (eds.), *The Treaty of Versailles: A Reassessment after 75 Years* (Washington, DC, 1998) investigates the treaty and the judgements made on it from various points of view. An overall account of the reparations question, which summarizes the many particular studies with pointed judgements, is Bruce Kent, *The Spoils of War: The Politics, Economics, and Diplomacy of Reparations, 1918–1932* (Oxford, 1989; rev. paperback 1991). On the interrelation of Lloyd George's plans for European reconstruction, the Genoa conference, and the Rapallo Treaty of 1922 there are important contributions in Carole Fink, Axel Frohn, and Jürgen Heideking (eds.), *Genoa, Rapallo, and European Reconstruction in 1922* (Washington, DC, 1991).

On the occupation of the Ruhr and the *Ruhrkampf*, especially the disastrous consequences for German domestic politics and Franco-German relations, see the detailed study by Conan Fischer, *The Ruhr Crisis, 1923–1924* (Oxford, 2003). Gustav Stresemann is one of the German politicians who has the most biographies and studies of particular aspects of his policies, but the situation with regard to personal sources is poor: an edition published immediately after his death and translated into English, *Gustav Stresemann: His Diaries, Letters and Papers*, ed. and trans. Eric

Sutton, 3 vols. (London, 1935–40; repr. New York, 1982), is unsatisfactory as regards source criticism. By contrast, after several swings of the pendulum in the academic assessment of Stresemann's foreign policy, a broad consensus has been reached in international scholarship that recognizes the national orientation of all foreign-policy makers between the wars (which went without saying at the time), but stresses the potential for stabilizing peace in Stresemann's efforts; this is well elaborated in Jonathan Wright, *Gustav Stresemann: Weimar's Greatest Statesman* (Oxford, 2002; paperback 2004), which offers a comprehensive political biography centred on his time as chancellor and foreign minister from 1923 to 1929, which thus sheds concentrated light on the years after the Locarno Treaties and Stresemann's policy of entente. Henry Ashby Turner, *Stresemann and the Politics of the Weimar Republic* (Westport, Conn., 1979) is older but still useful.

Again, the most recent literature on Germany's foreign policy is in German. Scholarship on the presidential cabinets from 1930 onwards has mostly foregrounded domestic politics, leaving more intensive study of foreign policy to a few specialist works; therefore the diplomatic history covering the entire period from 1930 to Hitler's acquisition of power in January 1933 by Hermann Graml, *Zwischen Stresemann und Hitler: Die Außenpolitik der Präsidialkabinette Brüning, Papen und Schechter* (Munich, 2001) is to be much welcomed.

Chapter 3

Gordon A. Craig, *The Politics of the Prussian Army 1640–1945* (Oxford, 1955) and F. C. L. Carsten, *The Reichswehr and Politics, 1918–1933* (Oxford, 1966) are the classic studies of the military in this period. There are a number of accounts of the role of the army in society: Arthur L. Smith, Jr., 'General von Seeckt and the Weimar Republic', *Review of Politics*, 20/3 (July 1958), 347–57 and Gaines Post, *The Civil-Military Fabric of Weimar Foreign Policy* (Princeton, 1973) are among the earliest; while William Mulligan, 'Civil–military relations in the early Weimar Republic', *Historical Journal*, 45/4 (2002), 819–41, and idem, 'The Reichswehr, the republic and the primacy of foreign policy, 1918–1923', *German History*, 21/3 (2003), 346–67, Matthias Strohn, 'Hans von Seeckt and his vision of a modern army', *War in History*, 12/3 (2005), 318–37, offer more up-to-date accounts. William Mulligan, *The Creation of the Modern German Army: General Walther Reinhardt and the Weimar Republic, 1914–1930* (New York, 2005) is comprehensive.

An important collection of essays is Wilhelm Deist (ed.), *The German Military in the Age of Total War* (Leamington Spa, 1985); while Klaus-Jürgen

Müller (ed.), *The Military in Politics and Society in France and Germany in the Twentieth Century* (Oxford, 1995) and Roger Chickering and Stig Förster (eds.), *The Shadows of Total War: Europe, East Asia, and the United States, 1919–1939* (Cambridge, 2005) provide useful comparative perspective. Richard J. Shuster, *German Disarmament after World War I: The Diplomacy of International Arms Inspections, 1920–1931* (New York, 2006) deals with an often neglected aspect of the military under the republic.

Michael Geyer, 'The past as future: the German officer corps as profession', in Geoffrey Cocks and Konrad Jarausch (eds.), *German Professions, 1800–1950* (New York, 1990) looks at the changing self-perception and role of the military in society. James M. Diehl, *Paramilitary Politics in Weimar Germany* (Bloomington, Ind., 1977) is one of the earliest and most important studies of militarism and mobilization, as too is Peter Fritzsche, *Rehearsals for Fascism: Populism and Political Mobilization in Weimar Germany* (New York, 1990). These two classic studies can be supplemented by Benjamin Ziemann, *War Experiences in Rural Germany 1914–1923* (Oxford, 2007).

Chapter 4

There are two major epochs described in this chapter: first the inflation (1918–23), and then stabilization and depression (1924–33). For the inflation, the classic account is that of Costantino Bresciani-Turroni, *The Economics of Inflation: A Study of Currency Depreciation in Post-war Germany* (London, 1937); there is also a good modern econometric study by Steven B. Webb, *Hyperinflation and Stabilization in Weimar Germany* (New York, 1989). Karsten Laursen and Jørgen Pedersen, *The German Inflation 1918–1923* (Amsterdam, 1964), give a grotesquely rosy Keynesian interpretation of the inflation; while Carl-Ludwig Holtfrerich, *The German Inflation 1914–1923: Causes and Effects in International Perspective* (Berlin, 1986), has a much more nuanced and subtle Keynesian account. Gerald D. Feldman has written a definitive account of the interaction of economics and politics with social developments in *The Great Disorder: Politics, Economics, and Society in the German Inflation, 1914–1924* (New York, 1993). The logic of investment in the inflation is dealt with by Dieter Lindenlaub, 'Maschinenbauunternehmen in der Inflation 1919–1923: Unternehmenshistorische Überlegungen zu einigen Theorien der Inflationswirkungen und Erklärungen', in Gerald D. Feldman (ed.), *Die deutsche Inflation: Eine Zwischenbilanz* (Berlin, 1982); with a fuller exposition in Dieter Lindenlaub, *Maschinenbauunternehmen in der deutschen Inflation 1919–1923: Unternehmenshistorische Untersuchungen zu einigen Inflationstheorien* (Berlin, 1985).

On the depression, see Knut Borchardt, *Perspectives on Modern German Economic History and Policy*, translated by Peter Lambert (Cambridge, 1991); Harold James, *The German Slump: Politics and Economics 1924–1936* (Oxford, 1986); Theo Balderston, *The Origins and Course of the German Economic Crisis: November 1923 to May 1932* (Berlin, 1993). The Borchardt interpretation was first formulated in a celebrated lecture of 1978, which is translated in the volume mentioned above: it produced a major interpretative debate, which is recorded in Jürgen Baron von Kruedener (ed.), *Economic Crisis and Political Collapse: The Weimar Republic, 1924–1933* (New York, 1990), and in Ian Kershaw (ed.), *Weimar: Why did German Democracy Fail?* (London, 1990). Two important works which emphasize the reparations issue are: Stephen A. Schuker, *American 'Reparations' to Germany, 1919–33: Implications for the Third-World Debt Crisis* (Princeton, 1988) and Albrecht Ritschl, *Deutschlands Krise und Konjunktur 1924–1934: Binnenkonjunktur, Auslandsverschuldung und Reparationsproblem zwischen Dawes-Plan und Transfersperre* (Berlin, 2002). Theo Balderston's *Economics and Politics in the Weimer Republic* (Cambridge, 2002), is a good short recent summary.

On 1933 as a change of economic regimes, see Peter Temin, 'Soviet and Nazi economic planning in the 1930s', *Economic History Review*, NS 44/4 (Nov. 1991); see also Chritoph Buchheim, 'Zur Natur des Wirtschaftsaufschwungs in der NS-Zeit', in Christoph Buchheim, Michael Hutter, and Harold James (eds.), *Zerrissene Zwischenkriegszeit: Wirtschaftshistorische Beiträge: Knut Borchardt zum 65. Geburtstag* (Baden-Baden, 1994).

On technology and innovation, a useful introduction is David Landes, *The Unbound Prometheus: Technological Change and Industrial Development in Western Europe from 1750 to Present* (2nd edn. Cambridge, 2003); see also Robert A. Brady, *The Rationalization Movement in German Industry: A Study in the Evolution of Economic Planning* (Berkeley, 1933). Elias Canetti's revealing memoirs only recently became available in an English translation: *Memoirs of Elias Canetti* (New York, 2000).

Chapter 5

The politics and economics of cities in Weimar have not received anything approaching the attention that historians, literary theorists, film specialists, and others have devoted to their cultural aspects, particularly in English. See Ben Lieberman, *From Recovery to Catastrophe: Municipal Stabilization and Political Crisis in Weimar Germany* (Oxford, 1998) and Anthony McElligott, *Contested City: Municipal Politics and the Rise of Nazism in Altona, 1917–1937* (Ann Arbor, 1998). Original source materials are collected in Anthony McElligott, *The German Urban*

Experience, 1900–1945 (London, 2001). A useful contemporary source remains Roger H. Wells, *German Cities: A Study of Contemporary Municipal Politics and Administration* (Princeton, 1932). Economic history is more plentiful. Specific treatment of municipal finance can be found in Theo Balderston, *The Origins and Course of the German Economic Crisis, November 1923 to May 1932* (Berlin, 1993), and is supplemented by W. H. T. Moss, 'Cities in the inflation: municipal government in Berlin, Cologne, and Frankfurt am Main during the early years of the Weimar Republic' (Ph.D. diss., Oxford, 1992). An important summary from the period is by Städtetag president Oskar Mulert, 'The economic activities of German municipalities', *Annals of Collective Economy*, 5 (1929), 209–70. There is hardly anything at all in English on the *Reichsreform*; the indispensable work is Gerhard Schulz, *Zwischen Demokratie und Diktatur: Verfassungspolitik und Reichsreform in der Weimarer Republik*, 3 vols. (Berlin, 1963–91). English speakers must rely on the account of Prussian constitutional expert Arnold Brecht, *Federalism and Regionalism in Germany: The Division of Prussia* (Oxford, 1945), and Brecht's memoir, *The Political Education of Arnold Brecht: An Autobiography, 1884–1970* (Princeton, 1970). The first history of the Städtetag was provided by Otto Ziebill, its president after the Second World War, in *Geschichte des Deutschen Städtetages: Fünfzig Jahre Deutsche Kommunalpolitik* (Stuttgart, 1956). Scholarly treatments are Hermann Beckstein, *Städtische Interessenpolitik: Organisation und Politik der Städtetage in Bayern, Preussen und im Deutschen Reich, 1896–1923* (Düsseldorf, 1991); and for Weimar, Wolfgang Hofmann's still excellent *Städtetag und Verfassungsordnung: Position und Politik der Hauptgeschäftsführer eines kommunalen Spitzenverbandes* (Stuttgart, 1966). But these all require familiarity with the German language!

Chapter 6

The literature on women and specifically the 'New Woman' of Weimar Germany is now vast. But the starting point is still Renate Bridenthal and Claudia Koonz, 'Beyond *Kinder, Küche, Kirche*: Weimar women in politics and work', in Renate Bridenthal, Anita Grossmann, and Marion Kaplan (eds.), *When Biology became Destiny: Women in Weimar and Nazi Germany* (New York, 1984); Katharina von Ankum (ed.), *Women in the Metropolis: Gender and Modernity in Weimar Culture* (Berkeley and Los Angeles, 1997) reflects a revisionist feminist approach that critically tackles the lived experience of women; Günter Berghaus, '"Girlkultur": feminism, Americanism and popular entertainment in Weimar', *Journal of Design History*, 1/3–4 (1988), 193–219, is accessible, while Atina Grossmann, ' "Girlkultur" or thoroughly rationalized female: a new woman in Weimar Germany?', in Judith Friedlander (ed.), *Women in Culture and Politics: A Century of Change* (Bloomington, Ind., 1986), is a thought-provoking essay that changed the way historians approached the phenomenon of the 'new woman'. Cornelie Usborne's essay 'The New Woman and generational conflict: perceptions of young women's sexual mores in the Weimar Republic', in Mark Roseman (ed.), *Generations in Conflict: Youth Revolt and Generation Formation in Germany 1770–1968* (Cambridge, 1995), also tackles the question of whether or not the 'new woman' was a media invention or a real person. Women and career opportunities under the republic (but also before and after) are dealt with by Jill Stephenson, 'Women and the professions: 1900–1945', in Geoffrey Cocks and Konrad Jarausch (eds.), *German Professions, 1800–1950* (New York, 1990). Representations of women in the arts and media are dealt with in Richard W. McCormick, *Gender and Sexuality in Weimar Modernity: Film, Literature, and the 'New Objectivity'* (New York, 2001); Sandra Frieden, Richard W. McCormick, Vibeke R. Petersen, and Laurie Melissa Vogelsang (eds.), *Gender and German Cinema*, vol. ii (London, 1993). Kate Lacey, *Feminine Frequencies: Gender, German Radio, and the Public Sphere, 1923–1945* (Ann Arbor, 1996) is an excellent study of the relationship of new mass communication and gender, while Patrice Petro, *Joyless Streets: Women and Melodramatic Representation in Weimar Germany* (Princeton, 1989) tackles the gender, media, and women as both objects and subjects of consumption. Mary Nolan, 'Housework made easy: the Taylorized housewife in Weimar Germany', *Feminist Studies*, 16/3 (1990), 549–77, is a path-breaking essay; idem, *Visions of Modernity: American Business and the Modernization of Germany* (New York, 1994). An important contribution to the history of the female body as a site of conflict has been made by Cornelie Usborne, *The Politics of the Body in Weimar Germany* (London, 1992), and her *Cultures of Abortion in Weimar Germany* (Oxford, 2007).

The experience of women in the First World War and their politicization has been tackled by Ute Daniel, *The War Within: German Working-Class Women in the First World War*, translated by Margaret Ries (Oxford, 1997), and Belinda Davis, *Home Fires Burning: Food, Politics, and Everyday Life in World War I Berlin* (Chapel Hill, NC, 2000). On women in Weimar politics the following three essays by Helen Boak, 'Women in Weimar Germany: the "Frauenfrage" and the female vote', in Richard Bessel and E. J. Feuchtwanger (eds.), *Social Change and Political Development in Weimar Germany* (London, 1981), 'Women in Weimar politics', *European History Quarterly*, 20/3 (1990), 369–99, and 'Mobilising women for Hitler: the female Nazi voter', in Anthony McElligott and Tim Kirk (eds.), *Working Towards the Führer: Essays in Honour of Sir Ian Kershaw* (Manchester, 2003), are good introductions to women as political actors, as too is the important study by Julia Sneeringer, *Winning Women's Votes: Propaganda and Politics in Weimar Germany* (Chapel Hill, NC, 2002). Raffael Scheck, 'German conservatism and female political activism in the early Weimar Republic', *German History*, 15/1 (1997), 34–55; idem, 'Women against Versailles: maternalism and nationalism of female bourgeois politicians in the early Weimar Republic', *German Studies Review*, 22 (1999), 21–42; idem, 'Women on the Weimar right: the role of female politicians in the Deutschnationale Volkspartei (DNVP)', *Journal of Contemporary History*, 36/4 (Oct. 2001), 547–60, and her *Mothers of the Nation: Right-Wing Women in Weimar Germany* (Oxford, 2004), are important contributions to the history of women in right-wing politics. For Jewish women see Marion Kaplan, *The Jewish Feminist Movement in Germany: The Campaigns of the Jüdischer Frauenbund, 1904–1938* (Westport, Conn., 1979). On the bourgeois women's movement in general: Richard J. Evans, *The Feminist Movement in Germany 1894–1933* (London, 1976), while his *Comrades and Sisters: Feminism Socialism and Pacifism in Europe 1870–1945* (New York, 1987) can be consulted with profit. On working-class women, Brian Peterson, 'The politics of working-class women in the Weimar Republic', *Central European History*, 10 (1977), 87–111; Karen Hagemann, 'Men's demonstrations and women's protest: gender and collective action in urban working class milieu during the Weimar Republic', *Gender and History*, 5/1 (1993), 101–19, and her magisterial study of working-class women from Hamburg's Social Democratic milieu: *Frauenalltag und Männerpolitik: Alltagsleben und Gesellshaftliches Handeln von Arbeiterfrauen in der Weimarer Republik* (Bonn, 1990).

Chapter 7

For conceptual and empirical starting points for the study of Weimar welfarism see: Detlev Peukert, *Grenzen der Sozialdisziplinierung: Aufstieg und Krise der deutschen Jugendfürsorge 1878 bis 1932* (Berlin, 1986), *Max Webers Diagnose der Moderne* (Göttingen, 1989), and in English 'The genesis of the "final solution" from the spirit of science', in David Crew (ed.), *Nazism and German Society, 1933–1945* (London, 1994). Young-Sun Hong, 'Neither singular nor alternative: narratives of welfare and modernity in Germany, 1870–1945', *Social History*, 30/2 (May 2005) and Edward Ross Dickinson, 'Biopolitics, fascism, democracy: some reflections on our discourse about "modernity"', *Central European History*, 37/1 (Mar. 2004), 1–48; *Welfare, Modernity, and the Weimar State, 1919–1933* (Princeton, 1998). David Crew, *Germans on Welfare: From Weimar to*

Hitler (Oxford, 1998) applies the principles of the history of everyday life (*Alltagsgeschichte*) to recover and theorize the experiences of welfare clientele in their encounters with the new social bureaucracy. There is only limited English-language literature dealing with veterans or the other new poor: Robert Whalen, *Bitter Wounds: German Victims of the Great War 1914–1919* (Ithaca, NY, 1984), Greg Eghigian, *Making Security Social: Disability, Insurance, and the Birth of the Social Entitlement State in Germany* (Ann Arbor, 2000), chapters in the above-mentioned works by Hong and Crew, and Deborah Cohen, *The War Come Home: Disabled Veterans in Britain and Germany, 1914–1939* (Berkeley and Los Angeles, 2001). Edward Ross Dickinson, *The Politics of German Child Welfare from the Empire to the Federal Republic* (New Haven, 1996). Larry Frohman, *Poor Relief and Welfare in Germany from the Reformation to World War I* (Cambridge, 2008) and Larry Frohman, 'Prevention, Welfare, and Citizenship: The War on Tuberculosis and Infant Mortality in Germany, 1900–1930', *Central European History*, 39/3 (Sept. 2006), 431–81, provide the standard account of the transition from deterrant poor relief to preventive social welfare. While Dickinson focuses on policy debates, the best English-language account of the changing fortunes of Progressive youth welfare practice is Elizabeth Harvey, *Youth and the Welfare State in Weimar Germany* (Oxford, 1993). While youth welfare was a system of supplementary public education for endangered and wayward youth, there was also a broad spectrum of programmes (*Jugendpflege* rather than *Jugendfürsorge*) directed at the edification, protection, and social integration of 'normal' youth; see Derek Linton, *'Who Has the Youth, Has the Future': The Campaign to Save Youth Workers in Imperial Germany* (Cambridge, 1991); Margaret F. Stieg, 'The 1926 German law to protect youth against trash and dirt: moral protectionism in a democracy', *Central European History*, 23 (1990), 22–56; Klaus Petersen, 'The Harmful Publications (Young Persons) Act of 1926: literary censorship and the politics of morality in the Weimar Republic', *German Studies Review*, 15/3 (1992), 505–23.

On the body and sexuality, as well as Cornelie Usborne, *The Politics of the Body in Weimar Germany* and her *Cultures of Abortion in Weimar Germany* see Atina Grossmann, *Reforming Sex: The German Movement for Birth Control and Abortion Reform, 1920–1950* (Oxford, 1995). Michael Hau, *The Cult of Health and Beauty in Germany: A Social History, 1890–1930* (Chicago, 2003) and Chad Ross, *Naked Germany: Health, Race and Nation* (Oxford, 2005). The most important English-language account of the impact of authoritarian eugenics on German social welfare is Paul Weindling, *Health, Race and German Politics between National Unification and Nazism, 1870–1945* (Cambridge, 1989); Michelle Mouton, *From Nurturing the Nation to Purifying the Volk: Weimar and Nazi Family*

Policy, 1918–1945 (Cambridge, 2007) is a recent important contribution to the history of family policy that cuts across periodization.

Chapter 8

Adelheid von Saldern, *Häuserleben: Zur Geschichte städtischen Arbeiterwohnens vom Kaiserreich bis heute* (Bonn, 1995), and her 'The workers' movement and cultural patterns on urban housing estates and in rural settlements in Germany and Austria during the 1920s', *Social History*, 15/3 (Oct. 1990), 333–54, set out arguments put forward here. For Austria see Helmut Gruber, *Red Vienna: Experiment in Working-Class Culture 1919–1934* (New York, 1991). For a good general description of housing in inter-war Europe, see Elizabeth Denby, *Europe Re-housed* (London, 1938). Important recent studies include: Richard Pommer and Christian F. Otto, *Weissenhof 1927 and the Modern Movement in Architecture* (Chicago, 1991); Franziska Bollerey and Kristina Hartmann, 'A patriarchal utopia: the garden city and housing reform in Germany at the turn of the century', in Anthony Sutcliffe (ed.), *The Rise of Modern Urban Planning 1800–1914* (London, 1980); Nicholas Bullock, 'Housing in Frankfurt 1925 to 1931 and the New Wohnkultur', *Architectural Review*, 168/976 (1978), 335–42; and 'First the kitchen—then the facade', *Journal of Design History*, 1/3–4 (1988), 177–92; Gerhard Fehl, 'The Niddatal project', *Built Environment*, 9/3–4 (1983), 185–97; Ben Lieberman, 'Testing Peukert's paradigm: the "crisis of classical modernity" in the "new Frankfurt", 1925–1930', *German Studies Review*, 17/2 (May 1994), 287–303; Barbara Miller Lane, *Architecture and Politics in Germany 1918–1945* (2nd edn. Cambridge, Mass., 1985). Irene Stoehr, 'Housework and motherhood: debates and policies in the women's movement in imperial Germany and Weimar Republic', in Gisela Bock and Pat Thane (eds.), *Maternity and Gender Policies: Women and the Rise of the European Welfare State* (New York, 1991); Karen Hagemann, 'Of "old" and "new" housewives: everyday housework and the limits of household rationalization in the urban working-class milieu of the Weimar Republic', *International Review of Social History*, 41 (1996), 305–30, challenges the thesis of the 'Taylorized housewife'. On the ambiguities of modern science and welfare see above all and Detlev J. K. Peukert, 'The genesis of the "final solution" from the spirit of science', in Thomas Childers and Jane Caplan (eds.), *Reevaluating the Third Reich* (New York, 1993), 234–52.

Chapter 9

The best books on Weimar Jewry in the English language are Donald L. Niewyk, *The Jews in Weimar Germany* (2nd edn. New Brunswick, NJ,

2001) and Michael Brenner, *The Renaissance of Jewish Culture in Weimar Germany* (New Haven, 1996). The first work is primarily concerned with politics, the second with religion and culture. While Niewyk tends to focus on conflict within the community, Brenner stresses the uniform quest for identity. Both works can be complemented by two edited volumes that address the subject from similarly diverse standpoints. Wolfgang Benz, Arnold Paucker, and Peter Pulzer (eds.), *Jüdisches Leben in der Weimarer Republik: Jews in the Weimar Republic* (Tübingen, 1998) explores various issues without advancing an overarching theme. By contrast Michael Brenner and Derek J. Penslar, *In Search of Jewish Community: Jewish Identities in Germany and Austria 1918–1933* (Bloomington, Ind., 1998) is intent on highlighting a re-emerging sense of Jewish community, particularly in religious and cultural life.

W. E. Mosse, *Jews in the German Economy: The German-Jewish Economic Elite, 1870–1935* (Oxford, 1987) and *The German-Jewish Economic Elite, 1820–1935: A Socio-cultural Profile* (Oxford, 1989) are essential for Jewish economics; Peter J. Pulzer, *Jews and the German State: The Political History of a Minority, 1848–1933* (Oxford, 1992) is essential for Jewish politics, equally important, though only available in German, is Martin Liepach, *Das Wahlverhalten der jüdischen Bevölkerung: Zur politischen Orientierung der Juden in der Weimarer Republik* (Tübingen, 1996). For Zionism, a good starting point remains Stephen M. Poppel, *Zionism in Germany 1897–1933: The Shaping of a Jewish Identity* (Philadelphia, 1977). It should be supplemented by Michael Berkowitz, *Western Jewry and the Zionist Project, 1914–1933* (Cambridge, 1997) and Jörg Hackeschmidt, *Von Kurt Blumenfeld zu Norbert Elias: Die Erfindung einer jüdischen Nation* (Hamburg, 1997). The subject of eastern Jewry in Germany has been dealt with from different angles. Steven E. Aschheim, *Brothers and Strangers: The East European Jew in German and German Jewish Consciousness 1800–1923* (Madison, 1982) examines the cultural and intellectual perceptions of the *Ostjuden*; Jack Wertheimer, *Unwelcome Strangers: East European Jews in Imperial Germany* (Oxford, 1987), analyses the political and social history of the subject; and Trude Maurer, *Ostjuden in Deutschland 1918– 1933* (Hamburg, 1986), provides an exhaustive treatment in German.

For liberal Judaism, the Reform Movement, and Jewish Orthodoxy, two books should be consulted as background information: Michael A. Meyer, *Response to Modernity: A History of the Reform Movement in Judaism* (Oxford, 1988) and Mordechai Breuer, *Modernity within Tradition: The Social History of Orthodox Jewry in Imperial Germany* (New York, 1992). The most important recent publications on intellectual debate are Ulrich Sieg, *Jüdische Intellektuelle im Ersten Weltkrieg: Kriegserfahrungen, weltanschauliche Debatten und kulturelle Neuentwürfe* (Berlin, 2001) and David

N. Myers, *Resisting History: Historicism and its Discontents in German Jew-ish Thought* (Princeton, 2003). The best social history of German Jewry is available in German. Outstanding examples include Shulamit Volkov, *Das Jüdische Projekt der Moderne* (Munich, 2001); Andreas Gotzmann, Rainer Liedtke, and Till van Rahden (eds.), *Juden, Bürger, Deutsche: Zur Geschichte von Vielfalt und Differenz 1800–1933* (Tübingen, 2001); and Till van Rahden, *Juden und andere Breslauer: Die Beziehungen zwischen Juden, Protestanten und Katholiken in einer deutschen Großstadt von 1860 bis 1925* (Göttingen, 2000).

On the growth of anti-Semitism in the Weimar period, see Anthony Kauders, *German Politics and the Jews: Düsseldorf and Nuremberg, 1910–1933* (Oxford, 1996), as well as the following works in German: Dirk Walter, *Antisemitische Kriminalität und Gewalt. Judenfeindschaft in der Weimarer Republik* (Bonn 1999); Frank Bajohr, *'Unser Hotel ist juden-frei': Bäder-Antisemitismus im 19. und 20. Jahrhundert* (Frankfurt am Main, 2003); and Cornelia Hecht, *Deutsche Juden und der Antisemitismus in der Weimarer Republik* (Bonn, 2003).

Chapter 10

Indispensable both as a source and for a sharp analysis of Weimar culture: Siegfried Kracauer, *The Mass Ornament: Weimar Essays*, edited by Thomas Y. Levin (Cambridge, Mass., 1995); while the 'feel' of the 1920s is captured by Christopher Isherwood, *The Berlin Stories* (New York, 1954; 1st pub. 1935), idem, *Christopher and his Kind 1929–1939* (Aldershot, 1977), idem, *Goodbye to Berlin* (London, 1989), and Alfred Döblin, *Berlin Alexanderplatz* (Berlin, 1929).

Looking somewhat dated but still useful are Peter Gay, *Weimar Culture: The Outsider as Insider* (London, 1969), John Willett, *The New Sobriety: Art and Politics in the Weimar Period 1917–1933* (London, 1978), and Bürbel Schräder and Jürgen Schebera, *The Golden Twenties: Art and Literature in the Weimar Republic* (New Haven, 1990). For excellent introductions to Weimar culture students would be well advised to consult Eve Rosenhaft, 'Brecht's Germany: 1898–1933', in Peter Thomson and Glendyr Sacks (eds.), *The Cambridge Companion to Brecht* (Cambridge, 1994), Elizabeth Harvey, 'Culture and society in Weimar Germany: the impact of modernism and mass culture', in Mary Fulbrook (ed.), *German History since 1800* (London, 1997); Stephan Lamb and Anthony Phelan, 'Weimar culture: the birth of modernism', in Rob Burns (ed.), *German Cultural Studies* (Oxford, 1996), and Jost Hermand, 'Unity within diversity? The history of the concept "Neue Sachlichkeit"', in Keith Bullivant (ed.), *Culture and Society in the Weimar Republic* (Manchester,

1977). The contributions to Thomas W. Kniesche and Stephen Brockman (eds.), *Dancing on the Volcano: Essays on the Culture of the Weimar Republic* (Columbia, SC, 1994) are a sampling of newer approaches to Weimar's cultural history by the best of (at that time) younger scholars; similarly the contributions to Charles W. Haxthausen, and Heidrun Suhr (eds.), *Berlin: Culture and Metropolis* (Minneapolis, 1990) are excellent for their discussion of modernity and the capital from a wide interdisciplinary range. Excellent also is the recent study by Peter Jelavich, *Berlin Alexanderplatz: Radio, Film, and the Death of Weimar* (Berkeley, 2006) which should be read in conjunction with Döblin's novel cited above. His *Berlin Cabaret* (Cambridge, Mass., 1993) remains the standard work on popular stage productions and is complemented by Karl Toepfer, 'Nudity and modernity in German dance 1910–1930', *Journal of the History of Sexuality*, 3/1 (1992), 58–108; idem, *Empire of Ecstasy: Nudity and Movement in German Body Culture, 1910–1935* (Berkeley, 1997). On cinema Eric Rentschler (ed.), *The Films of G. W. Pabst: An Existential Cinema* (New Brunswick, NJ, 1990) is indispensable. Michael Minden and Holger Bachmann (eds.), *Fritz Lang's Metropolis: Cinematic Visions of Technology and Fear* (Rochester, NY, 2000) contains useful contemporary documentation and important essays on this iconic film. Janet Ward, *Weimar Surfaces: Urban Visual Culture in 1920s Germany* (Berkeley and Los Angeles, 2001) deals with the visual mediation of culture through advertising, shop windows, and cinema. M. Kay Flavell, 'Über alles die Liebe: food, sex, and money in the work of George Grosz', *Journal of European Studies*, 13 (1983), 268–88, and Karl-Christian Führer, 'A medium of modernity? Broadcasting in Weimar Germany, 1923–1932', *Journal of Modern History*, 69 (Dec. 1997), 722–53 are stimulating and important additions. Joachim Schlör, *Nights in the Big City: Paris, Berlin, London 1840–1930*, translated by Pierre Gottfried Imhof and Dafydd Rees Roberts (London, 1998) is a brilliant account by a historical anthropologist of culture under darkness. On the relationship between culture, crisis, and Weimar, see Karl-Christian Führer, 'German cultural life and the crisis of national identity during the depression, 1929–1933', *German Studies Review*, 24 (2001), 461–86. Irit Rogoff (ed.), *The Divided Heritage: Themes and Problems in German Modernism* (Cambridge, 1991) remains outstanding in its treatment of modernity and Weimar.

Chancellors of the Weimar Republic, 1919–1933

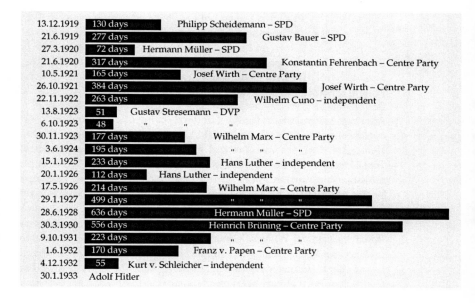

Date	Days	Chancellor
13.12.1919	130 days	Philipp Scheidemann – SPD
21.6.1919	277 days	Gustav Bauer – SPD
27.3.1920	72 days	Hermann Müller – SPD
21.6.1920	317 days	Konstantin Fehrenbach – Centre Party
10.5.1921	165 days	Josef Wirth – Centre Party
26.10.1921	384 days	Josef Wirth – Centre Party
22.11.1922	263 days	Wilhelm Cuno – independent
13.8.1923	51	Gustav Stresemann – DVP
6.10.1923	48	" " "
30.11.1923	177 days	Wilhelm Marx – Centre Party
3.6.1924	195 days	" " "
15.1.1925	233 days	Hans Luther – independent
20.1.1926	112 days	Hans Luther – independent
17.5.1926	214 days	Wilhelm Marx – Centre Party
29.1.1927	499 days	" " "
28.6.1928	636 days	Hermann Müller – SPD
30.3.1930	556 days	Heinrich Brüning – Centre Party
9.10.1931	223 days	" " "
1.6.1932	170 days	Franz v. Papen – Centre Party
4.12.1932	55	Kurt v. Schleicher – independent
30.1.1933		Adolf Hitler

Source: <http:/www.lsg.musin.de/geschichte/Material/karten/2/wr-reg.jpg>.

Chronology

Nadine Rossol

1918

Sailors' mutiny in Kiel at the end of October and early November. The formation of a workers' and soldiers' council sparks off uprisings all over Germany. Kurt Eisner, an Independent Socialist, proclaims a republic in Bavaria under a workers', soldiers', and peasants' council. Chancellor Max von Baden calls for Kaiser Wilhelm II to abdicate and the Social Democrat Philipp Scheidemann proclaims the German Republic on 9 November in Berlin. On the same day radical Socialists proclaim the Socialist republic. After rapid negotiations, fearing that the situation of strikes and uprisings could get out of control, the Social Democrat Friedrich Ebert becomes chancellor albeit for one day and forms a provisional government of Social Democrats (SPD) and Independent Socialists (USPD). The German armistice commission under Centre Party member Matthias Erzberger begins negotiations with the Allies. Workers' and soldiers' councils are formed. The Kaiser abdicates, flees to the Netherlands, and remains there until his death in 1941. To control and suppress revolutionary uprisings, General Wilhelm Groener puts the army at Ebert's disposal in exchange for Social Democratic support in maintaining order with armed forces (Ebert–Groener Pact). The armistice with the Allies is signed at Compiègne on 11 November. Foundation of the right-wing war veterans' organization Stahlhelm. Meeting of the National Congress of Workers' and Soldiers' Councils in Berlin. At the end of December the provisional government is reshuffled after the Independent Socialists walk out. The far left forms the German Communist Party (KPD). The split between Social Democrats and radical Socialists/Communists creates division lines within the political left-wing spectrum that remain for decades.

1919

Spartacist uprising in Berlin in January, attempting to overthrow the provisional government and to erect a Soviet Republic, is met with fear and overreactions from the SPD. The Social Democrat Gustav Noske heads all troops stationed in Berlin. Aided by *Freikorps* troops, he ends the uprising. Spartacist leaders Rosa Luxemburg and Karl Liebknecht are brutally murdered by *Freikorps*; Luxemburg's corpse is found months

Compiled by Nadine Rossol, Irish Research Council for the Humanities and Social Sciences Postdoctoral Fellow in the Centre for Historical Research, University of Limerick.

later in one of Berlin's canals. Radical Socialists hold the SPD responsible for the brutal use of force. Bitter resentment and hostility remain between the two left-wing groups. For most of the Weimar years the Communists refer to the Social Democrats as their worse enemy. In mid-January elections for deputies to the National Assembly are held and the SPD emerges as the majority party. The National Assembly opens in Weimar (hence the name Weimar Republic), away from the chaotic conditions in Berlin. Its delegates elect the Social Democrat Friedrich Ebert president. Ebert holds the highest office in the republic until his death in 1925. The SPD politician Scheidemann forms a coalition government of SPD, DDP, and Centre Party of which all parties support the republic and its Constitution (the so-called Weimar coalition). The Bavarian minister Kurt Eisner, a supporter of a Soviet Republic in Bavaria, is murdered by nationalists in Munich. In the chaotic situation after Eisner's death, a Soviet Republic is formed in Munich but crushed by Prussian and Württemberg troops and the *Freikorps* at the beginning of May. In June Scheidemann's government resigns, refusing to sign the peace treaty of Versailles. A new cabinet is formed under Social Democrat Gustav Bauer. At the end of June the German government signs the Treaty of Versailles which imposes heavy reparations, requires reduction of the German army, forbids German-Austrian unification, means a loss of German territories at home and abroad, separates East Prussia from the rest of the country, and insists upon German acceptance of the war guilt clause. Throughout the existence of the republic, anti-republicans use 'the shame of Versailles' as a propaganda slogan directed against the republic. In July the National Assembly in Weimar adopts the proposed democratic Constitution which offers equal and universal suffrage for men and women. The Constitution includes presidential as well as participatory elements. The powerful role of the Reich president, who can authorize the chancellor to govern by presidential decree without possessing a parliamentary majority, is due to the insecure social, political, and economic conditions at the beginning of the republic. On 11 August, President Ebert signs the Weimar Constitution. The date is commemorated with annually celebrated Constitution Day festivities in Weimar Germany.

1920
The German Workers' Party is founded and renamed the National Socialist Workers' Party (NSDAP). In March the nationalist Dr Wolfgang Kapp and General Freiherr von Lüttwitz lead a putsch in Berlin for the restoration of the monarchy. The government leaves the capital. A general strike and the refusal of leading civil servants and ministerial officials to follow the putschists' orders end the attempted overthrow of the republic.

Communist uprisings in the Ruhr area and central Germany continue until April. Eventually, they are defeated by the army. Elections for the Reichstag are held in the summer; 'the Weimar coalition' (SPD, DDP, Centre Party) loses support.

1921

At the Paris conference, German reparations are set at 132 billion gold Marks, payable over forty-two years. Communist uprisings in Saxony and Hamburg. The Centre Party member Joseph Wirth forms a new government. In August the United States signs peace treaties with Germany and Austria. Also in August, the politician Matthias Erzberger, held responsible for the German acceptance of the Treaty of Versailles, is assassinated by right-wing forces. As a consequence, the government declares a state of emergency until mid-December. Independent Socialists vote to merge with the Communist Party. The SA is established in November. The German currency begins to fall.

1922

In April Germany's foreign minister Walther Rathenau concludes the Treaty of Rapallo with the USSR which cancels the countries' reciprocal war debts and establishes diplomatic and economic relations. At the end of June, Rathenau is assassinated by right-wing nationalists. The republican public is shocked and regards the deed as an attack on the democratic state. Numerous demonstrations and protests, condemning the killing, show the indignation caused by the assassination. The republic passes the Law for the Protection of the Republic punishing anti-republican insults on the state form, state symbols, and members of the government. Chancellor Wirth resigns in November and Wilhelm Cuno succeeds him. The Allied Reparations Commission threatens sanctions against Germany because of the country's failure to meet its reparation obligations.

1923

French and Belgian troops occupy the Ruhr area to operate the mining industries for the victors. The German government objects and announces passive resistance to the occupation. This is in line with the sentiments of the German public which is united in its strong disapproval of the French action. However, the costly policy of passive resistance harms the weak German economy even more. It creates galloping hyperinflation and impoverishment. On 3 September a ticket on a Berlin streetcar costs 400,000 Marks. Chancellor Cuno resigns and Gustav Stresemann forms a new government which ends the passive resistance. Political uprisings characterize the autumn months and challenge the stability of the republic. In October Communists organize uprisings in Hamburg and Saxony and on 9 November Erich Ludendorff and Adolf Hitler lead the Beer Hall

Putsch in Munich. The putsch fails and Hitler is taken to court for high treason. The introduction of a new currency, the *Rentenmark*, stabilizes the currency and halts the inflation at the end of the year.

1924

At the end of February the republican war veterans' organization Reichsbanner schwarz-rot-gold is founded in Magdeburg. The Reichsbanner strongly supports the republic and counts 2 million members. In March Hitler is sentenced to five years confinement at Landsberg fortress, but he serves less than nine months of his sentence. The Allies meet in London to discuss the Dawes Plan proposing the evacuation of the Ruhr, the reduction of reparations, and loans to Germany. German delegates meet with the Allies, and the Dawes Plan is enacted in September. Reichstag elections show right-wing parties losing strength at the end of the year. A period of relative stability begins which the historian Sebastian Haffner calls 'the Stresemann years', due to the successful foreign policy conducted by Gustav Stresemann until his death in 1929.

1925

The NSDAP is re-established at the beginning of the year. President Ebert falls ill and dies unexpectedly at the end of February. The republic honours him with a state funeral. In April a relative majority of the German population elects General Field Marshal Paul von Hindenburg new president. Many republicans are shocked that the dedicated monarchist Hindenburg holds the highest office in the republican state. Removal of Allied troops from the Ruhr area in the summer. A commercial treaty between Germany and USSR is signed in October. The Nazi paramilitary organization the SS is formed. At the beginning of December France, Great Britain, Belgium, Italy, and Germany sign the Treaty of Locarno in which Germany recognizes the western borders of its country. The eastern borders are never officially accepted but Germany promises that the status quo will not be changed by force. The 'spirit of Locarno' represents for many contemporaries the beginning of peaceful and productive European foreign policy and cooperation after the disastrous First World War. Publication of Hitler's book *Mein Kampf* in December.

1926

The Treaty of Berlin promising friendship and neutrality between Germany and USSR is signed in April. Chancellor Luther resigns after a vote of no confidence triggered by the flag conflict. Marx becomes new chancellor. Plebiscite to extend the expropriation of princes throughout Germany fails. Germany becomes a member of the League of Nations in September. The French foreign minister Aristide Briand and the German foreign minister Gustav Stresemann receive the Nobel Peace Prize for their efforts to secure peace in Europe.

1927

Fritz Lang's film *Metropolis* has its première in Berlin. It is one of the most expensive films ever made and bankrupts its film studio. Chancellor Marx forms another cabinet including the Centre Party, the German People's Party, the Bavarian People's Party, and the German National People's Party. The law providing unemployment support for everyone passes in the summer.

1928

Reichstag elections in May with gains for the left-wing parties and losses for the right. The Social Democrat Hermann Müller forms a Grand Coalition of SPD, Centre Party, German Democratic Party, and German People's Party. Several republican and Social Democratic politicians hold important ministries in Müller's cabinet. At the end of the year the Allies form a delegation to examine Germany's ability to pay reparations.

1929

Berlin's police force overreacts to Communist demonstrations on the first of May. The event is labelled 'Bloody May' and leaves thirty-three dead, none of whom are police officers. In June the Dawes Plan is revised and replaced with the Young Plan. The Young Plan reduces the reparations but Germany is scheduled to pay until 1988. Germany is accorded full responsibility over its finances. The NSDAP, the Stahlhelm, and the German National People's Party oppose the Young Plan and call for a plebiscite against the agreement. It fails at the end of December. Death of foreign minister Gustav Stresemann at the beginning of October. Commentators in Germany and abroad honour Stresemann as an architect of European peace. At the end of October the stock market crashes in New York and touches off worldwide economic crisis and the withdrawal of loans to Germany. The following three years are characterized by bankruptcies and unemployment. More than 200,000 people witness the return of the *Graf Zeppelin* to Germany from its flight around the world. Publication of Alfred Döblin's novel *Berlin Alexanderplatz*. Erich Maria Remarque becomes the most successful contemporary writer. His anti-war novel *All Quiet on the Western Front* sells more than 300,000 copies within a few weeks. The novelist Thomas Mann receives the Nobel Prize for Literature.

1930

The National Socialist Wilhelm Frick becomes minister of the interior in Thuringia. He is also in charge of cultural matters and quickly implements Nazi cultural policy. This includes the banning of modernist artists on a local level. The government in Berlin accepts the Young Plan. At the end of March the Grand Coalition of the Social Democratic chancellor Müller resigns over the financing of unemployment benefits. The Centre Party delegate Heinrich Brüning forms a minority government and resorts to Article 48 to implement policies. The withdrawal of Allied troops from the Rhineland at the end of June is celebrated with popular festivities throughout the area. The Reichstag elections in September bring enormous success for the NSDAP. The Nazis win 18 per cent of the vote. However, the SPD is still the strongest party. Première of Josef von Sternberg's film *The Blue Angel*, which is one of Germany's first films with sound. It is Marlene Dietrich's breakthrough starring as seductive Lola Lola.

1931

Almost 5 million are unemployed in January. Berlin receives the Olympic Games for 1936. Several banks collapse in the summer. In Harzburg formation of a national front against Bolshevism and the republic including the NSDAP, the German National People's Party, the Stahlhelm, and representatives of right-wing economic and financial circles. As response to the nationalist 'Harzburg Front' Social Democrats and republicans found the Iron Front, which is supported by the SPD, the Reichsbanner, the unions, and the workers' sports organizations. Plans for an *Anschluss* with Austria.

1932

Over 6 million people are unemployed. At the beginning of April Hindenburg is re-elected president and wins against Hitler. Hindenburg's election is strongly supported by the democratic forces of the republic. Nazi paramilitary organizations, the SS and the SA, are banned. Elections in several German *Länder*; the NSDAP gains considerably. Advised by General Kurt von Schleicher, President Hindenburg dismisses the Brüning cabinet at the end of May. Hindenburg's protégé the nationalist Franz von Papen becomes chancellor and creates a cabinet of right-wing aristocrats and industrialists dubbed 'the cabinet of barons'. Kurt von Schleicher becomes minister of defence. In June Hindenburg dissolves the Reichstag and rescinds the ban on the SA and SS. Violent clashes between opposing political organizations, including the Communists, the Nazis, and, to a lesser degree, the republicans, reach a crescendo after the ban on the SA and the SS is lifted. In Hamburg-Altona, on 17 July, a clash between Communist and Nazi demonstrators leaves eighteen dead and sixty-eight wounded. Altona's 'bloody Sunday', which allegedly exemplifies the failure of the Prussian state to control political violence, provides the justification for a coup against the Prussian government. On 20 July, Chancellor von Papen seizes the Prussian government from the Social Democrats and governs as Commissioner of the Reich. Numerous republican and Social Democratic Prussian civil servants, police presidents, and ministers, responsible for Prussia's reputation as Weimar Germany's 'bulwark of democracy', are replaced by national conservatives. President Hoover announces a moratorium on reparations. At the end of July the NSDAP wins 37.8 per cent of the vote at the Reichstag elections. Hitler demands to be named chancellor but Hindenburg refuses. Chancellor von Papen calls for new elections and dissolves the Reichstag at the beginning of September. Despite Communist gains and Nazi losses, the NSDAP remains strongest party at the Reichstag elections in November. Chancellor von Papen resigns and Kurt von Schleicher becomes chancellor of yet another presidential government.

1933
At the end of January Kurt von Schleicher resigns as chancellor and on 30 January President Hindenburg appoints Hitler. Hitler heads a presidential government dominated by right-wing nationalists who wrongly believe they can manipulate him. Reichstag elections are announced for the beginning of March. Thomas Mann, like many artists, writers, and actors, leaves Germany. The Nazi Hermann Göring, newly appointed Prussian minister of the interior, orders that the Prussian police has to support the SA, the SS, and the *Stahlhelm*. On 27 February the Reichstag building burns down and Hitler presents the event as the beginning of an alleged Communist uprising. The Nazis use the Reichstag fire as the pretext for an emergency decree which suspends most civil liberties and legitimizes mass arrests of Communists and Social Democrats. At the Reichstag elections on 5 March, in intimidating conditions, the Nazis win 43.9 per cent of the vote. They fail to gain an overall majority. Throughout the country, swastika flags are placed on public buildings. Many republican politicians leave Germany after the March elections. The Day of Potsdam is celebrated at the end of March. The parliament meets, after the destruction of the Reichstag building, in the Garrison Church at Potsdam in a city symbolizing Prussian militarism. On the day Hitler deliberately demonstrates his respect for Hindenburg and for Prussian history. Two days later, on 23 March, the Enabling Act is passed spelling the end of parliamentary democracy. The government can pass laws and decrees without the approval of the Reichstag or the Reich president. Only the SPD—many of the Social Democratic delegates are threatened on their way to the parliament—opposes the act. Terror and brutal violence directed at political opponents of the Nazi state at Reich, state, and regional level characterize the first months after Hitler's appointment as chancellor. Germany withdraws from the League of Nations.

Map: Weimar Germany after the Versailles Treaty, 1919

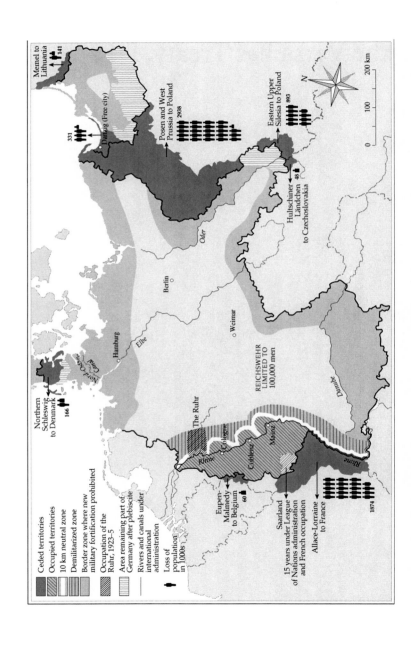

Memel to Lithuania 141

Danzig (Free city) 331

Posen and West Prussia to Poland 2938

Eastern Upper Silesia to Poland 893

Hultschiner Ländchen to Czechoslovakia 48

Northern Schleswig to Denmark 166

Hamburg

Nord-Ostsee Canal

Berlin

Weimar

Elbe

Oder

Danube

The Ruhr

Rhine

Cologne

Coblenz

Mainz

Rhine

Eupen-Malmedy to Belgium 60

Saarland 15 years under League of Nations administration and French occupation

Alsace-Lorraine to France 1874

REICHSWEHR LIMITED TO 100,000 men

N

0   100   200 km

Ceded territories

Occupied territories

10 km neutral zone

Demilitarized zone

Border zone where new military fortification prohibited

Occupation of the Ruhr, 1923–5

Area remaining part of Germany after plebiscite

Rivers and canals under international administration

Loss of population in 1000's

Index

poor relief (as deterrent) 187
Posen 50
postmodern 240
Potthoff, Heinz 217
pregnant women 197
Pretorius, Emil 224, 225, 226
Preuß, Hugo 26, 30–1, 34–5
presidential cabinets 71, 76, 116
preventive detention 202
Price, Morgan Philips, *Herald*
    journalist 4
price controls 112
print culture 165
procreation 218
productivity 105
progress 220
Progressives/ism *see* Weimar
    Progressives/ism
'proletarian hundreds' 91
proportional representation 5
prostitutes 202
Protestants 234–5, 240, 249, 250
provisional government 80
Prussia 11, 13, 26, 41, 78, 80, 84, 89, 97–8,
    139, 142, 245, 247, 263, 266
    Correctional Education Law
        (1900) 201
    government 95
    legislation 199
    militarism 5
    ministry of the interior 133
    three-class suffrage 150
    welfare decree (1929) 214
    youth, proposed welfare law 193
psychiatry 200
psychology 200
public assistance 189
public debt 109, 121
public health 214
public sector 119, 121
    deficit 113
Pünder, Hermann 33

Rabbis 241, 246
racial hygiene 14, 16
radio 216, 219, 269–70, 275
Rapallo 66 *see also* Treaty
rape 167

rapprochement 68
Rathenau, Walther 1, 33, 58–9, 102–3,
    234, 235
    assassination 110
    economic planning 125
rationality 195
rationalization 103–4, 159–62, 207, 213,
    215
reactionary modernists 10
rearmament 11, 99, 100
recession 115
Red Army 89
'red terror' 33
'Red Vienna' 212
reform schooling 201
reformers 225
regeneration 251
rehabilitative therapy 185
Reich 19, 29, 31, 41, 57, 61, 128, 130–8, 141,
    185
    court at Leipzig 56
    expenditure 109
    finances 183
    interior ministry 135, 139
    government 56–7, 60, 189, 262
    local government statute (1935) 20
    unemployment insurance law
        (1927) 127
Reich Economics Council 103, 135
Reich Federation of German Housewife
    Associations 213
Reich Pension Law (1920) 185–8, *see also*
    National Pension Law
Reich Youth Welfare Law (1922), 192–3,
    201, *see also* National Youth Welfare
    Law
Reichenau, Walther von, general 99
Reichsbahn 65, 113
Reichsbank 61, 108–10, 113, 119
Reichsexekution 31, 33, 91
Reichsmark 113, 120
Reichsrat 135, 139, 140
Reichsreform 20, 137, 141
Reichstädtebund 138
Reichstädteordnung 138
Reichstag 27, 32, 35–6, 38–9, 41, 44, 64,
    99, 113, 122, 135, 156–7, 169, 262
    elections 72, 119

Lightning Source UK Ltd.
Milton Keynes UK
UKOW03n0706081014

239771UK00008B/85/P